Nature Prose

Nature Prose

Writing in Ecological Crisis

DOMINIC HEAD

Great Clarendon Street, Oxford, OX2 6DP,
United Kingdom

Oxford University Press is a department of the University of Oxford.
It furthers the University's objective of excellence in research, scholarship,
and education by publishing worldwide. Oxford is a registered trade mark of
Oxford University Press in the UK and in certain other countries

© Dominic Head 2022

The moral rights of the author have been asserted

First Edition published in 2022

Impression: 1

All rights reserved. No part of this publication may be reproduced, stored in
a retrieval system, or transmitted, in any form or by any means, without the
prior permission in writing of Oxford University Press, or as expressly permitted
by law, by licence or under terms agreed with the appropriate reprographics
rights organization. Enquiries concerning reproduction outside the scope of the
above should be sent to the Rights Department, Oxford University Press, at the
address above

You must not circulate this work in any other form
and you must impose this same condition on any acquirer

Published in the United States of America by Oxford University Press
198 Madison Avenue, New York, NY 10016, United States of America

British Library Cataloguing in Publication Data

Data available

Library of Congress Control Number: 2022936456

ISBN 978-0-19-287087-2

DOI: 10.1093/oso/9780192870872.001.0001

Printed and bound by
CPI Group (UK) Ltd, Croydon, CR0 4YY

Links to third party websites are provided by Oxford in good faith and
for information only. Oxford disclaims any responsibility for the materials
contained in any third party website referenced in this work.

To Tricia,
for everything

To Felicity & Oliver,
our brightest stars

Preface

A vivid memory from my youth, in the mid-1970s, concerns identifying the red and orange butterflies that thronged in abundance on a *Buddleia davidii* on summer days in our Bedfordshire garden. In games of cricket with my father, our ball often had to be retrieved from under this dominant shrub: and then the game would be forgotten, we would fetch the Hamlyn concise guide to butterflies, and proceed to distinguish between the Peacocks, Commas, Gatekeepers, Painted Ladies, Red Admirals (and once, memorably, a White Admiral). When it came to the Small Tortoiseshell, we were less sure-footed because its colouring was very similar to that of the Large Tortoiseshell in the illustrations: 'how "small" is small, how "large" is large?', we wondered. The white markings on the wings of the Small would give it away; but we always hoped to spot a Large, intrigued by the scarcity in England recorded in the guidebook, dimly aware that it was more likely to be found in Europe, but buoyed by the note that 'gardens' were among its several habitats.[1] But we never did see one.

More than twenty-five years later, when that landmark study in butterfly conservation—*The Millennium Atlas of Butterflies in Britain and Europe* (2001)—was published, I had a queasy moment of grim discovery perusing it in Waterstones. I turned eagerly to the distribution map for the Large Tortoiseshell, remembering Dad, cricket on the lawn, and the flourishing butterfly bush. But that joyful recollection of nature-spotting instantly receded into an impossible past: the *Atlas* shows no sightings in the environs of Bedford between 1970 and 1982, and the Large Tortoiseshell is recorded as extinct in Britain from the 1980s, suffering one of the most serious losses of range of any British butterfly since 1800.[2] Our efforts to identify one had been futile.[3]

Over the years I have reflected on the sudden recognition of nature loss, which is a common experience for people of my generation. What does it mean to search for something in nature that is no longer there? What did it mean to live through a time of extinction in ignorance of it—before the evidence had been fully amassed? It seems to me important to hold those two moments together—the innocent

---

[1] Josef Moucha, *Butterflies: A Concise Guide in Colour*, illustrated by Vlastimil Choc (Feltham: Hamlyn, 1968), pp. 186–7, 193.

[2] Jim Asher et al., *The Millennium Atlas of Butterflies in Britain and Europe* (Oxford: Oxford University Press, 2001), pp. 333–4, 306.

[3] When Large Tortoiseshells are seen, the sightings have sometimes been put down to individual migrants from Europe (but see note 4 below), or the activities of breeders, perhaps making doomed efforts at reintroduction. See Asher, *Millennium Atlas*, p. 307.

quest for a scarce species, and the later moment of clarity that reconfigures the past. It's a way of bearing testimony, of reminding ourselves of what we have lost. Younger people will no longer expect or hope to see a native Large Tortoiseshell in Britain, a change in expectation that illustrates 'shifting baseline syndrome' or 'change blindness', the process by which species or habitat loss becomes *normalized*.[4]

The main reason, however, for dwelling on my realization about the true fate of the Large Tortoiseshell is that the doomed quest suggests several related paradoxes of the kind that this book is about, and which can have a more productive significance, even against the backdrop of species loss. First, there is the simple pleasure of observing nature, even if one's observations are not technically accurate or precise. Then there is the paradox of inverting the terror of extinction, which is displaced (if only momentarily) by the splendour of the species that you *do* see. And observation is an essential habit in conservation, leading to knowledge of how to act, especially where absence is noted. The horror of the 'revelation', then, can be conceived rather differently, as an example of the tendency that turns ignorance into knowledge. But the kind of paradox that interests me most goes beyond this suggestion of the contribution amateurs can make to conservation, in the spirit of 'citizen science'. The more important paradoxical tendency is rooted in feeling or affect, and the textual processes by which this is explored. When we observe nature now, we are acutely aware of conflicting narratives, joyful and fearful. The context of environmental crisis makes us fearful if (say) the Small Tortoiseshells don't appear at their usual time, mindful as we may be that they could be going the same way as the Large variety (at least in Britain), susceptible now to the effects of climate change.[5] But then when they *do* appear, the pleasure/relief they generate is intensified, and we may wish to record the experience all the more. That tension between fear and joy is one important component of contemporary writing about nature. It is an important source of a series of consequential kinds of paradox and contradiction that I discern in contemporary nature writing and nature fiction, effects caused by the self-conscious *doubleness* of enjoying nature while recording elements of its demise, of celebrating that from which we must also acknowledge our distance. While we may be familiar with the complex ways in which ecocriticism registers affect, it is not customary to see contradiction and paradox as a *fundamental element* of nature writing, which is often seen as urgent, earnest, 'on message'. If the tenor and orientation of nature writing is seen

---

[4] Jeremy Thomas writes that the '150 sightings...recorded in Britain since 1950' can be put down to imported specimens or misidentifications. He is sceptical of other explanations (such as immigrants from France) because there has been no record of Large Tortoiseshell caterpillar nests in Britain for sixty years. See Jeremy Thomas and Richard Lewington, *The Butterflies of Britain and Ireland*, rev. edn (Gillingham: British Wildlife Publishing, 2010), pp. 187, 188. J. B. MacKinnon writes of 'change blindness' in *The Once and Future World: Nature as it Was, as it Is, as it Could Be* (New York: Houghton Mifflin Harcourt, 2013), pp. 20–1.

[5] They are vulnerable to the increasing range of a parasitic fly—see Chapter 4.

only in these simple terms, we might be tempted to see elements of contradiction and paradox as unintended, a corollary of the contemporary moment, and something to be read off symptomatically. But paradox means more than this. It is an unavoidable element of the zeitgeist, something that has been *deeply embraced* by writers, giving rise to quite startling aesthetic effects.

While I was completing this book, the Covid-19 pandemic struck, killing millions of people and changing everyone's lives (including mine, as I decided to retire). It's a context that doesn't directly affect the discussion—this is not another Covid book—although it does add another dimension to the problems that ensue from the human interference with nature, and which figure prominently in the works I consider: the pandemic, in Dipesh Chakrabarty's words, 'is the most recent and tragic illustration of how the expanding and accelerating processes of globalization can trigger changes in the much longer-term history of life on the planet'.[6] The pandemic also colours our reading of particular texts, as in this notable example, a scene from *Horizon* by Barry Lopez, in which he recalls travelling down the Yangtze River in 1987, from Chongqing to Wuhan, and chances upon a night market at Yueyang:

> Live monkeys and other small mammals, hedgehogs among them, stared out from the confines of screened metal cages. In one booth, wicker trays of dead crickets and heaps of caterpillars were on display, beneath a kind of clothesline from which dozens of sparrow-like birds hung by their feet. This was more than the atavistic scenes of medieval meat markets that Pieter Aertsen painted in the sixteenth century. It was the future, the years to come, when we would begin killing and consuming every last living thing.[7]

Lopez's recollection has a chilling air of prescience about it. The issue here is not simply the later possibility of a 'wet market' in this region of China being identified as the source of transfer of the SARS-CoV-2 strain of coronavirus to humans (which may or may not be true), but rather the question of human appetite and unthinking disposal of the nonhuman, which remains constant: a cornucopia without restraint, all available living things reduced to commodities for consumption. The ethical lean of nature writing illustrated here reveals wisdom of great relevance to the post-pandemic world. Lopez appropriates earlier artistic expression—the exploitative abundance registered in celebratory fashion

---

[6] Dipesh Chakrabarty, *The Climate of History in a Planetary Age* (Chicago: University of Chicago Press, 2021), p. 1.

[7] Barry Lopez, *Horizon* (London: Bodley Head, 2019), p. 32. Aertsen's *A Meat Stall with the Holy Family Giving Alms* (1551) was available to view on 'Google Arts & Culture' at the time of writing: https://artsandculture.google.com/asset/fgF8j5tB3UFgAg (accessed 11 May 2021). As the painting's title suggests, it aims to convey a positive spiritual message. In this allusion Lopez draws a contrast, but also implies continuity and an inevitable bleak trajectory in the human appropriation of other animals.

by Aertsen repurposed to convey a contemporary horror, and a glimpse of the dystopian future—a tendency that recurs in the myriad ways in which nature writers embrace and refashion their artistic and literary heritage.

And yet, if the pandemic crystallizes for us the consequences of the careless human treatment of the nonhuman, it has also been a time of renewed appreciation, stimulating reflections on how lockdowns have revealed the impact of people on nature, as when Michael McCarthy sees buzzards for the first time above his house, in the airspace that usually comprises the Heathrow flight path: with all the planes grounded, nature returns.[8] Such moments of appreciation encapsulate the paradox we have come to internalize: these glimpses of wonder are sometimes afforded to us *because of*, not just in spite of, the damage we know we have done.

---

[8] Michael McCarthy, Jeremy Mynott, and Peter Marren, *The Consolation of Nature: Spring in the Time of Coronavirus* (London: Hodder Studio, 2020), pp. 30–1. This is from McCarthy's diary entry for Tuesday, 24 March 2020.

Acknowledgements

I am grateful to Svenja Adolphs and Lynda Pratt at the University of Nottingham who, while Head of School and Director of Research respectively, facilitated a period of leave during which this project was significantly advanced. *Nature Prose* has benefitted from the comments and suggestions of a number of critics, most notably the ever-perspicacious David James, who was kind enough to read draft material at several stages. Matthew Hart and Rebecca Walkowitz offered insightful comments on early draft chapters. Conversations with Richard Kerridge have helped calibrate my understanding of nature writing, and pertinent questions were put to me by Terry Gifford and Greg Garrard at the ASLE UKI conference at the University of Plymouth in 2019. I am especially grateful to Jacqueline Norton at OUP for taking time out of her busy schedule to read draft chapters and assess the project's merits, and to Jack McNichol for seeing the book through to contract. A special note of thanks must go to the three anonymous readers approached by Jack for their enthusiastic endorsements of the manuscript. I have been fortunate, as well, in the production phase: both Emma Varley, Title Manager at OUP, and Deva Thomas, at Straive project management, have been impeccably efficient and helpful, while in Neil Morris I was blessed with an 'old-style' copy editor, eagle-eyed, precise, and engaged with the topic. A number of people have helped to keep me on track: my sister Alison and her partner George have always succeeded in raising good cheer chez Head, in their joyful visits from the Isle of Skye or in upbeat online get-togethers; our best friends, Niall, Barbara, and Jessica Whitehead, have the unfailing knack of buoying us up after delightful visits or Skype calls; and, through the gloom of the pandemic, Jeremy Lewis has sent consistently hilarious emails from Coleraine, educating me in the art of facing down adversity with fortitude, a skill we all need at times in our lives. I am especially grateful for Jeremy's memories and anecdotes of the late Tony Bareham, who was a great friend, and significant influence at the beginning of my career. Finally, a special acknowledgement to my family, Tricia, Felicity, and Oliver, for their joie de vivre, and their constant love and support.

Contents

Introduction	1
The Critique of Nature Writing	8
Nature, Culture, and Indigenous Knowledge	13
Immersion in the Nonhuman	17
Fiction, Nonfiction, and Ecomimesis	21
1. Remoteness	27
The Question of Solitude	31
The Gavin Maxwell Myth	43
Maxwell's Followers	50
Neil Ansell: the Hebrides and Remoteness	60
2. Exclusivity	67
Nature Writing and Privilege	68
Reclaiming the Tropes of Nature Writing	74
Indigenous Lore	83
Remembering the Dead	95
3. Abundance	105
Flight Behaviour: Abundance and Climate Change	105
Parables and Parable Effects	111
Abundance and the Emergence of Environmental Consciousness	115
Cultural Memory	120
The Expressive Abundance of *Pilgrim at Tinker Creek*	125
The Opacity of the Parable Effect	133
Tim Dee's Starlings	137
4. Rarity	142
The Shadow of Extinction	144
Naming and Collecting	153
Quest Narratives	162
Rethinking Rarity	171
Conclusion: Transformations	180
Self-conscious Rewilding	182
Wolves and People	188
Intimations of (Im)mortality	194
Coda	201
Bibliography	205
Index	217

Introduction

This book seeks to explain the popularity and appeal of contemporary writing about nature. One explanation is obvious enough: ostensibly, the environmental crisis injects a fresh urgency to nature writing—and fiction about nature—and engenders a new piquancy for those readers seeking solace in the nonhuman, or for those looking to change their habits in the face of ecological catastrophe. With respect to nonfiction, this is the context that justifies the use of 'new' in the 'new nature writing'. However, behind this apparently strong and unequivocal match between the aims of nature writers and the desires of their readers, there is also a shared mood of radical uncertainty and insecurity. This is more than an extension of the bewildering experience of modernity, although it is connected to it, especially to the 'vital experience' characterized by Marshall Berman as a 'unity of disunity' in which citizens of the world exist in 'a maelstrom of perpetual disintegration and renewal'. But each effort of renewal is now perceived to be more difficult, made in an increasingly impoverished world. For Berman, 'to be modern' was 'to be part of a universe in which, as Marx said, "all that is solid melts into air"'.[1] For us, that metaphor won't work. We are obliged to be more literal-minded: inhabiting the environmental crisis requires a steady consciousness that all is being permanently compromised, if not destroyed, including the air.

For Berman, modernity inserts its citizens into a situation of radical doubleness, promising 'adventure, power, joy, growth, transformation of the world and ourselves', while at the same time threatening 'to destroy everything we have, everything we know, everything we are'.[2] The dichotomy of the current age, in which a step change is clearly visible, is determined by a dramatically reduced conception of human possibility. As we become increasingly aware of the dire prognosis for life on the planet, and ever more conscious of our own responsibility in the causes of environmental devastation—and, at the same time, keener than ever to experience and protect what remains of the wild—we are caught in a moment of profound self-division, drawn to revere that which we have helped to destroy. This is the contemporary predicament of ecological crisis, characterized by an increasing sense of doubleness, in which humanity must rapidly uncover, and even embrace, its own flaws and culpabilities, whilst fostering redemptive

---

[1] Marshall Berman, *All That is Solid Melts into Air: The Experience of Modernity* (London: Verso, 1983), p. 15.
[2] Ibid.

capacities of emotion and rationality, and the effects they stimulate: change through empathy, and scientific intervention. This new human consciousness is related to Dipesh Chakrabarty's account of how 'the figure of the human' has 'doubled' over a generation, as consciousness of the implications of the Anthropocene has dawned: first, there is 'the human of humanist histories... capable of struggling for equality and fairness among other humans while caring for the environment and certain forms of nonhuman life'; but there is also now 'this other human', figured as 'a geological agent', with a history outside 'purely humanocentric views'. Even while we might strive for environmental change, we are obliged to see ourselves as part of 'an impersonal and unconscious geophysical force, the consequence of collective human activity'.[3] In imaginative writing about nature, this context results in insecurities and contradictions that give the lie to the impression of a solid and shared platform of commitment between writers and their audience.

The overarching argument in this book is that nature writing, in its various formats, contains formal effects of a complexity that is not sufficiently recognized, and that these paradoxical or antithetical effects encapsulate our current ecological dilemma, and offer a fresh resource for critical thinking. Such *literary* effects become more easily discernible when the distinctions between fictional and nonfictional writing are (partly) set aside, so that 'nature writing' is set within the broader conception of 'nature prose'. More specifically, the treatment and construction of 'nature' in contemporary imaginative prose reveals some significant paradoxes beneath its dominant moods—moods which are usually earnest, sometimes celebratory, sometimes prophetic or cautionary. It is in these paradoxical or antithetical moments that the contemporary ecological predicament is formally encoded, in a progressive development of ecological consciousness from the late 1950s (or even earlier), but which is primarily illustrated in this work from texts published from the 1990s onwards. The ambiguity in the subtitle of this book—'Writing in Ecological Crisis'—is intended to capture a mode of writing that is both contemporaneous with a defining time of crisis for humanity, and also formally fashioned by that context: this is writing that emerges in a time of crisis, but which is also, in some ways, in crisis itself.

Literary expression is, of course, distinguished by its propensity to embrace/convey multifaceted or contradictory or paradoxical impressions, whether through complex images or symbols, or through narrative moments of indeterminate epiphany, or through hybridized reworkings of formal tradition/convention, or ambivalent use of—or allusion to—other writers, or any number of other distinctly literary techniques. Every symbol, image, motif, or theme conjoins different possibilities, revealing the capacity for skilful writers to cultivate a rich

---

[3] Dipesh Chakrabarty, *The Climate of History in a Planetary Age* (Chicago: University of Chicago Press, 2021), p. 3.

ambivalence which distinguishes literature from other forms of discourse. Literary criticism, in its developing complexity, has found ever more inventive ways of interpreting such effects, and the ambiguities and contradictions they give rise to. Literary critics and theorists have always been attuned to such complexity, sometimes placing stress on the fault lines in texts, where their moments of paradox or contradiction emerge as particularly revealing and significant, whether or not such fissures appear to be part of the design. The conception of nature prose identified here allows for the productive reading of contradiction in nature writing, as well as in nature fiction, and indicates that such moments embody a formal correlative to the predicament of contemporary ecological paradox I have outlined above; and this also implies a degree of design in the implementation and embrace of paradox in contemporary nature prose, a conscious (or at least semi-conscious) deployment of ambivalence as a sign of contemporary angst.

Turning a literary-critical eye to the ambiguities of contemporary nature prose, however, we might say that such effects simply take their place in a tradition as long as the history of imaginative writing. Yet what is distinctive about our moment is that the contradictions and paradoxes that abound in nature prose seem to crystallize a zeitgeist that has an air of finality about it, a new kind of aesthetic to capture a global mood in which the end of things and the fatal flaws of humanity are forced together in revelations that are hard to bear, a new sublime of terrifying force. If 'Stendhal syndrome' is the incapacity brought on by overexposure to aesthetic beauty, we might think of our new situation as one which evokes an analogous form of total response, but one in which incapacity must be overcome.[4] So, moving through the comparison, this is not a syndrome so much, since the impact stems from a pervasive and unavoidable quandary rather than a particularized condition. But the invocation of an illness, or medical condition, has purchase in understanding our required response to the irreducible paradox of this moment: because of the impression it creates of identifying the ultimate, the final nature of things—serving to uncover the flaws and redemptive responsiveness of humanity simultaneously—it requires of us a new kind of emotional register, robust enough to overcome paralysis.

Such a register is implicitly humanist rather than post-humanist, and this seems to me an obligatory position for any literary-critical project that seeks both to understand and to develop its intellectual heritage—which is also what the most notable nature prose writers do, as I aim to show. This register also requires a deep recognition of the cultural mediation and appropriation of nature, while preserving the category of the nonhuman. In this respect, *Nature Prose* is written in the

---

[4] Stendhal syndrome was named by psychiatrist Graziella Magherini, tracing the condition to the experience of Stendhal (nom de plume of Marie-Henri Beyle), who wrote in 1817 about being overwhelmed by Italian Renaissance art on a trip to Florence. See Magherini, *La Sindrome di Stendhal* (Milan: Feltrinelli, 1992).

spirit of Kate Soper's important resolution of the tension between 'nature-endorsing' and 'nature-sceptical' perspectives, while insisting on the 'extra-discursive reality of nature'.[5] In writing this, I acknowledge that imaginative writing about nature has frequently been seen as naïve in different ways by prominent ecocritics, and I engage with some of the important critiques in the following pages, especially concerning the ways in which the construction of nature may be seen as a hidden component, left unpacked in the haste to establish an (impossible) immediacy of affect. I seek to show that contemporary nature prose actually *re-presents* the paradoxes and contradictions that some nature writing has been accused of fostering unintentionally. This new brand of nature prose combines knowledge drawn from natural history with a range of literary effects, and a distinctively new form of ecomimesis emerges from this synthesis, which is *attuned* to the cultural mediation of nature, and not unaware of it, as is often assumed.

Nature Prose, then, challenges the view that nature writing relies on a deceptive form of mimesis. But several other negative appraisals in current ecocritical thinking are also disputed: that nature writing encourages a consumerist engagement with ideas of nature; that its central concerns are racially exclusive; and that it fails to address adequately the cultural construction of the nonhuman. Utilizing the expanded definition of nature prose, the book discovers diverse forms of ecomimesis which are overt rather than deceptive; which challenge our ideas of nature, while seeking to make us engage with a positive construction of it; and which reveal points of connection between writers of different backgrounds and ethnicities. The emphasis is on late twentieth-century and twenty-first-century writing in Britain and the US (with more examples drawn from Europe, Australia, and South Africa), and on the literary qualities, effects, and strategies of the chosen body of texts. But the emphasis is not on coverage, but rather on representative techniques and effects. Through its readings, *Nature Prose* seeks to offer ways of rethinking literary critical approaches to seminal ecological topics—including place, resources, and biodiversity—showing how these issues are mediated by literary tropes in ways that require a modified understanding of mimesis. The obvious blind spot in the publishing, reception and criticism of contemporary nature writing is clearly its ethnic exclusivity: while nature writing remains predominantly the province of white authors in the Anglophone world, the collective vision it promotes is undermined. This blind spot must be (and is being) addressed; so too must the question of *privilege* in gaining access to wild places. In each chapter I consider instances of nature prose in which inequality and/or ethnic exclusion are central concerns, showing how the ethical dimension of our predicament of paradox is amplified by the shadow of exclusivity.

---

[5] Kate Soper, *What is Nature? Culture, Politics and the Non-human* (Oxford: Blackwell, 1995), pp. 4, 8.

The case for a hybrid category of contemporary prose writing about nature, in which distinctions between fiction and nonfiction might be seen as ways of discriminating between sub-branches of a single phenomenon, is made not to ignore the different aesthetic effects of fiction and nonfiction but, rather, to argue that these distinctions become less significant in the field of nature prose, where a shared environmental consciousness is the governing principle of categorization. In making this case, the book seeks to intervene in several interlocking ecocritical debates which condition the reception of 'literary' writing about the environment and the nonhuman. Successive chapters explore the various kinds of intervention that nature prose offers, and the paradox that many of these texts seek to conjure versions of the nonhuman through complex forms of textual allusion, borrowing, or reinvention.

The first frame of engagement underpinning subsequent chapters is the nature/culture debate, and the suggestion that, in the Anthropocene-conscious age, and in the era of climate crisis, there no longer exists a 'natural' world unaffected in some measure by human interference. The second crucial area of debate is the objection that the kind of environmental ethical thinking that is almost universal in nature writing is compromised by its anthropocentric underpinnings, and that the aesthetic appreciation of nature is already a form of consumerism, and another way of reducing nature to culture. The argument put forward here is that the identification of a realm beyond culture has been (and continues to be) partly a *strategy* in nature prose seeking to demonstrate to us that the something we can still think of as nature can survive and reassert itself with the right kind of husbandry and political choice. The existence of 'nature' beyond culture seems to me irrefutable: no matter how delimited the nonhuman world becomes, as a consequence of human interference and despoliation, it still evolves in ways we cannot anticipate or fully comprehend. To think otherwise is a sign of the hubris that has produced our current plight. The literary effects of nature prose, and the aesthetic appreciation they foster—underpinned by natural history (which constantly seeks to improve its imperfect understanding)—are designed to raise environmental consciousness and activate a new sense of being-in-the-world rather than to encourage passive or escapist consumption. Yet these effects are often complex, revealing a dense reliance on long traditions of written expression, reconfigured in the context of new anxieties.

The close link between sensibility and social moment explains the markedly contemporary phase of nature writing. For the purposes of taxonomy at the outset of this discussion, Don Scheese's succinct definition helps to clarify what is held to be distinctive about this literary mode: 'a first-person, nonfiction account of an exploration, both physical (outward) and mental (inward), of a predominantly nonhuman environment, as the protagonist follows the spatial movement of pastoralism from civilization to nature'.[6] The first thing to note about this definition is that there is nothing specifically contemporary about it; and, along the way, I want to remain alert to the continuities evident in nature writing from different periods, even while I try to pinpoint examples of *transition* to something distinctively contemporary, betokened by a *concentration* of concerns about environmental crisis—especially from the 1960s onwards—and which become more acute in the twenty-first century. An essential addition to Scheese's definition is to observe that there has usually been a characteristic ethical *lean* in nature writing, a desire to induct the reader into a shared appreciation of the nonhuman, so that 'the spatial movement' in the deployment of pastoralism, 'from civilization to nature', carries with it a rhetorical imperative inviting us to question the basis of civilization. One key marker of contemporary nature writing is that, as this rhetorical imperative becomes more urgent, so does the first-person narrative position in such writing *appear* to become more confined: nature writers are increasingly under zeitgeist pressure, so to speak, to stay on message. Narrative confinement, of course, is the enemy of the messy, hybrid, dialogic, contradictory essence of the literary, an ideational straitjacket that can short-circuit creative exploration and manufacture dogma in its place. Perhaps the most significant and characteristic feature of contemporary nature writing has been its propensity to resist the straitjacket, to find new ways of finding space to convey contradiction and paradox.

Another objective of this book is to query the distinction between nonfictional nature writing and forms of fiction that wrestle with the same ideological confinement. This is not to deny the validity, in some cases, of separating fiction from nonfiction; nor is it to question the worth of the excellent taxonomical work that was done in the notional 'first generation' of ecocritical study to identify subtle differences between various formal manifestations of 'nature-oriented literature'.[7] While recognizing some of the key rhetorical differences between fiction and nonfiction, however, it is also useful to see how literary effects cross over from one mode to the other. The paradoxes evident in fiction about nature—involving myriad configurations of the nature/culture tension—have parallels in the more notable nonfictional attempts to wrestle with preconceptions about the nonhuman, and with the political impotence that naturalists feel in the face of successive failures. The hard knowledge of natural history and environmental science that now underpins so much contemporary nature writing has profoundly influenced the novel too, generating new challenges to absorb facticity within fictional realms. To the extent that nature writing, and novels about nature written within the

---

[6] Don Scheese, *Nature Writing: The Pastoral Impulse in America* (New York: Twayne Publishers, 1996), p. 6.
[7] See, for example, Patrick D. Murphy's *Farther Afield in the Study of Nature-Oriented Literature* (Charlottesville: University Press of Virginia, 2000), especially the Introduction, 'Toward a Taxonomy of American Nature-Oriented Literature', pp. 1–11.

broad conventions of realism, both find strategies to encompass shared problems and paradoxes thrown up by contemporary knowledge and aesthetic priorities, it seems to me important to investigate the extent of this common ground, and to think in terms of a collective category for this purpose, as signalled in the title of this book.

The focus on the plight of an individual protagonist is fundamental to this project, not just because that is a predominant feature of the best (and often voice-driven) contemporary nature prose, but also because it foregrounds the dilemma at the heart of this project, and which I have previously expressed reservations about in some of my earlier ecocritical work: the dilemma of competing anthropocentric and ecocentric needs and emphases, apparently compromised by the unavoidable anthropocentric underpinnings of narrative fiction.[8] One way in which novelists have ameliorated that effect in the past is by omitting the usual invitation to identify with particular *characters*, and by making *place* a more central component of fictional worlds instead.[9] I have previously suggested that some such attempts 'to make new kinds of connection for the novel between people and place' have been necessarily limited because the 'most affecting elements' of such experimental works are often 'produced by the social struggle with particular contextual forces', so that (broadly speaking) culture eclipses nature, as one might expect.[10] But that is also to highlight the human predicament, which generates the complex forms of nature–culture interaction that animate the best writing about the nonhuman. In this book I want to focus squarely on this dilemma of anthropocentrism, and its various modes of inflection in contemporary nature prose. The fluid conception of nature prose, which recognizes fictional techniques in ostensibly nonfictional writing, and which also traces the presence of informed natural history in fictional worlds, facilitates the identification of the predicament of contemporary paradox *within the formal components* of a text.

Before blurring the distinction between fiction and nonfiction, however, I will consider how nature writing (as conventionally understood) has been criticized in various ways by ecocritics for its simplistic construction of 'nature', for its anthropocentric emphasis on individual development or enlightenment, for its social blind spots, and for promulgating a too-simplistic narrative of apocalyptic extinction and ecological collapse. As I have indicated, I seek to show that, rather than peddling unexamined holier-than-thou messages, much nature writing reveals a vision of paradox, contradiction, and uncertainty, a vision that captures

---

[8] See, for example, 'Ecocriticism and the Novel', in *The Green Studies Reader: From Romanticism to Ecocriticism*, ed. Laurence Coupe (London: Routledge, 2000), pp. 235–41.

[9] See, for example, the first two volumes of Raymond Williams's unfinished trilogy, *People of the Black Mountains* (London: Chatto & Windus, 1989–90); or Adam Thorpe's *Ulverton* (London: Secker & Warburg, 1992).

[10] Dominic Head, *The Cambridge Introduction to Modern British Fiction, 1950–2000* (Cambridge: Cambridge University Press, 2002), p. 201.

the contemporary human predicament of seeking to make reparation for the ecological destruction we have caused (and continue to cause) as a species: this is our dilemma, the search for solutions from a position of undeniable culpability.

The Critique of Nature Writing

The recuperation of nature writing within the category of nature prose may need a more extended justification, however, most obviously because nature writing has sometimes been seen to exacerbate the problem of anthropocentrism I have referred to in connection with narrative fiction. Initially, this charge may seem counter-intuitive: one of the foundation stones of first-generation ecocriticism was that nonfictional nature writing should be the primary object of ecocritical attention. Lawrence Buell's examination of what 'might be said to comprise an environmentally oriented work' led him to conclude, in an influential account seeking to identify the works that 'qualify unequivocally and consistently' as 'environmental', that 'most of the clearest cases are so-called nonfictional works'.[11] A forceful challenge to this view was made later by Dana Phillips, who felt that the ecocritical construction of nature writing placed undue emphasis on the 'first-person narrator's efforts to establish an intensely felt emotional connection with the natural world'. Such an 'emotional connection' can only be 'idiosyncratic', dependent 'on the temperament of the individual nature writer, who often lives or at least writes in relative isolation ... and who may have no interest whatsoever in being tutored by the natural sciences'.[12] Phillips thereby asserts a distinction between nature writing and nature science based on their relative authority. Following the taxonomy established by earlier ecocritical writing about the American tradition, he suggests that 'nature writing is belletristic', whereas 'natural history, by contrast, is much less so'. This distinction is based partly on the question of narrative stance: in natural history writing 'the narrator, if there is one, is a much more neutral party, his character need not be all that strongly marked'.[13] But this is one of the binary oppositions that contemporary nature prose unravels: the supposed authority of the natural historian, which is actually equally susceptible to the limits of the personal view, and always vulnerable to scientific advance, is rendered less certain in the texts encountered in *Nature Prose*; and, in a reverse process, the increasing reliance on scientific concerns, in more personal impressionistic accounts, produces a hybrid that is more informed than Phillips's critique allows.

---

[11] Lawrence Buell, *The Environmental Imagination: Thoreau, Nature Writing, and the Formation of American Culture* (Cambridge, Mass.: Belknap Press, 1995), p. 8.

[12] Dana Phillips, *The Truth of Ecology: Nature, Culture, and Literature In America* (New York: Oxford University Press, 2003), p. 185.

[13] Ibid., pp. 186–7.

Yet it is the hybridity itself that Phillips sees as being particularly problematic. Where 'authors of so-called nature writing...do avail themselves of much that natural history and the natural sciences have to offer, and...are fully committed to standards of objectivity and to getting the facts straight', they do not have 'their own subjectivity completely in check when they write' and are prone to 'yield to sentiment'. Despite this caveat, he defines the 'most popular' nature writers as those who 'seem to regard natural history and natural science less as aids than as obstacles to achieving a spiritually satisfying relationship with nature', even if they are willing to make use of scientific information that is 'suggestive to the imagination'.[14] A key example of problematic nature writing for Phillips is Annie Dillard's *Pilgrim at Tinker Creek*, which he presents as representative of the central problem in the reception of nature writing—an assumption about its mimetic immediacy—because its artifice has not been properly registered by its 'many fans', among whom are numbered 'the book's academic fans'.[15] Phillips sees the paradoxes of *Pilgrim at Tinker Creek* as representative of nature writing more broadly, albeit in an exaggerated form. Like many nature writers, Dillard is 'seeking a nonverbal, sensual awareness of nature', which she needs to 'find some way to verbalize and to make sense of'. The heart of the paradox, for Phillips, lies in the fact that Dillard 'is trying to force essentially lyric thoughts into the prosaic container of the nature essay'.[16] Again, the generic blurring is felt to lead to incoherence. But how might our reading of *Pilgrim at Tinker Creek* change if we see its paradoxes as contributing to its effects, as indicative of literary complexity and not intellectual fuzziness?

Dillard's book features centrally in my third chapter; but it is worth considering here as an early illustration (1974) of the cultivated paradox that I see as the defining feature of contemporary nature prose. A famous—and famously problematic—example of the fiction/nonfiction boundary in nature writing is the episode in *Pilgrim at Tinker Creek* in which Dillard's encounter with a giant water bug devouring a frog is fashioned into one of her key revelatory moments.[17] It subsequently emerged that this was not a first-hand experience in the way it is presented. The problem is not that the observation itself is false—Dillard was drawing on the work of other naturalists—but rather that the personal experience of it was falsified. This 'furor', as Murphy glosses it, 'seems to derive not from the scientific accuracy, the non-fictionality, of the description of nature, but from the narrative means by which the author frames that information'. The fact that readers felt deceived by this discovery suggests that 'the claim of non-fictionality seems to be wrapped up in an idea of writing with a "scientific bent" and also in writing based on direct personal experience'.[18] For Murphy, the controversy

---

[14] Ibid., p. 187.   [15] Ibid., p. 188.   [16] Ibid., pp. 190–1.
[17] See Annie Dillard, *Pilgrim at Tinker Creek* (1974; London: Picador, 1976), p. 19.
[18] Murphy, *Farther Afield*, p. 50.

exposes 'the fiction of nonfictionality', and he suggests that, instead of worrying about the distinction, we should place emphasis on the 'narrative framing of the facts'.[19]

There is certainly much artifice in the nature prose that is presented to the world as 'nonfiction': as Richard Kerridge points out, in nature writing 'the writer-protagonist will become a partly fictional character, even when the events, and their place, time and order, remain factual. Just a few minutes between event and writing will introduce that fictional quality';[20] but we still have to reckon with the expectations that are deliberately cultivated when a writer not only presents an episode as having been experienced personally but also suggests that it has had a transformative effect on them. In the case of the Dillard example, this results in a complex effect that has now become part of the mythology of *Pilgrim at Tinker Creek*. Because of the power of the water bug episode, Dillard's readers may also share her horror, and experience a similar transformative effect in their understanding of the nonhuman; but with the extra-textual information about Dillard's fabrication, we must concede that her readers are not experiencing this vicariously in the way they might imagine—as Dillard's initiates. And yet, because our response presumably repeats Dillard's (also vicarious) response (she also read about it second-hand), we realize that she puts us through the same *intellectual* experience that inspired her to connect her reading with experience in the field. The effect of this moment is representative of a common procedure in nature prose, where the artifice of the writing draws us in to the experience—which is here felt to be shared with the author—without dissipating our sense of its reality, since it has the authority of natural history observation behind it. But we can reread the water bug episode, once we are alert to its artifice, and then see it as a *performance* of personal transformation underpinned by knowledge of species' behaviour. This performative quality becomes more overt in later nature prose, so that Phillips's opposition between belletrism and factual neutrality is refigured as a necessary fusion of modes in which a quasi-spiritual preoccupation with self-growth is inseparable from an engagement with knowledge of the world. This is the essence of the ecomimetic effects of nature prose, which situate the ethical individual response unavoidably within processes of recording nonhuman nature.

It might seem that here I am simply restating Phillips's point more favourably. The charge that 'most contemporary nature writing [contemporary up to 2003, that is]...is *too selfish*', in the sense that it is 'too preoccupied with the self as the formative and essential element of experience' to the detriment of ethical behaviour, is not necessarily answered by my emphasis on the performative.[21] However,

---

[19] Ibid., p. 51.
[20] Richard Kerridge, 'Nature Writing', in *The Cambridge Companion to Prose*, ed. Daniel Tyler (Cambridge: Cambridge University Press, 2021), pp. 214–32 (p. 214).
[21] Phillips, *The Truth of Ecology*, p. 195.

the elements that have perhaps become clearer in nature writing published since Phillips's survey are the more strenuous attempts to grapple with scientific knowledge. The juxtaposition of the personal experiential quest with factual understanding can be uneven, and often a source of the contradictory effects that this book is concerned with. But such juxtaposition serves to complicate the 'fundamental tension between psychology or spirituality and natural history' that preoccupies Phillips.[22] For him, the division between these things means that nature writing is often not 'about nature at all', but rather 'writing about a response to nature' which privileges 'the private, inner world of the self' over 'the outer world of nature and culture'.[23] This survey argues that the tension between private and outer worlds cannot be seen as an opposition but, rather, as the necessary nexus for ecological understanding, which may be glimpsed *because* of the contradictions of this aesthetic form rather than in spite of them.

What I am arguing for is the reclamation of the aesthetic effects of nature prose in such a way that the binary oppositions that have concerned—and continue to concern—the critics of nature writing are refigured as necessary features. Which means they are not 'oppositions' at all. Again, this is where literary criticism, with its propensity to focus on moments of discursive ambiguity, is a very helpful resource for rethinking the aesthetic rendering of nature. In a very familiar binary version of this aesthetic, the nonhuman world is perceived as a therapeutic escape from the excesses of the industrialized urban landscape in which most people spend most of their time. One problem with such an aesthetic of appreciation is that it smacks of consumerism rather than genuine engagement. An easy solution here is to see humans (and so human responses) as part of nature in the first place: such a view collapses the consumerism/engagement opposition by producing an aesthetics of the natural world in which 'natural beauty is not our projection of art-derived modes of seeing' because in fact 'aesthetic qualities are out there, objective presences registered by the human body as itself part of nature'.[24] Personally, I see no justification in dissolving this boundary of perception, or in suggesting that the human is absorbed into nature; indeed, the separation is the foundation of a very different aesthetic that thrives on the friction between nature and culture. The identification of such friction also addresses another risk noted by Timothy Clark—the risk that nature writing, by aestheticizing wilderness, might participate in the very process of taming that the writing ostensibly contests.[25] But *Nature Prose* is not simply designed to demonstrate this aesthetic of nature–culture friction. Beyond this, I am interested in a textual dynamic in

---

[22] Ibid., p. 203.   [23] Ibid., p. 210.
[24] This is Timothy Clark's summary of Gernot Böhme's work, published in German as *Für eine ökologische Naturästhetik* (Frankfurt am Main: Suhrkamp, 1989) and *Atmosphäre* (Frankfurt am Main: Suhrkamp, 1995). See Timothy Clark, *The Cambridge Introduction to Literature and the Environment* (Cambridge: Cambridge University Press, 2011), pp. 81–2.
[25] Clark, *The Cambridge Introduction to Literature and the Environment*, p. 40.

which such effects serve as a means to an end, a way of reconnecting readers with the nonhuman in such a way that the individual text ultimately recedes in importance, displaced by the referent it evokes.

The way in which this dynamic unfolds puts a fresh complexion on that perceived cliché in nature writing in which readers are seemingly led to share a moment of revelation—as in Dillard's account of the water bug—and are thereby cajoled into a vicarious appreciation of the terror/wonder of nature. Such a perceived rhetorical strategy is aimed at addressing the alienation of modern citizens from nature, a method that partly depends on emphasizing nature's otherness, even its inexpressible qualities: the pursuit of the ineffable seems to imply something elemental that we have lost in our dealings with nature, something that can be regained only by sloughing off our garb of intellectual preconception. For Phillips, writing of the American tradition, this tendency results in 'bad faith' in nature writing, which is 'most evident in its treatment of its own subject matter, the natural world, which it represents as alien, and therefore as something impossible to address, much less capture, in words – even when the words it uses to describe the natural world are in fact wonderfully eloquent and evocative'.[26] As a way of transcending this bad faith, Phillips calls for a form of cultural mediation, in which 'the difference between nature and culture doesn't have to be granted the grave philosophical significance that nature writers have granted it', so that culture can be correctly conceived as 'our means of negotiating our differences from nature and from each other, and not an outright impediment to our negotiations'.[27] The argument in this book is not just that such cultural mediation is foregrounded in contemporary nature prose but that the interaction of nature and culture is the very focus of its complex effects. Moments of apparent epiphany or revelation need to be approached in this way, and again the habits of literary-critical reading are useful here: James Joyce's *Dubliners* was a definitive demonstration (in a much longer literary history) that moments of epiphany can also be moments of compromised or non-epiphany, points of nexus in which perspectives or interpretations clash, cancel each other out, or point to various possibilities. Post-Joyce, no critic of contemporary fiction can take an 'epiphany' at face value; and neither should we do so when reading nonfictional nature writing, realizing the fusion of nature and culture.

For Timothy Morton the culture/nature opposition is problematic for 'environmental art'—which for him includes 'the literary criticism of environmental literature'—because 'the idea of "nature"' tends to obscure 'properly ecological forms of culture'.[28] This compounds the problem that writing about nature cannot put us directly in touch with the nonhuman in the ways it allegedly purports to do.

---

[26] Phillips, *The Truth of Ecology*, pp. 218–19.   [27] Ibid., p. 224.
[28] Timothy Morton, *Ecology without Nature: Rethinking Environmental Aesthetics* (Cambridge, Mass.: Harvard University Press, 2007), pp. 3, 1.

But if we see mediation as a necessary component of nature prose, often deployed knowingly in ways that foreground the *problems* of mediation, we can see the promise of direct access to the nonhuman as a consciously thwarted gesture, in which the performance is more important than the elusive union with the nonhuman other. Instead, the referent becomes the focus of debate and discussion, much in the spirit of Morton's invocation of avant-garde art, in his account of ecomimesis.[29] Thus, the reading of nature prose is analogous to the experience of stepping into a gallery, and engaging with a vibrant series of paintings, or an installation with an urgent political implication, and then emerging onto the street reflecting a little differently on the world, and perhaps feeling motivated to *act* on some front. In this way, nature writing has the capacity—as an integral facet of an aesthetic effect that can *seem* escapist, or consumerist, or sometimes dogmatic—to stimulate reflection and to enlarge understanding, but perhaps in unforeseen ways.

Nature, Culture, and Indigenous Knowledge

Such aesthetic complexity arises even in instances where a simple binary opposition seems to be in play. A clear example of this is the surprisingly equivocal treatment of indigenous knowledge, where such knowledge ostensibly requires holistic modes of living that are more in sympathy with the nonhuman environment than Western or colonial habits of living and development. This treatment leads in different directions in a discussion of the work of Louis Owens in Chapter 2. Here I want to introduce the topic through a consideration of another much-discussed text, the Chickasaw writer Linda Hogan's novel *Power* (1998).

There is a stereotypical idea of learning from traditional American Indian wisdom as a beneficent 'alternative response to the pervasive Western, techno-industrial attitudes toward and treatment of the land' (as well as nonhuman species).[30] However much value there may be in American Indian tradition, and however much wisdom may be gleaned from it, there is a central problem of mediation, because, as Lee Schweninger points out, the 'perspectives of environmentalism attributed to Native Americans' stem largely from 'representations both imposed on and culled from American Indian cultures by non-Natives'.[31] For Ursula Heise, the prioritization of indigenous wisdom results in a formulaic mode of environmentalist discourse which builds on a 'story template' established in the nineteenth century, 'the idea that modern society has degraded a natural world that used to be beautiful, harmonious, and self-sustaining and that might

---

[29] Ibid., p. 31.
[30] Lee Schweninger, *Listening to the Land: Native American Literary Responses to the Landscape* (Athens: University of Georgia Press, 2008), p. 16.
[31] Ibid., p. 17.

disappear completely if modern humans do not change their way of life'.[32] This template, when applied in connection with 'postcolonial societies', Heise argues, 'often contrasts an indigenous, ecologically grounded past with the degradation of nature European imperialism has brought about'. She argues further that 'Environmentalism inside and outside of recognizable social movements and organizations has relied' on such narratives of decline in which 'the awareness of nature's beauty and value is intimately linked to a foreboding sense of its looming destruction'. And 'environmentalist writers' have 'mobilized literary and aesthetic concepts and genres such as the sublime, the picturesque, pastoral, apocalyptic narrative, and…"toxic discourse" about polluted landscapes and deformed bodies so as to convey a sense of a precious, beautiful, and fragile natural world at risk'.[33] Environmental writing characterized in this way—rooted in a good/bad historical binary opposition, and dependent upon established narrative devices and rhetorical effects—is quite unlike the nature prose examined in this book.

A more complex approach to the matter of indigenous environmental wisdom is central to Hogan's *Power*. At the heart of the book is the relationship between Ama and Omishto, and their engagement with the customs and beliefs of the (fictional) Taiga tribe. Omishto, in a familiar trope of American Indian fiction, is caught between indigenous and settler/colonial cultures; but she is increasingly influenced by 'Aunt' Ama, who supplies the care and guidance her Westernized mother fails to provide. Ama, she feels, 'lives in a natural way' and is in touch 'with nature and the spirit world'.[34] But Ama is also living at the cusp of cultural change, believing herself called 'to living halfway between the modern world and the ancient one' (pp. 22-3). The central enigmatic act of the book is Ama's ritual killing of a Florida panther, drawing on tribal lore and with Omishto at her side, an episode that follows a hurricane, suggestive of a rift with nature that might be addressed by the sacrifice of the panther. Ama is arrested and put on trial, having admitted the slaughter of an endangered and protected animal. While Omishto understands Ama's motivation—her belief that 'someone had to find a way to renew the world' (p. 125), and that the sacrifice was the means to achieve this, according to Taiga belief (p. 111)—she also finds herself trying to reconcile contradictory truths, represented by 'the endangered cat' on one side and indigenous 'treaty rights' on the other. As a consequence, she realizes she is in 'the worst place', being 'on both sides now' (p. 115). The case against Ama is dismissed for lack of evidence (p. 143); but Ama is subsequently tried by a Taiga tribal court and banished from her people for failing to follow the sacrificial ritual

---

[32] Ursula K. Heise, *Imagining Extinction: The Cultural Meanings of Endangered Species* (Chicago: University of Chicago Press, 2016), p. 7.
[33] Ibid.
[34] Linda Hogan, *Power* (New York: Norton, 1998), p. 17. Subsequent references are given in parentheses.

appropriately: she should have brought the sacred animal to the Taiga people, the Panther Clan (pp. 172, 165). Ama willingly becomes a scapegoat, as Omishto surmises: she is deliberately concealing from the clan that the panther was a sick specimen, because they are 'intricately, intimately' connected to it, and to tell them of its 'ragged flea-bitten' state 'would cut their world in half' and 'break their hearts and lives' (p. 166). Thus Ama, according to Omishto, performs a sacrificial act of renewal and also sacrifices herself, both acts designed to save the tribe.

The sickness of the panther, its territory diminished by human encroachment, symbolizes the endangered status of the Panther Clan itself. At the same time, it foregrounds the literal environmental issue of modern conservation at odds with indigenous practice. But taken too literally, the connotations of the panther are inconsistent or unconvincing, according to Schweninger. For example, although it was a threatened species at the time, tracked specimens of the Florida panther were in good health.[35] Thus, if Hogan is making her panther sickly as a representation of the species (which conforms to a stereotype of the time), she is contradicting the published scientific record. Yet this is one example of how Hogan's method pursues a 'truth' that may be at odds 'with the facts of Western science'. In this case, she subverts the stereotype to indicate that 'even a diminished, sickly panther (like an old Taiga clan member) maintains enormous power on its own turf'.[36] Such a subversion invites us to think beyond the cultural oppositions that the book sets up, and which are complicated by the several connotations of the title. In the court case, Omishto reacts angrily, under cross-examination, to the suggestion that Ama was 'trying to get power' from 'the spirit world' by killing the panther: '"What for?" I say. Rude. "To get something she wanted? She didn't want anything. To have luck in gambling?"' (p. 130). Omishto's rudeness imputes a connection between acquisitiveness and power in the Western perspective, which is also enshrined in the courtroom. The line of questioning also reveals an ethnic stereotype in the perception that Taiga people believe they can gain power by eating panther meat (p. 132). Ultimately, the 'cold power' of the courtroom is produced by a blend of contradictory forces: first, the duplicitous nature of legal practitioners, 'those who believe in secrets and twists of truth, but call for honesty'; and second, the voyeuristic impulse to 'glimpse into another world' (p. 136). But the voyeurism also reveals the insecurity of the colonizer, because this other world of indigenous culture is 'a crack in the container of [white] history' (p. 136). Thus, the power of the white man's courtroom channels a fascination with the Other that might reveal the underlying insecurity of the colonizer's position.

During the 'trial by tribal court' (p. 160) Omishto ponders 'the old laws' of the Taiga people, which 'maybe... still had power' (p. 168). After Ama's banishment

---

[35] Schweninger, *Listening to the Land*, p. 191. Schweninger's authority here is David Maehr, *The Florida Panther: Life and Death of a Vanishing Carnivore* (Washington, DC: Island Press, 1997).

[36] Schweninger, *Listening to the Land*, pp. 192, 193.

is pronounced, Omishto thinks the tribal elders have acted in the belief that 'she wanted power' (p. 174)—the power of the old laws, that is—a mirror image of the white man's court, and also mistaken. A more positive sense of indigeneity emerges from Omishto's sense that the tribal elder Annie Hide, a relative of her birth mother (p. 158), 'has felt the power of healing' (p. 181), and this is an important staging post in Omishto's final decision to return to the fold of the clan, even though they have sentenced her mother figure Ama to exile, a 'walking death' (p. 176). There are no straightforward choices in *Power*. The two kinds of court, and the cultures they embody, are both compromised, so Omishto's choice to identify with the Taiga is an equivocal resolution. She remains 'halfway between the modern world and the ancient one' on the issue of species conservation (p. 23), and she must learn to live according to two contradictory truths (p. 115). The logic of embracing contradiction is flagged in the book's epigraph—'Mystery is a form of power'—which implies a transcendent form of power that resides beyond the impasse of contradictory, binary choice. In the spirit of the embrace of ambivalence, the response to ecological predicament that characterizes so much contemporary nature prose, Omishto recognizes 'a fracture in the world', which means that Ama is neither innocent nor guilty (p. 198).

In the preface to *Dwellings* (1995), a collection of essays and reflections, Hogan offers a simpler account of her inspiration, her 'lifelong work to seek an understanding of the two views of the world, one as seen by native people and the other as seen by those who are new and young on this continent'. But in this mediation between indigenous and settler views there is a clear emphasis on what she calls 'my native understanding that there is a terrestrial intelligence that lies beyond our human knowing and grasping'.[37] The 'mystery' here is avowedly spiritual, premised on the indigenous conviction that 'humankind is not separate from nature'.[38] In *Power*, the mystery that is evoked has additional dimensions, political and secular, which complicate Omishto's access to the spiritual contentment of Taiga ways. As Janie Soto (the Head of the Panther Clan) understands, the 'order of things', the 'mystery of how every single thing worked together' (p. 158), has been violated by the destruction of the panther's habitat: 'she knows that cutting the ground for the new highway was part of a terrible breaking that began long ago, the breaking of rules fixed from the start' (p. 183). The consequent mystery is not that of the spirituality of the kind Hogan celebrates in *Dwellings*, or the mystery of the ecosystem, but the mystery of finding a way forward in the current predicament, where both the religious system and the environment are known to be compromised, and where knowledge gleaned from both indigenous and settler people may be needed.

---

[37] Linda Hogan, *Dwellings* (New York: Norton, 1995), p. 11.   [38] Ibid., p. 12.

It is the insoluble difficulty of the contemporary moment that gives Ama's double sacrifice its power. Her self-destructive act, which transgresses Taiga law as well as white laws, is imagined as a paradoxically healing gesture: she 'acts against tradition in order to restore that tradition', as Carrie Bowen-Mercer puts it.[39] The reasoning remains mysterious, and this is Hogan's way of outlining the kind of act our predicament requires without prescribing its precise nature: such acts will be heroic, self-sacrificing, perhaps seeking solutions not yet defined or understood. But the power of *Power* is not as unhelpfully vague as this suggests: the mutual interrogation of indigenous and Western perceptions of power is a critique that pushes beyond the stereotypical presentation of indigenous wisdom and implies the need of a synthesis.

Immersion in the Nonhuman

Both Annie Dillard and Linda Hogan, in the texts I have considered above, emphasize the desirability of human immersion in, or integration with, the nonhuman, while also—implicitly or explicitly—showing that cultural mediation makes this impossible. Dillard's desire, in *Pilgrim at Tinker Creek*, to be 'in the clustering thick of things, rapt and enwrapped in the rising and falling world' cannot be realized, and this leads to some complex and powerful effects (as I try to show in Chapter 3).[40] In *Dwellings*, Hogan explains that she writes 'out of respect for the natural world, recognizing that humankind is not separate from nature', and in writing this she articulates a fundamental tenet of indigenous belief.[41] Yet *Power*, as we have seen, complicates this idealistic position, warning us against the stereotype of indigenous wisdom even while it seeks to reground the idealism within a dialectical process. Here, in an extension of the discussion so far, I want to consider the implications of still more extreme or insistent yearnings for immersion and integration: does a point come where the quest for oneness reveals its redundancy?

In any environmental literature a fundamental obstacle to the holy grail of immersion in the nonhuman is the tendency to anthropomorphize. Indeed, anthropocentric projection is apparent, to a degree, in different kinds of text— the more scientific natural histories, as well as the more lyrical—especially where the behaviour of animals is concerned. To an extent, this is *written into* the ethical principles of environmental thinking. If we consider Aldo Leopold's land ethic, in which our understanding of 'community' is extended to include 'soils, waters,

---

[39] Carrie Bowen-Mercer, 'Dancing the Chronotopes of Power: The Road to Survival in Linda Hogan's *Power*', in *From the Center of Tradition: Critical Perspectives on Linda Hogan*, ed. Barbara J. Cook (Boulder: University Press of Colorado, 2003), pp. 157–77 (p. 158).
[40] Dillard, *Pilgrim*, p. 195.   [41] Hogan, *Dwellings*, p. 12.

plants, and animals', we can see an obvious projection of human ethics, rooted in empathy for others, based on the assumption that the nonhuman realm comprises 'fellow members' of the land community. This is one of the founding principles of modern environmentalism, of course, the rhetoric of which hinges on its overt anthropocentrism, so that principles of human organization are used to construct a realm of protection: 'the role of *Homo sapiens*', as Leopold puts it, is reversed 'from conqueror of the land community to plain member and citizen of it'.[42] There is a significant blind spot in Leopold's thinking: not all people begin from the position of 'conqueror', a point enlarged upon in Chapter 2. Nevertheless, he identifies a general principle that underpins the ethics of environmental discourse, much of which implies the need to empathize with nonhuman 'citizens' and to try and understand their needs. Yet we are inclined to trace nonhuman motivation in anthropocentric terms, which can lead to unfounded assumptions, so the challenge then becomes recognizing the imperfections of anthropocentric projection in an ongoing process of recalibration. This is how natural history improves its understanding, in an unending programme of improvement; and this process informs other kinds of nature prose too.

One way of circumventing the difficulty of anthropocentrism is to see humanity as a part of nature by virtue of evolution, a species occupying 'a niche, adaptive fit'.[43] As I mentioned earlier, this is to deny the friction between nature and culture upon which nature writing depends. In this sense, *Nature Prose* is broadly in tune with Phillips's astute observation that 'culture is our means of negotiating our differences from nature and from each other, and not an outright impediment to our negotiations'.[44] Unlike Phillips, however, I find this cultural emphasis implicit in much nature writing, even those instances that make the gesture of decrying culture as an obstacle in the quest for immersion. Invariably, in the most keenly pursued immersive narratives, in which the holy grail of integration with the outer world is the primary motivation, the apparent impediment of cultural mediation emerges as a vital resource. This is not to make the obvious point that any text is a cultural product, but rather to signal how those nature writers who seek, ostensibly, to relinquish their cultural ties—and often in innovative and startling ways—still rely on the paradox, which is so distinctively resonant in nature prose, that their quest becomes vital only through its cultural rootedness.

My example to illustrate this section of the discussion is Peter Matthiessen's enigmatic quest narrative *The Snow Leopard* (1978), an account of extreme natural history exploration in the Himalayas that is also an inner journey, the quest for the 'ultimate perception' of Zen Buddhism, one aspect of which is an

---

[42] Aldo Leopold, *A Sand County Almanac and Sketches Here and There* (1949; Oxford: Oxford University Press, 1987), p. 204.

[43] Jim Cheney, 'Truth, Knowledge and the Wild World', *Environmental Ethics*, 10 (2005), 2, pp. 101–35 (p. 116).

[44] Phillips, *The Truth of Ecology*, p. 224.

immersive mode of being-in-nature, in pursuit of a mystical state beyond dualism and non-dualism.[45] For Matthiessen this is a lifelong quest that can never be achieved—at least, this is the implication of *The Snow Leopard*. He gives an indication of the impossibility of the quest when he describes a *koan*, 'a Zen paradox, not to be solved by intellect, that may bring about a sudden dissolution of logical thought and clear the way for direct *seeing* into the heart of existence' (p. 125). But Matthiessen's book demonstrates the paradox behind the paradox: the attempt to progress beyond logical thought and advance towards ultimate existence requires intellectual application in the first place. His particular achievement is to build a contemporary travel/nature narrative around this age-old enigma. But this already reveals the self-conscious textual confines of the creative moment: for Tim Youngs, *The Snow Leopard* is a clear example of how 'modern quests may be a search for the meaning of a quest'.[46] The outward journey is an account of Matthiessen's journey with zoologist George Schaller in 1973 on an expedition to Tibet to study 'the bharal, or Himalayan blue sheep' (p. 13). Matthiessen, however, is more compelled by the journey to the Buddhist 'Crystal Monastery' near Shey Gompa; and by the possibility of encountering a rare snow leopard on the way.

The book is artfully constructed. Matthiessen primes his reader to see the quest to find the snow leopard, 'that rarest and most beautiful of the great cats', as the focus of the journey: they are reputed to be found where the bharal are 'numerous and easily observed', and his 'hope of glimpsing this near-mythic beast' is 'reason enough for the entire journey' (p. 13). Throughout the book we are enticed with provocative signs of the leopard—prints, scat, reports of their habitat, accounts of sightings—and we are encouraged to anticipate a revelatory encounter in which the spiritual journey may intertwine with the climax of the expedition. It will eventually dawn on every reader, however, that Matthiessen is not going to be rewarded with a glimpse of the leopard. This is signalled clearly when he makes the *not-seeing* part of the inner quest:

> If the snow leopard should manifest itself, then I am ready to see the snow leopard. If not, then somehow (and I don't understand this instinct, even now) I am not ready to perceive it, in the same way that I am not ready to resolve my *koan*; and in the not-seeing, I am content. I think I must be disappointed, having come so far, and yet I do not feel that way. I am disappointed, and also, I am not disappointed. That the snow leopard *is*, that it is here, that its frosty eyes watch us from the mountain – that is enough. (p. 221)

---

[45] Peter Matthiessen, *The Snow Leopard* (1978; London: Vintage, 1998), p. 42. Subsequent references are given in parentheses.

[46] Tim Youngs, *The Cambridge Introduction to Travel Writing* (Cambridge: Cambridge University Press, 2013), p. 98.

Even after this significant prolepsis about not-seeing—which is also one of the most arresting passages in contemporary nature prose, as I hope to show—we are still encouraged to believe there is a last hope of Matthiessen seeing the snow leopard (p. 265); but it is Schaller who sees it, after Matthiessen has left the expedition, and Schaller's encounter with the leopard is reported in perfunctory fashion. (We are simply told that it 'jumped up ahead' of him 'in patchy snow' (p. 290), a second-hand account presented as if barely worth mentioning.)

To understand fully the effect of the not-seeing passage we need to consider the resonances of the snow leopard. As my summary of Matthiessen's book so far suggests, the leopard, the 'near-mythical beast', is linked profoundly to the author's quest for enlightenment according to the principles of Zen Buddhism. And the contradictory feelings of disappointment *and* contentment in the not-seeing is part of his spiritual journey, an acceptance of contradiction that signals a personal advance. But the snow leopard is also the focus of a wildlife explorer's tale, a life-and-blood rare species, and 'not some kind of facile symbol' as Richard Mabey puts it. Mabey observes that Matthiessen is 'desperate to glimpse' the animal, 'but also desperate to allow [it] to remain invisible, secretly itself, untouched by his cravings'.[47] The use of language, often seen as a barrier to immersion in the nonhuman in nature writing—and which is, Mabey points out, particularly 'suspect in Buddhism', perceived as 'one of the layers of illusion to be transcended'—emerges as the book's clear strength. Matthiessen's expression is 'direct, an unadorned outgrowth of what he is describing and an embodiment of its significance'. For Mabey, this pinpoints 'the central paradox of the book' in that 'the author's meditative disciplines, his search for a purity of understanding beyond words, has led him to a supreme clarity of language'.[48] I will say more about the problem of language in Chapter 4 in a consideration of the relationship between nature writing and natural history. The point I want to extract and extend from Mabey's analysis here is that Matthiessen's quest produces a classic of (secular) nature writing about a rare animal. Yet because it is also a spiritual quest, the sense of reverence infuses a secular world view in a way that is prototypical of contemporary nature writing. It is not that reverence of nature per se is new, but rather that the embrace of contradiction that combines with it gives it a distinctive hue. To return to the not-seeing passage, there are elements that chime with a contemporary environmentalist reader's stance: the contentment in simply knowing the snow leopard is there, and the instinct not to intrude upon wild nature. But the not-seeing also evokes the shadow of extinction, which implies another reason why the disappointment is double-edged. And there is also a non-literal element to the snow leopard—not the facile symbol that Mabey

---

[47] Richard Mabey, *Turning the Boat for Home: A Life Writing About Nature* (London: Chatto & Windus, 2019), p. 9.
[48] Ibid., pp. 13, 14.

fears, but rather an emblematic dimension that grows out of the literal quest, revealing a dynamic of extrapolation: as the embodiment of nonhuman nature, the snow leopard is that which is elusive, vulnerable, but which cannot be contained or controlled. Part of Matthiessen's complex paradox thus evokes the contemporary predicament I am concerned with in this book.

Fiction, Nonfiction, and Ecomimesis

I have already made some reference to the problematic distinction between fiction and nonfiction in defining an 'environmental text' (in Buell's term), and blurring that distinction is fundamental to all of the readings I offer. I want to conclude this survey of topics by considering this issue in more detail, and I return here to the 'checklist' drawn up by Buell concerning the four key principles that might 'comprise an environmentally oriented work', since this is a landmark exercise in establishing the differences, but also the common features, between environmental nonfiction and fiction.[49] The principles are inclusive—as Buell observes, 'few works fail to qualify at least marginally'—but, at the same time, 'few qualify unequivocally and consistently', nonfictional works comprising 'most of the clearest cases'.[50] With respect to contemporary nature prose, there are grounds to revise the extent of this inclusivity. All of Buell's principles apply to the texts selected for discussion in this book, I think, whether published as fiction or nonfiction; indeed, there is a good deal of self-conscious reflection on these principles *within* these texts. And while this kind of artful self-consciousness is not entirely new to nonfictional writing, the extent of it—marked by distinctive kinds of formal hybridity—seems to be a key element in an epochal shift.

Here it is worth remarking upon the literary credentials of contemporary nature writing, and that seminal text, Jason Cowley's editorial letter in the landmark *Granta* issue devoted to 'The New Nature Writing' (2008), where Cowley distinguishes between 'old nature writing', defined as 'the lyrical pastoral tradition of the romantic wanderer', and new 'heterodox and experimental' methods of treatment: 'the best new nature writing is also an experiment in forms: the field report, the essay, the memoir, the travelogue. If travel writing can often seem like a debased and exhausted genre, nature writing is its opposite:

---

[49] The principles are (i) that '*the nonhuman environment is present not merely as a framing device but as a presence that begins to suggest that human history is implicated in natural history*'; (ii) that '*the human interest is not understood to be the only legitimate interest*'; (iii) that '*human accountability to the environment is part of the text's ethical orientation*'; and (iv) that '*some sense of the environment as a process rather than as a constant or given is at least implicit in the text*'. See Buell, *The Environmental Imagination*, pp. 7–8.

[50] Ibid., p. 8.

something urgent, vital and alert to the defining particulars of our times.'[51] The context of 'our times' is defined in relation to the pressing environmental concerns that now govern consciousness about the world and our place in it. More broadly, this 'time of emergency' is what some environmentalists refer to as the Anthropocene (discussed above in Chakrabarty's account of a 'geophysical force' produced by 'collective human activity'), the current geological epoch commencing with the Industrial Revolution (or earlier in some definitions), the period in which geology and ecology are directly affected by the activities of humankind.[52] While *consciousness* of that epoch is relatively recent, nature writers have been responding directly to what we think of as contemporary environmental issues certainly since the 1960s. To add to the necessity of experimentation and generic reinvention, the proposed new nature writing is infused with an understanding of this complex time of crisis.

As the previous sections of this Introduction indicate, I am interested in the use made by nature writers of a wide range of cultural sources, whether taken from natural history, or pastoralism, or traditions of personal reflection—this is the 'experiment in forms' that Cowley writes of—sources that can all be seen as problematically anthropocentric in one way or another, but which are put to new uses. This makes principles such as those brilliantly drawn up by Buell, before this era of creativity emerged, seem de rigueur: all of them can now be taken as given, necessary focal points of self-conscious reflection. The literary-critical questions that seem relevant now concern the new ways in which contemporary writers make their consciousness about these ethical problems part of their formal effects. The redeployment of, especially, literary tropes and forms may often be undertaken in the spirit of accepting the anthropocentric taint they 'import' into a work. This is an essential dimension of contemporary nature prose, an ambivalent characteristic that demands a recalibration of critical comprehension: writers in the contemporary moment, even if they seem to be striving for some kind of ecocentric purity, bring with them an understanding of the inescapable cultural past. Declining to jettison that heritage, they investigate ways in which it might be reworked.

A good example of some aspects of this hybridity is Adam Thorpe's *On Silbury Hill* (2014), an instance of new nature writing which includes the author's reflections on his formative influences, and the importance of Silbury Hill in Wiltshire to his ongoing reflections on the human inhabitation of place. He recalls an event from his younger days with the travelling theatre company Equinox, which is recounted in his poem 'Drama Workshop, Avebury', concerning a drama

---

[51] Jason Cowley, 'Editor's letter: the new nature writing', *Granta*, 102, Summer 2008, pp. 7–12 (p. 10).

[52] Ibid., pp. 9–10. The landmark essay in defining the Anthropocene is Paul J. Crutzen and Eugene F. Stoermer's 'The Anthropocene', *IGBP Newsletter*, 41(2000), pp. 17–18.

workshop for children, culminating in a performance using the Avebury stone circle as a 'Brookeian empty space'.[53] Thorpe remembers an 8-year-old running towards the horizon, instead of turning for the finale. The child's enigmatic explanation of her behaviour—she says there is 'too much space'—is a key moment in Thorpe's inspiration: 'what the child said still strikes me as profound: the stone circle creates its own space, a space that has nothing to do with normal space. The circle of infinity concentrates our attention on above and below, like a tube, a microscope or a telescope. Above, it really is more or less infinite. And below?' (p. 169). The question opens up the distinctive Thorpeian territory and its archaeological proclivity: that which is 'below' is the residue of human history and endeavour. Reflecting on this takes Thorpe's work in many directions, but *On Silbury Hill* shows that his personal investment in the Wiltshire landscape, from his schooldays, is a primary creative resource. The focus of Thorpe's (sometimes mystical) investment in place is to evoke its hidden human history, a process fuelled by his undergraduate 'passion for Amerindians', especially 'the wisdom of the Hopi', and an experimental phase 'visiting past lives under hypnosis' (pp. 113–14). But Thorpe is also equivocal about his creativity: 'invasive archaeology is a metaphor for our whole current situation: the process of discovery necessitates destruction' (p. 201). Such ambivalence is quintessentially contemporary; and the archaeological motif, as here, can be simultaneously literal and metaphorical in Thorpe's writing, in his nonfiction as well as his fiction (most notably in his novel *Ulverton* (1988)). Arguably, the most powerful moment in *On Silbury Hill* occurs away from Wiltshire, in Italy, at the South Tyrol Museum of Archaeology in Bolzano, and stems from Thorpe's reaction to the 5000-year-old remains of 'Ötzi the Iceman'. It is not the mummified corpse of 'Ötzi' that Thorpe finds affecting, however, but rather the incredibly well-preserved artefacts, the clothes and tools, found with him:

> But what was it that moved me most of all in this museum, so I was swallowing back the tears?
>
> The knots.
>
> These were *his* knots: they show his thought, his care, even his imagination.
>
> ...
>
> For me, it was a revelation. Although Ötzi had been lying in the ice for many hundreds of years before the first turf stack was put into place [at Silbury Hill], the first sarsen lifted, I now think of the builders of Silbury and Avebury as people, not as ghostly mysteries or supermen or magicians or even as vague forms smoked from foetal skeletons. It was the knots that did it. And his torn, dangling chinstraps.   (p. 106)

---

[53] Adam Thorpe, *On Silbury Hill* (Toller Fratrum: Little Toller Books, 2014), p. 168. Subsequent references are given in parentheses.

This is a celebration of the significance of archaeology, in the personal testimony of its ability to inspire imagination and to stimulate a more vital connection with the places we are inclined to think of as 'native' to us; but it is also a demonstration of the poet/novelist's sensibility, transcending the essence of history as a discipline to realize a moment of acute empathy: there are many very similar moments in *Ulverton* where affect is generated by the resurfacing of personal history. But if we visit the corpse named 'Ötzi', on public display in Bolzano, we may also think of Thorpe's idea that 'invasive archaeology is a metaphor for our whole current situation' (p. 201).[54] That which has the power to move us and make connections may also bring with it other ethical and ecological concerns. In the case of 'Ötzi', the remains were discovered in the Ötztal Alps in 1991, when the glacier in which they were encased 'had shrunk to its lowest level in thousands of years':[55] global warming facilitates the astonishing discovery.

The power Thorpe assigns to 'Ötzi's' knots in a museum exhibit is a very clear example of literary affect stimulating a connection with the world outside the text: the knots make Thorpe reimagine the reality of one ancient person's struggle to survive in a harsh environment, which, in turn, revitalizes his engagement with the human history of Silbury Hill. The same bridging tendency also defines ecomimesis, which does not instigate a simple process of referentiality; rather, it involves a range of rhetorical strategies that invite a reader to reflect on the extra-textual world. Buell's theory of stylization, the mechanism through which outer mimesis is prioritized, remains a good way of summarizing such bridging effects. To illustrate the purpose of stylization in environmental nonfiction, Buell uses the comparison of ornithological field guides, in which schematic drawings or paintings assist identification more swiftly than photographs: 'the capacity of the stylised image to put the reader or viewer in touch with the environment is precisely what needs stressing as a counter to the assumptions that stylisation must somehow work against outer mimesis or take precedence over it'.[56] In a very broad sense, the ecomimesis of contemporary nature prose seems to me to rely on such gestures of stylization.

This understanding of ecomimesis is comparable to the way it has been characterized by Timothy Morton, for whom the problematic evocation of an authentic reality outside the text in nature writing is what defines ecomimesis, the desire 'to go beyond the aesthetic dimension altogether', an impossible gesture in a mode of writing prone to devices that pull it more deeply 'into the orbit of writing'.[57] Morton undertakes a sophisticated rethinking of ecomimesis, especially

---

[54] On my own visit to the Ötzi exhibition in 2016 I found the main attraction, the mummified remains, and the queue to view them through a small window onto a sealed chamber, rather ghoulish. The other artefacts were certainly more engaging.
[55] Angelika Fleckinger, *Ötzi, the Iceman* (Vienna and Bolzano: Folio, 2014), p. 23.
[56] Buell, *The Environmental Imagination*, pp. 97–8.
[57] Morton, *Ecology without Nature*, pp. 30, 31.

by developing the connotations of ambience and ambient art. At a more mundane level, however, it is worth asking whether the effects of the ecomimesis Morton associates with the conventions of nature writing can be seen as more *consciously deployed* than is often assumed. Are the illusions of ecomimesis an integral part of how nature writing is conceived and received, rather than effects only to be found through 'critical close reading'?[58] And if such illusions are, ordinarily, a feature of the reading experience, does this establish a contract between text and reader that stimulates productive environmental awareness and action, through a less immediate bridging process, rather than the passive consumerism that is implied in the trap of textual aesthetics? For Morton, ecomimesis works to obscure its artifice rather than to emphasize it, so that 'all signals that we are in a constructed realm have been minimized'. Morton cites Buell's principle of stylization in nature writing, problematizing the idea that 'language can render real things, that is, ecological ones';[59] for him, the 'lack of believability' in ecomimesis 'penetrates to the very core', complicating 'the most potent rhetorical device for establishing a sense of nature'. Necessarily restricted by 'the inherent instability of language', we must recognize that 'ecomimesis fails to deliver' a 'solidly real nature'.[60] My contention is simply that good nature writing has often internalized this essential paradox, which becomes a distinctive sign of the contemporary predicament. If we see the imperfections of ecomimesis as an integral part of the contract—that its failure to deliver is a *textual feature* alongside the apparently opposing cultivation of belief in the *idea* of referentiality—then we may be closer to an understanding of the most powerful instances of contemporary nature writing. This, I think, is the essence of the key examples I have discussed in this Introduction: the shiver Dillard makes us feel when the water bug slips away from the devoured frog in *Pilgrim at Tinker Creek* (the performance of a defining experience); the tragedy of Ama's self-sacrifice in Hogan's *Power* (a destructive act of regeneration); the force of Matthiessen's not-seeing in *The Snow Leopard* (the revelation of non-revelation); and the emotional charge of 'Ötzi's' knots in Thorpe's *On Silbury Hill* (the life revealed in death). Most significantly, it is the *artifice* of each moment, or the artifice which gives rise to each moment, that constitutes its bridge to the extra-textual world.

The various ecocritical debates considered in this Introduction concerning nature and culture, fiction and nonfiction, text and referent underpin the remainder of the book. The four main chapters address recurring preoccupations—for both nature writers and ecocritics—each one linked to an aspect of the current crisis, but which also reveal in each case a longer tradition of expression: (1) remoteness, (2) exclusivity, (3) abundance, (4) rarity, and, in the Conclusion, transformations. This thematic organization allows for a thorough illustration of

---

[58] Ibid., p. 77. [59] Ibid., p. 35. [60] Ibid., pp. 77–8.

the reconnective principles outlined above. The four main chapters are presented as pairs ('Remoteness' and 'Exclusivity'; 'Abundance' and 'Rarity'), in dialogue with each other, testing the limits of the writing strategies discovered in each chapter. To me, these topics seem self-selecting by virtue of their recurrence in contemporary nature prose; but it is also important to note that each one points to planetary issues while simultaneously evoking a personal response, a psychological state. From this fusion of inner and outer worlds, each chapter builds a contribution to the understanding of mimesis in nature prose. At the same time, because every topic is suggestive of both personal experience and worldly geography, each chapter addresses aspects of the tensions discussed in this Introduction between objectivity and subjectivity, scientific writing and belletrism, fact and affect. A complication of these binaries, and an embrace of contemporary paradox, inhere in the complex literary effects I trace under each heading.

The extended close readings concern late twentieth- and early twenty-first-century texts, with appropriate reference to their most significant antecedents. *Nature Prose* also aims to do more than make a case to defend or recuperate the claims of nature writing: beyond this, the emphasis is on the formal—and social/political—implications of the new creative energies unleashed as nature writing cuts across generic boundaries. Chapter 1, for example, examines texts in which the appeal of remoteness is reconfigured to embrace its apparent omissions (depredation, sickness, inequality); while the texts analysed in Chapter 2 eschew the conventions of aesthetic appreciation and reinsert the people excluded in much anglophone nature writing. In such ways, contemporary nature prose occasions a recalibration of critical thinking and becomes a fresh resource for this procedure. Thus, in Chapter 3 the connotations of abundance are shown to be, irreducibly, both literal and metaphorical, requiring a reappraisal of secular parable; and in Chapter 4 the interrelationship between the discipline of natural history and the shadow of extinctions necessitates the reinvention of responsible—and responsive—protagonists. The book concludes with a consideration of the nature prose about the wild and 'rewilding', which often posits a radical transformation of both environment and consciousness. Some of these texts represent perhaps the most significant test of the claim that culture can be embraced as a conduit, not a barrier to productive understanding of nonhuman nature.

1
Remoteness

A familiar form of nature writing is the account of a sojourn in a remote or wild place, presented in a mood of contemplative withdrawal. The temporary retirement from the alienating effects of urban life notionally affords the nature writer the insight from which to experience some kind of healing growth, to experience immersion in the 'wild', and to expose the blithe disregard of the nonhuman enshrined and perpetuated in the practices of modernity. By the early twentieth century this manoeuvre had become a cliché, the 'customary going off to write in a cottage', as Ronald Blythe put it.[1] But the familiarity of this literary trope makes it a constant vehicle of self-reflection. At the end of *Copsford* (1948), Walter J. C. Murray's recollection of a ten-month stay in a derelict Sussex cottage in the 1920s, there is a moment in which the book's scaffolding is laid bare. Battling through the snow, in a severe winter that is about to defeat Murray and terminate his sojourn, he recalls a snow globe at his grandmother's house that had delighted him as a boy, depicting 'a house, a garden, a tree and a tiny figure':

> I suddenly realised that one of my childish dreams had there and then come true. I was that little figure in the globe. As I floundered, so the lantern cast a grotesque and gigantic shadow of myself upon the outside of the sphere of flying flakes with which I was by light imprisoned; and by a strange inversion, I, the puny figure within, thus saw projected an enormous phantom of myself without, whereas in those far-off childhood days I, without, had imagined myself the Lilliputian figure within.[2]

The adventure is exposed as the subconscious adult realization of a childhood fantasy, a staged event that cannot quite escape the kitschiness that is suddenly revealed. The experiment in remote living, which Raynor Winn describes as the 'story of [Murray's] discovery of a spiritual connection to nature', is thus recontained within the cultural codes that determine his psyche.[3] And yet, despite the

---

[1] Ronald Blythe, 'Introduction' to Adrian Bell's *Silver Ley*, 'Twentieth Century Classics' edition (Oxford: Oxford University Press, 1983), pp. vii–xx (p. ix). Blythe is here trying to distinguish between Adrian Bell's thorough engagement with rural East Anglia and the less immersive projects that were common in the 1920s and 1930s.
[2] Walter J. C. Murray, *Copsford*, introd. Raynor Winn (1948; Toller Fratrum: Little Toller Books, 2019), pp. 152, 153.
[3] Raynor Winn, 'Introduction' to Murray, *Copsford*, pp. 7–11 (p. 7).

kitschiness, it is a curiously oppressive epiphany/non-epiphany: in the moment of his defeat by the weather, Murray realizes that his fantasy has been realized and dismantled in the same instant, his adult hindsight recalling and quashing the childhood dream in a revelatory flashback. But, as a dramatic autobiographical abridgment, it is also a carefully staged moment.

Building on the kind of demythologizing self-consciousness illustrated at the end of Murray's book, this chapter shows how the retreat narrative is a format that has been the subject of much revision in contemporary nature prose, so that the apparently outmoded idea of remoteness as a resource of replenishment has been revitalized. The paradox of seeking seclusion, in an era dominated by a collective consciousness of global overcrowding and rapid urbanization, produces new ways of seeing our shared predicament, and also ways of understanding how contemporary social problems, such as homelessness, are connected to environmental catastrophe, as I will show in the final section of this chapter.[4] The productive paradoxical effects of the literature of remoteness hinge on two key features: first, an unexpected sense of the dislocated self; and, second—in common with much of the nature prose examined in this book—a pronounced form of self-consciousness, signalling an extended interrogation of the underpinning cultural and literary antecedents.

Dislocation occurs when the expected focus on contemplative advancement, the facility to set the ego aside in the process of attaining a higher philosophical plane of understanding, is disappointed. As Neil Ansell puts it: 'the great gift of solitude is that although you might think it provokes introspection, actually the very opposite is true – you can lose all sense of self'. This is brought home to him when he is making his way to camp on an isolated beach, but finds a kayaker already there: as he scrambles on the rocks, he knows he 'must have looked clumsy and graceless'. It is 'the mere presence of an observer' that 'return[s] [him] to self-consciousness': 'a stranger in the distance was all it took to change my perspective, so that instead of seeing a landscape, I saw myself within it'.[5] The further paradox, however, is that—even without an intrusion into the bubble of remoteness—losing 'all sense of self' does eventually lead to a form of productive introspection, when the experience is written down in such a way as to articulate its wider social and ecological relevance: when examined with hindsight, the 'loss' of self becomes a way of reframing the relationship between the self and the body politic. By this

---

[4] These associations have pertinence in the treatment of contemporary dilemmas. The shed that Catrina Davies makes her home may not be particularly remote, but hers is a distinctive contemporary account of basic, solitary living that is made to highlight questions of land ownership and homelessness. Davies uses the ubiquitous *Walden* 'as a lens to help [her] understand how the current [international] housing crisis...is a symptom of a deeper homesickness' made manifest 'as crises in ecology, social justice and mental health'. See Catrina Davies, *Homesick: Why I Live in a Shed* (London: riverrun, 2019), p. 4.

[5] Neil Ansell, *The Last Wilderness: A Journey Into Silence* (London: Tinder Press, 2018), p. 178. Subsequent references are given in the text.

I do not mean to evoke the cliché of 'finding oneself' through retreat in any straightforward sense: very often the insights gained are dependent upon dismantling that procedure and the assumptions that surround it.

The second feature referred to above, cultural and literary self-consciousness, is often the means through which the notional procedure of gaining wisdom in the wild is complicated. For example, the necessary interaction of social conscience and remoteness is given a self-reflexive literary dimension in Ansell's invocation of George Orwell, first in his own treatment of homelessness—he reminds us of *Down and Out in Paris and London*, which 'had depicted life on the streets 50 years earlier'—and, second, in following Orwell's steps to Jura, where he went to live in 1946, drawn by 'its impeccable remoteness', to write *Nineteen Eighty-Four* before returning 'to London where he died soon after of TB', still a common ailment of the homeless in the 1980s.[6] Ansell's account of his own trip to Jura will provide an important illustration later in this chapter. Such echoes and reconsiderations of the earlier instances of remote nature writing are apparent throughout the examples considered here, and this reveals a principle of reflexiveness that is not just unavoidable but actually a formative component of this branch of contemporary nature prose. This goes beyond the question of influence that conditions all literature, because the emphasis on textuality is so emphatically at odds with the idea of an escape from cultural influence. Insofar as the contemporary nature writing of remoteness can make unexpected and counter-intuitive connections with our most pressing environmental concerns, this is done through its reliance on a foundation of historical allusiveness, so that past and present, culture and nature, cannot be seen as opposing elements.

Understandably, perhaps, the inseparability of place and writing in this connection has not always been registered when the evocation of place as a source of insight has been subjected to ecocritical scrutiny. The literature of remoteness usually focuses on specific sites as sources of inspiration. Indeed, such writing often seems to be, definitively, about the genius loci so that its textual basis can be obscured. Most of the examples I cite describe experiences in the Hebridean islands, or on the north-west coast of Scotland—as a kind of case study—the better to demonstrate the interplay between the specificity of place and what can be extrapolated from that specificity in contemporary writing. But it is the very idea of placing stress on specific locales as a source of environmental consciousness in nature writing that has been questioned, notably by Ursula Heise. Her examination of the perceived 'need to reconnect to local places as a way of overcoming the alienation from nature that modern societies generate' seems to chime with a particular concern of some contemporary nature prose, taken at face value. Looking at the longer history of this tendency in America, Heise accurately

---

[6] Neil Ansell, *Deer Island* (Toller Fratrum: Little Toller Books, 2013), pp. 20, 103, 29. Subsequent references are given in the text.

identifies a recurring trope in which 'physical immersion in the landscape', presented as 'wild', leads nature writers to 'epiphanic fusions with their natural surroundings', especially in the 'more literary versions'. The emphasis on the withdrawal into nature, as a form of personal development, and even transformation, is problematic for Heise because the 'ethic of proximity' may have inadequate purchase on 'larger contexts such as the nation or the transnational realm'.[7] This difficulty, which is obviously intensified in the literature of remoteness, hinges on the perception of the opposition between individual experience and collective action, between remote and global geographies.

Dana Phillips makes a similar series of objections, analysing the way in which ecocritics have constructed nature writing to identify 'a non-fiction prose essay describing the first-person narrator's efforts to establish an intensely felt emotional connection with the natural world', in which the 'relative isolation' of the nature writer privileges first-hand experience over knowledge gleaned from 'the natural sciences'.[8] This leads Phillips to make the distinction I mentioned in the Introduction, between the suspect 'belletristic' tendencies of nature writing and the more objective narrative stance in natural history writing;[9] but the main objection is against 'the selfishness or self-absorption implicit in the very form of nature writing', which does not produce 'an ethically responsible entity and a citizen of the world'.[10] Such a responsible person, for Phillips, ought to draw on the objectivity of natural history: the psychology or spiritual emphases of nature writing are in tension with it, and with the biological, social, and political urgency of ecological and environmental issues.[11] The contemporary nature writing of place, following the readings of Heise and Phillips, might be read and judged according to these negative/positive binary opposites: selfish/responsible, psychological/biological, spiritual/political, individual/collective, remote/global, and belletristic/objective. Phillips is surely right that the self in contemporary nature writing 'has been shaped by different cultural and historical forces than those that shaped the selves of earlier nature writers';[12] in particular, we must bear in mind the oppressive sense of impending environmental collapse that has gradually intensified. But this may not behove contemporary writers to think in terms of

---

[7] Ursula K. Heise, *Sense of Place and Sense of Planet* (Oxford: Oxford University Press, 2008), pp. 29, 33, 34.
[8] Phillips, *The Truth Of Ecology*, p. 185.
[9] Ibid., pp. 186–7. Phillips is aware 'that there are authors of so-called nature writing who do avail themselves of much that natural history in the natural sciences have to offer'; but he defines the 'most popular' nature writers as those who 'seem to regard natural history and natural science less as aids than as obstacles to achieving a spiritually satisfying relationship with nature' (p. 187). Phillips is also distinguishing between 'the self at the center of recent nature writing essays' and 'the self at the center of the essays of Thoreau, [John] Burroughs, and [John] Muir': the former, he argues, 'is represented as incapable of sustaining the intense, life-long involvement in a particular place that gave definition to the characters of Thoreau and Burroughs – that, in effect, made them characters' (p. 197). The examples that follow in this chapter tend to blur that distinction.
[10] Ibid., pp. 196, 195.   [11] Ibid., p. 203.   [12] Ibid., p. 197.

problems/solutions in quite the way that Heise and Phillips suggest. This is not the way that contemporary nature writing seems to work. Rather, it often absorbs the kind of binary opposites that the astute analyses of Heise and Phillips reveal, producing contradictions and paradoxes in which selfish and responsible, spiritual and political, individual and collective, remote and global emphases are examined in tension, or are even made to seem indivisible, sometimes resulting in stylistically hybrid forms, by turns belletristic and objective.

The Question of Solitude

An important component of remoteness, although not its only aspect, is solitude. The association of art and solitude exceeds the bounds of nature writing, of course, and has deep roots in literary history; and it is not my intention to rehearse the long history of anchorites—hermits and recluses—and their evolving relevance to cultural sensibility.[13] More specifically, I am focusing on that post-Romantic legacy in which solitude in nature is seen as a source of succour through retreat from worldly cares, but also, by virtue of that, a primary source of creative inspiration.[14] Anthony Storr, with a psychiatrist's perspective, gives substance to the familiar connection between solitude and creativity: the 'creative person is constantly seeking to discover himself, to remodel his own identity...his most significant moments are those in which he attains some new insight, or makes some new discovery; and these moments are chiefly, if not invariably, those in which he is alone'.[15] A specific kind of creative psyche is identified in Storr's argument that significant advancements in science, philosophy, and the arts have been made by those who not only 'are bound to spend a great deal of their time alone' but have also been unsuccessful in forming 'interpersonal relationships of an intimate kind' (p. ix). However, if 'major talent is rare', the creative genius still betrays 'the same needs and wishes as the rest of us', which means that 'the need of the creative person for solitude...can reveal something about the needs of the less gifted, more ordinary human being' (pp. xiv–xv). This democratic sentiment may lend importance to the significance of remoteness in nature writing: if there is a relationship between the solitude that engenders creativity, and the more general

---

[13] Anchorites were a feature of life in the Middle Ages, for example. See Tom Licence, *Hermits and Recluses in English Society, 950–1200* (Oxford: Oxford University Press, 2011), and E. A. Jones, ed., *Hermits and Anchorites in England, 1200–1500* (Manchester: Manchester University Press, 2019). The religious anchorite had an afterlife in the fad for the secular hermit in the eighteenth century. See Gordon Campbell, *The Hermit in The Garden: from Imperial Rome to Ornamental Gnome* (Oxford: Oxford University Press 2013).

[14] There is a succinct account of this in Wordsworth's *Prelude*: 'When from our better selves we have too long / Been parted by the hurrying world, and droop, / Sick of its business, of its pleasures tired, / How gracious, how benign, is Solitude'; *The Prelude* (1850), IV, ll. 354–7.

[15] Anthony Storr, *Solitude* (1988; London: HarperCollins, 1997), p. xiv. Subsequent references are given in parentheses.

psychological need, we can draw wider conclusions from the uses of solitude. For Storr, 'the capacity to be alone is a valuable resource when changes of mental attitude are required'. Solitude serves a purpose 'after major alterations in circumstances', such as bereavement, when a 'fundamental reappraisal of the significance and meaning of existence may be needed'. Questioning the way in which, in Western culture, 'interpersonal relationships are generally considered to provide the answer to every form of distress' (p. 29), Storr shows how different forms of social withdrawal in bereavement—for example, in rural Greece, or amongst orthodox Jews—are deemed to be a fundamental part of 'coming to terms with loss' (pp. 30–1). One of the possibilities I'd like to suggest is that solitude is used in nature writing precisely to advance a change in attitude, in the face of what should be seen as our collective 'bereavement' for the loss of a functioning natural world.

The very idea of solitude, however, seems increasingly anachronistic, difficult to get a purchase on in contemporary experience. Michael Harris's experiment inhabiting 'the cabin in the woods'—in his case 'an old A-frame, built by [his] grandparents', on Pender Island off the coast of British Columbia—emphasizes the contemporary difficulty of finding solitude.[16] Overshadowed by the realization that he has never 'been completely alone for longer than twenty-four hours' (p. 215), his week-long stay in isolation is beset by difficulties and fears; he finds the first few days 'torture', deprived as he is of television, his partner, 'and dear old Google' (p. 220). His reflections are punctuated by the thoughts of other solitary writers—notably Thoreau—and this gives him a framework for articulating what is 'rare' and 'therefore precious' in his encounters with wildlife, and his discovery of ancient features in the landscape (p. 227); but the episode emphasizes the struggle of being alone, as much as its value.

Yet Harris wants to resuscitate the potential of solitude, and finds three productive outcomes in its uses: 'new ideas; an understanding of the self; and closeness to others' (p. 40). This last use is a consequence of separation, and the reflection that causes us to reaffirm our bonds with friends (p. 39). The emphasis in Harris's accent on solitude, however, is to recoup something that is lost in the contemporary moment. In keeping with this retrospective mood, both Storr and Harris refer to the same historical touchstone in the experience of Admiral Richard E. Byrd, alone on an Antarctic weather base in the winter of 1934. In a celebrated passage, Byrd responds to the 'imponderable processes and forces of the cosmos, harmonious and soundless'. Out of the silence he detects 'a gentle rhythm, the strain of the perfect chord, the music of the spheres', and feels 'momentarily to be myself a part of it'. The experience makes him certain 'of man's oneness with the universe'. This feeling of harmony, he realizes,

---

[16] Michael Harris, *Solitude: In Pursuit of a Singular Life in a Crowded World* (London: Random House, 2017), p. 215. Subsequent references are given in parentheses.

'transcended reason': it goes 'to the heart of man's despair and found it groundless'.[17] For Storr, this is a representative mystic religious experience (p. 37); but it is also, as Harris observes, the discovery, through 'solitude in nature', of 'a human impulse that our progress has all but quashed' (p. 135). The emphasis is repeatedly on the desirability of elusive—or even unattainable—communion. In contemporary nature prose, solitude in nature attains a new kind of vitality. Harris's emphasis on fresh discovery, and the means of social reconnection through solitude; and Storr's comparison between the isolation of the creative genius, and the more generally beneficent and healing properties of social withdrawal, all remain in view. But we are increasingly aware of the heightened, self-conscious performance, and the inventive ways in which remoteness is made to speak to the goal of reconnection, even while we are alerted to the fraught difficulties of such a project.

It is important to note that the performative dimension of remote nature writing is not, in itself, a contemporary phenomenon; rather, it is part of a continuum of allusive writing that has become progressively more reflexive, as it registers the climate predicament. This is an anxiety of influence that registers an anxiety of being. In Randall Roorda's study of American nature writing, 'the writer's movement from human society toward a state of solitude in nature' is held to be 'the central dynamic of the genre'.[18] This 'movement of retreat' results in 'dramas of solitude', the appeal of which highlights the obvious paradox I have identified above, between remoteness and the goal of reconnection. 'What good can it be to retreat in this way?' asks Roorda: 'what can it mean to turn away from other people, to evade all sign of them for purposes that exclude them by design, then turn back toward them in writing, reporting upon, accounting for, even recommending to them the condition of their absence?' The exploration of this paradox pinpoints the 'social' and 'ethical purposes of solitude', and also reveals something about what 'stories of solitude reveal of the "character" of nonhuman nature'.[19] This may involve 'finding analogues to human character and action among the narrative's nonhuman elements'; but it might equally involve an impulse to 'resist or complicate or sidestep this correspondence'.[20]

In such dramas of solitude, we may be restricted to the perspective of one protagonist, but this does not preclude an interrogation of that protagonist's cognitive processes even while we share in the perceptions recounted, so that the 'drama of the writer's understanding becomes our own as we deem these figurations interesting and apt, or mechanistic, pathetic, sentimental, or enfeebled, as the case may be'. It is in the recognition of 'the writer as a protagonist' in this

---

[17] Richard E. Byrd, *Alone* (New York: G. P. Putnam's Sons, 1938), p. 85.
[18] Randall Roorda, *Dramas of Solitude: Narratives of Retreat in American Nature Writing* (Albany: SUNY Press, 1998), p. xiii.
[19] Ibid., p. xiii.   [20] Ibid., p. 16.

genre of nature writing that an important overlap with the habits of reading fiction is clearly evident: 'we are posed in dramatic contradistinction to the writer', and 'we both "move through with" and come up against that writer'. For Roorda this is true of narrators with contrasting demeanours, whether the 'extravagantly standoffish personae of writers like Thoreau and Edward Abbey' or more self-effacing authors: all 'exhibit bents of style, action, and attention that have the effect if not the purpose of self-characterisation', so that we engage in a dramatic encounter with them.[21] If the drama of solitude is an established tradition in nineteenth- and twentieth-century landmark texts, and if reading them requires us to draw on our skills as readers of fiction, it may be that the contemporary manifestations of nature prose differ in *degree* rather than *kind* from their antecedents.

The distinctive accent of the contemporary nature retreat may be located in a more complex form of self-effacement, or dissolution of self. Roorda describes this as 'a sort of willed purposelessness', but suggests there may be an element of 'heroism' to it, if this betokens a rethinking of the self in relation to 'the greater biotic community'.[22] In Roorda's survey, 'the destination of retreat' in these texts is 'figured *as* a community or web of relations that the writer feels implicated in and is concerned to comprehend – figured, in a word, ecologically'.[23] In contemporary nature prose the same kind of relationship is desired and explored, but the grounds of its possibility are questioned more overtly.

Robert Macfarlane's admirable *The Wild Places* (2007) illustrates this contemporary reworking through its attempt to find and experience the remaining 'wild' places of Britain and Ireland, and to reimagine the map imprinted on most of our minds by the modern road atlas, which, he suggests, 'encourages us to imagine the land itself only as a context for motorised travel', and which 'warps its readers away from the natural world', with its 'priorities of... transit and displacement'.[24] *The Wild Places* enacts an intellectual journey that summarizes the shift of emphasis that is held to be central to the new nature writing. Macfarlane's project is initially premised on making trips to a series of wild places 'outside history' (p. 7); but it is to be pursued through the flatly contradictory means of emulating the 'Celtic Christian culture of retreat' that 'originated in the Ireland of the fifth and sixth centuries', a 'practice of retreat' that 'spread to what are now western Scotland and coastal Wales' (p. 24). Thus, Macfarlane's project is actually conducted inside, not outside, history, and in a systematic way that generates the book's central insight that 'the human and the wild cannot be partitioned' (p. 127). Macfarlane's other 'revelation'—both are really knowingly performative 'discoveries' that challenge the popular mindset, rather than Macfarlane's own—is that wildness does not occur only in remote, large landscapes. On a trip to the Burren

---

[21] Ibid., p. 18.   [22] Ibid., pp. 19–20.   [23] Ibid., p. 11.
[24] Robert Macfarlane, *The Wild Places* (London: Granta Books, 2007), p. 11. Subsequent references are to this edition.

on the mid-west coast of Ireland with Roger Deakin, looking down into a fissure or 'gryke' in the limestone pavement, Deakin makes him realize that the gryke is itself 'a wild place', with its thriving plant life (p. 168). This recalibration of where to look for the wild, and on what scale, leads Macfarlane to a fresh 'understanding of wildness not as something which was hived off from human life, but which existed unexpectedly around and within it: in cities, backyards, roadsides, hedges, field boundaries or spinnies' (p. 226).[25]

In her infamous review of *The Wild Places*, Kathleen Jamie pinpoints the tradition of retreat as the flaw in Macfarlane's thinking:

> The early Christian monks would have been the first literate people in this country and the first we know of to seek out remote places qua remote for some spiritual quest. Literature began with them, and a tradition developed which has persisted ever since and remains largely uninterrogated: the association of literature, remoteness, wildness and spiritually uplifted men. It must be connected with the elevated tone characteristic of so much nature writing.[26]

Jamie presumably means to invoke a literary history that embraces the British archipelago as a whole—although in the phrase 'this country' (she is writing in the *London Review of Books*) there is a hint that the problematic nature of this tradition has its roots, or at least persists most prominently, in England. That aside, there are two aspects of this critique which are equally forcefully put, and which identify concerns I wish to keep in view, and to complicate or contest, and which resonate beyond the British context: that nature writing has a central importance in the development of a particular brand of literary articulation; and that it is a mode that lends itself to a privileged and quasi-spiritual mode of expression, with the putative potential to register personal transformation for an elect group. We can resist this implication by remembering the bridge Anthony Storr builds between creative 'genius' and the commonplace experience of rejuvenation through retreat: does contemporary nature prose achieve the same ends, dismantling the inbuilt privileges of its codes in the pursuit of biotic community thinking? That is certainly the impetus of Macfarlane's shared remapping of places, a potentially collective enterprise that might transform the tradition of retreat.

---

[25] Macfarlane is here writing in the tradition of writing about 'edgelands' established by Richard Mabey in *The Unofficial Countryside* (1973; repr. Wimborne Minster: Little Toller Books, 2010).

[26] Kathleen Jamie, 'A Lone Enraptured Male', *London Review of Books*, 30: 5, 6 March 2008, pp. 25–7 (p. 26). Jamie's objection to *The Wild Places* seems partly that a privileged white English male of Macfarlane's class may presume too much by exhibiting 'rapture' in ancient Celtic places. The question of exclusivity and privilege in nature writing is the subject of the next chapter. For a balanced account of the Macfarlane–Jamie controversy, see Jos Smith, *The New Nature Writing: Rethinking the Literature of Place* (London: Bloomsbury, 2017), pp. 84–6.

Kathleen Jamie exemplifies this movement, even if she doesn't recognize the elements of it in Macfarlane's work. In *Findings* (2005), she overcomes the risk of making remoteness a canvas of personal revelation by placing emphasis on the history of inhabitation in remote Scottish places. The clearest example of this is her account of the 'shielings, and shieling grounds' she encounters 'in the hills' in 'the Central Highlands'—these were human shelters built in 'the high summer pastures' when cattle were driven to new pastures in the system of transhumance, a practice that 'died out at the time of the Improvements, in the latter half of the eighteenth century'.[27] Earlier in her walk, Jamie encounters Neolithic carvings on a rock face (p. 116), an observation that enables her to reflect on 'four or five thousand years of human subsistence' in this landscape, to remind us of human suffering, and to reject terms like 'natural', 'wild', and especially 'wilderness', which she hears as an 'affront to those many generations who took their living on that land' (p. 126). Jamie's approach to remote places is to discover within them the inscription of (often domestic) human history, disproving the apparent remoteness, and displacing the moment of personal revelation with a reminder of collective activity.

This corresponds with elements of Macfarlane's method in *The Wild Places*, especially where that method encourages comparison between different places—rather than the reverence of 'sacred' remoteness. Jos Smith characterizes this process as involving 'interactions and inter-animations of diverse and distinctive landscapes'. It is an outward-facing dynamic so that 'intimate topographical experiences' encourage 'dialogue with other areas of limestone, forest, moorland and so on, wherever they are in the world'. This emphasis on 'correspondences and dialogues', not tied to the specificity of place, suits a global ecocritical vision.[28] Jamie's emphasis on human traces—like Macfarlane's, I think—circumvents the magnified anthropocentric problems she associates with the pursuit of remoteness and solitude, and eschews parochialism. There is, however, a rather different strand of nature writing, in which particular remote places are deliberately sought—a modern equivalent of the spiritual quest that Jamie wants to interrogate. To approach such texts we need to see how they dismantle the binaries that order Jamie's critique, and which, as we have seen, underpin the ecocritical objections of critics such as Ursula Heise and Dana Phillips. Specifically, we need to understand how the retreat is also a social gesture; and how more general implications may be inherent in the quest for the genius loci.

The remainder of this chapter examines the literary effects in some key examples of the later twentieth-century and contemporary nature prose of remoteness; but I want to set the scene for this by considering the extent to

---

[27] Kathleen Jamie, *Findings* (London: Sort Of Books, 2005), p. 122. Subsequent references are given in parentheses. The Highland Clearances of inhabitants and traditional practices to make way for sheep were the central plank of agricultural 'improvements' in the eighteenth and nineteenth centuries.

[28] Smith, *The New Nature Writing*, p. 84.

which Henry Thoreau's *Walden* anticipates more contemporary inflections that place remoteness at the centre of the inquiry. *Walden* is unquestionably the urtext in modern nature writing predicated on the withdrawal from human society as the route to engagement with the nonhuman. Often the reliance on, or allusion to, *Walden* can seem to be anachronistic, a retrograde attempt to recapture a lost moment—before the full implications of environmental crisis were clear—when immersion in nature as a form of succour still seemed a viable means of self-definition. The pursuit of solitude on a crowded planet can seem irresponsive, if not irresponsible. Michael Harris suggests that *Walden* marks the end of an epoch: 'how swiftly, how irrevocably the world swung toward permanent social contact after that moment'. Consequently, '*Walden* is a swan song for an antique enjoyment of time alone' (p. 40). In this view, *Walden* is consigned to the ideological past, and any attempt to replicate elements of it are tainted with a failure of historical vision. It may not be the case, however, that contemporary nature writers inspired by Thoreau are necessarily hampered by the backward look: perhaps, instead, we should focus on the ways in which *Walden* was ahead of its time, anticipating our contemporary concerns. Indeed, for Roorda, 'Thoreau's *Walden* marks the "birth" of the retreat narrative genre'.[29]

The decision to retreat to a hut in the woods—and write about it—is a way of making two narratives, and two experiments in living, come together: the testing of the isolated self in communion with the nonhuman; and the discovery about civilization revealed by that isolation. Jane Bennett traces the self-conscious foundation of Thoreau's project, explaining his effort of self-definition as the pursuit of the identity of a 'sojourner'.[30] I used the word 'sojourn' at the beginning of this chapter, anticipating Bennett's very particular application of this term, which seems to me to get to the essence of the persona in the retreat narrative. 'Sojourners', she explains, 'are artificial beings who come to construe themselves – through minute observations of plant and animal cultures, through writing about wilderness, through bodily disciplines – as belonging to a universe that articulates through them and extends beyond them.' The sojourner also courts 'what Thoreau calls *the Wild*, that which disturbs and confounds settled projects, techniques, and myths'. The sojourner is a constructed 'ideal self', and someone who, far from being settled in a revered place, is 'in search of a home', valuing 'the sense of estrangement that propels' the quest. Along the way, the sojourner seeks 'to inflect the world as Nature', alert to the 'cultured character of nature' anticipating a fundamental principle of contemporary nature writing.[31]

---

[29] Roorda, *Dramas of Solitude*, p. 4.
[30] At the outset of *Walden* Thoreau describes himself as 'a sojourner in civilized life again'. See *The Portable Thoreau*, ed. Carl Bode (London: Penguin, 1982), p. 258.
[31] Jane Bennett, *Thoreau's Nature: Ethics, Politics, and the Wild* (London: Sage, 1994), p. xxi. Bennett explains that she capitalizes Nature 'when it refers to the magical reality of Thoreau's making, to the outdoor life he inflects as Nature' (p. xxvi).

In this overview, Thoreau's writing seems to anticipate not just our fraught nature–culture debates, but also the problematic aspects of self-definition implicit in the contrived encounter with the nonhuman. Thoreau's self-consciousness, in particular, seems peculiarly contemporary. He is '*double*', Bennett suggests, 'in that he is both a subjective agent with the potential for submersion in intense personal experience and an objective agent capable of recording, with minimum mediation, the facts of Nature'. Under the sign of self-consciousness, this double identity, 'both a chanticleer of sentiment and a chronicler of data', is intensified, so that 'the sojourning self... is doubly double'.[32] The identity that emerges from this reflexive intellectual effort—'character' in Thoreau's terminology—'is an artifice', Bennett suggests, 'that, if properly constructed and maintained, functions as if it was always there'. But it is a theoretical identity: 'sojourners are individuals because they posit a core of self that renders them whole', perhaps overcoming, by means of such artifice, 'the central tension driving Thoreau's work', which is 'the tension between his ideal of a deliberate life and his ideal of a Wild life'.[33]

The self-consciousness of writers who are inspired by Thoreau to emulate his withdrawal to a hut in the woods may need some reconsideration in light of the artifice of self at the core of Thoreau's own experiment. Henry Beston's account of a year spent in a wooden hut on the beach at Cape Cod, *The Outermost House* (1928), is not replete with literary reference, but it is firmly in the Thoreauvian tradition, as Philip Hoare points out.[34] Beston's book is a classic example of the old paradox that remote living is made to reveal a common good, that 'nature is part of our humanity';[35] but it also contributes to the developing Thoreauvian paradox that the vitality of nature is revealed vicariously, through a literary tradition. The impermanence of Beston's hut, eventually washed away by the tide in 1978, encapsulates the predicament of remote writing, the authority of its insights tempered by our perception of its ideational precarity, and the staged and temporary basis of withdrawal.[36] A more distinctively contemporary text is *Consolations of the Forest* (2011), Sylvain Tesson's account of six months spent in a cabin on the shores of Lake Baikal in Siberia. Tesson's work is a bookish enterprise, and couched in self-irony, as when he offers his long 'LIST OF IDEAL READING MATERIAL CAREFULLY COMPOSED IN PARIS FOR A SIX-MONTH STAY IN THE SIBERIAN FOREST', a list that includes *Walden*, of course.[37] Tesson pursues the idea of 'the *genius loci*' (p. 12), but ultimately questions the motivations of the would-be hermit. His ambivalence is

---

[32] Ibid., pp. 30–1.   [33] Ibid., pp. 32, 34.
[34] Philip Hoare, 'Introduction' to Henry Beston, *The Outermost House: A Year of Life on the Great Beach of Cape Cod* (1928; London: Pushkin Press, 2019), pp. ix–xxiii (p. xvi).
[35] Henry Beston, 'Foreword to the 1949 Edition', *The Outermost House*, pp. xxv–xxvii (p. xxvi).
[36] Ibid., p. xxiii.
[37] Sylvain Tesson, *Consolations of the Forest: Alone in a Cabin in the Middle Taiga*, trans. Linda Coverdale (2011; London: Penguin, 2014), pp. 14–17. Subsequent references are given in parentheses.

encapsulated in his final diary entry, and a very different mood. While he is hoping for some final benediction, as he bids 'farewell to the lake', his dog disturbs an eider duck and savages its ducklings before he can intervene: he has to 'finish off the downy little things with a stone', and is then haunted by the cries of the mother duck, grieving 'for her lost offspring' and 'for the thousands of miles travelled for nothing' (pp. 230–1). The book ends with this shocking instance of the violence enacted upon nature by human carelessness—which is shown to be a consequence of the withdrawal to a cabin in the woods as much as any other human activity. The doubleness here is conditioned by a gloomy perspective on the environmental crisis—'why this desire to remake the world just when it's going out?' (p. 217), Tesson asks—and this is what dissolves his pursuit of the genius loci, producing an inverse revelation, or non-epiphany in the killing of the eider ducklings, and the implied discrediting of Tesson's presence in Siberia in the era of extinctions: the experience of withdrawal ultimately produces an insight that discredits the circumstances of its production.

A less pessimistic contemporary sojourner of the wild is Neil Ansell, who constructs his persona as being defined by his observational habits and skills; his writing; and his bodily discipline and capacity for endurance. He also wishes (to a degree) 'to inflect the world as Nature', while still conscious of the trespass of culture upon nature; and he is much preoccupied with the effect of remoteness on the understanding of the self. The tensions between nature and culture, self and other, immediate experience and the artifice of rendering result in an ambivalent form. Ansell's *Deep Country* (2011), the key text here, is a distinctly contemporary version of remote nature writing. This record of living alone in a Welsh cottage for five years, 'summer and winter, with no transport, no phone', is, he says, 'the story of what it means to live in a place so remote that you may not see another soul for weeks on end', and also 'the story of the hidden places that I came to call my own, and the wild creatures that became my society'.[38] But to define this perfect crucible for his experiment with the self, in the tradition of Thoreau's artistic licence, Ansell exaggerates (and so manufactures) the remoteness of Penlan Cottage, to some extent.[39] There is a village in the vicinity (a lengthy walk away, admittedly); and the nearest town is 'only seven miles away', but that is rendered inaccessible by Ansell's decision not to keep a vehicle. Hence 'the pocket of wild country [he] lived in felt remote': a point clinched by the selective statistic that in five years there are no passers-by walking up the track past the cottage (p. 26). Ansell also keeps the pertinent social history in view, although this becomes more prominent in his later books, as I'll show at the end of this chapter. An abandoned remote

---

[38] Neil Ansell, *Deep Country: Five Years in the Welsh Hills* (London: Penguin, 2011), p. xi. Subsequent references are given in parentheses.

[39] *Walden* is generally recognized as an instance of 'creative non-fiction'. See https://www.walden.org/education/for-students/myths-and-misconceptions/ (accessed 10 June 2021).

cottage in Wales tells a story of rural impoverishment, something Ansell hints at in his observation that 'it was over forty years since anyone had lived here year-round', although 'the cottage had been used in summer' (p. 24)—a familiar story of rural community life displaced by second-home owners.

Self-imposed solitude is a personal experiment for Ansell: 'I ... wanted to know who I was when I could no longer define myself in terms of my relation to others' (p. 27). This is not a test of his psychological resistance as such: he does not feel lonely because, he believes, 'loneliness is the product of an isolation that has not been freely chosen'. To his mind, 'solitude embraced is the opposite of loneliness' (p. 30). The process of self-discovery is presented as having unexpected outcomes: Ansell does not find that the five years 'free of social obligations, free of work commitments' give him the time to reflect on his 'personal development', even though this seems an ideal opportunity 'to work out your goals in life, your true ambitions'. Because his days are 'spent outside, immersed in nature', the 'solitude [does] not breed introspection'. Rather, his 'attention [is] constantly focused away from [him]self and onto the natural world around [him]'. Never having 'practised meditation', he yet believes he has attained by accident the 'goal in Buddhist practice of achieving a condition of no-mind, a state of being free of thought'. In a familiar metaphor of nature prose, he feels he 'had become a part of the landscape, a stone' (pp. 44–5). This impersonal state of being facilitates his activities as a nature observer, managing bird boxes in the woods, recording laying dates, ringing fledglings, and monitoring 'a four-mile beat of the river ... for the river-bird survey' (p. 28). In the course of his observations, he discovers two new nesting species for the Cambrian Mountains.[40] Yet there is some vacillation about this purpose. He makes many, varied observations about the avian life in his environment; but he cautions us that his 'methods may not always have been scientifically rigorous', and that he 'was not attempting a scientific study, rather an experiment in life' (p. 82). This emphasis apparently downplays the significance of his 'observations of individual birds', even though this 'meant the most to [him] personally'—and comprises a significant component of *Deep Country*—and valorizes instead the 'scientific validity' that 'comes from the slow accretion of small facts' of the kind generated through his own workmanlike projects monitoring sites and ringing fledglings, contributing to the 'tens of thousands of nesting records' required to 'reveal a population slump or a change in the distribution of the species' (pp. 99–100). But such a disavowal of what the amateur naturalist observes in and around the collection of data—the speculative account of behaviour, the anthropomorphized narratives—is also a denial of the personal journey, the immersion in remote nature. A tension thus emerges between his role as citizen-scientist and his identity as nature writer.

---

[40] The species in question are the mandarin duck (p. 155) and the red-breasted merganser (p. 158).

This is analogous to Dana Phillips's distinction which I considered earlier, between the belletrism of nature writing and the objectivity of natural history—the latter being, for him, more valuable. Ansell intensifies the tension between the two modes by ostensibly privileging the significance of scientific recording, while encouraging us to privilege the anthropomorphic speculations, which are the stuff of his tentative outward projections of self. Indeed, the descriptions in this vein are often compelling. For example, his account of a family of thirteen goosanders, fishing in a line stretched 'across the entire width' of a river, 40 feet across, resembling 'a line of pheasant-beaters', reveals the automatic recourse to human codes in nature description, which can announce itself as an inadequate approximation rather than anthropomorphic appropriation. We are primed to see the flaw; yet this enhances Ansell's wonderment at the goosanders' 'co-ordinated teamwork', which is repeated and modified when the birds 'formed themselves into a tight semicircle' as they corral, Ansell assumes, 'a whole shoal of tiny fish' (pp. 165–6). This passage works because Ansell is an invisible observer—the naturalist's goal. Yet he makes us realize how unusual this is: his 'most memorable encounters with wildlife were those occasions when there was a breakdown in the natural order of things', when 'wild creatures' were unable to flee from him, when injured or while protecting their young—'those moments that felt to me like intimacy, like closeness to nature, must undoubtedly have seemed quite different to the animals involved.... Even the garden birds that we watch with pleasure at our bird-feeders are in a state of conflict: safety or hunger' (p. 162). The subjective inadequacies of the perceiving self paradoxically become the conduit for something we sense to be more objective.

At the end of *Deep Country* there is a shift of focus back to the social self of the author, another common manoeuvre in contemporary nature writing. Ansell's sojourn is disrupted by illness: an overactive thyroid puts his 'whole life out of balance', leaving him with insufficient 'concentration to keep my journal, or even to read'. In his isolation, without a support network, 'habituated to the solitary life', his experiment must eventually come to an end, although he stubbornly persists with it for a further eighteen months (pp. 186–7). The illness makes Ansell re-evaluate his experiment in remote living, and the nature of the self that is revealed through it. Before his stay at Penlan, he believed that 'your true self' would be revealed once 'you strip away your cultural choices'. What he discovered, to the contrary, was that he 'rapidly became less and less self-aware', with his attention 'on the outside'. The circumstances of his illness force him 'to look inward once again', and 'to discover that there was perhaps no fixed self to find'. And it is this realization, in his new state of vulnerability, that gives him 'the sense that my life was not so very different from that of the birds fluttering on my bird-feeder, as though a boundary between us had been broken' (p. 188). Another paradox emerges: in order to reflect on his connection with the nonhuman he has to re-enter the social world of medical science to give social meaning to his vulnerable state. Ansell wants to present this as a transformative experience, and to imbue Penlan Cottage with the special quality of genius loci justified by its remoteness, and after five years of observation, of looking outwards at the local wildlife getting the impression of 'deeper and deeper understanding', in a seemingly unending process (pp. 198-9). And the capacity of this place to return him to this state endures: on his occasional returns to Penlan, Ansell is, he writes, able to 'forget myself', to recapture the relinquishment of self that came over him through his five-year adventure (p. 206).

In his epilogue Ansell relates his experiences at Penlan Cottage to the process of nature writing. This process is registered in the journal he kept, which is 'erratic' and not, he claims, written in the expectation 'that I might one day want to make use of those notes'. However, the journal shows the 'dramatic change' (p. 204) in the author, mirrored in its changing format:

> The first year, it is a fairly straightforward diary, an account of where I went, what I did, and how I felt. By the second year it is strictly a nature Journal: a record of my sightings and perhaps some notes on the weather. And by the third year it is virtually an almanac: arrival dates for spring and autumn migrants; nesting records; perhaps interspersed with an occasional piece of prose capturing a fragmentary moment, say a description of the flight of a single bird. I have disappeared entirely from my own narrative; my ego has dissolved into the mist. I came to the hills to find myself, and ended up losing myself instead. And that was immeasurably better. (pp. 204-5)

This posits a linear progression in which the writing persona is refined out of existence; but this doesn't reflect the book that is made from the journal. Ansell emerges as more like a sojourner in Bennett's sense, irreducibly double in his dependence on subjectivity as he strives for an objective record. He is also double in that artful sense of constructing a Thoreauvian 'character' for us to reflect on, a figure who combines these apparently opposing traits. This construction of the experience of nature in a remote setting is complicated, then, by the tensions and paradoxes that persist, and which remain prominent in the book Ansell has made from his journal. It is not so much that the book records the *process* outlined above, the means by which contradiction and paradox are refined out of existence, just as the self is discarded in Ansell's notebooks. Rather, *Deep Country* makes contradiction and paradox an aspect of its form, further evidence that paradox is a fundamental principle of contemporary voice-driven nature prose, and an attribute of a state of complex being, rather than a method of wrestling with binary opposites.

The Gavin Maxwell Myth

As I suggested in the Introduction, the demonstrable acceptance of paradox as the psychological status quo for reflecting on environmental questions is an important appropriation of an inherently literary quality, since literary language is characterized by paradox and ambiguity. It is also a way of locating the contemporary milieu; but can we detect the historical moment where this form of paradox emerges in the literature of remoteness, a point in time, that is, where Thoreauvian doubleness becomes tinged with the sense of crisis? There may be no indisputable singular instance of this transition to the conflicted appreciation of place determined by ecological crisis; but the work and life of Gavin Maxwell embody a very clear example of this transition. Maxwell is important because his evolution as a nature writer is an illuminating component of the paradigm shift from an empathic engagement with the nonhuman, to an ecological world view informed by the urgency of conservation.

Maxwell's status as a barometer of changing consciousness has partly to do with his social position. His biographer Douglas Botting shows that he was born into the landed gentry: his father, Colonel Ayer Maxwell, was 'heir presumptive to the baronetcy of Monreith'; his mother, Lady Mary Percy, was the 'fifth daughter of the seventh Duke of Northumberland'. Maxwell learned to appreciate 'natural beauty that was spare, austere and wild' on the rugged Elrig estate of his childhood; but he also gained a passion for shooting, against his more sensitive boyhood inclinations, so that he came to see 'no contradiction in loving the creatures he killed'.[41] In this, he embodied a pragmatic sensibility that endures in estate husbandry. His first venture after the Second World War was an ill-fated enterprise in shark fishing, based on the Isle of Soay, which he had acquired in 1944.[42] The basking shark increased in numbers in Hebridean waters from the 1930s onwards; and their livers are a bountiful source of oil, which was the focus of Maxwell's venture, eventually formalized as 'Island of Soay Shark Fisheries Ltd'.[43] From a contemporary perspective, it seems incredible that Maxwell, a figure associated so strongly with conservation, should have run such a gruesome and destructive business, if only for a brief while.[44] Botting explains this in terms of the sea change in environmental awareness that interests me here: Maxwell's erstwhile drive to hunt 'found expression at a time when public opinion imposed no moral constraints on it (big-game hunting was still approved and whale hunting

---

[41] Douglas Botting, *Gavin Maxwell: A Life* (1993: London: HarperCollins, 1994), pp. 3, 6, 14.
[42] Ibid., p. 67.
[43] See Gavin Maxwell, *Harpoon at a Venture* (1952; Harmondsworth: Penguin, 1984).
[44] Botting includes a photograph depicting 'the cartilag[i]nous vertebrae of processed sharks laid out to dry in the factory "boneyard" on Soay', which gives a hint of the grisliness (see Botting, *Gavin Maxwell*, plates between pp. 106 and 107). The shark-fishing business was wound up in 1949 (Maxwell, *Harpoon at a Venture*, p. 184).

condoned)'.[45] The change in his consciousness began in 1956, according to Botting, on Maxwell's trip with renowned explorer Wilfred Thesiger to the region of the Marsh Arabs in Iraq, where he witnessed 'the widespread and innumerable manifestations of pain and horror and dying that characterised the life of both man and nature in the marshes'. Having witnessed the cruel death of an owl he had wanted to adopt, and with the death of a pet otter he had acquired on the trip imminently to occur, Maxwell was on the cusp of 'a philosophical shift that was to lead, step by step, to the ardent conservationist of future years'.[46] As we'll see in Chapter 3, reckoning with the ambivalent response that abundant nature has always prompted instigates a gear shift in contemporary nature prose.

Maxwell's fame is intimately bound up with specific sites on the north-east Scottish coast and the Hebridean islands, and the remainder of this chapter is concerned with the different ways in which the remoteness of this region has been infused with meaning. It is important to bear in mind that the appeal of the rugged remoteness has a long artistic history, but a history which becomes intensified in twentieth-century British rural writing. As Madeleine Bunting points out, 'the islands inspired a wealth of books during the 1930s and 1940s, with readers hungry to hear more of their beauty, distinctive culture and echoes of the peasant life now long lost'. Such books, 'sometimes sentimental, sometimes purple in their prose...fed the British imagination'.[47] The appropriation of Scottish experience in this populist genre must be kept in view. Indeed, the nature of the Highland landscape in the twentieth century has been produced by a form of class (if not English) colonialism which celebrated its sterility. For Iain Stewart, the 'magnificent wilderness' of the north-west Highlands is 'a delusion', effectively 'a romantic idyll of the sublime and picturesque carefully cultured by a Victorian nobility that adored the landscape but did precious little to protect it'. The preservation of game habitats, 'deer forest and grouse moor', came at the cost of forfeiting the Highlands' 'ecological richness', as well as the traditional activities of subsistence: the planting and cutting of woods; mining; farming and fishing. The production of this rugged sublimity, where 'less people meant more beauty', means that its

---

[45] Botting, *Gavin Maxwell*, pp. 101–2.
[46] Ibid., pp. 183–4. This trip supplied the material for Maxwell's acclaimed travel book, *A Reed Shaken by the Wind* (London: Longmans, Green & Co., 1957). The Iraq marshes, inhabited by the Ma'dan people (the term 'Ma'dan' can be disparaging), 'were one of the world's great unspoiled wetlands' (Botting, *Gavin Maxwell*, p. 172). This ancient culture and habitation were both destroyed by Saddam Hussein's regime, the people persecuted, the marshes drained. See Michael Wood, 'Saddam Drains the Life of the Marsh Arabs', *The Independent*, 27 August 1993. However, in more recent times the Iraqi government has made efforts to reinstate the habitat and the Marsh Arabs: see Peter Schwartzstein, 'Iraq's Marsh Arabs Test the Waters as Wetlands Ruined by Saddam are Reborn', *The Guardian*, 18 January 2017, https://www.theguardian.com/global-development/2017/jan/18/iraq-marsh-arabs-test-the-waters-wetlands-ruined-by-saddam-reborn-southern-marshes (accessed 27 February 2018).
[47] Madeleine Bunting, *Love of Country: A Hebridean Journey* (London: Granta, 2016), p. 51.

remoteness is also a sign of moral culpability.[48] The human cost signalled by the abandoned or empty dwellings adopted by some of the writers considered in this chapter is a visible sign of this history, where remoteness can be romanticized and the signs in the landscape misperceived. However, it is also important to understand that contemporary Scots identify with the remote landscape of the Highlands and islands, seeing something other than just the legacy of desolation caused by the Clearances. Moreover, the concept of rewilding now produces a slightly altered framework for understanding remoteness in nature writing— abandoned places *become* wild, and so a different prospect for the naturalist or nature writer who takes up residence in once inhabited places, but who is not occupying a place that anyone else might wish to inhabit. We need, then, to allow for this notion of the wild in the perception of Highland remoteness, but without forgetting the social history that remote living inevitably tends to obscure.

In the foreword (1959) to *Ring of Bright Water* (1960), the first book in a trilogy, Gavin Maxwell explains something of how the mythology of his sojourn in the Western Highlands of Scotland was constructed. For the setting of his remote cottage he used the fictional name Camusfeàrna (which translates from the Gaelic as 'the Bay of Alders') rather than the actual location, Sandaig—not 'to create mystery' he writes, realizing 'it will be easy enough for the curious to discover where I live', but rather 'because identification in print would seem in a sense a sacrifice, a betrayal of its remoteness and isolation, as if by doing so I were to bring nearer its enemies of industry and urban life'.[49] The protection of remoteness and isolation as an antidote to twentieth-century modernity is historically significant, anticipating both the counterculture and the environmental movement of the 1960s. Camusfeàrna, Maxwell suggests, calls to mind many 'such bays and houses, empty and long disused', which are 'scattered throughout the wild sea lochs of the Western Highlands and the Hebrides', places which are 'symbols, for me and for many, of freedom, whether it be from the prison of over-dense communities and the close confines of human relationships, from the less complex incarceration of office walls and hours, or simply freedom from the prison of adult life and an escape into the forgotten world of childhood, of the individual or the race'. Abandoned dwellings, a sign of urbanization and rural decay throughout the British archipelago, now become a resource for escaping from—and reflecting on—the effects of that historical trend. Here Maxwell articulates a conundrum that informs contemporary expression: the abandoned cottage, the site of remote nature writing is, invariably, a sign of historical rural impoverishment; yet Maxwell, and others who have followed him, appropriate these places as symbols

---

[48] Iain Stewart, 'Introduction' to Frank Fraser Darling, *Island Years, Island Farm* (1940, 1943; Toller Fratrum: Little Toller Books, 2011), pp. 13–17 (p. 13).
[49] Gavin Maxwell, *Ring of Bright Water* (London: Longmans, 1960), p. vii. Subsequent references are given in parentheses.

of freedom, but a freedom predicated on challenging the long historical process that rendered them empty (and available for the nature sojourn) in the first place. Maxwell's rationale for the Camusfeàrna story, then, lies in the desire to generalize his experiences of this place, and make them speak to the general predicament of alienation 'that man has suffered in his separation from the soil and from the other living creatures of the world'; and, as a consequence of that generalizing tendency, *Ring of Bright Water* is clearly distinguishable from more recent instances of writing about place, where it has become commonplace for writers to excavate social history (and prehistory). But Maxwell is distinctly contemporary in the ecological colouring he gives to the shared human plight: true to the continuing conventions of remote nature writing, the Maxwell myth foregrounds the healing potential of 'look[ing] long at some portion of the earth as it was' before humanity 'tampered with it' (p. vii).

As well as helping to usher in a new contemporary mood, the nature of this idealism is also historically specific. It suffuses the first book, and this is partly achieved by the account of Maxwell's pet otters and his affecting bond with them, and in this dimension Maxwell caught the sensibility of his age, and an emergent mood, as Botting makes clear: '*Ring of Bright Water* struck a chord' with 'a large swathe of the public'. It was a book that 'met a yearning in the heart of urbanised, industrialised man, creating not readers but fans, who could retreat into its world'. Anticipating 'the revolutionary changes of the sixties', *Ring of Bright Water* 'appealed to many trapped in the old post-war system, who seized on it as depicting an alternative ideal way of life and an escape option'.[50] The apparent 'timelessness' of *Ring of Bright Water*, then, was very much of its time; and one marker of this historical specificity was the sentimental depiction of animals.[51] For Maxwell, the value in Camusfeàrna's remoteness is bestowed upon it only when the otter Mij is installed and his presence becomes an essential part of 'the waterfall, the burn, the white beaches and the islands': 'he seemed so absolute a part of his surroundings that I wondered how they could ever have seemed to me complete before his arrival' (p. 121). So necessary is the presence of the otters to the significance of the remote scene for Maxwell (and so, too, for a reading 'with the grain'), that Maxwell has to spend a year away from Camusfeàrna when Mij is killed, feeling the place now 'hollow and insufficient' (p. 150). All Maxwell's otters relish the chance to roam wild, if only temporarily—and this adds another important dimension to the blending of animal and landscape: the domestication of a species felt to be at one with this particular place lends great potential to Maxwell's isolated dwelling, a place where inside and outside become

---

[50] Botting, *Gavin Maxwell: A Life*, p. 296.
[51] As Dan Boothby points out, utopian 'books about wild places and living with wild animals were "in"' in the 1950s and 1960s. See *Island of Dreams: A Personal History of a Remarkable Place* (London: Picador, 2015), p. 15.

indeterminate, producing a blurring of nature and culture, and the possibility of a fusion between the two.[52]

Yet, if remoteness is the underpinning condition of Maxwell's utopia, it is also a fantasy. The important aspect of this is that Maxwell exposes the fantasy, as the trilogy progresses. It's not that he doesn't invest in the idea of Camusfeàrna as an idyll of human–nature interaction—that is central to its conception, and to the popularity of the first volume; rather, it is through trying to live the idyll that it turns sour. Maxwell's perception is revised in the second volume, *The Rocks Remain* (1963), for several reasons. High on the list is a series of violent episodes involving the otters Edal and Teko, expressing their instinctive aggression. In the worst of these episodes, one of Maxwell's entourage, the naturalist Terry Nutkins, then a 15-year-old, loses the top of two of his fingers.[53] Maxwell finds a behavioural rationale for each of the attacks, but the dream of human–animal cohabitation mooted in *Ring of Bright Water* rapidly fades. There, the otter Mij, despite his habit of piercing people's ears with a sharp bite, is perceived to display different brands of 'demonstrative love' to his three favourite humans (pp. 139–40). This is certainly a book that transformed perceptions of the otter in Britain, playing a central role in adding it to the list of protected species.[54] For all the scenes of lovable domesticity, however, the most arresting description of Mij is when Maxwell has arranged for him to swim and catch fish in a large glass tank at the zoo in Regent's Park. Mij swims with

> a zeal and a display of virtuosity for which even my long hours of watching him from above had left me unprepared. His speed was bewildering, his grace breathtaking; he was boneless, mercurial, sinuous, wonderful. I thought of a trapeze artist, of a ballet dancer, of a bird or an aircraft in aerobatics, but in all these I was comparing him to lesser grandeurs; he was an otter in his own element, and he was the most beautiful thing in nature that I had ever seen. (p. 145)

This intimation of the otter's otherness, for which no comparison in human endeavour is adequate, prepares us for the collapse of the Camusfeàrna experiment. The seeds of this are apparent in *The Rocks Remain*, when Camusfeàrna is besieged by Maxwell fans, enamoured of the first book, and enraptured by the

---

[52] Mij, brought back from Maxwell's travels in Iraq, was from a species found not to have been named previously, and which was named after Maxwell, much to his satisfaction: *Lutrogale perspicillata maxwelli* (pp. 102–3). This raises the question of native species and human interference; but in the context of Maxwell's writing, there is something seemingly apposite about *any* otter in this environment.

[53] Gavin Maxwell, *The Rocks Remain* (London: Longmans, 1963), pp. 96–9. Subsequent references are given in parentheses.

[54] As Douglas Botting observes, *Ring of Right Water* 'marked the beginning of a groundswell of worldwide support for otter conservation'. Botting goes on to claim that Maxwell's 'contribution to saving the otter was immeasurable, and was probably the greatest achievement of his life'. Botting, *Gavin Maxwell: A Life*, pp. 509–10.

remote idyll. Camusfeàrna becomes a site of pilgrimage: 'a steady stream of rubbernecks arrived daily, often with loose and undisciplined dogs, to bang on the single door of the house and demand, as if it were their right, to see the otters and all that had figured in the story' (pp. 88–9). The house at Sandaig is difficult to access, and this produces a deluded sense of specialness in each of the uninvited visitors, a conviction 'that he or she, and he or she alone, was the pioneer; that it could not have been possible for any other to have discovered the true location of Camusfeàrna, or for any other to have wished to do so'. Maxwell finds this 'revealing' (p. 89), alerting us to the pursuit of remoteness he shares with these intruders. It is their deluded self-importance he finds significant, but what is also revealed by this episode is a fault at the heart of the project. In a practical sense, his anger is understandable, because the endless interruptions stop the household from functioning, putting 'the very life of the place ... at stake' (p. 90). Yet it is on account of the success of the first book—the realization of its vision—that the pilgrims arrive. They have been inspired by Maxwell, and the idea of a special remote place which stages the interaction of its human and animal inhabitants, and where the house is absorbed by its wild surroundings. If we assume that some of the pilgrims have been urged by the sentiment of Maxwell's foreword to *Ring of Bright Water*, with its claim that life at Camusfeàrna demonstrates how to repair humanity's fatal 'separation from the soil and from the other living creatures of the world' (p. vii), we can understand their desire to witness this nirvana for themselves, if not their need to feel something unique in their pilgrimage to it.

If we try to disentangle the several overlapping paradoxes in play here, we should probably set aside the paradox that the broad appeal of remoteness in this instance is destructive of it: it is obvious enough that a remote place has value for a select few, or even one individual. The more interesting tension is between what Camusfeàrna *represents* and how the actual experiment in living there is played out. The pilgrims took Maxwell too literally. As the foreword makes clear, Camusfeàrna is intended as a 'symbol' of an alternative way of living; and that's another reason for the invented name: Sandaig is the actual place, Camusfeàrna, although anchored to it, is also the *idea* of the place, released as a source of inspiration that might find other literal manifestations. Yet to convince us—such is the convention, the credo of realism in nature writing about remote places—the actual life described must retain its inspiring credentials. This is why the collapse of Camusfeàrna through the course of the trilogy acquires an element of tragic force. Maxwell gives us a vision of a place transformed after nineteen years of occupancy, with changing retinues, schemes, and financial pressures, and inevitable signs of development. In the final book, *Raven Seek Thy Brother* (1968), he realizes that the remote site has been transformed from 'a four-roomed cottage, two rooms upstairs and two down', now with its 'straggling pre-fabricated wings built with the ugliness born of what had seemed necessity'. There are 'broken-down jeeps', his 'motor launch Polar Star ... high and dry on her massive wheeled cradle', 'telegraph posts and wires descended the hill from one direction, electric conveyances from another', and 'around the house itself were high wooden palings confining two otters that had once been house-living pets'. He is, he reports, 'surveying what I had done to Camusfeàrna – what I had done to the animals and what I had done to myself'.[55] Amidst vacillating plans to close down Camusfeàrna and rehouse the remaining otters in a zoo, the general scene of dilapidation reveals further depressing evidence of human activity over a generation: 'all along the dunes between the house and the sea lay rubbish dumps of rusty cans and bottles, exposed, perhaps, by the wind's lifting of the sand that had originally covered our deep-dug pits' (pp. 185–6). There is an effort in the final chapter of *Raven Seek Thy Brother* to rekindle the dream: the otters Teko and Edal are no longer to be sent away, and Maxwell consorts with them, recapturing, he writes, 'the vision that I had lost' (p. 209). But it is a short interlude: Maxwell ponders the impending extinction of the human species—'the evidence is all there' (p. 209)—and the terse epilogue that follows describes the fire of January 1968 that destroyed Camusfeàrna, and killed Edal, whose remains were buried at the foot of the rowan tree that also figures prominently in the Maxwell myth (p. 210).[56] The rowan tree becomes the symbol of the inversion of remoteness in the trilogy, as misfortune displaces idealism.

Central to the literary resonance of Maxwell's work, and to the significance of that rowan tree, is the poet Kathleen Raine, who was profoundly in love with the homosexual Maxwell, who did not reciprocate her deep passion.[57] Believing herself badly mistreated by his mercurial behaviour, she placed a curse on the rowan tree beside the house one night: 'weeping I laid my hands upon the trunk, calling upon the tree for justice: "Let Gavin suffer, in this place, as I am suffering now".' Maxwell became aware of the curse a few years later.[58] The importance of this for the trilogy is that Maxwell gives the impression of a firm belief in Raine's curse, so that it seems to orchestrate the spiral of misfortune recounted in *Raven*

---

[55] Gavin Maxwell, *Raven Seek Thy Brother* (London: Longmans, 1968), pp. 2–3. Subsequent references are given in parentheses.

[56] This is a new focus of pilgrimage for Maxwell fans. Edal's burial is marked by a carved stone that exhorts visitors: 'whatever joy she gave to you, give back to nature'. See Virginia McKenna, 'Afterword' to Gavin Maxwell, *The Ring of Bright Water Trilogy*, ed. Austin Chinn (London: Puffin Books, 2001), pp. 405–8 (p. 407). After Maxwell's death, in accordance with his wishes, his ashes were buried on the site of the house at Sandaig, beneath a large boulder with an inset memorial plate. See Botting, *Gavin Maxwell: A Life*, p. 553.

[57] It was Raine who supplied the title for Maxwell's most famous book, which comes from her poem 'The Marriage of Psyche', used by Maxwell as his epigraph. The ring of bright water in the poem refers to the reflection from the encircling burn at Sandaig.

[58] Kathleen Raine, *The Lion's Mouth: Concluding Chapters of Autobiography* (London: Hamish Hamilton, 1977), p. 73. For Maxwell's perturbed reaction to the news see Botting, *Gavin Maxwell: A Life*, p. 286. The actual wording of the curse in *Raven Seek Thy Brother* was a matter of dispute between Maxwell and Raine, and was amended from the manuscript version. See Botting, *Gavin Maxwell: A Life*, p. 535. Writing his preface in 1992, Botting records that 'the rowan tree – the source of so much myth and conflict in years gone by – finally died this summer' (p. xv).

Seek Thy Brother. Here the discovery of the curse comes when Maxwell is reading the manuscript of Raine's autobiography. He reports that 'she had always believed that she possessed great and terrible occult powers, and in that moment of hatred she had not doubted her ability to blight the years ahead of me'. He pictures her uttering her curse on 'a wild night of wind and sleet-storm, roaring surf, and a witch's moon', and reflects 'how exactly the pattern of the last years had paralleled her blind desire for destruction', wondering 'if she had exulted' in his woes (*Raven Seek Thy Brother*, p. 5). The foreboding mood of this book is also implicit in its title, drawn from the Bedouin belief that a single raven is an evil omen, which must be annulled by the cry, 'Raven, seek thy brother!' (p. 266). Maxwell's death on 7 September 1969, in the year following the destruction by fire of the house at Sandaig—and on the very day the remains of the house were being razed by a bulldozer—completes the myth of the inextricable connection of a remarkable place, and a remarkable nature writer, making Camusfeàrna one of the most special sites in the British nature-writing tradition, but also a potent illustration of the contradictory mythology at the heart of this tradition. Camusfeàrna was a fiction, and was exposed as such even before the dwelling that inspired it was destroyed; and yet it has inspired successive followers, drawn to north-west Scotland and the Hebrides in the hope of reproducing Maxwell's fantasy of remote living.

Maxwell's Followers

Maxwell's followers—those who have been inspired to emulate or extend his work—have fashioned different kinds of ambivalent expression. The first writer I want to consider from this group is Mike Tomkies, someone for whom the goal of remote living overshadows the writing of it. His work aspires to belong to the genre of the nature retreat, but we have to stretch our understanding of the genre to see how his literal-mindedness achieves its potency: endurance and observation take precedence over literary craft, but that ultimately produces a kind of naïve purity of engagement and, as we shall see, another characteristic instance of contradiction in the work of a contemporary environmentalist. Tomkies was a seasoned wilderness dweller, who then decided to try and emulate Maxwell's experience: first in a cottage on Eilean Shona, and then in a still more remote cottage on the shores of a loch in Inverness-shire (as the county was known until 1975). His desire to live in the remote Scottish Highlands and study wildlife was inspired by *Ring of Bright Water*, which, he recalled, 'had suggested to me wilderness life in Britain was really possible'.[59] On his pilgrimage to Sandaig/

---

[59] Mike Tomkies, *Between Earth and Paradise* (1981; London: Jonathan Cape, 1991), pp. 12–13. Subsequent references are given in parentheses.

Camusfeàrna, in homage to 'the man who had created a concept of paradise for so many', he is temporarily moved by the 'impulse to try and breathe new life into the place, fill it with love, resurrect it', even though the house has gone, but he finally abandons the plan to buy the old croft still remaining on the site, after weeks of 'fruitless negotiations' (p. 16).[60] The dilapidated cottage he settles on, in 'a secluded natural bay' on Eilean Shona, a few miles south of Sandaig, is suitably remote and basic: 'there was no road, no electricity, gas, phone, bathroom, kitchen, sanitation or even piped water. Sheep dung five inches thick covered the floor. A dead sheep's carcass propped up the shattered door' (p. 19). Tomkies finds it spellbinding, however, with its 'vast 180-degree panorama with not a house, road or sign of human habitation in sight', and so sets about the task of renovation (p. 19). After three-and-a-half years on Eilean Shona, he relocated to a small crofter's cottage on the shores of Loch Shiel, a dwelling which he renamed 'Wildernesse'.

Tomkies' own myth of remote living is recorded in a series of books; but this is a different kind of 'performance' to the dramas of solitude that more usually characterize the retreat narrative. Tomkies is unique in that his withdrawal from society to define himself in relation to wilderness is a lifetime commitment—or, at least, something he determined to devote the rest of his working life to, at the age of 42 (p. 9).[61] He is not a self-conscious writer in the way that some of Maxwell's other followers are; yet he still feels the need to situate his project in relation to literary antecedents. He is very pleased to be given the use of the 'superb mahogany four-drawer desk' on which J. M. Barrie had written the first film script for his book *Peter Pan* during his stay on the island (pp. 18, 21); and he finds a kindred spirit in Henry Williamson and the autobiographical figure of Willie Maddison, whose withdrawal to 'a lonely Devon cottage to be at one with nature' (p. 79) in Williamson's *Flax of Dream* tetralogy is the most important influence on him: he accepts its challenge to modernity, unaware of the partly hidden fascist leanings, which have escaped many of Williamson's readers. Tomkies refers to the third and fourth volumes in the tetralogy, *The Dream of Fair Women* (1924) and *The Pathway* (1928).[62] He also discovers *Walden*, 'where thoughts similar to mine,

---

[60] A croft in Scotland is a special kind of property, with attached land that the owner must farm, or maintain in approved ways. The owner must also live on the croft or within its locale.

[61] I calculate that he moved to Scotland in 1970, and then from Eilean Shona to Loch Shiel in the autumn of 1973. See Tomkies, *Between Earth and Paradise*, pp. 9, 16, and Tomkies, *A Last Wild Place* (London: Jonathan Cape, 1984), p. 18. Subsequent references are given in parentheses. The duration of three-and-a-half years is from Tomkies' voice-over for the documentary *Look Stranger*, dir. Colin Morris, BBC 1975, https://www.youtube.com/watch?v=zDRW8HOygD0 (accessed 15 October 2018).

[62] When the tetralogy was published in a single volume, in 1936, Williamson took the chance in his foreword to 'salute the great man across the Rhine': see *The Flax of Dream* (London: Faber & Faber, 1936), p. 7. In *Goodbye West Country* (Boston, MA: Little, Brown & Co., 1938) Williamson drew a comparison between Hitler and Willie Maddison (p. 38). These books are dominated by Maddison's

so well expressed, made me feel less alone' (p. 72). Yet, in the same breath, he distinguishes between his own life immersed in nature—at a very early stage at this point—and Thoreau's experiment: 'to find I had already spent more than twice as long in the wilds as he had in his cabin in the woods of Concord renewed my resolve to carry on' (p. 72). This signals what is distinctive about Tomkies: for him, remote living is primarily a feat of endurance, and only secondarily inspiration for the written record.

The paying of dues to Williamson and Thoreau seems a little ready-made, an attempt by Tomkies to claim a place in a literary tradition in which he doesn't fully belong: reportage is his main strength. Immediacy of expression is the usual effect, as when Tomkies reflects on his intense loneliness: 'alone in the wilds, a man's conscience and self-awareness increase, hang over him like a hawk. The psychological effect of one's opinion of oneself can be overwhelming in its ability to destroy—and also to preserve. Self-respect is the only foundation upon which one can survive' (p. 55). More usually, as we have seen, the contemplative retreat into nature produces varieties of immersive experience, a process that necessarily entails a degree of dissolution of the self (however self-conscious that may be in the writing of it), so Tomkies' emphasis here is intriguing. The intensified self-awareness, or vital self-assertion, that Tomkies experiences may be down to the *permanence* of his time in the wild. He is not a sojourner in Bennett's sense of someone self-consciously constructing an ideal self and searching for a home: the emphasis on the search in Bennett's sojourner—which cannot be completed without destroying the sojourner's questing identity—is not an accurate way of accounting for Tomkies' life, working out the process of survival in a state of permanent adjustment to remoteness. He is, rather, a case study of the sojourner's antipole.

In Tomkies' literal presentation, remoteness facilitates immediacy for the appreciation of his wild surroundings, and enables him to advocate the experience as the route to a more general healing, in the spirit of Maxwell: 'how meaningful life suddenly seemed. I felt happy again. Loneliness in the wilds, if only for a spell, should be compulsory for everyone!' (p. 87). However, it is only when he discovers the still more remote site of his second Highland home that he perceives the true value of his work, pared down to its essential ingredients. As this reflection gathers shape, he experiences 'the strange and wonderful surge of total solitude' in a place 'totally devoid of human life' (pp. 173–4). On the loch, however, he visits a 'green Island' containing 'the ruins of a tiny church built to the memory of a local saint', 'an ancient brass bell' upon the stone altar (p. 174), and this reveals the fault line in his presentation of remoteness. Tomkies is less interested in the human history of

---

plans to write his visionary programme of political renewal from his position of remoteness—ultimately a rather different objective to the blazing message of wisdom-found-in-nature that Tomkies perceives, and which moves him 'profoundly' (*Between Earth and Paradise*, p. 80).

this place than in the wildness it now plays host to. He emphasizes its remoteness, but without denying the human history of a place where 'no one had lived... all year round, since 1912': an 'old steamer... had once plied the loch', but with its removal 'so had died the human life along its shores' (*A Last Wild Place*, p. 1). Now Wildernesse is 'the only surviving dwelling in fifteen miles of roadless loch shore' and 'the wildest, and loneliest place in which [he] had ever lived' (p. 1). Its extreme remoteness, inaccessible by road, is indicated by the '13-mile return boat trip' required whenever he needs supplies (*Between Earth and Paradise*, p. 213). But the signs of former inhabitation have been glimpsed, making us desirous of a more sustained engagement with the relationship between this remote place and its history of impoverishment, that tension which we saw to be inherent in Maxwell's conception of the 'freedom' to be pursued in derelict cottages.

Tomkies advanced a simple message of reconnection through his own detailed observations and photography of a range of birds and species, notably wild cats, black-throated divers, and golden eagles. His efforts constitute an exemplary instance of becoming 'close to the animal state oneself' (*A Last Wild Place*, p. 225). His was a life dedicated to a feat of extraordinary endurance;[63] yet the flip side of this lifelong commitment to remoteness is its precarity, its lack of domestic security. In the convention of remote nature prose, he makes a 'home' from a derelict dwelling, but the shadow of homelessness is ever-present, if unexamined. Tomkies eventually gave up at Wildernesse in 1986, after thirteen years.[64] In his final memoir of this phase of his life, *Last Wild Years*, the presiding mood is that of a defeat that echoes Walter Murray's experience at the end of his time at Copsford, but without the self-reflexivity: enduring a winter with the lowest temperatures for thirty years, his health failing, Tomkies decides he 'had really had enough' (pp. 48, 49). It is not just the elements that make his dwelling unhomely. He is also disillusioned about fresh encroachments into his wilderness: fish farms on the loch (p. 84); open-cast mining (p. 85); and ecotourists looking for the eagle eyries he is authorized to monitor and film (p. 96). These intrusions into his last wild place—some of which his writing has stimulated, of course, in an ironic repetition of Maxwell's unintended lure—cause him to conclude that 'the end is coming here' (p. 85). But it is a personal ending, drawing together conflicting moods, now following some of the conventions of remote nature writing. As the sheep encroach on his 'hard-won patch', he reflects on 'the scandalous Highland Clearances' that 'brought the sheep to these hills' (p. 88),

---

[63] Tomkies died on 6 October 2016. See Jim Crumley, 'Mike Tomkies, Nature Writer Who Immersed Himself in the Wildest of Terrain', *The Scotsman*, 21 October 2016, https://www.scotsman.com/news/obituary-mike-tomkies-nature-writer-who-immersed-himself-wildest-terrain-647953 (accessed 30 June 2021).
[64] Mike Tomkies, *Last Wild Years* (London: Jonathan Cape, 1992). Subsequent references are given in parentheses.

as if that thought can no longer be deferred.[65] What Tomkies' books reveal, in summary, is the fundamental contradiction of this subgenre of nature writing, but without the enriching self-reflexivity: the tension between remote living pursued in extremis, and the literature of retreat, which must always return us to questions of human history and culture.

Douglas Botting offers a helpful distinction between Maxwell and Tomkies, based on their differing responses to remoteness. Maxwell, he writes, 'was an infinitely more complex and versatile human being' than the popular image of him as 'a guru of the wilds would suggest'. The 'claim that he was bogus – not a real wilderness man at all but a kind of dilettante eco-tourist' is partly supported in Mike Tomkies' re-evaluation of him 'as a "great, great writer but a wilderness fool"'.[66] This distinction, based on survival skills, is instructive. For Botting, Maxwell was 'an artist rather than a rugged outdoor man', and '*Ring of Bright Water* was more a work of the imagination than a documentary', which, 'like the best works of literary creativity,... selected, compressed and transposed pieces of his experience into a work of truth rather than a simple catalogue of facts'.[67] This is well said, although rather than seeing a nebulous concept of 'truth' in the appreciation of nature, emerging from selective creativity, our attention should be centred on the interpretation of experience that emerges from Maxwell's writing, and in the trilogy as a whole, so that the 'truth' about remote living constructed in *Ring of Bright Water* is destroyed literally, and dissipated figuratively, in the next two volumes. Yet it is a truth that lingers, and not just as an idea, since it has a literal afterlife in the efforts of Maxwell's followers. Understanding that contradiction—the persisting value apprehended in a way of life exposed as an artifice—gets us to the ideational heart of this branch of contemporary nature prose.

Although the Maxwell myth constructed in the *Ring of Bright Water* trilogy places Sandaig/Camusfeàrna at the centre of the ultimately tragic adventure of building a haven of remoteness, there is another site of particular importance that allowed Maxwell's adventure to persist for a little longer, and which has inspired another group of writers, notably from among his associates. The site in question is Kyleakin Island, or Eilean Bàn ('White Island'), the island over which the Skye Bridge projects, although it was separate from the mainland in Maxwell's lifetime:[68] I'll give a little background to this phase of Maxwell's life, as it gives the context for

---

[65] His first Highland home is now advertised as one of a series of holiday cottages for rent on Eilean Shona. Tomkies' cottage, called 'Ballindona' in his time of residence, is now called 'Red Cottage'. See: http://eileanshona.com/the-cottages/red-cottage (accessed 16 October 2018).

[66] Botting, *Gavin Maxwell: A Life*, p. 301. Botting is drawing on correspondence and/or interviews with Tomkies (p. 576).

[67] Ibid., p. 301.

[68] This is the island between the Kyle of Lochalsh and the Isle of Skye. Douglas Botting observes that the correct Gaelic name for Kyleakin Island is actually Eilean na Gil[l]ean ('Island of Boys'). The muddle, he suggests, stems from the 1903 Ordnance Survey map which confused it 'with the larger island to the north, properly called Eilean Bàn, and the wrong names have stuck to the wrong islands

the most recent instance of remote writing inspired by him. Maxwell had bought the lighthouse keeper's cottage on this island, and also the one on Isle Ornsay, in 1963;[69] but it was the White Island that became his final home. Richard Frere, who converted the Kyleakin lighthouse cottages to Maxwell's specifications, has adjusted the Maxwell myth in his memoir, which gives an insight into Maxwell's unpredictable moods, but also seeks to cement Maxwell's place in British nature writing, finding 'a strong literary kinship' between Maxwell and Richard Jefferies.[70]

John Lister-Kaye was appointed to oversee Maxwell's post-Camusfeàrna project on the White Island, which was to be home to a private zoo, 'a park of Scottish mammals and birds to which the tourist and visiting naturalist might come and observe at close quarters a representative selection of Highland wildlife which it would be virtually impossible to see in the wild state'. This planned 'oasis of tamed animal life' was the logical development of Camusfeàrna, and the epitome of Maxwell's nature-culture project.[71] The collaboration between Maxwell and Lister-Kaye was short-lived, however: Lister-Kaye 'was just beginning to get to grips with his duties when the news came that his employer and mentor was dead'.[72] Yet his testimony about Maxwell's enduring zeal for the post-Camusfeàrna project, in his final weeks, is compelling: he found 'Gavin's enthusiasm...boundless and infectious', determined as he was to assemble a menagerie 'of some twenty species of Scottish mammals and birds'; and it seems significant that the new scheme was conceived together with plans for a new exhaustive reference work, 'a book on the mammals of Britain' which Maxwell and Lister-Kaye were to co-author.[73] The zoo and the book bespeak Maxwell's continuing efforts to popularize nature, the effect of which was to bring remoteness and culture into greater proximity.

Remoteness, however, retained its allure for Maxwell's followers. Indeed, Lister-Kaye reinforces the function of remoteness as the means of refashioning the self through an immersive encounter with the nonhuman, recalling how his first experience living on Kyleakin prompted in him 'a complete mental reshuffle', finding himself suddenly able 'to respond naturally to the demands of an existence free from pretence and devious motivation'. Such an 'entire reassessment of

---

ever since'. See Botting, *Gavin Maxwell: A Life*, p. 407. (Dan Boothby pinpoints the cartography error as having occurred in 1872. See note 77 below.) Eilean nan Gillean, as it appears on maps now, is attached to the mainland, at the point where the Skye Bridge heads towards the White Island.

[69] Botting, *Gavin Maxwell: A Life*, p. 434.

[70] Richard Frere, *Maxwell's Ghost: An Epilogue to Gavin Maxwell's Camusfeàrna* (1976; Edinburgh: Birlinn, 2011), p. 28. Frere, who resembled Maxwell, was mistaken for him after the author's death, hence the title of his memoir—which also, of course, suggests his continuing presence in the places revered by Maxwell pilgrims. Frere also gives some insight into Maxwell's views about homosexuality, notably Maxwell's defence of the 'custom', in Morocco, 'that young men of position spend some years in the houses of elder men as adopted sons', receiving 'advancement and worldliness' in exchange 'for love and affection' (p. 66).

[71] John Lister-Kaye, *The White Island* (London: Longman, 1972), p. 30.

[72] Botting, *Gavin Maxwell: A Life*, p. 557. [73] Lister-Kaye, *The White Island*, pp. 2, 30–1.

purpose and direction' depends on 'monastic' isolation, with any distractions coming only 'direct from nature'.[74] This manifesto for wild living, however, is not something that Lister-Kaye really explores in his memoir. It has more relevance to the Maxwell myth—the ambitions, if not the actuality—and *The White Island* is really a tribute to Maxwell, and an account of the winding up of his final venture. Describing the interment of Maxwell's ashes at Sandaig, Lister-Kaye writes: 'the simple ceremony marked the tragic ending of a saga and the beginning of a legend', a saga and a legend he perpetuates.[75]

The last Maxwell follower I shall consider is Dan Boothby; his experience reliving and reflecting on the Maxwell myth brings together the emphasis on artifice and literary construction that we find in Maxwell's own writing, set against the more insistent expression of, and involvement with, the wild that is the preoccupation of Tomkies, at the other extreme. For Boothby, the Maxwell myth was a lifelong obsession, from his schoolboy reading of the *Ring of Bright Water* trilogy, through successive visits to Sandaig, beginning in the year he left school, to his tenure as warden on Kyleakin Island for two summers from 2005. His account of this experience, *Island of Dreams* (2015), is an important reconsideration of the Maxwell story's contemporary relevance, not least because the presence of the Skye Bridge compromises the island's remoteness.[76] Boothby cultivates the allure of place in his account of his first impressions of Maxwell's former house on Kyleakin Island.[77] He recounts being overcome by 'a strange feeling', which he compares to being left alone in the apartment of a new lover in Damascus, when he had been left wondering 'if I wasn't going a little insane. For it *is* a kind of insanity, falling in love' (pp. 28–9). This is a roundabout way of saying that he was falling in love with the place, which also alerts us—in that suggestion of 'insanity'—to a state that is both irrational and evanescent. In the spirit of this embrace of Maxwell's world, Boothby's first sighting of an otter dispels his former aversion to them: enraptured by the creature's 'stealth', 'flowing fluid motion', and 'charisma', he becomes 'an immediate convert' (p. 46).

Boothby, however, vacillates in his response to Maxwell: he remains drawn to the romance, but is equally inclined to expose the myth. The ambivalence is carefully cultivated, and it extends to the idea of remoteness. His repeated pilgrimages to Sandaig are made because of his 'obsession' with Maxwell (p. 117); but they are always conditioned by a sense of the extreme feelings that seem to be enshrined in this remote site, with its particular history, as on one visit when he is frightened by 'the silence and the violence and the beauty and the

---

[74] Ibid., p. 56.   [75] Ibid., p. 109.
[76] Dan Boothby, *Island of Dreams: A Personal History of a Remarkable Place* (London: Picador, 2015). Subsequent references are given in parentheses.
[77] Like Botting, Boothby points out that 'Eilean Bàn is not the island's original "given" name, which is in fact Eilean nan Gillean', a mistake he traces to a cartographer's error of 1872. Given the misnaming, he prefers to call it Kyleakin Lighthouse Island (p. 289).

ferocity of that place', 'an isolated intense arena', and the thought that 'a heaven can so easily become hell' (p. 115). The uncertainty is felt at Kyleakin Island too, but here Boothby is more concerned with the paradox that the island both is, and is not, remote. It is certainly 'an elemental place', 'a rocky outcrop in the middle of the sea, hammered by salt-laden winds and lashed by rain', making 'any habitation' a challenge to maintain (p. 61); and yet it is also in sight of Kyle on the mainland, to the east, and Kyleakin village on Skye, to the south. Boothby recalls how Maxwell would often sit with a telescope 'spying on Kyle and Kyleakin', and is himself 'cheered in [his] solitude by the sights and sounds, and by the companionship, of the villagers' (p. 21). For him, the island is not a place of creative solitude, chiefly because of the demands on his time in his duty as a warden: the island is too much present, 'a project without end' (p. 80). Here Boothby pinpoints the tension between immersion in place and the artifice of literary creation: his memoir as a whole is a rehearsal of the personal experience of rethinking the idea of capturing, in writing, the essence of place and its transformative potential.

The ambivalence of Boothby's book can be traced to a granular level, and notably in the passages of natural description. The purple patches of belletrism are few, however, in keeping with a book that is overtly interrogating its own procedures. In one arresting section, Boothby condenses the wildlife memories of his second summer on the island, giving us a breathless catalogue of wildlife: a blackbird singing; a hedge sparrow hopping; a wood mouse negotiating 'the jungly grass behind the house'. There are knots, curlews and sandpipers, terns and gulls, puffins, flocks of guillemots and razorbills; a dog otter catching crabs; bats by the lighthouse; two species of jellyfish; Common Blue and Scotch Argus butterflies and Six-spot Burnet moths. The flora is especially noteworthy on this rocky outcrop: there are 'hanging locks of honeysuckle'; a rose bush; 'bramble bushes and rushes... spotted with cuckoo spit', and wild grasses edge the paths; wild roses and foxgloves attract the butterflies, and the flowers of bell heather provide the backdrop, turning 'the surrounding mountainsides the colour of blackcurrant coulis' (pp. 231–2). What is notable is the way in which these memories of a full summer are condensed into two paragraphs. They create the impression of an idyll, but an idyll that is falsified through compression. Boothby goes on to explore the wildlife 'mysteries' of that summer: the appearance of a roe deer that may have swum across to the island, or used the bridge, as toads are now doing; and then the inexplicable mass slaughter of voles, finally explained by 'a very fat ginger tomcat' that has escaped to the island from its domestic confines (pp. 233–5). Boothby shares, temporarily, the sense of a remote island ecosystem—Kyleakin had a self-contained remoteness in Maxwell's era, despite its proximity to the neighbouring villages—but he presents his foreshortened nature idyll in order to undermine it, making us see how the bridge compromises its remoteness.

In the analysis of his feelings about Kyleakin Island, Boothby tries to progress beyond the kind of vicarious identification displayed by the 'Maxwell nuts', the devoted fans that he has to conduct tours for, as one of his duties as warden (p. 266). He acquires a dinghy to emulate Maxwell's experience of the island, even though the bridge makes this a whim, not a necessity, 'a preposterous nostalgia for a way of life I'd never known' (p. 212). In working out what is 'preposterous' in his nostalgic hankering after Maxwell's life, he comes to a significant realization in which the nostalgia is not for the life Maxwell lived—because he increasingly comes to understand its constructed nature—but for a moment when such a construction was possible. The appeal of remoteness for Maxwell comes under scrutiny as Boothby deconstructs the myth;[78] but he retains his nostalgia for an earlier intellectual moment, at the birth of the conservation movement of the 1960s, and this governs the self-divided mood that characterizes *Island of Dreams*.

Boothby wrestles with the 'thought that [he] had found home' on the island, even though he is aware that 'the island could never be home, not truly' (p. 262). He feels that 'part of the myth' (p. 65) surrounding Maxwell will remain on the island, but Sandaig also retains its allure, and figures in the closing pages when Boothby's role as warden is coming to an end and, in melancholy mood, he makes a farewell visit to Sandaig. The melancholy has partly to do with inevitable generational change: 'the older generation of Glenelg and the surrounding villages still retain memories of the odd, highly strung spendthrift "otter man", but they are hazy memories now, mired by the mists of time' (p. 283). This is purposive nostalgia for the moment when starting up a programme of conservation—of participating in the vitality of that movement—was a source of hope, rather than a rearguard action. Boothby presents the plastic detritus that now washes ashore at Sandaig as visible evidence of this change: 'the beaches are littered with...globally available crap. Where once almost everything was biodegradable nowadays almost nothing is' (p. 280). But this is another instance of continuity, further evidence of Maxwell's instigation of the contemporary zeitgeist: as we have seen, the accumulation of buried refuse, exposed by the elements, was already a feature of Maxwell's tenure, and one source of his eventual disillusionment.

If Boothby's nostalgia establishes a continuity that he doesn't fully register, it also pinpoints discontinuity. In the closing pages he lays bare the rhetorical guile of Maxwell, by reflecting on the intimacy of reading, and the 'powerful but always one-sided bond' that can occur; but this is based on a re-evaluation of himself as a teenage reader, susceptible to Maxwell's 'carefully constructed version of himself', which was 'compelling, but also quite false' (p. 284). The romance persists, however, despite the artifice:

---

[78] For example, he posits the idea that Maxwell's homosexuality 'provoked the way he lived his life', including his pursuit of remoteness: in the very different era of the 1960s, with homosexuality outlawed in England and Wales until 1967, and in Scotland until 1980, 'a homosexual stayed in the closet to stay out of gaol and out of the press' (p. 238).

Part of his genius was to create a semblance of honesty in his books, enchanting and involving the reader by telling us all about it. He made us feel like we were his *intimates*. It was all a mirage in the end, of course, just *Art*, but Gavin Maxwell introduced me to the Highlands and the Hebrides, and he showed me the power of the written word. (pp. 284–5)

I'll return in a moment to the value produced by this combination of place and literary artifice, revealed as paradoxical. It is also a stage beyond an 'innocent' or untutored reading. Boothby also registers the disappointment he feels in Maxwell as his 'surrogate father', whose works fed his 'credulousness and innocence' as 'a shy, bookish, country-bred boy'. The emphasis here is on disillusionment:

I am a dreamer. But dreams aren't sustainable, and they're never as good in reality as they are in your head. All my life I have been led on by writers whose words on a page I have fallen in love with. We think of books as tablets of stone, but all writing, even the autobiographical, is full of fiction: a fraudulent, transmuted reality; a distorted projection of truth. I got lost early on. (p. 285)

The idea of 'fraud' in the puncturing of his dreams coincides with the ending of the narrative and his departure from the Highlands. The despondency is offset, however, by Boothby's own artifice, his version of Walter Murray's studied snow-globe (non-)epiphany. In his note of clarification at the end of the book, it emerges that he has learned from the selective use of autobiographical material for the sake of artifice: people have been omitted, names have been changed, and, crucially, 'the timeframe of [his] sojourn on the island has been rearranged', in order to serve 'the needs of the memoir form, and *story*' (p. 289). The artifice of *Island of Dreams*, in other words, helps implement the debunking of the Maxwell myth of value and self-realization in remoteness, by using similarly selective processes. A different myth of personal development through remote living is installed, which paradoxically supplies fresh oxygen to the Maxwell myth: like Maxwell, Boothby relies on the contemporary ecomimetic fusion of place and textuality, in which our engagement with his pilgrimage, and the insights it affords, is inseparable from our understanding of the debate about constructed value. And readers of *Island of Dreams* will be no less inclined to visit Eilean Bàn/Eilean nan Gillean as a consequence of reading the book. In this way, Boothby invites his readers to share in the irreducible doubleness of his project, conceived in reverence for a place and the myth that makes it special, despite its 'fraudulence'. The value resides in the recognition that deceit is inherent in the genre of remote nature writing and then reproducing that artifice *overtly*, so that the reader cannot resist the simultaneous 'push-and-pull' of the writing, cultivating and denying the representation of an appealing and significant place.

Neil Ansell: the Hebrides and Remoteness

In the discussion of Neil Ansell's *Deep Country* above, I suggested that this work is an exemplary instance of a tendency central to this survey: the tendency to embrace contradiction and paradox so that they become something else, a fusion of opposites, melded in such a way as to push us beyond the binary thinking that makes us think of that which is 'contradictory'. This is a development of the ambiguity inherent in all literary language, a contemporary synthesis that registers the predicament of environmental crisis, which can be recognized but not escaped, and where blame cannot be attributed without admitting culpability. I will conclude this chapter by turning to Ansell's subsequent books, which illustrate this contemporary coalescence very well in relation to the reconceptualization of remote nature writing. An enhanced understanding of Ansell's pursuit of remoteness in *Deep Country* emerged after the publication of his retrospective account of working with, and living amongst, homeless people in London in the 1980s: *Deer Island* (2013). This is also a book about remote nature, in which Ansell juxtaposes his accounts of homelessness with periodic trips to the Isle of Jura, in a startling reappraisal of the literature of solitude.

Ansell spent three years working as an unpaid volunteer for a small community charity, serving the needs of the homeless, a phase of his life that left him mentally exhausted, 'worn out from making friends with people and then having to watch them die'.[79] His charity work in Camden Town is recounted in a section dated 1980; and he subsequently lives in a squat between 1988 and 1989. These episodes of homelessness contain moments of human camaraderie and resistance amidst the urban squalor; but the juxtaposed episodes on Jura emerge as a form of repair, escape from the trauma Ansell feels. The effect of this can be to make Jura/Deer Island—Ansell's favourite place—a form of antidote as a place remote from oppressive London.[80] Yet Ansell uses this effect in order to question it, without quite dissipating the impression altogether. On the 'wild west coast' of Jura Ansell explores a series of caves 'a hundred feet above the shore', which 'had all once been sea caves' and which now provide shelter for the prolific red deer (p. 105), which outnumber the human population on the island by 25:1 (p. 42). The caves are full of what seems to be earth, 'ten or more feet high', but which in reality is 'the dung of generation after generation of deer' that, he reckons, probably predate 'the very first Picts' to settle the island (p. 105). He comes across two skeletons of otter cubs, apparently abandoned, imagining 'that this must have been the exact spot where

---

[79] Neil Ansell, *Deer Island* (Toller Fratrum: Little Toller Books, 2013), p. 31. Subsequent references are given in parentheses. Ansell worked for the Simon Community, which is run on the principle that volunteers and homeless people live together.

[80] Ansell explains that 'the name Jura comes from the old Norse and means deer island' (p. 42). There are other explanations of the meaning and origins of the name 'Jura', however. For a summary see https://isleofjura.scot/jura-island-of-deer-or-the-cursed-isle/ (accessed 30 June 2021).

they had lived and died' (p. 106). His empathy for the sheltering deer and the dead otters parallels his sympathy for the hardened drinkers he encounters in a derelict house in the 'Sunset Strip' chapter—'winos, by their own description'—a gathering hosted by a Belfast Catholic named Casey, who wears 'a chunky crucifix', and who makes him 'feel welcome' in this 'induction into the world of the homeless', even though Casey is grieving for his partner, who died two weeks earlier (pp. 17–18).

Casey, who will shortly be dead himself, haunts the narrative. Ansell is entrusted with his stainless-steel Catholic crucifix, 'an ugly thing' (p. 89), that becomes the vehicle for his attempt to connect the two disparate environments of his book. As soon as he feels the squatters' community has dissolved, Ansell hitches back to Jura as 'the keeper of memory' (pp. 93–114), on a mission, he eventually reveals, to find a suitable place to bury Casey's cross. He finds 'a beautiful spot on a rocky promontory facing out to sea', somewhere he imagines he 'would want to come back to'. He dismantles the seaward side of a cairn, and buries the cross inside before replacing all the rocks. But he is uncertain about his motivation—the cross has 'no meaning for [him] as a religious symbol'—but he has promised to keep it safe (p. 112). In retrospect, he comes 'to realise that what I was really being asked to keep safe was a memory, not a physical object' (p. 113). The force of this moment is given by the more focused reflection-with-hindsight that Ansell offers in the opening section, 'The Drift', dated 2013. Here he names the Isle of Jura as 'a favourite place' (p. 9) because, as he puts it, 'it is a place that I cannot forget, because I have left a little piece of myself there, a fragment of who I am'. Without explaining the full significance of what he is doing at this point in the narrative, he indicates that he has chosen 'an ancient cairn', possibly 'built in memory of the long-ago dead' or 'simply...accumulated...by passing walkers, rock by rock', to secrete something (p. 10):

> I decided that this would be the place. Remote, isolated. I can still picture the spot perfectly, a place where the otters play. I began to dismantle the little cairn; to find its heart, and then to rebuild it with my talisman at its core. I could not have explained quite why I was doing what I was doing, not to myself let alone to others. But sometimes a symbolic gesture is all that we have to give. (pp. 10–11)

It is Maxwell, of course, who must be credited with alerting us to the play of otters, and this allusion (whether deliberate or subconscious) borrows from his creation of the genius loci in this region, and it puts Ansell's examination of his quest for 'the wildest of wild places' (p. 54)—which is presented in *Deer Island* as a puzzle to be solved—clearly in the tradition of Maxwell and his followers. How might we solve this puzzle? The obvious way of explaining Ansell's gesture is that he is staking a claim for the homeless, the impoverished, by secreting Casey's crucifix where he does. Like Orwell before him, he imports his consciousness of homelessness into his work on Jura, so that this renowned site of privileged artistic withdrawal and creativity is marked with this 'talisman' of deprivation. For Casey, who is otherwise totally impoverished and without kin, the crucifix is the only thing of value he has when he dies. There is a connection here with the way Maxwell sought to infuse abandoned and derelict cottages with 'freedom', that is, to reclaim them as sites of reflection on ecological modes of being, so that these places—the poignant reminders of lost rural communities now inhabitable chiefly by those with ambitions to realize intellectual capital—might inspire a rejection of the more chaotic flows of capital that rendered them obsolete. This forced correspondence of privilege and deprivation, which involves making an intellectual home in unhomely places, is a statement of aesthetic intent in which worldly advantage is acknowledged but is overtaken by the urgency of ecological purpose.[81] A parallel concrescence of purposes is signalled by Ansell placing the crucifix in the cairn on Jura.

Ansell's next book, *The Last Wilderness* (2018), is another powerful work of wilderness writing, the geographical focus this time being the Rough Bounds of Lochaber, or *Na Garbh Chriochan*, the area of West Inverness-shire between Loch Hourn and Loch Shiel, which is in between Maxwell's Sandaig to the north and Tomkies' Wildernesse, on the shores of Loch Shiel, to the south. Ansell chooses the Rough Bounds because of 'their remoteness and inaccessibility, their sense of being a place apart'. The northernmost peninsular of the region, Knoydart, 'is notorious for having no road access whatsoever and has been dubbed Britain's last great wilderness', a description he wants us to feel the force of, while simultaneously alerting us to Knoydart's 'long history of settlement by crofters, of emigration, of forced clearances', which the thought of wilderness tends to disregard or downplay.[82] The book is constructed as five separate journeys to the Rough Bounds within the space of the year, a fresh investigation—if we read his books in sequence—of the 'life as a solitary wanderer' to which he is increasingly drawn (p. 4). And it is another bold attempt to bring nature observation, and ideas of eviction and homelessness together into a mutually informing pattern.[83]

---

[81] I do not intend expressly to invoke the concept of the uncanny or 'unheimlich' (as developed by Heidegger from Freud) in speaking of the unhomeliness of abandoned dwellings. It is true that the sudden revelation of hidden relations through uncanny effects has some purchase on the idealization of the remote cottage, when it is exposed as an historical reminder of economic hardship and suffering. Yet, for most of the writers examined here, that history is self-evident, and the paradox of making a home from places that have *become* unhomely is an acknowledged component of their creative enterprises.

[82] Neil Ansell, *The Last Wilderness: A Journey into Silence* (London: Tinder Press, 2018), p. 3. Subsequent references are given in parentheses.

[83] While I was preparing this manuscript, Ansell's *The Circling Sky: On Nature and Belonging in an Ancient Forest* was published (London: Tinder Press, 2021). Again, Ansell juxtaposes a remote place (the New Forest) with questions of access, reflecting on the Romany people who were expelled from this place, their home for centuries.

Like Richard Mabey's *Nature Cure*, *The Last Wilderness* makes an explicit connection between the ill health of its author and the broader 'eco-sickness' of humanity's disconnection from the nonhuman. Ansell punctuates his narrative with two developing serious illnesses: a heart condition eventually diagnosed as a variant form of angina, 'provoked not by exertion but by rest' (p. 252); and his progressive loss of hearing. The encroaching deafness may be less life-threatening than the angina, but it is the true tragedy for a nature writer attuned to the sounds of the wild, and especially birdsong. Ansell continually reminds us of the sounds he cannot hear: the 'high-pitched whistle' of the otter (p. 16); the songs and calls of meadow pipits (pp. 107, 157); the songs of wood and willow warblers (p. 167), of wrens (p. 205); and the 'shrill, loud call' of sandpipers, which provokes a reflection on 'loss in a wider sense' and 'a sense of nostalgia even for things that are not yet gone', which behoves him to 'pay close attention' (pp. 146–7). Ostensibly, Ansell makes this a personal reflection, a sense that 'it is not the world that is leaving me, it is me that is leaving the world' (p. 147), as he approaches his 'own personal silent spring' (p. 167).[84] Yet in a book preoccupied with the 'needless extinction' consequent upon the human depredation of natural habitats, a process that 'impoverishes us all' (pp. 54–5), the personal loss of birdsong makes us think of the vulnerability of all species quite without his careful allusion to Rachel Carson.

Such self-consciousness, involving the deliberate fusion of apparent opposites, is Ansell's modus operandi. Thus, for example, he sets the falsity of cultivating the trust of animals through feeding them, or seeing them 'up close and personal' in a zoo, or gaining 'an intimate insight' into their private lives by watching television documentaries against the incomparable 'joy inspired by even a brief encounter with a scarce and beautiful wild animal in its natural element', which forges 'a momentary connection with the wild', and through which he discovers 'a place in the world for [his] own wild heart' (p. 29). This easy opposition between 'the value' assigned to an encounter by virtue of 'the raw experience of the moment, rather than the representation of it' produces 'a dilemma' for 'observational nature writing', which can only offer 'second-hand experience'. The acknowledgement of this limitation, however, is turned into a virtue, from an ecological perspective, because the distancing process of mediating the 'wild' encounter in prose leads him to question the validity of the personal 'connection' that cannot anyway be rendered: 'I can talk about my response to this encounter, the thoughts and memories it evokes, while never forgetting that the natural world has not been placed here for my benefit; it is not here to teach us life lessons, but exist always and only for itself' (p. 30). In this way, the dilemma of dilution through mediation

---

[84] For Ansell birdsong becomes something he has to summon from within: 'if I closed my eyes and concentrated, I could just about make out the echo of them preserved in memory; the piercing call of a sandpiper on a mountain river, the endlessly repeated descending trill of a willow warbler in a spring wood; the winter wren suddenly breaking the silence of a frosty morning' (pp. 305–6).

is not overcome but, rather, embraced as a necessary (self-correcting) aspect of the writer's method. While this is not new in itself, the degree of self-reflexivity produced by the consciousness of ecological crisis—and facilitated by the experience of remoteness—is distinctly contemporary.

Another contemporary marker in the literature of remoteness, and a notable development of the Highland nature writing of Maxwell and Tomkies, is Ansell's continued insistence on the social history of place. Concerning the Rhu of Arisaig, one of the peninsulas that make up this landscape, Ansell describes its southern shores as 'completely depopulated' rather than 'uninhabited', cautioning us against easy assumptions when confronted with an apparently wild landscape. In recent history—'two hundred years ago'—a community of 'perhaps fifty crofts' existed on the Rhu of Arisaig, which was displaced by sheep farming. After the Clearances, 'the whole of this peninsula became a single sheep farm'. The evidence of a once 'thriving community' is in the place names: 'almost every little hill and tiny lochan has a name, showing it was once of significance to someone' (pp. 171–2). And the human history is extensive: a 'Neolithic relic' on 'the south side of the peninsula' shows 'there were people here five thousand years ago' (p. 172). More than once, Ansell fights against the impression of remoteness in the Rough Bounds. Further north, on the Knoydart peninsula, there may once have been 'over a thousand crofters' before 'one of the most notorious instances of the Highland clearances'. The small population that 'has slowly begun to build up again' gives the remoteness of this place a special significance: 'everybody here has consciously chosen to isolate themselves from the world, to live in a small community cut off from the mainland. Everybody is an incomer, even the Scots who live here' (p. 214). An isolated community, established through choice and in the shadow of historical oppression, reclaims the social story of remoteness, and demonstrates the portability of Ansell's social vision, inspired by the Camden Town homeless.

The recognition of the social history of place requires this understanding of remoteness: 'for those of us who are drawn to the wild, it may be hard to acknowledge that what looks like wilderness may really be a simulacrum, just a place of temporary neglect. Almost everywhere is to some extent the product of land management' (pp. 43–4). At the same time, however, Ansell pursues a more pristine conception of remoteness, so that competing understandings are yoked together. When he reaches the northern slopes of Loch Hourn—on the northernmost segment of his expeditions into the Rough Bounds—he finally reaches something approaching genuine wilderness, a place where 'the woods remained... while they had been stripped from almost everywhere else, for precisely the reason that the location was too remote for human exploitation' (p. 228). It is in this region, where 'pine trees hung right over the water', that he believes he has found 'tiny surviving fragments of the great wood' that 'reach all the way to the sea' (p. 234). The persistence of the search for remoteness in *The Last Wilderness* enables Ansell to recalibrate his understanding of this quest, and its significance for him, by reconsidering the phases of his life recorded in his earlier books. From his five-year sojourn in Wales 'what stands out most', he writes, 'is my long solitary walks in the hills, the long weeks when every night was spent sitting alone in front of a log fire, in silence, seeing no one' (p. 56). In the same breath, however, he reminds himself of the 'many years living and working among rough sleepers, and among drug users and street drinkers, the dispossessed'. Turning to remote nature is not a turning away from empathy, but rather 'a matter of self-sufficiency' (pp. 56–7). The remote nature writer's vocation depends upon self-deprivation, upon the pursuit of elemental living that has much in common with the homeless state.

Ansell is also aware of a further insoluble paradox in his pursuit of remote wild places. On the one hand he feels 'it is fundamental human nature to roam in a landscape' such as those he finds in the Rough Bounds (p. 102). Eyeing up the 'chain of islands near the head of Loch Morar', he ponders kayaking over to one to explore it, camp overnight, 'and have it all to myself, my own little piece of wilderness' (pp. 99, 102). But he decides that the islands should be sacrosanct in a reflection that has implications for the whole project: 'if they are truly wild, perhaps the best thing I can do is to admire them from afar, and leave them in perfect peace'. It is a chastening resistance of 'that exploratory desire to possess the wild for ourselves' that has resulted in its disappearance (pp. 102–3). Nature writing requires an invasive orientation to the wild, of course, so the contradiction is absorbed, again, in Ansell's circular vision; and he projects this vision onto the reader through the metaphorical connotations of his illnesses. In this way, his September journey to Knoydart is given particular significance, as 'far more of a physical challenge than it would normally have been'; but his expedition, to places where he would be 'unreachable', is made more intense by his vulnerability, as solitude makes him feel independent: 'My body might be failing me but it somehow made me stronger rather than weaker, more sure of myself than ever' (p. 210). And yet, we know that the journey, potentially destructive of the individual traveller, is also emblematic of the destruction of the wild consequent upon the desire to explore.

Ansell resolves the contradiction by placing emphasis on his internal journey; and the pursuit of self-discovery also has traction as a general predicament, so that his concluding reflection might strike a personal chord with his readers: 'I had been looking for the last wilderness, and had found it, even if it had largely been a wilderness of my own mind' (pp. 303–4). To some extent this contradicts the assertion Ansell is apt to make about his pursuit of remoteness, countering the suspicion that 'the lure of the cabin in the woods' is 'a negative desire; the desire to escape from social commitments and pressures': 'when I tell people about my years of solitude in Wales, they will often respond by asking what it was that I was running away from. But it never felt like that, not to me. I was never running away;

always running towards' (p. 216). And yet the idea of running towards the wild is also, in Ansell's work, a way of embracing precarity, vulnerability, and through that process establishing solidarity with the dispossessed, and the homeless. In this presentation, personal rewilding is simultaneously a process of integration with the nonhuman and a reminder of human frailty—and dependence upon the nonhuman—that necessarily embraces human suffering because that, ultimately, is produced by the iniquity of unequal access to the nonhuman. In this way, the idea of synthesis or coalescence that I have been working with in this chapter is partly transcended: what is ostensibly a fusion of opposites—the pursuit of personal repair in a remote wild place, and the cultivation of an ethical social vision—is revealed to be a way of presenting indivisible aspects of a single predicament. The writer's personal illness merges with the eco-sickness around him; and the vulnerability thereby revealed is a way of asserting his bond with the human dispossessed, whether evicted from the Rough Bounds in the past, or excluded from such remote places, and their ambivalent beneficence in the present.

2
Exclusivity

The previous chapter demonstrated how the convention in nature writing of the contemplative withdrawal to remote wild places has been subject to significant revision in contemporary nature prose, and that this process of revision has sometimes involved the retrieval or amplification of a crucial element of *self-impoverishment* that may be implicit in the convention: the decision to deprive oneself of worldly goods and a conventional home opens up the question of social inequality, and reveals an element of sensitivity about class in the writing persona—sometimes overtly, as in the ways in which homelessness becomes the shadow of the solitary nature writer in Neil Ansell's work. Under the pressure of contemporary ecological anxieties, this may be a significantly fractured or ambivalent deployment of Romantic and transcendentalist legacies, most notably, a development of the figure of the vagrant in the tradition of the contemplative Romantic wanderer. However, the extent to which inequality is registered in the literature of remoteness is sometimes a matter of stage-managed *choice* for the writer, who usually still enjoys the freedom to access remote places and the confidence to work within traditions of writing that are readily available to him or her. Despite these caveats, however, it is a significant trend which suggests that nature writing has the capacity to treat other areas of exclusion, the most important of which is exclusivity drawn along ethnic lines. How does contemporary nature prose dismantle the perception of an ethnically exclusive club? This chapter illustrates how writers of colour have accessed and revised literary traditions that historically have excluded them;[1] and also, in the process, how they rework indigenous traditions that require us to question the construction of 'the nonhuman environment' in ways that both complement and challenge the ambivalent modes accounted for in the last chapter.[2] In the texts considered here, the tensions and contradictions of hybrid cultural interactions also suggest

---

[1] In using the term 'people or person(s) of colour' in this chapter I am sensitive to the ease with which labels denoting race or ethnicity can be variously appropriated, and become inappropriate: I grew up in an era when the term 'coloured' evoked the categorizations of apartheid. But I follow the self-defining gestures of writers themselves, such as Anita Sethi's decision to define herself as a 'woman of colour' even while pondering the way in which terms like 'coloured' and 'BAME' can become offensive or reductive. See Anita Sethi, *I Belong Here: A Journey Along the Backbone of England* (London: Bloomsbury, 2021), p. 75.

[2] The term 'nonhuman' is used throughout this survey since it registers a sense of otherness that structures much nature prose, as the Introduction makes clear. However, specific constructions of the nonhuman are sometimes revealed as flimsy or inadequate in contemporary writing, and especially in the examples considered in this chapter.

connections, most especially in the ecological significance of mourning practices and responses to death.

Nature Writing and Privilege

In *The Sharpest Sight* (1992), a novel by Louis Owens (1948–2002), a writer of Choctaw-Cherokee-Irish descent (and who will emerge as a key figure of cultural hybridity in the following pages), the character Mundo Morales offers a vision of remote living quite different from the situations discussed in the previous chapter:

> You know, sometimes I have this fantasy about being way the hell and gone out in some wilderness, Alaska maybe. I'm in a little plane flying over this huge wilderness, and the plane crashes. I'm the only survivor, and I have to live out there all by myself for months and months. It's just me, no family, no job, no name, no nothing. Just me and what I can do to survive.[3]

The fantasy of complete social withdrawal is explicitly Crusoesque, reminiscent of his retrieval of as many tools as possible from the wrecked ship: in his fantasy, Morales strips everything of use from the plane, making snowshoes from seat covers, snares from electrical wire, and an axe and a stove from broken metal. And he retains civilized values, even in complete isolation—'I'm the only one that knows I exist, the only thing that knows who I am'—making his shelter 'two-day's hike away from the corpses in the plane' to ensure he doesn't 'get desperate and turn cannibal' (p. 184). A European fantasy—which is partly his heritage—has (at this moment) colonized the consciousness of Morales, and, in exposing this, Owens is parodying a dynamic he sees as characteristic of Western literature, in a way that is analogous to Ian Watt's link between the origins of the novel in the Crusoe story and the emergence of modern economic individualism.[4] He is also alerting us to the contradiction inherent in this individualism, the pursuit of which depends upon the trappings of civilization in the form of tools that facilitate the fantasy of withdrawal, and where uncultivated or wilderness spaces are perceived to be ripe for appropriation, if only as the stage for a drama of self-realization: in this orientation to wilderness, privilege is an unspoken assumption. Nature writing by white authors, as we shall see, is sometimes perceived to perpetuate a

---

[3] Louis Owens, *The Sharpest Sight* (Norman: University of Oklahoma Press, 1992), p. 184. Subsequent references are given in parentheses. The character Mundo Morales is (in Owens's words) 'a young mestizo...who discovers in his own blood an inextricable web of inherited identities'. See Louis Owens, *Mixedblood Messages: Literature, Film, Family, Place* (Norman: University of Oklahoma Press, 1998), p. 182. Such identity quests are at the heart of Owens's writing, and are usually undertaken by 'mixedblood' characters, in search of their Native American origins.

[4] See Ian Watt, *The Rise of the Novel: Studies in Defoe, Richardson and Fielding* (London: Chatto & Windus, 1957).

fantasy in which the facilitating presence of a society riven by inequality and oppression is obscured. By contrast, Owens's explorations of how indigenous culture emphasizes community is a challenge to white constructions of nature as separate—as 'nonhuman'—and so also a challenge to European literary approaches to nature, which he subverts as he writes. But his work also exhibits an ambivalence about indigenous wisdom which has affinities with the paradox illustrated in the reading of Linda Hogan's *Power* in the Introduction: for Owens, as for Hogan, the challenge is to resuscitate the traditional ecological knowledge that has been diminished.

The discussions that follow show various ways in which writers of colour have faced this kind of paradox, which involves not just the resuscitation of indigenous wisdom but also the need to revitalize traditions of writing that apparently exclude them. These cultural paradoxes stem, of course, from more fundamental experiences of exclusion. Writing of the African American experience, Kimberley Ruffin identifies what she calls the 'ecological burden-and-beauty paradox'. The burden is that which is placed 'on those who are racialized negatively' so that they 'suffer economically and environmentally because of their degraded status'. At the same time, however, there is 'the experience of ecological beauty' resulting from 'attitudes toward nature' that may 'undercut the experience of racism and its related evils'.[5] The aesthetic forms that emerge from the ecological burden-and-beauty paradox make no attempt to cultivate a pristine nature; rather, in exposing and negotiating the problems of exclusion, the focus is on reasserting the human presences in nature that have been effaced historically, or which are currently edged out of the frame. In wrestling with this paradox, human engagement and struggle are primary, and the conception of 'nonhuman' nature is sometimes seen to be complicitous with ethnic exclusion.

Efforts to increase ethnic diversity have been made in many areas of cultural and social life over the past decade, and one of the most notable of such efforts in Britain has resulted in a loosening of the white monopoly on presenting nature programmes, and in nature reporting.[6] This is a significant shift, given the great social importance of diverse role models. At the same time, it must be recognized that the project of inclusivity cannot be adequately prosecuted by such simple means, because the problems of exclusivity may be *written into* the forms and conventions of nature programmes or nature writing, determining their orientation. Where nature writing is concerned, its aesthetic limitations reveal significant

---

[5] Kimberley N. Ruffin, *Black on Earth: African American Ecoliterary Traditions* (Athens: University of Georgia Press, 2010), pp. 2–3.

[6] For example, since 2017 Kenyan-born Gillian Burke has been a regular presenter on the BBC programmes *Springwatch* and *Autumnwatch*; David Lindo, who styles himself 'The Urban Birder', and who has also appeared on *Springwatch*, has successfully broken into a white male preserve. He published *The Urban Birder* in 2011 (repr. London: Bloomsbury, 2018). His ornithological journalism was collected in *Tales From Concrete Jungles: Urban Birding Around the World* (London: Bloomsbury, 2015).

and continuing problems in relation to ethnicity. In the introduction to a recent commissioned anthology of nature writing, Tim Dee seeks to address inequality, pinpointing the culpability of 'masking economic and social collapse with digitised verdancy': yet this acute recognition of the social problems masked in any filmic (or word-processed) paean to nature does not register the kinds of inequality that are bound up with ethnic exclusivity. Dee signs off this introduction by confessing that he 'failed to find anything other than white contributors'. He is not to blame for this state of affairs; but the revealing (and disarmingly honest) admission, in a state-of-the-art anthology, obliges us to question the institution of nature writing in Britain, if we see it as a source of hope and inspiration for a heterogeneous populace.[7]

The problem of place and privilege in the evaluation of nature writing has been addressed more extensively in the US. In the introduction to a very different anthology to Tim Dee's, Alison Deming and Lauret Savoy observe that while 'African-American, Latino, Asian-American, Native, and mixedblood voices have profoundly enriched our national literary identity over the past fifty years... nature writing remains, for the most part, the precinct of the Euro-American privileged class'. The conviction of these editors is that 'the "lack" of nature writing by people of color reflects the limited perspective of both the defining audience and the publishing community more than the lack of interest in the natural world by writers of color'.[8] Unenlightened perceptions result in generic conventions that are too restrictive, obstructing other ways of approaching the nonhuman. Savoy poses the searching questions that identify the key issues here:

> What falls within the frame of nature writing in America, and what is considered outside of it? Whose definitions or distinctions are these? As someone who thus far has looked at the genre from the outside, I've wondered if any perceived 'lack' of other voices beyond a traditional Anglo-American context was in part a reflection of a societal structure of inclusion and exclusion based on color, class, and culture.[9]

Savoy seeks to uncover the extent to which conventional nature writing, as a form of privileged contemplative withdrawal, might be founded on forms of ethnic oppression, especially where the historical brutalization of indigenous inhabitants facilitated the appropriation of space for aesthetic appreciation: we must recognize

---

[7] Tim Dee, 'Introduction', *Ground Work: Writings on Places and People*, ed. T. Dee (London: Jonathan Cape, 2018), pp. 1–14 (pp. 3, 14).

[8] Alison H. Deming and Lauret E. Savoy, 'Introduction as a Conversation', in *The Colors of Nature: Culture, Identity, and the Natural World*, ed. Deming and Savoy (Minneapolis: Milkweed Editions, 2002), pp. 3–15 (p. 6).

[9] Deming and Savoy, 'Introduction as a Conversation', p. 7. After the first section of this introduction, the two editors' contributions appear as separate interspersed voices, so it is possible to individuate the attributions.

the degree to which modern nature writing unwittingly continues an aesthetic practice which is built on the history of colonial exploitation.

The compromised historical background of these literary modes, which are commonly thought of as relatively 'free' from social and political conflict, requires that they undergo a radical and sometimes surprising reconceptualization; and not just in critical analysis, since such a reconceptualization might be part of a writer's project, and can erupt in unexpected places. For example, we might expect a certain political detachment in the discourse of garden writing; yet, as Jamaica Kincaid implies in a book of essays about plants and gardens, such 'innocence' may be unavailable if we refuse to overlook the colonial roots of gardening. She associates the foundation of natural history as a discipline—the efforts of Carl Linnaeus to bring an 'objective standard' to the task of naming and classifying 'the vegetable kingdom'—with the emergence of colonialism, and the historical European assertion of power. She asks, 'who has an interest in an objective standard?' And also, 'what should history mean to someone who looks like me?' She gives two alternatives, one signalling a perpetual trauma, the other seeking its explanation in the 'discovery' of America, and the beginning of European colonization: 'should it be an open wound, each breath I take in and expel healing and opening the wound again, over and over, or is it a long moment that begins anew each day since 1492?' With specific reference to Linnaeus, and the inception of natural history, the challenge is to understand that natural history nomenclature 'has been a good thing', the foundation of ecologically responsible knowledge, without losing sight of the vested interests and the centuries of oppression since Europeans arrived in America.[10] This is the essence of the challenging paradox that, as Kincaid shows, must be embraced by nature writers who are the victims of environmental injustice, whether in the contemporary moment or through familial history. But this necessity—to extract the ecological good from centuries of thought rooted in imperialism—suggests an important addition to the range of ambivalent modes and paradoxical forms that are encountered throughout this survey. Indeed, that larger narrative, about a reconceptualized and expanding nature *prose* as an equivocal phenomenon, capable of revealing its own paradoxes and insecurities, already descries a cultural territory that has progressed beyond the parameters of a privileged, white-dominated tradition of nature writing. Kincaid's *My Garden (Book)* is less radical: it looks like a conventional artefact of nature writing, with its coffee-table credentials—cream paper with a leaf-border design, gentle illustrations of plants and gardens—so that its subversiveness is a Trojan Horse strategy, softened by its generic packaging. It may participate in the

---

[10] Jamaica Kincaid, *My Garden (Book)* (New York: Farrar, Straus & Giroux, 1999), p. 166. In Chapter 4, I trace the more positive inspiration drawn from natural history in nature writing, in its implications not just for conservation but also for considering how impulses in natural history, such as collecting, can signal a redeeming human imperative.

challenge articulated by Savoy, to look 'beyond a traditional Anglo-American context', and to identify writers with approaches to nature that may confound generic conventions; but this objective is often pursued more emphatically.

A recalibration of the literary-critical taxonomy of nature writing is required: if the leisured exploration and appreciation of rural and wilderness spaces is associated with white privilege, such spaces have been unavailable, historically, to people of colour. In the spirit of this re-evaluation, which is given impetus by reflecting on fictional as well as nonfictional modes, Lawrence Buell detects 'a strain of African American pastoralism', from Jean Toomer's *Cane* to Toni Morrison's *Song of Solomon*, but acknowledges the persuasive argument of Melvin Dixon that dissociates 'African-American literary culture' from the 'Anglo-American romanticization of nature wilderness', and points out that in 'African American history, the countryside is what you escape from, an area of chance violence and enslavement'.[11] Alison Deming confirms the contemporaneity of this sense of ethnic exclusion, where past injustices condition perceptions of the rural environment: 'I recalled an African-American friend cajoling me to see that in his familial past the woods were not a place one might go for solace and recreation but a place where one might be dragged, beaten, or lynched.'[12]

Paul Outka argues that 'the wilderness' in America 'is constructed as a white-only space', a principle of exclusivity that has its roots in imperialism and slavery. Outka is concerned with that legacy 'in which whites viewed black people as part of the natural world, and then proceeded to treat them with the same mixture of contempt, false reverence, and real exploitation that also marks American environmental history'.[13] With this historical burden, African Americans cannot identify with the natural world as easily as white nature writers have. The Environmental Justice movement has brought about a significant adjustment in ecocritical practice which is relevant here, most notably by 'bring[ing] attention to ways in which environmental degradation and hazards unequally affect poor people and people of color'.[14] The impact of pollution and spatial dispossession upon African-American and Native American sensibilities is central to several of the texts considered in this chapter, all of which put questions of social justice at the heart of an ethnically inclusive poetics of the 'nonhuman', which is thereby reconceptualized; and it is the sense of displacement, whether physical, psychological, or both, that is the primary point of emphasis.

---

[11] Buell, *The Environmental Imagination*, p. 17. See Melvin Dixon, *Ride Out the Wilderness: Geography and Identity in Afro-American Literature* (Urbana: University of Illinois Press, 1987).

[12] Deming and Savoy, 'Introduction as a Conversation', p. 12.

[13] Paul Outka, *Race and Nature from Transcendentalism to the Harlem Renaissance* (New York: Palgrave Macmillan, 2008), p. 3.

[14] T. V. Reed, 'Toward an Environmental Justice Ecocriticism', in the *Environmental Justice Reader: Politics Poetics and Pedagogy*, ed. Joni Adamson, Mei Mei Evans, and Rachel Stein (Tucson: University of Arizona Press, 2002), pp. 145–62 (p. 149).

Two notable attempts in Britain to reclaim a particular mode of nature writing are worth considering here: *Wanderland* (2020) by Jini Reddy (a Londoner), and *I Belong Here* (2021) by Anita Sethi (a Mancunian). Both books fall into the category of nature walking literature, and each writer asserts her claim to this tradition, and her right to wander in rural England in the face of racism. In *Wanderland*, Reddy ponders the 'generalisation' that 'people whose skin colour is not white... never connect with nature', and she draws attention to the racial bias of nature publishing, lamenting the opportunities not afforded to writers of colour, those 'whose voices are never heard'.[15] A paradoxical component emerges in her ambivalent attitude to nature taxonomy: in the spirit of Kincaid's concern about Linnaeus and the colonial origin of natural history, Reddy feels it is not in her DNA to become a taxonomist (pp. 119–20). Nevertheless, she is determined to learn the names of trees (p. 119); and later she feels her 'ignorance keenly' when she is unable to name plants in Cornwall, and wants to 'make amends', now viewing naming as a 'simple act of courtesy' (p. 138). A similar ambivalence emerges when she is walking in Snowdonia, in her response to the notional appeal of feeling rooted in 'the Welsh mythic landscape': 'which specific culture am I meant to identify with?' she asks, implying that the question is unanswerable for those 'from a multicultural background' (p. 248). Non-identification here is simultaneously a sign of exclusion *and* a rebuke to those who mythologize their sense of belonging.

Sethi's *I Belong Here* responds more explicitly to racism, and her Pennine journey becomes a defiant response to a race-hate crime, as she asserts her right to belong, invoking the Kinder Scout Mass Trespass of 1932, in her reworking of protest walking.[16] She is at pains to reorientate a tradition, and articulates her affinity with other walking writers.[17] One of Sethi's preferred compositional methods is to use literal/metaphorical wordplay to link external landscapes with internal landscapes: 'scars' in rock formations, for example, inspire her to reflect on the healing of psychological scars through immersion in nature, so that wounds/body markings become self-defining and a way of linking landscape and body (pp. 203–7). When Sethi reflects on 'faults' in the limestone pavement at Malham Cove, there is an echo of (or riposte to) Robert Macfarlane's account of a 'wild place' in a fissure or 'gryke' in the limestone pavement on the Burren in Ireland;[18] here, the focus is as much on the matter of exclusion as it is on marvelling at the wild. Sethi makes us rethink 'fault-lines' by association with

---

[15] Jini Reddy, *Wanderland: A Search for Magic in the Landscape* (London: Bloomsbury, 2020), p. 109. Subsequent references are given in parentheses.

[16] Anita Sethi, *I Belong Here: A Journey Along the Backbone of England* (London: Bloomsbury, 2021), p. 14. Subsequent references are given in parentheses.

[17] For example, she expresses the 'strong companionship' she feels for Raynor Winn, Robert Macfarlane, Edward Thomas, and George Borrow (p. 70).

[18] Macfarlane, *The Wild Places*, p. 168. See Chapter 1.

her experience of standing up to race hatred, which also means showing how you have been hurt: 'being brave and strong also paradoxically means allowing yourself to reveal your vulnerabilities' (|p. 148). Sethi draws an analogy between the grykes of Malham Cove, deepened by time, 'seemingly barren and yet teeming with life' (p. 150), and the 'fault-lines' in society and the complex sense of victimhood that must be resolved before personal regeneration is possible.

Wanderland and *I Belong Here* are important and innovative works, each one staking a claim for inclusivity; but the fault line that is also revealed is one of current exclusion, in those moments where the tropes and conventions of nature writing are felt to be exclusive, as when Reddy feels ambivalence about nature taxonomy; or when both authors must fight the sense of hostility, or the questioning about their simple *presence* in the landscape (*Wanderland*, p. 148; *I Belong Here*, p. 275). The predicament these authors lay bare for us is the ecological urgency of reclaiming a literary mode, the desire to render it inclusive, while paradoxically having to express the limits of its formal responsiveness. These are necessary but preliminary gestures. In the section that follows I consider one writer who has taken forward the project of formal reclamation in deeply impressive ways: Lauret Savoy.

Reclaiming the Tropes of Nature Writing

The perception of physical exclusion from the landscape is the key obstacle to Sethi's and Reddy's formal inventiveness. In the US context, Lauret Savoy has confronted this problem in *Trace* when she interrogates the divide between the American wilderness constructed in white traditions of nature writing and the impoverished places in which people of colour have been obliged to dwell. She reconsiders sites and texts that are central to the white-dominated traditions of wilderness, in what is an understated invitation for us to reshape American nature writing. Such a process of reconfiguration, she shows, must begin with human time, personal history. The book opens with a childhood memory: her father drives the family to Point Sublime in the Grand Canyon National Park, and, as Savoy puts it, 'the memory of what we found shapes me still'.[19] There is the expected awe in the face of natural grandeur: 'the suddenness stunned. No single camera frame could contain the expanse or play of light' (p. 10); and this inspires her to stake a claim against the racist construction of the appreciation of the nonhuman in European thought—'in Kant's view, neither I nor my dark ancestors could ever reach the sublime, so debased were our origins' (p. 10)—and this is the only moment of 'scenic' appreciation in the book. I will return to the racism

---

[19] Lauret Savoy, *Trace: Memory, History, Race, and the American Landscape* (Berkeley: Counterpoint, 2015), p. 5. Subsequent references are given in parentheses.

inherent in Kant's conception of the sublime. Here I want to focus on how quickly Savoy turns away from the conventions of nature writing—away from place per se and towards the social history of places. It's a deliberate refusal at this site, the Grand Canyon, inextricably linked with the attempts of Europeans to convey in words the majesty of nature.[20] Savoy immediately makes us see the significance of the episode in relation to her family's history, thus establishing the tone of the book. The family is relocating from the West Coast to the East, away from the environment Savoy has come to identify as 'home', and back to Washington DC: 'back', that is, to the place her father associates with 'origins and dignity'. It is in this episode that 'history began' for Savoy (p. 12), an understanding that obliges her to investigate questions of place and belonging by binding together personal/familial time and nonhuman/geological time, and through a cultural fusion in which she rechannels the creative challenge embodied in her father's work. This 'beginning of history' is also the beginning of another narrative mode, a form of nature writing in which awestruck admiration for natural beauty is studiously avoided: the fact that this doesn't *look* like nature writing is precisely the point.

In part, this is an attempt to go beyond another dichotomy, also observed by Outka in arguing that 'sublimity and trauma represent two racially disjunct resolutions of a similar moment', a disjunction that means 'the sublime white subject possesses the scene; the traumatised black subject is possessed by it'. In this view, the sublime is a troubling vehicle of racial difference, especially if it is found in visions of untamed wilderness, unwittingly racial constructions with 'intellectual and aesthetic origins in Romantic sublimity and American transcendentalism'.[21] This is not to say that the sublime cannot embrace an inclusive ecological mode of writing; but first we need a clear sense of its limits, signalled most obviously in the inherent racism of Kant's conception, which attracts Lauret Savoy's ire, as noted above. In Kant's exposition, Outka shows, 'the ability to produce the sublime is a triumphant mark of the subject's intrinsic freedom'. However, this freedom, this ability—as Kant's earlier writing indicates—is not universal, which makes 'the failure to produce the sublime...a mark of the subject's bondage and degradation'. In Kant's *Observations on the Feeling of the Beautiful and Sublime* (1764), writes Outka, 'this failure becomes a sign of black racial inferiority'. This locates an element of implicit racial mastery in the Kantian sublime, which is also a form of textual mastery as the disorientation of the sublime encounter is contained within—and tamed by—the structures of artistic convention, and so divested of its terrors.[22]

---

[20] Louis Owens considers García López de Cárdenas to have been the first in a long line of Europeans to be confronted by 'the problems of proportion and description presented by the Grand Canyon' in 1540. See Louis Owens, *I Hear the Train: Reflections, Inventions, Refractions* (Norman: University of Oklahoma Press, 2001), p. 69.

[21] Outka, *Race and Nature*, pp. 2, 26.   [22] Ibid., pp. 19, 20, 17.

Setting the matter of racist underpinning aside for a moment, the experience that produces the sublime is made subordinate to the aesthetic forms that, through this process of recontainment, will inevitably fail in their attempts to register it fully. The aesthetic 'capture' of the sublime in isolation is thus a refusal of its inherent paradox, which stems from the fact that it is simultaneously experiential *and* textual. But this doubleness can be cultivated, made into an important resource for the mediation of nature: the sublime is predicated on the sense of the ineffable otherness of nature eluding its textual frame, but in such a way that the textual frame concentrates our impression of this alterity. This is another way of explaining many of the strangely dissonant effects I identify throughout this survey: it takes a powerful literary effect, a concentrated form of ecomimesis, to make us register and appreciate the piquant *demonstration of inefficacy* in the text's efforts to convey nature in textual form.

Such effects are more complicated if we include a perception of the racist underpinning of the sublime, which I have briefly set aside. A modified form of ecomimesis, with an ethnic inflection, is at stake in Savoy's attempt to undermine the racist implications of the Kantian sublime by *refusing* a position of awestruck admiration for pure natural beauty. Instead, as we have seen, she insists on the interplay of landscape and human history. This is a familiar procedure in the 'new' nature writing more generally, but here it has a specific sociopolitical purchase. The effect is to overlay the traumatic experience of African American oppression on natural space, so that the unsettling effect of the originating experience of sublimity—obscured in its aesthetic form—is retrieved, now with an explanation in racist structures. And this is a very different kind of awe than we are used to seeing glimpsed and then aestheticized in the conventional sublime. It is not just that we are made to sense a history of oppression in the landscape; beyond that, the parallel kinds of troubling and irresolvable perception—the trauma of racism, the irreducible alterity of the nonhuman—are also presented as separate (though interrelated) kinds of ethical challenge. This is also a vision rooted in personal experience, and, to give a full sense of this, I need to devote some space to the key strands of Savoy's remarkable book.

Reflecting on the geology of the Devil's Punchbowl in the San Gabriel Mountains, Savoy considers how its 'texture and makeup' reveals much about its origins, and 'about climate through time', and then asks: 'what of Us? What of who we are is owed to memories of blood or culture, custom or circumstance? To hardness? What makes an individual in a sequence of generations?' (p. 18). There are several such moments in *Trace*, analogies between geological and family time. But the cumulative effect of this analogical process is to break down its obvious metaphoricity: as the slow and partial recovery of Savoy's personal history becomes increasingly dependent on the rediscovery of place, her sense of self is intertwined with her reading of the landscape. Savoy makes her complicated ancestry an essential foundation for her quest:

I descend from Africans who came in chains and Africans who may never have known bondage. From European colonists who tried to make a new start in a world new to them. As well as from Native peoples who were displaced by those colonists from homelands that had defined their essential being. (p. 20)

In one chapter, pursuing the roots of her mother's family, Savoy visits Boley, in rural Oklahoma, established in 1903 as an 'African American Town' (p. 25). She imagines 'some of my mother's forebears relocating from Alabama's water-thick air, plantation fields, and dark woods', speculating on 'their response to expanses of grass and sky, to the opening of distance to the eye, to a land on which they hoped to live on their own terms'. Savoy has to invent and project to align her own sense of inhabitation with that of her forbears—'I imagined the felt attachment to place that one generation could make' (p. 27)—and, as in much of the book, she is left in uncertainty about her ancestors: 'did any arrive in bondage decades earlier?...I imagined but did not know' (p. 27); yet the projection of a shared responsiveness to place asserts kinship. Crucial to the meaning of such kinship is the way Savoy reclaims landscape appreciation. From her childhood, the idea of the American landscape becomes a form of surety against the horrors of racism: 'one idea stood firm: The American land preceded hate. My child-sense of its antiquity became as much a refuge as any place, whether the Devil's Punchbowl or a canyon called Grand' (p. 29). This is a carefully cultivated paradox: places of natural beauty, the revered sites of conventional nature writing, are appreciated in a way that *imitates* the apolitical withdrawal often associated with the genre; yet that very withdrawal is here made political, a refusal to engage with the hatred and resentment consequent upon victimhood.

Aloof aestheticism is thus *re-presented* as an ethical social foundation: and this ethical remaking is given an explicitly self-conscious literary hue, which leads to the central intellectual paradox of Savoy's book, where she condemns the text that is also an important inspiration for her new environmental ethics. Indeed, she finds herself having to critique and cherish a tradition simultaneously. The focus of this contradiction is her reckoning with Aldo Leopold's *A Sand County Almanac* (1949), that key work in the making of modern American environmentalism. This was an important book in her personal development: 'what appealed to my fourteen-year-old sensibilities were the intimate images of land and seasons in place...what also appealed was the seeming openness of this man's struggle to frame a personal truth' (pp. 32–3). Rearticulating that teenage intuition, she detects in 'his call for an extension of ethics to land relations' a 'sense of responsibility and reciprocity not yet embraced by this country but embedded in many Indigenous peoples' traditions of experience—that land is fully inhabited, intimate with immediate presence' (p. 33). The early encounter with Leopold's land ethic stimulates Savoy's burgeoning social awareness: the conventional aesthetic—contained in the 'images of land and seasons in place'—has to be developed to address racism. It is this process of formal reconfiguration that *Trace* undertakes, its dissatisfaction with the landscape aesthetic bound up with Savoy's identification of the blind spots in Leopold's vision, notably that while he refers to slavery in ancient Greece, he fails to acknowledge slavery in America's past (p. 33). She began to fear, she recalls, that 'his "we" and "us" excluded me and other Americans with ancestral roots in Africa, Asia, or Native America' (pp. 33–4).

This dialogue with Leopold takes on a special and personal dimension when she discovers, after her father Willard Savoy's death, that he had published a novel, *Alien Land*, in the same year as Leopold's landmark work (1949). Willard Savoy was burdened with that acutely problematic identity in any racist culture, as (in Lauret's description) 'a man who in appearance would be accepted without question by those calling themselves "white." Pale of complexion with gray-blue eyes, he'd not be seen or treated as other until he admitted "Negro" blood' (p. 35). The novel, in Lauret's summary, concerns 'an embittered "mulatto" boy-becomes-man who thinks he might escape prejudice, and his own demons, by redefining himself as white' (p. 35). The topic strikes a deep chord in her: she reflects that Kern Roberts, the protagonist, 'the boy-becomes-man, and I shared too many experiences of hurt, too many questions' (p. 35). There is a powerful moment in *Trace* where Lauret recalls applying for a job, in her teens, as a summer assistant to 'a collector and trader of Civil War memorabilia'. After impressing in a phone interview, she travels to meet her prospective employer in person: 'I remember the heavy door opening, my practised "Hello, I'm Lauret Savoy," and his single word as the door closed. *Sorry.*' Her immediate reaction, returning home to watch 'an ancient rerun of *The Mickey Mouse Club*', follows the classic pattern of burying traumatic experience. But this turns out to be a day of still greater trauma, the day of her father's death; and in recounting the tragic sequence, her early encounter with the affront of racism is a prelude to the account of his lifelong struggle with it (p. 34).

In his foreword to the 2006 reissue of *Alien Land*, Robert Stepto recalls how the novel's publication was 'met with immediate attention and considerable fanfare' in 1949.[23] Willard Savoy was dubbed 'the newest Negro novelist' by the *New York Herald Tribune*, but Stepto shows how his decision to identify in this way—he was given the choice by his publisher's publicity department to identify as white instead—may have had a profound effect on his short-lived literary career.[24] Stepto speculates that Willard may have had a white mother, and may have experienced 'what it was like for the Young Kern Roberts to grow up with a white mother in black Washington'. Kern's experiences in New York evoke 'modern African American "passing" novels': he becomes, as Stepto puts it, 'a

---

[23] Robert B. Stepto, 'Foreword' to Willard Savoy, *Alien Land* (1949; Boston: Northeastern University Press, 2006), pp. vii–xix (p. vii).

[24] Ibid., p. viii.

white man who has made a little money – who is also a black man a white woman is willing to marry'.[25] At the novel's end Kern is content with his 'bargain with Life', avoiding the violence and disruption his father's 'role' brings upon the family, 'as a light-skinned civil rights lawyer who has suddenly discovered his blackness'.[26] But the final scene of reconciliation with his father is also a sign of Kern's accommodation to his mixed-race identity.

Her father's novel, which she discovers only after his death, helps crystallize Lauret Savoy's own thinking about the 'alien land' that America frequently becomes for people of colour. But it also helps her to focus her reading of nature writing's blind spots, specifically through the comparison with Leopold, and these overlapping titles: '*alien. land. ethic.* Three words published midway through a century of world wars – as a young man's semi-autobiographical novel, and as "The Land Ethic," climax essay in an older man's "end-result of a lifetime journey"' (p. 38).[27] By bringing these two visions into dialogue, her father's alienation in America and Leopold's imperfect projection of benign human interaction with the land—'I want *alien land* and *land ethic* to meet and answer to each other' (p. 47), she states—Savoy is able to suggest how a proper reckoning with racism should refashion ecological perceptions of America. But this involves a profound personal awakening:

> ALIEN LAND. LAND ethic. What is the distance between them? As a young adult I felt little integrity or wholeness of living because so much of my acquired knowledge came from inculcated divisions. Only slowly did I come to see that I would remain complicit in my own diminishment unless I stepped out of the *separate* trap: me from you, us from them, brown skin from depigmented skin, relations among people from relations with the land.   (p. 43)

Escaping from 'the *separate* trap', and thereby attaining the moral high ground, is also the route to self-realization and social evolution—the refusal to remain complicit in one's own diminishment—and Savoy is able to retrieve Leopold in this venture, because she focuses on his presentation of 'the land ethic as a product of social evolution' (p. 43).[28] Conscious that Leopold was concerned about 'the inadequacies of dis-integrated thinking and living' (p. 44), she is able to make his blueprint speak to her concerns, despite its inadequacies. It is, however, a gradual

---

[25] Ibid., pp. ix, xii.   [26] Ibid., pp. 320, xiv.
[27] Leopold's exact phrase, I think, is 'end-result of a life-journey', which comes from the original foreword (1947) to the collection of essays, which then had the title *Great Possessions*. See Richard L. Knight and Suzanne Riedel, 'Introduction' to *Aldo Leopold and the Ecological Conscience*, ed. Knight and Riedel (Oxford: Oxford University Press, 2002), pp. 3–11 (p. 8).
[28] Savoy is quoting from Leopold, *A Sand County Almanac*, p. 225.

and piecemeal undertaking, in which Savoy allows her motifs to convey her meaning through an indirect, cumulative process.[29]

Through the preceding discussion, traumatic experiences or realizations are shown to punctuate Savoy's intellectual journey, and to reveal a potential point of contact between trauma and the sublime, where the element of terror in the sublime, its unsettling essence, is not made subordinate to aesthetic forms, as is usually the case. For Outka, sublimity and trauma can be perceived as 'two racially distinct resolutions of a single moment'. Indeed, the numbness produced by traumatic experience and the inability to process it immediately—resulting in the 'delayed reaction' of post-traumatic stress—reveal an important point of connection with the sublime: 'the failure of witnessing', and the inability to process the traumatic event fully, find 'analogues in the sublime's definitional experience of potent ambiguity'.[30] These analogues are rooted in the idea of parallel kinds of dissonant textual processing. Most relevant here is the duality of the past, which is irrecoverable in the sense that it cannot be rectified; and yet, even as a repository of trauma, it remains a paradoxical resource for the future. Savoy makes extensive use of this paradox in *Trace*, as we have seen: her inevitably incomplete search for her ancestry makes her familial past irrecoverable, for example, even while the reverberations of suffering and oppression are indelibly present. In its refusal of conventional depictions of natural beauty, and its recalibration of dissonance, *Trace* embodies a significant development. The eco-mimetic demonstration of *inefficacy* in the text's efforts to convey nature in textual form now also evokes the *concealment* of racial repression. It challenges the norm that, in African American experience, trauma produces the 'inverse of white sublimity, rendering both the subject and nature abject, commodified, subaltern'.[31] Savoy invites us to reconsider the relationship between sublimity and trauma and hints that trauma can transform 'white sublimity' into a more productive resource. For Savoy, when questions of ethnic identity are placed at the forefront of environmental concerns, a recalibration of what she calls the 'interwoven fabric of nature and culture' is required;[32] and the central component of that recalibration is a steady confrontation with the traumatic past, and the legacy of colonial subjugation.

In the work of other writers, such a confrontation often issues in the recovery or recuperation of elements of traditional ethnic resources to recover self-dignity. Different forms of ambivalence are consequent upon this process, as we'll see in the next section. The root purpose is clear in outline, however: the reclaiming of identity through the deliberate confrontation of the traumatic past addresses the

---

[29] The motif of place-names allows her to make running comparisons between colonial and indigenous thinking, for example.
[30] Outka, *Race and Nature*, pp. 21–2.   [31] Ibid., p. 25.
[32] Deming and Savoy, 'Introduction as a Conversation', p. 14.

fundamental question of *belonging*, so that the *awe* inherent in the experience produces righteous anger at the brutality of displacement, and the violence done to one's ancestors and one's ancestral rights or heritage. This chain of connection may not always be explicit, and may not envisage a particular lost 'homeland'; rather, the reclamation of identity is a process of assertion in which the interpellation 'alien' is refused, perhaps as a prelude to the exposure of the historical injustice of place.

One instructive example of this process is found in the self-construction of the Chicano poet Francisco X. Alarcón, who identifies as 'a Mestizo', glossing this as 'a Spanish word that identified a person of mixed racial/ethnic background' and a positive term of 'self-identity'.[33] Yet this assertion of identity in his adult life follows a traumatic past, in which, as Alarcón puts it, he felt unable to 'identify or associate myself with this body of mine when almost everything around negated me'.[34] The process of finding his identity involved exorcizing the past by reliving it: 'we need to reconnect all the misunderstandings, confrontations and contradictions, all the suffering and havoc brought about by the so-called discovery of this continent by Europeans'.[35] The longer history of human activity in the American continent, traced to migrations 'from Asia at least 60,000 years ago', brings home the impact of the arrival of Europeans on well-established indigenous populations, and inspires in Alarcón a sense of kinship, a process of 'reclaiming ourselves' as well as 'reclaiming America'.[36] Identity politics, in this conception, is thus both the means of bearing witness and the route to self-affirmation, and, by extension, the route to the resuscitation of the body politic.

Alarcón cites Gloria Anzaldúa's interpretation of the mestizo/mestiza identity; but her projection seems to be less rooted in identification with indigenous culture, and so less oppositional; more concerned with negotiating a path of cultural hybridity, partly as a means of survival—'the new *mestiza* copes by developing a tolerance for contradictions... She learns to juggle cultures... she turns the ambivalence into something else.'[37] These are different models of embracing paradox, Alarcón's governed by a long history of injustice, Anzaldúa's by cultural reinvention. The most persuasive hybridizations in nature prose by writers of colour combine elements from these two positions, turning traumatic historical oppression into a productive resource by revealing the significance of such histories for an individual writer's identity, while at the same time finding ways of reclaiming a sense of place as a prelude to reinventing the traditions of nature prose, and establishing new homes within it.

---

[33] Francisco X. Alarcón, 'Reclaiming Ourselves, Reclaiming America', in *The Colors of Nature*, ed. Deming and Savoy, pp. 28–48 (pp. 29, 48).
[34] Ibid., p. 28. [35] Ibid., p. 31. [36] Ibid., pp. 32–3.
[37] Gloria Anzaldúa, *Borderlands/La Frontera: The New Mestiza*, 2nd edn (1987; San Francisco: Aunt Lute Books, 1999), p. 101.

The manner in which the ambivalence of trauma is refashioned by writers like Alarcón, Anzaldúa, and Savoy, as a resource of *collective* hope—for that is an intrinsic component of hybridized identity and synthesized cultural forms—implies the need for this model to be understood and cultivated by all writers regardless of ethnicity. A comparable position emerges in *Animal Dreams* (1990), a novel by Barbara Kingsolver, whose work embodies one of the touchstones and linking strands in this book. Sheryl Stevenson finds in *Animal Dreams* an exemplary instance of trauma fiction: following Judith Lewis Herman, Stevenson hones in on the 'catch-22 Herman calls the "dialectic of trauma"', by which the necessity to recall terrible events, as part of the necessary healing process for individuals and societies, can be both painful and disturbing, prompting resistance and denial.[38] Addressing trauma will probably cause further trauma, and this irresolvable paradox parallels the burden of responsibility in full ecological consciousness. In *Animal Dreams* this encumbrance originates in American Indian indigenous lore, but is generalized and established as a shared contemporary trauma. Kingsolver's central character, Cosima Noline (Codi), is the locus of the recuperation of personal past in *Animal Dreams*, and of the parallel collective assertion of ecological responsibility. The collective memory is rediscovered partly through Codi's relationship with Loyd—who identifies as Pueblo (he is of Pueblo, Navajo, and Apache descent), and who introduces her to both Pueblo and Navajo traditions—and partly through her involvement in the community defeat of the polluting Black Mountain Mining Company.

Most of the novel is Codi's first-person narrative, in which personal trauma abounds as she returns to her home town (Grace, Arizona) and comes to terms with successive events of the past: the death of her mother when she was small; a difficult upbringing, and a sense of estrangement from the people of Grace; and her teenage pregnancy, which ended in a stillbirth. The trauma continues in the present, as she struggles with her father Doc Homer's rapid decline suffering from Alzheimer's disease, and then, most tragically of all, with the death of her sister Hallie, killed by the US-backed Contras in Nicaragua. Unsurprisingly, 'Codi's narrative is one of gaps, evasions, and sudden fissures of erupting emotion', as Stevenson points out, so that her 'unstable discourse' comes to resemble that 'of traumatized people'.[39] Literary discourse is partly defined, of course, by the gaps and fissures in a text; but Kingsolver's method is one in which omissions and points of dissonance are partly resolved by other textual features, and this is a defining characteristic of her resolution of the ecological paradox produced by the predicament of ethnic oppression.

---

[38] Sheryl Stevenson, 'Trauma And Memory In *Animal Dreams*', in *Seeds Of Change: Critical Essays On Barbara Kingsolver*, ed. Priscilla Leder (Knoxville: University of Tennessee Press, 2013), pp. 87–108 (p. 88). See Judith Lewis Herman, *Trauma And Recovery: The Aftermath of Violence—From Domestic Abuse to Political Terror* (New York: Basic Books, 1992).

[39] Stevenson, 'Trauma and Memory', p. 89.

Such transcendence of irresolution, in the novel's design, echoes Savoy's resistance of 'the *separate* trap', which Kingsolver avoids through the union of Codi and Loyd. Codi's personal story is retrieved from the obfuscation of self-deception partly by the corrective memories of other characters; but her progression is also punctuated by more obvious ecological markers. Thus, despite her refusal for most of the novel to commit to life in Grace, or to her relationship with Loyd, we are made to see the 'rightness' of her role in this place, and with this person (who, unbeknownst to him, was the father of her stillborn child in high school), and to see the value (which she does not recognize) of her civic contributions. Thus, as a temporary teacher in her old school, she raises her pupils' awareness of impending ecological crisis by implicating them in environmental damage.[40] On another day she has them read *Silent Spring*, when she is too upset to teach (p. 271). Much earlier in the novel, another character compares her to Thoreau, the patron saint, so to speak, of dwelling in place in American nature writing (p. 76). Such signals of Codi's ecological credentials can seem too obvious; but they function—in a manner typical of Kingsolver's method—to provide a structure of inevitability, clearly anticipating the eventual outcome, despite the gaps in Codi's self-understanding and the vacillation caused by her traumatic experiences. This is the resolution of the book's environmental paradox: despite the feeling of being overwhelmed by her predicament, Codi's path of responsibility is clear. Such responsibility involves an appeal to traditional ecologically responsive indigenous practices, and this also demands an exposure of their limitations, and further equivocation, as the next section of this chapter demonstrates.

Indigenous Lore

An established branch of anthropology emphasizes how indigenous practices, or 'Traditional Ecological Knowledge' (sometimes shortened to 'TEK') can inform efforts to conserve biodiversity and to protect ecosystems. It is the 'subsistence basis' of 'traditional Indigenous economies' that requires them 'to understand the way that the different plants and animals interrelate'—a 'small-scale yet system-wide understanding' that reveals the shortcomings of 'the intensive, isolated, single resource use that characterizes industrial capitalist economies'.[41] Indigenous interaction with the nonhuman is not always harmonious, of course. To take an extreme example, the use of the plumage of birds of paradise for

---

[40] Barbara Kingsolver, *Animal Dreams* (1990; London: Abacus, 1992), pp. 254-7. Subsequent references are given in parentheses.
[41] Charles R. Menzies and Caroline Butler, 'Introduction: Understanding Ecological Knowledge', in *Traditional Ecological Knowledge and Natural Resource Management*, ed. Charles R. Menzies (Lincoln: University of Nebraska Press, 2006), pp. 1-17 (p. 5).

headdresses in New Guinea, where 'beauty and extreme rarity...often coincide', has resulted in the eradication of some species in areas around villages.[42] It is the scientific understanding of ecosystems that might prevent such unintended consequences, and the task that Kingsolver and others set themselves is to establish the guarantee of indigenous lore by blending it with the insights of natural history.

Native American wisdom has been a frequent inspiration for these investigations, and it is usually established as the privileged component, with a sacrosanct air. In the most significant such scene in *Animal Dreams*, Loyd takes Codi to Kinishba, a prehistoric site of Puebloan dwellings. Primed to see this as a heritage site, Codi is reluctant to venture in: 'can we go inside?' she asks; 'is it allowed?' Feeling the proprietorship of ancestral kinship, Loyd replies, 'it's allowed. I allow it' (p. 127). His ease and comfort are apposite, at one with the philosophy of Pueblo architecture. As Codi recognizes, the tessellation of these simple structures makes the site seem organic: 'it looks like something alive that just *grew* here' (p. 129). The education that Loyd offers is didactic in essence. When he is explaining the beliefs behind the traditional native dances they witness in his home village on Christmas Day, he says, 'it has to do with keeping things in balance' (p. 239). This is the perspective of those who see themselves as 'permanent houseguests' on earth, and it occasions a realization for Codi, where character and author speak as one: 'to people who think of themselves as God's houseguests, American enterprise must seem arrogant beyond belief. Or stupid. A nation of amnesiacs, proceeding as if there were no other day but today. Assuming the land could also forget what had been done to it' (p. 241). The indigenous perspective of humility adds another dimension to the way in which the sublime experience of nature is configured, which also embraces (as here) an overarching environmental consciousness.

The contiguity with trauma in the sublime, as we have seen, uncovers a form of terror concealed in the European awe of a nonhuman pristine nature.[43] If the encounter with nature is receptive rather than assertive, open to the unknown and not seeking to impose order, a different kind of awe can be experienced, which, again, admits a conditioning contemporary perspective. In one of his memoir essays in *I Hear the Train*, Louis Owens recalls a camping trip to the Grand Canyon in the 1970s, on a break from his daredevil work for a forest-firefighting team.[44] With typical derring-do, he descends in the dusk along a trail with 'a near-vertical drop' on his left and rock on his right. Out of necessity, he camps in 'a

---

[42] Eric Dinerstein, *The Kingdom of Rarities* (Washington, DC: Island Press, 2013), p. 35.

[43] The term 'pristine' can be infused with new meaning in such a way that it incorporates, rather than excludes, indigenous practices. On this point see the reading of Vernon R. L. Head's *The Search for the Rarest Bird in the World* in Chapter 4.

[44] Owens worked for the US Forest Service for seven years, from 1969, and as 'a sawyer on a hotshot fire crew in the Prescott National Forest' towards the end of that time. See Jacquelyn Kilpatrick, 'Introduction' to *Louis Owens: Literary Reflections on His Life and Work* (Norman: University of Oklahoma Press, 2004), ed. Kilpatrick pp. 3–17 (pp. 9–10).

three-sided stone shelter built into the rock wall beside the trail, its open face looking out into the black air above Hermit Creek a long, long way below'.[45] He settles down in his sleeping bag as 'a great disc of moon began to rise over the canyon', and in this perilous perch he has a frightening encounter with the wild:

> Shadows unfurled around me, and each line and crease was abruptly present, hard edged and clear.... And then a black and hairy hand appeared, groping at the end of a sinewy arm slowly down from the shelter roof, enormous, spidery fingers given full, terrifying dimension in the great moon. For what seemed a very long time the sooty hand probed, monstrous fingers flexing toward me, and then it was gone. (p. 65)

In a state of 'pure fear' he is driven to investigate, and sees a ringtail scurrying away, 'whose delicate, prehensile hand had been made abruptly monstrous by the framing moon and infinitude of canyon' (p. 65).[46] It is this encounter that frames Owens's deliberation on questions of aesthetics and perspective in relation to the Canyon, and, by implication, a rethinking of the sublime. In his recollection, 'reality had fractured' momentarily, so that 'the impossible – a grasping black hand as big as the moon – had been conceivable, full of meaning and significance and capable of reshaping a lifetime of knowledge of how the world works into something utterly new and transforming' (p. 66). It is this openness to the new, to a radical alteration of one's knowledge base, that signals the *native* sublime from which Owens borrows, and which also suggests an important point of contact with modern ecology (and natural history) which ceaselessly produce fresh understanding of ecosystems and their pressure points.

As does Savoy, Owens makes the Grand Canyon a prime site for illustrating ethnic environmental understanding. He puts his experience in the context of several centuries of attempts to make sense of this place, indicating that some inherited cultural wisdom might help to situate the viewer. He traces the disorientation of Europeans and Euro-Americans who, since the sixteenth century, have tried to find words to describe how 'the Canyon reaches great, hairy hands out of its bloated moon to grasp your soul, wrenching it out of common experience' (p. 68). But the Canyon requires the passivity that is born of native acceptance, the relinquishment of words of measurement or containment, since 'only the Native holds the measure of the place, because the Native, the Indian, has had many, many generations in which to learn resistance to the jealousy of measure and voice, the futile desire for words to reach up and over' (p. 68). This superior

---

[45] Owens, *I Hear the Train*, p. 65. Subsequent references are given in parentheses.
[46] For Owens, ringtails—'small, catlike creatures...related to the raccoon'—'attain proper dimension only in the Canyon, where the world speaks to us in its real form, undisguised, sincere, forever' (p. 76).

ability to negotiate the sublime involves the prior claim of inhabitation. The overwhelming otherness of this astounding, and confounding, natural feature, 'up to 6,000 feet deep', has to be stoically accepted. Upon its rock, some of which is 'more than 1.7 billion' years old, 'Native people lived and worshipped long before the first European despaired of perspective and proportion there, and upon that rock Native people still live and pray' (p. 75). The despair of Europeans, who cannot avail themselves of such stoicism, implies a fatally flawed world view and, perhaps, a certain bankruptcy in the very concept of the sublime, which must be remodelled to register this wisdom. But, like Savoy, Owens is also partly wedded to the Western tradition he critiques—indeed, he performs the disorientation of the European sensibility in his own encounter with the ringtail's 'monstrous fingers'— and this generates a significant intellectual tension, where cultural hybridity seems to result in inevitably (and often self-consciously) contradictory modes of expression.[47]

In Louis Owens's writing there is an intellectual crux combining place and ethnicity; and the place that crystallises what is at stake in his work is a mountain in northern Washington, in the region of the North Cascades, which he describes here:

> At the center of the Glacier Peak Wilderness... is the vastly beautiful mountain named on maps, most unimaginatively, Glacier Peak. We look at the peak and see glaciers, and the text of the mountain is laid bare. There are other names for the peak, however, one of which is Dakobed, a Salish word meaning something like Great Mother. The local Indian people, the Suiattle, look at Dakobed and see the place from which they came, the place where they were born, the mother earth.... There is an important and invaluable message in this knowledge, for whereas a society may well mine the heart out of something called a natural resource, one does not violate one's mother.[48]

Euro-American superficial habits of naming, revealing a predisposition to exploitation, are starkly contrasted with the empathic indigenous culture of naming, rooted in deep-historical inhabitation. It is precisely this bald cultural choice that Owens's fiction wrestles with, but without allowing us to make the easy choice adumbrated in this essay.[49]

---

[47] In a comparable instance of negotiating different traditions, Melissa Nelson has described her own intellectual journey away from deep ecology and towards an appreciation of Native American philosophy, after recognizing an unhelpful binary division in deep ecology, 'a distinction between an anthropocentric worldview and a "biocentric" one', a distinction that divides people from nature. See Melissa Nelson, 'Becoming Métis', in *The Colors of Nature*, ed. Deming and Savoy, pp. 146–52 (pp. 148, 149).
[48] Owens, *Mixedblood Messages*, p. 211.
[49] Owens does not question the gendering of the mountain in Suiattle culture.

In a short essay/story—Owens is one of the earliest 'new' nature writers to engage self-consciously with the fictionalization of first-hand experience—he recalls an instructive episode from 1976, when he was 'working as a seasonal ranger for the US forest service' and was given the job of burning a dilapidated shelter, in a place called White Pass, on the side of the mountain in the Glacier Peak Wilderness. As in the essay quoted above, Owens establishes the significant difference between the cartographer's limited description—Glacier Peak—and the indigenous understanding of this 'glaciated white volcano' as 'the place of emergence', which embraces both the threat and the fecundity of the mountain. But this is a story of destruction and culpability. Owens recalls dismantling and burning the White Pass shelter over a period of five days, until 'not a trace' of it remained: he plays his efficient part in 'a Forest Service plan to remove all human-made objects from wilderness areas, a plan of which I heartily approved'.[50] His satisfaction at a job well done is short-lived, however. On his way back down the mountain trail he encounters two elderly 'Indi'n' ladies, 'silver braids hanging below thick wool caps', who 'seemed ancient, each weighted with at least seventy years as well as a small backpack'. They are, it transpires, the daughters of the Forest Service worker who originally built the 'little house', before they were born: they are undertaking an annual pilgrimage to this site of familial significance, which affords them the chance to view what was once 'all Indi'n land everywhere you can see'. He has to tell them that 'the shelter is gone'; but his incomplete explanation that 'it was crushed by snow, so I was sent up to burn it' does not elicit the 'outrage, anger, sadness' he expects from the sisters, who 'continue to smile up at me', adjusting their plans to use tarpaulin instead, now that the shelter isn't there.[51]

The episode draws contradictory responses from Owens. His main reaction is one of self-condemnation: he realizes that in defending something called 'wilderness' he is working to buttress 'a figment of the European imagination', because 'before the European invasion, there was no wilderness in North America; there was only the fertile continent, where people lived in a hard-learned balance with the natural world'. The sisters are a surviving remnant of that 'ancient' mode of inhabitation, their father's 'little house' a reminder of that way of life. Consequently, Owens experiences a seemingly profound epiphany: 'in embracing a philosophy that saw the White Pass shelter – and all traces of humanity – as a shameful stain upon the "pure" wilderness, I had succumbed to a five-hundred-year-old pattern of deadly thinking that separates us from the natural world'. The realization, however, is held in tension with a pragmatic acceptance 'that what we call wilderness today does need careful safeguarding': the epiphany is qualified, containing within it an inverse non-epiphany. Despite this internal debate,

---

[50] Louis Owens, 'Burning the Shelter', in *The Colors of Nature*, ed. Deming and Savoy, pp. 142–5 (p. 142).
[51] Ibid., pp. 143, 144.

however, matters of conservation do not deflect the final judgement. The resonant conclusion drawn from the episode involves a comparison between the destroyed shelter and the 'faint traces of log shelters' that Owens has come across, 'built by Suiattle and Upper Skagit people for berry harvesting a century or more ago', and inspires him to celebrate 'our native ancestors all over this continent [who] lived within a complex web of relations with the natural world', assuming 'a responsibility for their world that contemporary Americans cannot even imagine'. Without the recovery of such an ethos, 'a few square miles of something called wilderness will become the sign of failure everywhere'. And yet, despite the explicit message, the episode still obliges us to compare perspectives, so that the celebration of native wisdom is not as straightforward as it might seem. Owens is shamed into a round condemnation of his conservation work; but he also recognizes the necessity of it as a defence against the worst ravages of ecotourism. We also see a parallel between Owens and the sisters' father, who had also been in the employ of the Forest Service two generations before him. Idealism is thus tempered by pragmatism, so that the exhortation for us to 'learn what the indigenous peoples of the Americas knew and often still know' as the route to saving the earth is already overshadowed by the impression of a different context.[52]

Owens's self-division, but with the ethical balance tipped towards the claims of indigenous responses to nature, is also discernible in the distinctively dissonant form of his fiction, where Dakobed/Glacier Peak becomes a site of more complex contestation. In his first novel, *Wolfsong* (1991), it is a site of both ethnic struggle and personal transformation. The full significance of Dakobed is revealed at the novel's end, a conclusion that is emblematic of the central dilemma inherent in Owens's life and work, at the nexus of Euro-American and Native American culture. He is torn between embracing this hybrid situation and making the latter critique the former. Ostensibly, *Wolfsong* follows a plot line familiar from many Native American novels, in staging the conflict between Euro-American and Native American perspectives, and tracing an identity quest for a protagonist in pursuit of ancestral roots. But it also explores ways in which traditional indigenous culture might be merged with Western intellectualism. As we shall see, it is a notably self-conscious work, as one might expect from a novelist who was also a leading scholar of the American Indian novel;[53] and a key aspect of that self-

---

[52] Ibid., pp. 144, 145. An alternative, and clearly fictionalized, version of 'Burning the Shelter' underscores Owens's feeling of culpability. This version, titled simply 'Shelter', was originally published separately in 1988, but it is included as a short story in *I Hear the Train*. The story concentrates on the kernel of the memoir: the falsity of constructing 'wilderness', and the violence inherent in the denial of native tradition. It is a 'single effect' story in the tradition of Poe, rather than a story that explores ambivalence. See Owens, *I Hear the Train*, pp. 189–93.

[53] Owens's pioneering study was *Other Destinies: Understanding the American Indian Novel* (Norman: University of Oklahoma Press, 1992). *Wolfsong* was published in 1991, but was begun much earlier while he was working as a Forest Ranger, during the same formative period as the shelter-burning episode. See John Purdy, '*Wolfsong* and Pacific Refrains', in *Louis Owens: Literary Reflections on His Life and Work*, ed. Kilpatrick, pp. 175–94 (p. 179).

consciousness is a rethinking of apparent oppositions, particularly those arising from connotations of 'wilderness'. In Susan Bernardin's words, '*Wolfsong* traces the ecologically and spiritually devastating consequences of America's invention of the wilderness for Euro-Americans and Native Americans alike'.[54] The novel begins with the death of Jim Joseph, the last member of the 'Stehemish' tribe to understand the tribal lore and to uphold its values (although much of it is already lost to him), and who dies while protesting against mining operations on unspoilt land.[55] Jim's nephew Tom Joseph returns from university for the funeral, and the novel thereafter is concerned with Tom, chosen by Jim as the conduit of tribal continuity, and with Tom's struggle to engage with his heritage.

There are, then, structural elements to *Wolfsong* that are familiar to the American Indian novel, notably the idea of an ecocentric vision embedded in indigenous culture, and the loss of that vision experienced by a displaced protagonist. The opposition of world views, however, leads to 'complicated tensions between dominant Euroamerican environmental practices and ideologies on one hand, and indigenous tribal ways of inhabiting and representing the landscape on the other', as David Brande puts it.[56] The tensions are complex not because the concept of wilderness serves to conceal real historical relations, the fact of Native dwelling (and displacement) erased from the landscape: that concealment can be readily exposed. Indeed, the catastrophic European misperception of 'wilderness' is a seminal feature of the Native American literary tradition in Owens's account. Viewed in this oppositional way, this is an established tradition that has proved its credentials by offering 'a way of looking at the world that is new to Western culture', through 'a holistic, ecological perspective'.[57] But Owens does not find easy access to that tradition in *Wolfsong*. It is not just that the indigenous holistic view has been submerged: Owens also questions the extent to which that view still embodies the requisite resource of hope. Tom's inadequate understanding of Salish culture is his great limitation for much of the narrative, and this is especially significant in relation to his knowledge of place. The fact that he doesn't know 'the old, real names' of all the mountains is keenly felt.[58] At one point, we read: 'he stared at the White Mountain, the center, the great mother, and tried to feel what it had meant to his tribe' (p. 92). This echoes the familiar trope of cultural loss in the Native American novel; but it is also a sign of Owens acknowledging the fact that indigenous wisdom is fading.

---

[54] Susan Bernardin, 'Wilderness Conditions: Ranging for Place and Identity in Louis Owens' *Wolfsong*', *Studies in American Indian Literatures*, 10 (1998), 2, pp. 79–93 (p. 79).

[55] The 'Stehemish' is a fictional coastal Salishan tribe; Bernardin, 'Wilderness Conditions', p. 80.

[56] David, Brande, 'Not the Call of the Wild: The Idea of Wilderness in Louis Owens's *Wolfsong* And *Mixedblood Messages*', *American Indian Quarterly*, 24 (2000), 2, pp. 247–63 (p. 247).

[57] Owens, *Other Destinies*, p. 29.

[58] Louis Owens, *Wolfsong* (1991; Norman: University of Oklahoma Press, 1995), p. 94. Subsequent references are given in parentheses.

The vacillating effect serves, partly, to reassert indigenous authority by making us see the consequences of its loss. Thus, Lee Schweninger is right in his observation that Owens is writing in the spirit of N. Scott Momaday when he addresses the spiritual disconnection implicit in environmental destruction: 'as we lose sight of our fundamental connection to the land, we invite spiritual death'.[59] The ethical idea embodied in Momaday's 'An American Land Ethic' clearly influenced Owens's understanding. Momaday argued that Americans must come 'to moral terms' with 'the physical world', generating the desired land ethic, rooted in a latent 'deep, ethical regard for the land', through 'an act of the imagination'.[60] Momaday's essay contrasts with Leopold's land ethic in its greater emphasis on established human wisdom: the recovery of a latent ethical immersion in place also hinges on the recuperation of ancestral lore, memory handed down, and *Wolfsong* is partly an exploration of the extent to which such recuperation is possible.

Tom's journey to discover his legacy through such lore involves the ongoing attempt to make himself able to receive the guardian wolf spirit, or *staka'yu*, passed on by his uncle, and which he attempts to open himself to by seeking visionary experiences in the landscape, attempts which are unsuccessful until the very end of the novel, on Dakobed Mountain. It is an ambiguous ending because Tom's apparent salvation seems too easy, relying on a switch of modes to transcend the complicating levels of ambiguity that remain—stemming, perhaps, from Owens's grasp of the impossibility of *living* the indigenous world view.[61] There is more at stake in this ending, however, the very ambiguity of which concentrates the cultural sources Owens is seeking to fuse together. One of these sources is the constructed nature of the Native American, 'a product of literature, history, and art' in Owens's own summary, and 'an invention'.[62] The recuperation of identity is thus especially complex since the available cultural models betray a 'disjuncture between myth and reality'.[63] This means that 'the recovering or rearticulation of an identity', a process that is 'at the center of American Indian fiction', becomes 'a truly enormous undertaking',

---

[59] Lee Schweninger, 'Landscape and Cultural Identity in Louis Owens' *Wolfsong*', *Studies in American Indian Literatures*, 10 (1998), 2, pp. 94–110 (pp. 94–5). Schweninger points out the values on which Owens's fictional tribe is based: 'the coastal Salish – like Northwest Coast Indians in general – recognize a critical, reciprocal relationship... generally between the human and the non-human community. Hence the Snohomish (Stehemish in the novel) can be seen to abide by moral principles that promote such a respectful and spiritual relationship' (p. 97).

[60] N. Scott Momaday, *The Man Made of Words: Essays, Stories, Passages* (New York: St. Martin's Press, 1997), pp. 47, 49.

[61] Owens acknowledges his own ambiguous position in relation to the plans to mine copper in the middle of the Glacier Peak Wilderness. In his work for the Forest Service he had 'participated in the mining companies' ultimate goal: to exploit the wilderness'. He 'had cut out windfalls and blasted rockslides to open trails', and 'most unforgivably... had felled a magnificent, centuries-old hemlock to make a bridge across a big creek that should never have been bridged'. See Owens, *Mixedblood Messages*, p. 210.

[62] Owens, *Other Destinies*, p. 4.   [63] Ibid., pp. 4–5.

perhaps an impossible one, with implications for the very survival of holistic ecological being.[64]

An indication of Owens's own vacillation on this point is found in *Mixedblood Messages*, where he writes disparagingly of the construction of 'American Indians as something like genetically predetermined environmentalists', blaming the 'dominant discourse' of Euro-Americans especially, but implicating 'Native Indians' as well to a degree.[65] However, despite calling attention to the stereotype, Owens concludes *Mixedblood Messages* by underscoring the 'closeness of vision, reciprocity, and respect' of the Native American world view, arguing that these are 'powerful medicines, the only medicines that may, perhaps, save humanity from itself'.[66] Working broadly *with the grain* of this ecological message, Owens's fiction explores how far such a construction is plausible, and what its useful components might be. But this also obliges us to keep the prospect of falsification in view.

Owens is also making something new by drawing together Western intellectualism and native literary codes. In his criticism, Owens is influenced by Bakhtin's concept of hybridization, which he defines as 'a mixture of two social languages within the limits of a single utterance, an encounter, within the arena of utterance, between two different linguistic consciousnesses';[67] and, for Owens, the dialogic potential of the Native American novel is linked to the figure of the traditional trickster, the figure who is 'in dialogue with himself, embodies contradictions, challenges authority, mocks and tricks us into self-knowledge';[68] the trickster, whether human or animal, 'mocks, ridicules, and challenges every fixed meaning or static definition'.[69] Owens is especially influenced by Gerald Vizenor's work, and the ways in which 'the mixedblood and the trickster become metaphors that seek to balance contradictions and shatter static certainties'.[70] The form of intellectual fusion Owens works to achieve stems from the affinity between the radical relativization of perspective implicit in the trickster world view and the cultural hybridization central to the Bakhtinian model. But this involves an interesting contrast: where the trickster can serve to undermine all fixed concepts—including that of the ecological American Indian—dialogism keeps all constructions in play. Here Owens finds his own way of pursuing Vizenor's crucial challenge to the myth of the death of Indian culture: 'the liberation of language and consciousness is Vizenor/trickster's aim, particularly the liberation of the signifier "Indian" from the entropic myth surrounding it'.[71]

---

[64] Ibid., p. 5.   [65] Owens, *Mixedblood Messages*, p. 220.   [66] Ibid., p. 236.
[67] Owens, *Other Destinies*, p. 110. Owens is quoting from *The Dialogic Imagination*. See M. M. Bakhtin, *The Dialogic Imagination*, trans. Caryl Emerson and Michael Holquist (Austin: University of Texas Press, 1981), p. 358.
[68] Owens, *Other Destinies*, p. 108. The 'himself' here is specific, not generic: Owens is discussing the role of John Big Bluff Tosamah in N. Scott Momaday's novel *House Made of Dawn* (1968).
[69] Owens, *Other Destinies*, p. 109.   [70] Ibid., p. 225.   [71] Ibid., p. 226.

The ending of *Wolfsong* trades on this entropic myth. After his gesture of sabotage, blowing up the mining company's water tank—and in the process accidentally killing the town's wealthy entrepreneur J. D. Hill—Tom becomes a fugitive, chased across the mountains by a helicopter, trying to escape to Canada. The odds are stacked against him in very difficult terrain, especially after he is wounded by a gunshot in the chase. It all seems desperate; but in the final passages the grim realism of the fugitive episode, which conveys the harshness of the terrain, the impairment of the wound, the apparent impossibility of escape, gives way to a different mood as Tom is finally at one with the wolf:

> He turned to run just as the wolf began to call again, and this time it kept growing, louder and louder and spinning in ever-widening circles through the thin air until it was deafening and seemed a part of the air he breathed. He ran with long, smooth strides down the mountain, the moon hurling his shadow northward before him, listening to the rising howl of the wolf that went on and on until the night seemed ready to burst. (p. 249)

After pages describing a predicament of grim foreboding, with progress almost impossible, and capture or death virtually certain, Tom suddenly finds he can run down the mountain 'with long, smooth strides'. This is an ending that wrong-foots the reader in several respects. Whether or not he successfully escapes the retribution of the law, there is a sense that he has failed: he has continued his uncle's protest, but the protest is merely gestural and cannot stop the mine; he has failed to find a community on his return to his home town; his uncle and mother are both dead; and, with his brother culturally compromised, he is alone in his (consequently impossible) attempt to uphold Stehemish values. As a novel of ecological protest, *Wolfsong*'s prognosis is bleak. And yet, Tom's great achievement is to have joined with the wolf spirit, and it is this that makes the night so full of potential, and which gives him his apparently superhuman strength. Even if we read this as a moment of feverish insight moments before death—and that is one possible reading, given the sudden switch from the code of realism in the chase episode to something like magic realism—Tom's victory, the recovery of his heritage, remains intact. In the mythic logic detected by Brande, it becomes irrelevant whether or not the character Tom is deemed likely to survive. Rather, the emphasis is on Owens's demonstration of the recovery of tribal values, which survive beyond the deaths of individuals.[72]

We realize, however, that Tom is banished from Dakobed, the mountain that is his spiritual home, and this is of huge significance given the central importance of this place to Owens. Such a major equivocation, premised on the clash (broadly

---

[72] Brande, 'Not the Call of the Wild', p. 259.

speaking) of Euro-American interests and the remnants of indigenous culture, seems problematic, if not disastrous. But such equivocation epitomizes Owens's work at a formal level, too. He saw himself as working in a long tradition of Native American writing, in which the effects of colonization are resisted, as he put it, by using 'the colonizer's language...to articulate our own worlds and find ourselves whole'.[73] The difficulty of the task is exacerbated, for Owens, because 'the dominant culture...has constructed the Indian' so that 'resisting the "absolute fake" self that is thrust so powerfully upon us' is a major obstacle in trying to 'bring together the nearly schizophrenic parts of the self into a coherent personal identity'.[74] The Euro-American appropriation of the Indian makes the revitalization of Amerindian identity, for the prosecution of environmental justice, essential—but also impossible, perhaps.

Vizenor's 'trickster discourse' constitutes the principal resource in the endeavour to bridge the binary divide. Vizenor is able to celebrate 'the boundless zone of transculturation from a perspective beginning deeply within the traditional trickster narratives of native America'. The result is a difficult form of writing, and another variety of paradoxical nature prose. Vizenor, Owens suggests, 'has long been involved in an effort to move native American studies in the direction of what [Arnold] Krupat has called the "project of ethnocriticism"', which inspires Owens as a 'critical enterprise' deemed to be 'of the frontier'—a term he is at pains to appropriate—and an enterprise that has a compelling structural ambiguity at its heart: the 'trope most typical of ethnic critical discourse...is the *oxymoron*, that figure which offers apparently oppositional, paradoxical, or incompatible terms in a manner that nonetheless allows for decidable, if polysemous and complex, meaning'.[75] It's worth noting in passing that Krupat is actually ambivalent about the potential of Vizenor's trickster discourse, and this is understandable given the style in which Vizenor articulates his ideas in the relevant essays.[76] Consequently, for Krupat, the language games of structuralist-inspired postmodernism limit the potential of 'Vizenor's sense of postmodern/trickster/comic "liberations"' by virtue of his emphasis on 'the absolute difference of all linguistic acts and all texts one from another' which results in 'a form of radical epistemological relativism'.[77] Yet Krupat argues that there are 'ways in which Vizenor's "loosening the bounds" of Western discursive categories could be reoriented for ethnocritical

---

[73] Owens, *Mixedblood Messages*, p. xiii.   [74] Ibid., pp. 21–2.
[75] Ibid., p. 55. Owens is quoting from Arnold Krupat, *Ethnocriticism: Ethnograohy, History, Literature* (Berkeley: University of California Press, 1992), p. 28.
[76] Vizenor's 'Trickster Discourse: Comic Holotropes and Language Games', for example, comprises a series of repeated but evolving assertions, punctuated by relevant theoretical ideas drawn especially from structuralism and semiotics, so that the trickster is defined as no more than 'a semiotic sign for "social antagonism" and "aesthetic activism" in postmodern criticism and the avant-garde'. See 'A Postmodern Introduction' (pp. 3–16) and 'Trickster Discourse: Comic Holotropes and Language Games' (pp. 187–211 (p. 192)), in *Narrative Chance: Postmodern Discourse on Native American Indian Literatures*, ed. Gerald Vizenor (Albuquerque: University of New Mexico Press, 1989).
[77] Krupat, *Ethnocriticism*, p. 184.

purposes'. Like Owens, he is inspired by Vizenor's 'fascinating conjunction' of 'postmodern "trickster" fluidities' with 'his commitment to...premodern tribal identities', which afford 'a view of the natural world utterly and entirely different from the postmodern alienation of late capitalism'.[78] In this account, which chimes with Owens's, the postmodern attributes of Vizenor's trickster discourse are a means of exposing the alienation of postmodernity, which must include the alienation produced by ecological collapse, environmental injustice, and the eclipse of holistic indigenous traditions.

In Owens's development of Krupat's terms, via Vizenor, it is the ethnocritical oxymoron that can produce appropriately complex, but *decidable*, meaning. As in the previous section of this chapter, it is the process of transcending ethnic exclusivity that is ultimately at stake. Chris LaLonde argues persuasively that Owens's fictions put the construction of the American Indian at the heart of 'the narrative of the nation', because he understands that the *invented* Indian 'is vitally important to the construction of Euroamerican identity and America'.[79] Unsettling that process of colonial self-definition, at the frontier of conflicting cultures, is then of great importance to the health of the nation as a whole. Owens was keen to appropriate the term 'frontier', which he considered a 'deadly cliché' of territorial colonialism, by following the 'trickster's strategies' of 'appropriation, inversion, and abrogation of authority', so that 'frontier' is understood as being 'always unstable, multidirectional, hybridized, characterized by heteroglossia, and indeterminate'.[80] At the end of *Wolfsong* Owens generates these characteristics through the trickster strategy of allowing Tom Joseph to elude the capture that might confirm a cultural death, on the US/Canada frontier. As his several references to Krupat indicate, Owens was producing his own version of ethnocriticism. LaLonde shows that, in following Vizenor, Owens relies upon the ways in which trickster discourse 'introduces chance and possibility, upsets binaries, counters terminal creeds'. This latter point is important, because it enables Owens to interrogate not just the construction of the Indian but also the trope of 'the vanishing Native' as he creates an 'affirmation of Native identity'. In this way, trickster discourse is a survival tool for Amerindian culture.[81]

This is important in transcending ethnic exclusivity because the entropic myth is also a colonizer's myth. 'The trope of the vanishing Native tribe', as LaLonde observes, 'is the phrasing of an ideal created and then clung to by the dominant culture.'[82] The point of this 'ideal' in white thinking is simultaneously to bring about, and yet to deny responsibility for, the displacement of indigenous people, a concealment produced in popular consciousness by romanticizing the

---

[78] Ibid., p. 191.
[79] Chris LaLonde, *Grave Concerns, Trickster Turns: The Novels of Louis Owens* (Norman: University of Oklahoma Press, 2002), p. 9.
[80] Owens, *Mixedblood Messages*, p. 26.
[81] LaLonde, *Grave Concerns, Trickster Turns*, pp. 19, 22.   [82] Ibid., p. 47.

disappearing figure of the noble savage, and lamenting the cultural loss it betokens. What is particularly striking in Owens's vision is the imperative to lay bare this fantasy of postcolonial denial, on behalf not just of the victims, but of the oppressors (or their successors) too: that is the point of making this recuperative quest part of the national narrative. Ostensibly, however, *Wolfsong* corroborates the story of the vanishing American Indian: Tom's whole tribe has gone (p. 120), so that he is now a 'one-man tribe' (p. 195). But the postmodern incredulity implicit in Vizenor's trickster discourse is deployed by Owens in such a way to make us start questioning this master narrative. It is not so much that we adopt a position of complete incredulity towards it but that we seek to understand how and why such a terminal narrative comes into being, so that its hold on us is loosened.[83] This is not necessarily to discount its real-world purchase, but to open up a consideration of alternative afterlives for indigenous philosophy, for the enhancement of the national narrative. In this way, the 'social antagonism' and 'aesthetic activism' that Vizenor sees as being contained within the 'semiotic sign' of the trickster figure are given leverage in relation to the ecological vision that Tom's quest rediscovers. The implied reinvention of Tom's heritage is part of Owens's contribution to the 'unending battle' of Native American writers 'to affirm their own identities, to resist the metamorphoses insisted upon by European intruders', but most especially a significant contribution to the collective indigenous resistance of 'the great Western myth of cultural extinction'.[84] Challenging the extinction myth requires the affirmation of indigenous practices, and chief among these—in another apparent paradox—are the rituals and traditions surrounding death and mourning.

Remembering the Dead

This section is concerned with how cultural extinction evolves in Owens's work into an exploration of the ecological significance of death and mourning, a connection that is also central to the texts by Lauret Savoy and Barbara Kingsolver discussed in this chapter. Mourning also offers a way of bridging the divide between Western and indigenous cultures, the amalgamation that is of great concern to Savoy, Kingsolver, and Owens in different ways. The importance of death and mourning is well illustrated in Owens's second novel, *The Sharpest*

---

[83] Perhaps the central mantra of postmodernism is contained in Jean-François Lyotard's definition of it as 'incredulity toward metanarratives'. (By 'metanarratives' Lyotard means grand overarching cultural stories that tend to suppress social contradictions, rather than the self-reflexive 'stories about stories' which became staple features of postmodernist fiction.) See Jean-François Lyotard, *The Postmodern Condition: A Report on Knowledge*, trans. Geoff Bennington and Brian Massumi (1979; Manchester: Manchester University Press, 1984), p. xxiv.
[84] Owens, *Other Destinies*, p. 21.

Sight, which is a highly autobiographical work.[85] The core action of this novel is the search made by Cole McCurtain—the Owens figure—for the murdered body of his brother Attis, and his enactment of the Choctaw tradition of picking the flesh from the bones and taking care of them. As Margaret Dwyer explains, 'Choctaw did not bury or burn their dead, but instead placed a scaffold atop oak supports some yards from the deceased's house, where the body was placed, wrapped in a blanket or bark to keep birds and animals away, and left for several months until the flesh decayed to such a point that it could be removed easily from the bones'.[86] Dwyer's authority here is H. B. Cushman, who is also Owens's authority.[87] Cole's Uncle Luther, who is one of two significant elders in this novel, has a copy of Cushman's book (p. 87); and this is clearly an important intertext for Owens, a book lauded by Luther for its accuracy: 'this here writer was a man of rare intelligence. For a white man' (p. 88). In this qualified praise Owens anticipates a familiar objection in the deployment of anthropological texts, where they are governed by a white perspective: the most detailed available written accounts of indigenous practices are often infused with an external (and sometimes a colonial) perspective, so that the reliance on them—necessary where such accounts are the most authoritative available—is always paradoxical, since the authority must be disentangled from the misperceptions and appropriations that the position of the outsider invariably produces.[88] *The Sharpest Sight* hinges on Choctaw mythology, but this caveat about sources, which is a self-conscious component of the book, conditions how it is read.

Cole's mission is to return Attis's bones to Mississippi, the home of the Choctaw people, so that his *shilombish*, or 'inside shadow', can proceed to its proper resting place, and his *shilup*, or 'outside shadow' (pp. 110–11)—a ghostly and sometimes threatening presence, seen by several characters—can finally rest. This act is also crucial for the Choctaw who, according to the migration myth of their origins, carried the bones of their ancestors east to what is known today as Mississippi.[89] Luther explains to Cole that he must retrieve Attis's bones in order to follow the pattern of this migration story, and to restore order (p. 98). The social function of the bone-picker is already established in Cole's mind from his

---

[85] Owens reveals the extent of the autobiographical background to the novel in *Mixedblood Messages*, pp. 181–2.

[86] Margaret Dwyer, 'The Syncretic Impulse: Louis Owens' Use of Autobiography, Ethnology, and Blended Mythologies in *The Sharpest Sight*', in *Studies in American Indian Literatures*, series 2, 10 (1998), 2, pp. 43–60 (p. 48).

[87] See H. B. Cushman, *History of the Choctaw, Chickasaw and Natchez Indians*, ed. Angie Debo (1899; Stillwater: Redlands Press, 1962).

[88] A comparable instance is Nadine Gordimer's extended use of the Reverend Henry Callaway's *The Religious System of the Amazulu* (1870) as a source to give presence to the Zulu cult of the ancestor in her Booker Prize-winning novel *The Conservationist* (1974). Callaway's transcriptions of first-hand accounts of Zulu codes, customs, and beliefs is an invaluable historical document; but we have to wonder how Zulu practices may have been mediated by Callaway, a nineteenth-century British missionary.

[89] See, for example, John P. Bowes, *The Choctaw* (New York: Chelsea House, 2010), pp. 16, 98.

father's stories 'of Choctaw things' (p. 54), so his adoption of this role is well anticipated. Cole finds Attis's drowned body 'cupped in the branches' of 'four small oaks', and 'ten feet off the ground' (p. 251), carried there by the river in spate, a consequence of environmental damage. This accidental occurrence performs the role of the traditional scaffold of oak supports in Choctaw traditional burial, so that Cole finds his brother's remains ready to be picked clean of flesh.

To this extent, Owens relies on his source in Cushman for Choctaw ritual, but is aware of the problems consequent upon this reliance. As LaLonde suggests, we are reminded that Cushman's history 'must be read carefully' to recognize its 'connection to the dominant culture's story'.[90] In particular, Cushman at times sees the Indian tribes he examines as both 'noble *and* vanishing', thus playing his part in establishing the dominant white mythology of extinction.[91] Considerable nuance is needed here, because there *is* a kind of nobility in the Choctaw figures that Owens depicts—as there is in the depiction of many indigenous characters in American Indian literature—and there *is* a clear recognition that tribes and indigenous practices are, indeed, vanishing. But the problem is that a certain kind of romanticization of the noble savage, evolving in the cultural perceptions that come after works such as Cushman's, coupled with a sentimental perspective on cultural loss, can be a way of concealing culpability, and projecting the death of the Indian—the subconscious white desire—as inevitable. We need to realize that seemingly identical reflections on cultural extinction can have opposing motivations, both of which are in play in Owens's interrogation of this myth, which is linked to his examination of the tropes of canonical American literature.

The Sharpest Sight is an overtly metafictional text, both in its self-consciousness about its own procedures and through its allusions to the canon of American literature. The two elders, Uncle Luther and Onatima, function as a chorus, managing the behaviour of Attis's *shilup*, and anticipating or commenting on the novel's action. They also supply the route to the novel's interrogation of the American literary canon. Among the books that Onatima has given Luther to read are Melville's *Moby Dick* and Twain's *Adventures of Huckleberry Finn*, and he proves an astute reader, recognizing the power of these stories, but also (from a Choctaw perspective) the white cult of death discernible in them (pp. 90–1, 113). For example, this is his reading of the end of *Huckleberry Finn*, when (says Luther) 'the boy thinks he's going to light out for Indian territory all by himself': 'I think that white boy knew he was part of something that wouldn't let him live with no Indians. It's like these white people want to keep killing off everything so's one day they'll be alone, no parents, no family, not even mother earth. Just one kid out there all alone somewhere' (p. 113).[92] Luther suggests that, in these classics of

---

[90] LaLonde, *Grave Concerns, Trickster Turns*, p. 85. [91] Ibid., p. 86.
[92] This analysis of *Huckleberry Finn* echoes the plane-survivor fantasy of the character Mundo Morales quoted at the beginning of this chapter.

mainstream American literature, there is an aestheticization of death that is inherently antipathetic to holistic environmental living; and Owens is here anticipating the emerging ecocritical theme concerning good and bad ways of conceptualizing death. Compare, for example, Timothy Morton's reflection on death at the end of *Ecology without Nature* where he exhorts us to 'choose and accept our own death, and the fact of mortality among species and ecosystems'. Morton sees this as 'the ultimate rationality: holding our mind open for the absolutely unknown that is to come', in contrast with the tendency to 'aestheticize this acceptance', which results in 'fascism, the cult of death'.[93] Such formulations about stoicism in the face of death, which are becoming quite frequent in discussions of the time of extinctions, can sometimes seem to replicate the cultish aestheticization of death that they would resist; here I simply wish to observe that, without the same acute pressure of twenty-first-century climate crisis, Owens anticipates contemporary concerns about the Western cult of death in a way that illustrates well why indigenous understandings of the environment are frequently drawn on in ecological thought. As Robert Bringhurst writes, 'those of us who care about the earth, and who keep recalibrating our minds by spending time in the wild, find ourselves siding, more and more, with marginal cultures – old, sustainable cultures – against the unsustainable mainstream, and with other species against our own'.[94] Yet the holistic understanding of death that is often retrieved from indigenous wisdom is harder to co-opt than Bringhurst implies.

I will return here to Kingsolver's *Animal Dreams*, in which memorializing the dead is the central motif. For Codi, the key moment of grieving comes in the improvised ceremony for her dead sister Hallie, towards the end of the book: without a body to inter, she and the other women of Grace 'bring something that reminded them of Hallie' to decorate 'a blanket with icons from the past' (p. 325). The novel is actually replete with the idea of human grieving and memorialization, and this is made the central aspect of self-definition, especially through Codi's coming-to-terms with the loss of her mother, signalled when she is helped to recover the memory of her presence on her mother's death day, recalling the emergency helicopter carrying her away (pp. 48, 342). Such self-definition is also self-abnegation in the sense that the novel places emphasis on the individual's temporary role in a longer continuum. The memory is recalled on the Day of All Souls, and Kingsolver is scrupulous is giving memorialization a ritualistic dimension.

Human continuity is associated with the ecological theme in the episode at Kinishba, when Loyd explains that 'the walls are graveyards. When a baby died, they'd mortar its bones right into the wall. Or under the floor' (p. 128). Codi

---

[93] Morton, *Ecology without Nature*, p. 205.
[94] Robert Bringhurst and Jan Zwicky, *Learning to Die: Wisdom in the Age of Climate Crisis* (Saskatchewan: University of Regina Press, 2018), p. 38.

shudders at the thought and asks why the Puebloans would have done this. 'So it would still be near its family', Loyd explains, surprised at the question (p. 128). Kingsolver is not ultimately focusing on the cultural difference implied in Codi's reaction; rather, she is working towards an accommodation between Western and indigenous mourning practices, and between divers cultural perceptions of the impact of the dead upon the living. In this respect, *Animal Dreams* anticipates Robert Pogue Harrison's reflection that 'the foundational authority of the predecessor' is present everywhere 'across the spectrum of human cultures'. He argues: 'humanity in its distinctive features is through and through necrocratic. Whether we are conscious of it or not we do the will of the ancestors'.[95] Harrison is concerned with 'the manifold relations the living maintain with the giant family of the dead in Western culture, both in past and present times';[96] and these reflections on Western culture are hugely significant for the cultural fusion I am tracing in the ecological recalibration of death. For Harrison, 'burial does not mean only the laying of bodies to rest in the ground'. Rather, 'it means to store, preserve, and put the past on hold'. Burial sites are analogues for 'our psyches', which are 'the graveyards of impressions, traumas, desires, and archetypes that confound the law of obsolescence'.[97] In this sense, the closure sought by the grief-stricken, ostensibly embodied in burial, is also a form of continuity, of preservation, a denial of chronological time. And burial has a spatial significance too, because 'humans bury...above all to humanize the ground on which they build their worlds and found their histories'. Fundamentally, being human 'is a way of being mortal and relating to the dead'; which is also our route to humanizing place: 'to be human means above all to bury'.[98]

These concerns—the spatial and temporal dimensions of burial, and its ecological significance in a framework of cultural rapprochement—are prominent in Savoy's *Trace*, where, again, the most powerful motif is that of burial, and the theme of honouring one's ancestors, a central strand that draws together her treatments of geology, place, belonging, and power. Sometimes these things are linked by a process of analogy, and sometimes through a more literal or metonymic process. In her consideration of heritage tourism Savoy finds the story of slavery often unrecorded, or quietly suppressed (p. 109); and a defining moment occurs on her visit to 'Walnut Grove Plantation, in Spartanburg County... one of South Carolina's heritage sites' (p. 89). At the Walnut Grove Cemetery there are marked and elaborate graves commemorating the family elders, Charles and Mary Moore, and their family. Savoy then chokes on a realization: 'turning back, we paused. Unnoticed at first, angular rocks spread like stepping-stones beyond the footpath, through an understory tangle of leaf litter and vinca.

---

[95] Robert Pogue Harrison, *The Dominion of the Dead* (Chicago: University of Chicago Press, 2003), p. ix.
[96] Ibid., p. x.   [97] Ibid., p. xi.   [98] Ibid., p. xi.

One...two...three...four...I stopped counting at thirty' (p. 89). The guide confirms her suspicion: 'some fieldstones mark the graves of family slaves'. This realization elicits a visceral response from Savoy: 'walking by so many untended, unnamed graves I felt as if part of me lay beneath fieldstones, buried by a whitewashed past' (p. 91). The sense of historical erasure is still more keenly felt at the burying ground at Deerfield, western Massachusetts, 'colonial New England's north-westernmost frontier settlement' for 'several decades' (p. 103). Here, 'of three centuries of stone markers at the burying ground, not one is known to stand over the grave of an African American' (p. 105), despite 'the long presence of people of African ancestry who helped build the community' (p. 104). Such 'silence', as Savoy says of Walnut Grove's burying grounds, 'seemed to belie the enslaver's power to extract work without consent from the enslaved. Not just work, but blood, breath, life itself' (p. 111).

This disregard inherent in the semi-concealed exercise of power, but which is revealed by the discovery of inadequate memorial sites, requires an ethical response that is necessarily prior to Leopold's land ethic (in which humanity is seen as just another member of the ecological community), and more focused on oppression than N. Scott Momaday's (in which indigenous wisdom is the guarantor of an ethical regard for the land). What Savoy takes from these 'burying grounds' is the realization 'that each of us is implicated in locating the past-to-present', charged with 'the task...to uncover the strata of securing language and acts, of meanings shrouded over generations' (p. 113). Savoy's excavation of the personal past begins with her genealogical search, a difficult process because of the scanty records. Giving the process of excavation a metaphorical dimension—which is central to Savoy's writing method, to unleash the associated freedom of psychological growth—is hampered by the literal dishonouring revealed in the burial sites. The task, then, is to find a way of 'honoring the lives of those so often unacknowledged by taking responsibility for the past-in-present' (p. 113), a necessary precursor to any meaningful land ethic. This undertaking involves another notable instance of ecomimetic enactment—the distinctive blending of the literal with the textual or metaphorical, with an emphasis on grounding, on the *earth*. In this sense the *humus* is literally claimed for us by the dead, and simultaneously understood to inspire the culture of sustainable inhabitation. For Harrison, Western burial bridges nature and culture, and this is the germ of its ecological significance: 'human bodies, when they perish, share in [the] organic afterlife of the dead....human culture, unlike nature, institutes a living memory, and not just a mineral retention, of the dead'. In this way, 'culture is the condensed residue of such perpetuation, unless we prefer to think of it as the nonorganic residue-forming process itself'.[99] Of course, where organic replenishment has an

---

[99] Ibid., p. 2.

immediate beneficial environmental effect, its nonorganic metaphorical equivalent in the cultural realm needs to be consciously constructed to reveal its ecological purport; and this is what Savoy attempts in *Trace*.

Relinquishing her childhood attachment to California, Savoy concludes her book with an account of her visits to Washington DC, 'the place [her] father's kin call home' (p. 161), as well as successive visits to the Woodlawn Cemetery in Washington, 'a cemetery overgrown and eroded' (p. 179), where she knows her great-great-grandparents, Elizabeth and Edward Savoy, are buried.[100] It is an important place in itself: listed on the National Register of Historic Places, it contains 'mortal remains of some of the most prominent and noteworthy African-Americans of the last century and a half' (p. 179). The site betrays a different kind of disregard to that embodied in the burial grounds encountered earlier in the book, where perfunctory anonymous memorials—or their complete absence— signalled the exercise of the slaver's power. Here, the 'neglect may reflect many things: commitment but lack of means; amnesia or apathy; perhaps forces more complex and sinister'. But, Savoy insists, 'to preserve a burial ground is an act of remembrance'. She asks, 'at what point does a burial ground lose its sanctity?' (p. 180), a rhetorical question that promotes the honouring of ancestors as a way of contesting those 'sinister' forces of dispossession.

This historical investment in place, through the humanizing of ancestors, is the foundation of a proper land ethic, in Savoy's conception. In an earlier chapter alluded to above she remarks that 'Leopold began "The Land Ethic" with a reference to the "slave-girls" in Homer's *Odyssey*, noting that the "ethical structure of the day...had not yet been extended to human chattels"' (pp. 39–40). Savoy ponders the 'we' Leopold appeals to in his case for an extended ethics, quietly drawing our attention to the fact that the legacy of slavery in Leopold's own time and place make the collective 'we' he asserts more problematic than he is prepared to recognize. Yet, at the end of *Trace*, Savoy makes her own appropriation of Homer, to put the structure of her journey in a longer literary history. She writes: 'Odysseus said, *I belong in the place of my departure and I belong in the place that is my destination.* To reach from California, the place of my birth, to this place and deeper origins, where roots began to twine, is a belated coming home' (p. 181). In contrast to the parodic impetus of modernism—encapsulated in Joyce's domestication of Odysseus' epic homecoming in *Ulysses*—Savoy recuperates the sense of an epic sweep, that which is denied in her refusal to look at the Grand Canyon through the lens of the sublime. But the homecoming is gestural, a momentary glimpse, betrayed by Savoy's recognition that 'the past and its landscapes lie close'; they only 'linger in eroded, scattered pieces, both becoming and passing into what I am, what I think we are' (p. 181). And so we realize that this is not a true

---

[100] There is also a famous 'Woodlawn Cemetery' in the Bronx, New York.

homecoming, but merely a stage in an endless process: 'at the bank of the Potomac River I watch ripples rise, sun-jeweled for an instant, then disappear into the current. I must continue the search' (p. 181). Savoy's careful reworking of traditional texts and concepts—Leopold's 'land ethic', Kant's sublime, *Ulysses*—corresponds with Anne Raine's reading of W. E. B. Du Bois' *The Souls of Black Folk* (1903), in which his responsiveness to evocations of nature in Romantic and Victorian literature is shown to be 'compatible with, or even integral to, a critique of capitalist and racist exploitation'. In particular, it is the 'simultaneous resistance to and affinity with the Romantic tradition' that makes *Souls* 'compelling as an environmental text'. It is important to register, in that paradox of 'resistance and affinity', the crucial underlying point that the traditional forms of nature writing, left unchallenged, continue to exclude work by writers of colour.[101]

Savoy's final rhetorical strategy is to change the temporal frame by making us think about her personal dilemma of ethnic exclusion in relation to geological time. Such temporal shifts have become a feature of the literature of environmental crisis. One strategy has been to put the demise of the earth in a cosmic perspective, as Robert Bringhurst does in reminding us about current theories of the death of the Sun, on its way to becoming a supernova: 'In six billion years or thereabouts, the diameter of the sun will be about the same as the earth's orbit... Your books, your bones, your lichen-covered headstones, and your dreams will be a plasma of broken atoms.'[102] Such rhetoric often functions as a brief respite from the grim facts under scrutiny. In this case, Bringhurst's real purpose is to encourage us to accept the inevitability of the sixth mass extinction, and the death of our species, and to make this the foundation of a new mode of morality: 'let's have more meaning and less control. Let's have more truth, more birdsong, more reverential silence, and less jabber. You, your species, your entire evolutionary family, and your planet will die tomorrow. How do you want to spend today?'[103] But this paradoxical juxtaposition of temporal scales—designed to clear the head—is not the principal perspective of Savoy, for whom questions of dispossession in the past and present are primary; and her own experiment in temporality leads us away from Bringhurst's grim pessimism, and towards a different moral focus and a different kind of redemption. Harrison's work on the dead is again relevant here. He also juxtaposes 'the great span of geological time' with 'human history', which 'figures as no more than the briefest, evanescent instant'; however, he is clear that 'it is in that self-sedimenting instant that we nevertheless dwell insofar as we are human'.[104] There is no meaningful escape from human history into geological time, at least as far as a purposive reckoning with death is

---

[101] Anne Raine, 'Du Bois's Ambient Poetics: Rethinking Environmental Imagination in *The Souls of Black Folk*', *Callaloo*, 36 (2013), 2, pp. 322–41 (pp. 339, 323).
[102] Bringhurst and Zwicky, *Learning to Die*, p. 25.   [103] Ibid., p. 30.
[104] Harrison, *The Dominion of the Dead*, p. 2.

concerned. Harrison is very much against the idea of consolation in the juxtaposition of these timescales, an emphasis justified by the way we respond to ruins: 'by revealing what human building ultimately is up against – natural or geological time – ruins have a way of recalling us to the very ground of our human worlds, namely the earth, whose foundations are so solid and so reliable that they presumably will outlast any edifices that we build on them'.[105] For 'ruins' we might substitute leaning headstones in unkempt cemeteries, which intensify this perception so that (in this case) a narrower temporal juxtaposition serves to re-emphasize our frailty, rather than to offer respite from it.

Savoy's evocation of geological time suggests something of this frailty; but it has still more in common with the perspective of Jan Zwicky, in the book co-authored with Bringhurst. Zwicky puts a different complexion on these mind-expanding temporal juxtapositions by reminding us that 'industrialized humans are not destroying everything. Being will be here. Beauty will be here.' And a different kind of hope, on a temporal scale we are not accustomed to considering, might then emerge to allow us some kind of continuing empathetic link with the earth, in the knowledge 'that the earth is prodigious', and that 'after other mass extinctions, life has proliferated again'. Zwicky allows us to hope that 'perhaps there will be some new species with many of our talents and fewer of our vices'.[106]

Something of this implied planetary kinship emerges in Savoy's own rhetorical shift into the realm of geology. In her epilogue Savoy gives us another version of herself, as a graduate student fossil-hunting for evidence of 'an interval of great environmental change... 360 million years ago' (p. 183). North of the US border, a few miles from Owens's Dakobed, on the divide between southern Alberta and British Columbia, she found some unidentified fossils 'at Crowsnest Pass, on the flank of Sentry Mountain' (p. 184). These 'soft-body remains bore no compelling affinity with any other recognised organism alive or extinct', she reports. There is genuine wonder in the discovery of specimens whose 'mere existence highlighted the mysteries of life's past'. They 'were named a new genus and species', but named 'without assurance of relationship, *Incertae sedis*. Homeless. Alien' (p. 184).[107] This leads to an arresting, and intensely personal, juxtaposition of time frames: 'we – fossils and woman – arrived to meet that day in the field, a chance moment of exposure together' (p. 185). Savoy wants us to recognize that her past, like the fossils', is 'pitted by gaps left by silences stretched across generations'. But she foregrounds what is distinctive about *human* alienation, characterized 'by losses of language and voice. By human displacements.... And by dismembering narratives of who "we" are to each other in this land' (185). The analogy leads us back to recognizable human time, not least because the fossil

---

[105] Ibid., p. 3.   [106] Bringhurst and Zwicky, *Learning to Die*, p. 51.
[107] *Incertae sedis*, 'of uncertain placement', is the taxonomic term attached to species that cannot be placed because a broader set of relationships has not yet been defined.

discovery also quietly asserts Savoy's authority in place through professional accomplishment, and her role in a significant natural history find.

As we read this epilogue we descry how the motif of geology provides a frame in *Trace*, from the opening memory of the childhood trip to the Grand Canyon to this episode of scientific discovery. The 'alien' fossilized species is a clear metaphor for Savoy's own experiences, a link she makes explicitly. But it also allows her to reorientate the idea of alienation, away from the racist alien land in her father's novel—but without forgetting that connotation—and towards the spectre of a shared human alienation. Geology, in the twenty-first century, brings with it the idea of the Anthropocene, our own geological era (so posited) of human-induced mass extinction, written into the sedimented layers of our time, and which introduces a new kind of human that we observe with a kind of horrified schizophrenia (as I discussed in the Introduction): the impersonal 'geological agent', in Dipesh Chakrabarty's phrase.[108] But the definition of 'trace' Savoy wants us to remember places emphasis on a different kind of agency and process: 'Active search. Path taken', as well as 'Track or vestige of what once was' (p. 185). Savoy champions '*re-remembering*' as 'an alternative to extinction', and this is also a recognition that 'home indeed lies among the ruins and shards that surround us all' (p. 186). And it is specifically in the memorial to her father, and in the excavation of the family's past—and claim to place—that we are made to see how the dead reinvigorate the living, disavowing the impersonal aestheticization of death, and forcing us to see the environment through the lens of human time and remembered injustice.

In nature writing now, the fact of loss—of habitats and species—is a permanent presence; and this creates a mood of mourning that is another distinguishing feature of the contemporary mode. But, as we shall see in the next two chapters, it is those texts that consciously cultivate the connections between personal grief and grief in the face of extinction and environmental catastrophe that avoid the death drive. These texts, written in the paradoxical contemporary moment that obliges them to celebrate nature, while at the same time articulating a sense of bereavement for its passing, also adopt something of the dynamic that fires the paradox of grief in the literature of ethnic exclusion: they refuse impersonality, and insist on individual uncertainty, vulnerability, culpability, as the necessary components of an ethical response to a dying world.

---

[108] Chakrabarty, *The Climate of History in a Planetary Age*, p. 3.

3
Abundance

Creative reflections on nature often present images of abundance; but it is always a troubling topic. Abundance in nature can be evoked to inspire joy and reverence; but, at the same time, abundance now always brings with it the spectre of scarcity, in a more literal apprehension of the global predicament, and the travesty of the unequal distribution of resources. The extremity of these contrasting reflections stretches the principle of paradox in nature prose, the means through which apparently contradictory impulses and meanings are brought together in a layered mode of apprehension: nature prose treating of abundance is, potentially, a self-defeating form of ecomimesis, where the textual resonance leads inevitably back to a bleak comprehension of the world. Abundance, however, also connotes knowledge and understanding by association with the spiritual enlightenment of the elect in biblical parable.[1] For the secular purposes of nature prose in the Western tradition, this association produces rich effects, in which cultural knowledge (rather than spiritual certitude) is assigned the decisive role in bestowing enlightenment, a dynamic that privileges knowledge as our resource of hope in otherwise complex and enigmatic moments of deliberation.

Flight Behaviour: Abundance and Climate Change

A striking image of abundance in twenty-first century fiction is that of the monarch butterflies in Barbara Kingsolver's *Flight Behaviour* (2012), a novel that has attracted much ecocritical interest as an important climate change novel. Indeed, Greg Garrard considers *Flight Behaviour* a 'climate change masterpiece'.[2] Its importance has to do with how it presents the problem of addressing its topic, so that climate-change denial (itself a form of 'flight behaviour') is refigured in class terms, after the 2008 financial crisis. This adds a contemporaneous social dimension to the novel's central ecocritical dilemma: how to address the problem of the general political inertia about global warming and the difficulty, on a

---

[1] This topic is explored below in the section on 'Parables and Parable Effects'.
[2] Greg Garrard, 'Conciliation and Consilience: Climate Change in Barbara Kingsolver's *Flight Behaviour*', in *Handbook of Ecocriticism and Cultural Ecology*, ed. Hubert Zapf (Berlin: de Gruyter, 2016), pp. 295–312, https://www.academia.edu/39752480/Conciliation_and_Consilience_Climate_Change_in_Barbara_Kingsolvers_Flight_Behaviour (accessed 2 December 2018).

personal level, of maintaining a steady focus on bewildering, overwhelming—and in many ways *ineffable*—climatic changes.

The premise of Kingsolver's novel is that, following the actual devastation of the monarchs' usual overwintering mountain site in Mexico, after 'unprecedented rainfall' in 2010 caused 'mudslides and catastrophic flooding', the overwintering colonies are relocated to southern Appalachia.[3] In truth, the monarchs still return to their usual mountaintops in central Mexico for the winter; but the premise allows Kingsolver to imagine the sudden arrival of 'the entire migratory population of North American monarchs' in an impoverished farming community in Tennessee, a site that may be too cold for their survival, so that the prospect of the extinction of a species intersects with the competing social and cultural claims that their arrival exposes: religious, environmental, and commercial.[4] But the most significant element of the book, in relation to the motif of abundance, concerns the self-realization of the central character, Dellarobia Turnbow, whose experiences refract each of the other themes.

Dellarobia, trapped in a stifling marriage, first encounters the monarchs when she is hiking on the mountain road behind her house, on her way to an adulterous tryst. Vanity has prompted her to 'shed her glasses' (p. 3), so that the reader shares her befuddlement when she comes upon the monarchs in a forested valley. Kingsolver is able to draw out this initially inexplicable encounter, as Dellarobia struggles to focus on the strange 'brownish clumps' that hang from the trees, 'their branches droopy and bulbous', boughs 'speckled and scaly like trees covered with corn flakes' (p. 13). The myopia is metaphorical—signalling a broader concern with the failure to engage with nature (and to address the consequences of climate change)—as well as literal, so that Kingsolver puts her initial readers in Dellarobia's position of moral uncertainty. She finds the phenomenon uninterpretable, so her perception is an unmediated sensory record:

> The forest blazed with its own internal flame...The sun slipped out by another degree, passing its warmth across the land, and the mountain seemed to explode with light. Brightness of a new intensity moved up the valley in a rippling wave, like the disturbed surface of a lake. Every bough glowed with an orange blaze.
>
> (p. 14)

---

[3] Barbara Kingsolver, *Flight Behaviour* (London: Faber & Faber, 2012), 'Author's Note', p. 435. Subsequent references are given in parentheses.

[4] Kingsolver is concerned with the eastern population of North American monarchs. However, there is also a western population in California, which overwinters along the Pacific coast. See Kurt Johnson and Steve Coates, *Nabokov's Blues: The Scientific Odyssey of a Literary Genius* (Cambridge, Mass.: Zoland Books, 1999), pp. 235–8. Concerning the eastern population at their overwintering site in central Mexico, Johnson and Coates observe: 'the clustering butterflies, in the millions, make one of nature's most breathtakingly beautiful sights' (p. 236).

This passage demonstrates clearly how a contemporary response to natural abundance can still echo Romanticism's sublime, in combining wonder with awe, fear with trepidation: contemporary nature prose often reclaims the sublime, as we saw in Chapter 2, most notably in Lauret Savoy's exposure of its racist underpinnings. Here the sublime is invested with another new connotation, signalling ultimate fear in the unimaginable consequences of climate catastrophe. Dellarobia struggles for natural metaphors to explain this 'lake of fire', which is 'far more fierce and wondrous than either of those elements alone' (p. 16). Deciding that the 'burning trees were put here to save her', Dellarobia abandons the tryst and returns to her family. Sharing her sense of divine intervention, her church community is persuaded that she has had some kind of vision that foretold of the arrival of the butterflies (pp. 70–1). In one sense, she *is* 'saved' by the experience: her involvement with the team of entomologists that comes to Tennessee to study the monarchs leads eventually to her (amicable) planned separation from her husband, in order to undertake the college study she had been unable to pursue when she fell pregnant in high school. The ending, however, casts doubt on this felicitous outcome: as we shall see, nature displaces the social theme.[5]

This is not, in any case, a simple story of class mobility through education. The scientific understanding of the abundance is complex, requiring us to adjust our understanding as we read. Ovid Byron, the lepidopterist who has devoted his professional career to studying the monarchs, explains the substance of Dellarobia's vision: it comprises 'a significant proportion of the entire North American monarch butterfly population'—most of the migratory population, in fact, so that the probable demise of this colony (of more than fifteen million) indicates 'a continental ecosystem breaking down' (pp. 258, 354). Ovid sees his task in impersonal terms, to gather evidence of how 'climate change has disrupted this system' before the species (and the evidence) disappears (pp. 228–9). Dellarobia, however, is apt to see things in more personal terms, and this also involves a series of readjustments. Initially, she is resentful of Ovid's explanation of the monarchs' arrival as an unnatural event: 'why did the one rare, spectacular thing in her life have to be a sickness of nature?' The scientists, she feels, have made them 'theirs' (p. 149). Later, she recognizes the folly of 'wanting the butterflies to be hers alone', a self-serving response mirrored in the deluded local plans for a monarch theme park of some kind (p. 255). As a lab assistant, she comes to understand and respect the importance of the science, and she learns to adopt a more impersonal demeanour; but when Dellarobia understands that Ovid has arrived at the dire prognosis for the monarchs, she reflects on the

---

[5] I am aware that a flood caused by climate change could be seen as 'culturally' produced. This is a matter of emphasis; but, as rehearsed in the discussion of the term 'nature' in the Introduction, ultimately it seems to me a false appropriation to consider such climatic events as cultural, rather than as a sign of nature damaged.

personal significance it has for *him*, having 'chased this life for all his years'. His 'grief' makes us reflect on the paradox of the human investment in nature, always inclining towards the egotistical and the proprietary, even in seemingly disinterested activities (p. 229).

As all of this suggests, the fact of the monarchs' abundance allows Kingsolver to convey a series of changing perceptions. From Dellarobia's initial awe-inspiring visionary moment, the presence of the monarchs becomes oppressive, emphasizing for us their jeopardy. Dellarobia initially finds it hard to adopt the unsentimental view of the scientists, disturbed by the abundance, which is now an abundance of death rather than burning visionary light:

> The ground was completely covered with flattened bodies lying every which way, like a strange linoleum pattern. The butterflies never lay open, as she'd seen them at rest or flying, but invariably were dead in the folded position, like praying hands. She hated walking on them, but that's what the others did. (p. 138)

The simile of the linoleum is arresting, its 'strangeness' registering both the oddity (to Dellarobia) of the scientists' lack of sentiment and the squeamishness she is learning to overcome by emulating them. As she adjusts to the demands of laboratory evidence gathering, she is introduced to various techniques and methods, including the cooking of butterfly remains, and using a powerful blender to make 'butterfly soup' for analysis (p. 217). Snow brings death to the monarchs, and the abundance of corpses now more clearly signals not the wastefulness of a natural cycle, but the eerie portent of a species' demise, as 'insect bodies lay in heaps...like mounds of withered tomatoes fallen from the vines in a failed harvest' (p. 269). The simile of the ruined crop scarcely seems adequate to register the enormity of a species' extinction; but its inadequacy serves to emphasize the failure of human imagination that preoccupies Kingsolver throughout.

A different abundance is ultimately the saviour of the monarchs. In February, those that have survived the cold discover 'abundant' numbers of harbinger flowers as a source of nectar (p. 348), so that the next stages of their complex, multigenerational migratory life cycle can continue: they mate (p. 373), then finally gather in a 'bud colony' ready to fly (pp. 420–1). Dellarobia fears there are not enough of them—not a million, and so not a big enough 'gene pool to get them through' (p. 421)—but in the closing pages, while a catastrophic flood is destroying her home, Dellarobia sees a more hopeful sight, as the surviving monarchs are forced into flight by the rising waters: 'the vivid blur of their reflections glowed on the rumpled surface of the water, not clearly defined as individual butterflies but as masses of pooled, streaky color, like the sheen of floating oil, only brighter, like a lava flow. That many' (p. 433). Here, the echo of the sublime resurfaces, the re-emergence of abundant life inspiring wonder, but with the vague sense of threat signalled by the lava flow simile. Dellarobia is 'astonished' by the numbers, 'maybe a million' (p. 433). The magic number leaves survival a possibility for the monarchs, their odds 'probably no better or worse than hers', she reflects (p. 433).

I will return to the significance of the novel's ambiguous ending later in the chapter. Here I want to register the pressing contextual questions *Flight Behaviour* forces us to address—in this respect Kingsolver inevitably courts the danger of didacticism—to give a better sense of the tenor that characterizes a contemporary ecological consciousness. The novel makes the impact of climate change its central preoccupation, and this is underpinned by some thorough research.[6] The real challenge, from an environmental point of view, is to put that long-term history meaningfully into the twenty-first-century social context, and to make these two frames illuminate each other. The wider social purview for American politics— with obvious global resonances—is easily evoked by the motif of migrancy. As Christopher Lloyd and Jessica Rapson show, 'the butterflies bridge disparate geographies and cultures'.[7] More challenging is their argument that Kingsolver charts 'interactions between local and planetary environments, prompting readers to contextualise the micro – geographically bounded human experience and memory – within the macro context of the Anthropocene'.[8] This is an astute suggestion, but it may be that Kingsolver encourages us to make the connection while implicitly acknowledging the wishful impulse behind it. The attempt to reconcile 'scales of memory, knowledge, and experience' may be presented as essential and yet nigh impossible.[9]

Heather Houser's reading suggests that Kingsolver finds a way of making this connection more emphatically: her treatment of memory, knowledge, and experience make it possible to perceive a bridge between the micro political world of *Flight Behaviour* and the overwhelming macro environmental moment. Houser argues (admirably, if ambitiously) that Dellarobia becomes a version of 'Antonio Gramsci's organic intellectual', through her role in 'recovering common space out of alienation', in a presentation of how 'loss generates shared space and

---

[6] Axel Goodbody deftly summarizes the complex of 'sober scientific facts' that climate change has produced to disrupt the migratory pattern of the monarchs in the novel: 'changes on the Mexican mountainsides where they normally overwinter, drought affecting the plants they eat, an increase in pesticide spraying because global warming has brought in new mosquitos, changes in weather patterns, the northward spread of fire ants, and higher infection rates from parasites which limit their flying ability'. See Axel Goodbody, 'Risk, Denial and Narrative Form in Climate Change Fiction: Barbara Kingsolver's *Flight Behaviour* and Ilija Trojanow's *Melting Ice*', in *The Anticipation of Catastrophe: Environmental Risk in North American Literature and Culture*, ed. S. Mayer and A. Weik von Mossner (Heidelberg: Universitätsverlag Winter, 2014), pp. 39–58, https://purehost.bath.ac.uk/ws/portalfiles/portal/123429557 (accessed 12 February 2018).

[7] Christopher Lloyd and Jessica Rapson, '"Family Territory" to the "Circumference of the Earth": Local and Planetary Memories of Climate Change in Barbara Kingsolver's *Flight Behaviour*', *Textual Practice*, 31 (2017), 5, pp. 911–31 (p. 917).

[8] Ibid., p. 911. [9] Ibid., pp. 924, 926.

experiential knowledge that serve environmentalist goals'.[10] Partly, this is a question of unpacking the gender-based cultural misapprehension of nature, that 'powerful, pervasive trope that equates maternity with care for and closeness to the earth'. Dellarobia's work as a lab assistant 'revises her labor position' so that the reversal of 'environmental estrangement' in her case 'occurs because she seeks escape from wifedom and motherhood'.[11] Crucial to this argument is that a recuperation of 'the commons', now conceived as 'a threatened space that is productive for knowledge work', foregrounds cooperation, and especially the integration of 'local and expert intelligences'.[12] The key moment here involves the salvation of the monarchs: to find winter food for the monarchs, Dellarobia turns to her mother-in-law Hester's botanical knowledge, for it is Hester who identifies the 'late winter flowers necessary for the insects' survival'.[13] This is a vital aspect of the way the book requires us to re-evaluate the oppressive matriarch Hester, as she comes to occupy the heart of local knowledge and potential. Yet this is another equivocal instance of hope: Hester's memory and knowledge of local flora, rooted in a lifetime's experience of this locale, explains the source of the monarchs' possible survival. But it has no causal role to play in this (perhaps) felicitous outcome: the monarchs find the harbingers for themselves.

The signification of the abundant monarchs shifts, then, as the novel unfolds. Initially they are taken by Dellarobia as a sign of wonder, and a form of divine intervention, leading her back to a path of conventional moral rectitude. Through the lens of scientific understanding—which is the novel's mimetic framework—they signal ecological collapse; yet the final image of their abundance connotes resilience, a natural resilience that is serendipitous, and quite independent of human interference: the monarchs may survive, while the human protagonist is left to face a flood of catastrophic proportions. The flood is biblical, in fact, denoting the consequences of our environmental 'sins'. The swarming insects, too, have biblical connotations, evoking terror and retribution. These cultural echoes of terrifying abundance are opposed by the scientific appreciation of abundance in nature, and the unceasing—though ineffectual—effort to help put things back in kilter. These resonances lend certain qualities of parable to Kingsolver's novel, notably in the interplay between the pursuit of knowledge and the spectre of extinction connoted by abundance gone awry. It is a setting of contemporary anxiety; but it restages some of the established—and paradoxical— aspects of biblical parable.

---

[10] Heather Houser, 'Knowledge Work and the Commons in Barbara Kingsolver's and Ann Pancake's Appalachia', *Modern Fiction Studies*, 63 (2017), 1, pp. 95–115 (p. 96).
[11] Ibid., p. 102.   [12] Ibid., p. 106.   [13] Ibid., pp. 111–12.

Parables and Parable Effects

This contemporary anxiety about abundance is anticipated and succinctly condensed in the Parable of the Talents, and the servant who fails to invest (Matthew 25:14–30).[14] In the parable, a man entrusts his goods to his servants, according to their ability: five 'talents' are given to one servant, two to another, and one to another (the unfortunate member of the retinue). The servant with five talents trades with them and doubles his tally; the servant with two talents achieves the same result, gaining another two. The servants' lord, returning from his travels, is happy with the prudence of these two; but not with the unfortunate final servant, who, fearful of losing the single talent entrusted to him, has hidden it in the earth. His master takes the talent from him and gives it to the servant who has doubled his tally to ten, with this resonant judgement: 'For unto every one that hath shall be given, and he shall have abundance: but from him that hath not shall be taken away even that which he hath' (Matthew 25:29).[15]

In a crude capitalist model, this parable may seem to convey a message about prudent investment, wealth accruing wealth (and the devil take the hindmost). Of course, as Jesus explains to the disciples in an earlier verse—using the same language about abundance—the intent of the parables concerns a different kind of wealth: spiritual enlightenment for his followers. Jesus does not explain the parables to those who fail to hear or to see—indeed, the parables seem designed to enshrine the dichotomy between the elect and the others. There is no effort of conversion to enable others to share the ability of the disciples to redouble their wisdom: 'For whosoever hath, to him shall be given, and he shall have more abundance: but whosoever hath not, from him shall be taken away even that he hath' (Matthew 13:12).[16] This *opacity* as a defining quality of parable will be significant in the discussion throughout this chapter. Yet, if 'abundance' is a spiritual capacity that lends itself to exponential growth, in this originating biblical conception (at least for the elect) it has proved difficult to disentangle from its more literal connotations, not least, perhaps, because these parables in Matthew are dominated by agricultural and food metaphors (the Parables of the Sower, the Mustard Seed, and the Yeast; Matthew 13:18–43).[17]

Andrew Pearse, evaluating the effect of international policies on global agriculture from the perspective of the 1970s, saw precisely this more literal resonance. Pearse presents the Parable of the Talents as, in effect, an allegory for the failed 'Green Revolution', the international programme pursued from 1940

---

[14] I do not presume to enter the lists of biblical scholarship and interpretation, here, but rather to highlight a quality of this parable that has a direct relevance to what I call the 'parable effect' in contemporary nature prose.
[15] *The New Cambridge Paragraph Bible*, ed. David Norton (Cambridge: Cambridge University Press, 2005), p. 1582. There is a similar parable in Luke 19:11–27 (ibid., p. 1648).
[16] Ibid., p. 1564.   [17] Ibid., pp. 1564–5.

through to the 1960s 'aimed at increasing the productivity of land by means of a science-based technology... in the production of foodgrains'.[18] What Pearse calls the 'talents-effect' counted against the 'small tenant cultivators in Malaysia, the Philippines, Indonesia, Sri Lanka, and even India', often peasants who were unable to compete with 'agriculturalists' or the 'local élite': for the peasant, like the servant burying his single talent in the parable, 'the economic fragility of his enterprise due to his penurious supply of land' turned 'the excellent agronomic potential of the new technology into an indifferent bargain', making 'low-cost technology' a 'safer option'.[19] The 'talents-effect' is a disastrous and unintended consequence of international development, by which inequality was exacerbated rather than ameliorated.

In the modern era of ecological consciousness, it is impossible (morally speaking) not to think of abundance in terms of global food inequality, so that abundance and plenty must evoke want, scarcity, and famine. This is partly, as we have seen, because of the counterproductive consequences of the Green Revolution (continued by initiatives in international development since the 1960s), which left 'unsustainable monocultures and ecological destruction in its wake'.[20] Considered from an ecological standpoint, abundance is a chimera, as world agriculture is stretched by the twin pressures of population growth (even if global birth rates are slowing) and climate change.[21] It is not just that rising temperatures will reduce dramatically the available arable land: the 'ultimate irony', as Joel Bourne puts it, is that agriculture is one of the most significant contributors to greenhouse gas emissions, so that 'we are literally farming ourselves out of food'.[22] In this context, it is hard to invest reflections on abundance with anything other than the starkest literalism.

As this chapter progresses, I'll be trying to retrieve abundance from this bleak setting—without losing sight of the urgent context it behoves us to address—by reflecting on the rhetorical resonances, as well as the formal and stylistic implications of abundance, characteristics which can reinvigorate our engagement with that urgent global context. Images of abundance in nature are not confined to the paradigm of subsistence, of course (though they may often lead us back to it), and they are often presented with a rhetorical intent to engage the reader profoundly.

---

[18] Andrew Pearse, *Seeds of Plenty, Seeds of Want: Social and Economic Implications of the Green Revolution* (Oxford: Oxford University Press, 1980), p. 1. Pearse quotes Matthew 25:29 in his introduction (p. 5).
[19] Ibid., pp. 166–7.
[20] Joel K. Bourne, *The End of Plenty: The Race to Feed a Crowded World* (New York: W. W. Norton, 2015), p. 12.
[21] The 2019 revision of the UN's 'World Population Prospects' suggests that the global birth rate is in a state of steady decline, a trend which will continue towards 2100, so that the total global population may start to fall at the turn of new century; https://population.un.org/wpp/ (accessed 26 May 2021). This does not immediately alter our perspective of global food inequality and the chimera of abundance, of course.
[22] Bourne, *The End of Plenty*, p. 18.

This is one way in which the sense of abundance has been reconfigured from the Parable of the Talents: the effort of conversion/persuasion, apparently absent from the prophet's work (though perhaps enshrined in the text), is undeniably apparent in the contemporary desire to widen appreciation of nature's bounty by means of an aesthetic or secular-spiritual response.[23] And yet the fullest appreciation of the significance of abundance also requires a comprehension of real-world finitude, of the fragility of the nonhuman, because the most overwhelming images of abundance usually signal something awry in the ecosphere.

The instances of nature prose considered here, however, operate by cultivating literary effects, and—in treating the topic of abundance—they frequently borrow something from parable for their secular contexts. I am not speaking here of *stories* in the sense that parables are contained stories requiring (and usually resisting) interpretation. Rather, I am concerned with *moments* that have the air of belonging to a parable, moments in which the idea of abundance evokes the originating biblical parable setting in which abundance signals knowledge and enlightenment, or their absence. These 'parable effects', as I shall call them, make us consider how actual natural abundance might inspire sudden insight, or personal growth, or a surfeit of 'abundant' knowledge: as with the parables in the Gospels, the literal referent is in some ways supplanted by the hidden knowledge it can inspire, when fully understood by those attuned to its meaning. This knowledge is not always welcome or celebratory—it may, rather, be cautionary, or even overwhelming. These parable effects are orientated towards secular reflection, but the distinction between religious and secular parable is not easy to make, for technical reasons that are considered below. And the examples themselves often obscure the distinction. In the case of Annie Dillard, as we shall see, the parable effects are integrated within a carefully designed Christian structure, even though their ongoing relevance for secular readings is indisputable. Even without the structures of organized religion, parable effects flowing from accounts of natural abundance can imply some kind of spiritual insight, or pantheistic understanding of the nonhuman environment.

Often the artful presentation of images of natural abundance create parable effects by making them lead to some form of insight or revelation that may be ineffable, or obscure, blurring the secular/religious dichotomy still further. In J. Hillis Miller's suggestive account of the distinction between secular and religious forms of parable, the emphasis is on the inexpressible, in both forms. For Hillis Miller, parable, whether in literature or in scripture, is 'a mode of figurative language which is the indirect indication, at a distance, of something that cannot

---

[23] Frank Kermode offers an overview of biblical scholarship concerning the translations of the parables in the Gospels, the difference between Mark and Matthew, and the extent to which Jesus is more forgiving in the latter. See *The Genesis of Secrecy: On the Interpretation of Narrative* (Cambridge, Mass.: Harvard University Press, 1979), pp. 28–47

be described directly, in literal language'.[24] In the case of the parables of Jesus, this gap between the literal referents and their 'spiritual or transcendent meaning' is bridged in the figure of 'Christ as Logos', the basis of 'the correspondence between visible vehicle and invisible and unnamed tenor in a parable'. Jesus, for believers— accepted as the Son of God—is the guarantor of the 'correspondence between his realistic narrative of sowing, fishing, or household care and those unseeable things of which the parable "really" speaks'. There is no such guarantee in secular parables, for their authors 'are down here with us', dependent on a more haphazard method through which 'their words about things visible can only be thrown beside things invisible in the hope that their narratives of what can be spoken about... will magically make appear the other invisible, perhaps imaginary, line to which their realistic stories, they hope, correspond'.[25]

The difficulty identified here, in the lack of authority in secular parable, can be sidestepped to a degree by considering the rhetorical intention and effect of *all* parable, approached as a 'speech act', so that in the parables of Jesus 'the performative word makes something happen in the minds and hearts of the hearers'. However, since 'this happening is a knowledge of a state of affairs already existing'—that is, 'the kingdom of heaven and the way to get there'—'a biblical parable is constative, not performative at all'. By contrast, secular parable is 'a genuine performative', because 'it creates something, a "meaning", that has no basis except in the words... a meaning based only on the language itself and on our confidence in it'.[26] The parable effects in nature prose are 'effects' partly because they resist the confines of textuality. They trade on the authority of 'abundance' as given wisdom or religious insight in biblical parable, but also, in a paradoxical manoeuvre, on the implicit *refusal* of the predetermination of this knowledge in their cultivation of the performative linguistic attributes of secular parable. These parable effects function through a dual operation by foregrounding the performative, the vital capacity to bring something new into existence, but with a nostalgic echo of absent divine authority to be appropriated. In so doing, they invite us to engage with the experiences of insight and revelation inspired by real-world events, encouraging us to build the gestural bridge to reality that the contextual circumstance demands. Occasionally this insight is inspired not by real-world events but by imagined events connected to experience; but, either way, the urgency of conservation (broadly understood) demands that we build that bridge. In the examples considered in this chapter, instances of abundance in nature allow us to glimpse, and try to grasp, an 'abundant' knowledge about the complex ecological predicament, effects replete with an urgency intensified by the authority of biblical echo. Yet these parable effects also depend on a progression

---

[24] J. Hillis Miller, *Tropes, Parables, Performatives: Essays on Twentieth-Century Literature* (Hemel Hempstead: Harvester, 1990), p. 135.
[25] Ibid., p. 137.   [26] Ibid., p. 139.

beyond the enclosed textuality of their biblical sources. The fundamental problem with biblical parables that I mentioned earlier—that they are presented not to convert non-believers, but to reinforce the faith of the disciples—means, as Hillis Miller puts it, 'the parables are posited on their own inefficacy', because 'if you have knowledge of the kingdom of heaven already, you do not need them', and 'if you do not have that knowledge, you will not understand the parables anyhow'. They do not generate new knowledge, they merely reinforce existing knowledge, and so are 'superfluous, a superabundance'.[27] My contention, to put it simply, is that the parable effects of nature prose gesture towards an abundance of knowledge (rather than a superabundance) precisely through the immediate correspondence of different conceptions of abundance—the literal examples from nature provoking or inspiring the metaphorical abundance of new understanding.[28]

Abundance and the Emergence of Environmental Consciousness

Abundant knowledge in this conception allows for the shifting and evolving bases of scientific understanding: indeed, abundance in this connection is also the burden of elusive comprehension, never finally reached. This potentially burdensome abundance—quite different from Hillis Miller's superfluous super-abundance, and overwhelming in its complexity but also in the responsibility it behoves us to embrace—has some relationship to the difficulty of grappling with the 'hyperobjects' of which Timothy Morton writes.[29] This paradoxical complexity is the marker of a distinctively contemporary world view, where literal and metaphorical conceptions of abundance/knowledge are welded together in a peculiarly tense relationship. But can we detect the moment of origin for this contemporary conceptualization? As a rough exercise in mapping out this chronology, but also to suggest the imaginary basis to which twenty-first-century writing responds, I will consider some examples of natural abundance in earlier twentieth-century writing.

In his autobiography, Leo Walmsley recalls an episode from July 1914 when he was fishing by moonlight with some friends on the beach at Robin Hood's Bay, on

---

[27] Ibid., p. 140.
[28] Readers of Hillis Miller may think I am escaping the linguistic loop too easily, and I acknowledge that I am not exploring the full implications of his argument that 'both kinds of parable', biblical and secular, 'tend to be parables about parable' (ibid., p. 139). His account of the paradoxical self-containment of parable, both in its own procedures and in the discourse of its commentators, is well illustrated in his discussion of Kafka (ibid., pp. 145–7). My conviction is that the urgency of the ecological crisis forces our attention away from contained textuality.
[29] Global warming is the most problematic example of these ungraspable things 'massively distributed in time and space relative to humans'. See Timothy Morton, *Hyperobjects: Philosophy and Ecology after the End of the World* (Minneapolis: University of Minnesota Press, 2013), p. 1.

the North Yorkshire coast. They make an astonishing discovery where the rock formation has formed a natural trap for sprats, forced ashore by larger predatory fish:

> For at least twenty yards above the end of the creek there lay a solid mass of dead or practically dead sprats, looking in the moonlight exactly like an immense snowdrift: and from the water's edge outwards, the creek was literally boiling with them and bigger fish. We saw one, it was either a billet or a cod, drive into the mass and shoot straight out of the water on to the shallow scaur and lie there stunned for a few seconds before jerking back into the water.[30]

Descriptive without being evaluative, Walmsley's prose registers the inevitable death of the trapped fish in his snowdrift simile, water in an inert state; but he watches with the hunter's opportunistic eye. The friends' attempts to catch the larger fish with line and hook are to no avail, because the fish are behaving erratically: 'they were mad. Time after time they were rushing practically ashore with half of their bodies out of the water. And *we* got slightly mad before too long.'[31] Pragmatic urgency in the text then ousts any lingering reflection on this infectious insanity, and—abandoning the conventions of angling—Walmsley utilizes 'a piece of old salmon net' to make the catch. The friends manoeuvre the net, 'wading through living sprats', and drag it 'not ... quite to the shore', as the net contains 'at least a hundredweight of fish'. For Walmsley, it is a once-in-a-lifetime catch in a native place: 'I have never seen anything like that haul. There were billets and codling by the dozen, but more exciting still, there were salmon trout (one a beauty of about four pounds) and there were flatfish, a real sole, plaice, dabs, flounders, and one big conger, only this managed to escape.'[32] Walmsley's naïve enthusiasm, the mood in which the fact of freak abundance is received without question, allows him to present this episode as an auspicious portent, with the three friends looking forward to their future ventures. Even though Walmsley is writing retrospectively, on the cusp of war, the tenor is not melancholy in connection with personal destiny.[33] As a piece of regional writing, it takes its place in Walmsley's complex nostalgic recreation of inshore fishing in North Yorkshire; but from the perspective of the 1940s there is no sense of foreboding about the depletion of fish in the North Sea.

A strikingly similar episode is recounted in Gavin Maxwell's *Ring of Bright Water*, occurring in the early 1950s towards the beginning of his years at Sandaig/Camusfeàrna. He is disturbed from his reading by a rumpus from the beach, caused by the twin sons of a neighbouring family, thigh-deep in the shallow water, 'edged with yellow' in the evening light:

---

[30] Leo Walmsley, *So Many Loves: An Autobiography* (London: Collins, 1944), p. 107.
[31] Ibid., p. 108. [32] Ibid., p. 109. [33] Ibid., p. 110.

They were shouting and laughing and dancing and scooping up the water with their hands, and all the time as they moved there shot up from the surface where they broke it a glittering spray of small gold and silver fish, so dense and brilliant as to blur the outline of the childish figures. It was as though the boys were the central décor of a strangely lit baroque fountain, and when they bent to the surface with cupped hands a new jet of sparks flew upward where their arms submerged, and fell back in brittle, dazzling cascade.[34]

The quality of the writing, perhaps more literary than Walmsley's above, fully deserves the praise Kathleen Jamie bestows upon *Ring of Bright Water* in her delighted, serendipitous encounter with his work.[35] What we might remark upon here is the way Maxwell subtly introduces a note of unease as he struggles to interpret the inexplicable: the boys are like carved figures in a resplendent scene of the human harnessing of nature (the baroque fountain), and this discordant effort to make sense of a wild scene is unnerving, making the laughter and the dancing redolent of some transgression, or—because these are boys—of some misapprehended danger. Maxwell enters the sea, 'like wading in silver treacle', and finds the boys' response to 'the packed mass of little fish' infectious:

To scoop and to scatter them, to shout and to laugh, were as irresistible as though we were treasure hunters of old who had stumbled upon a fabled emperor's jewel vaults and threw diamonds about us like chaff. We were fish-drunk, fish-crazy, fish-happy in that shining orange bubble of air and water.[36]

Now Maxwell is also under the spell, sharing in the madness, the natural abundance transformed in his mind's eye to a different kind of material abundance, evocative of human greed, but also of a cautionary fairy tale in which the actors' transgressive delight is a gasp away from mortal threat. After a few minutes Maxwell reflects on this circumstance, and looks out to sea, where at a hundred yards' distance he observes 'flurries of mackerel' that have 'driven the fry headlong before them into the narrow bay'; but the mackerel, too, have been 'harried from seaward by a school of porpoises who cruised the outermost limit of their shoals', and the 'porpoises' return to the open waters of the sound' has, in turn, been cut off by a bull killer whale, 'his single terrible form controlling by its mere presence the billions of lives between himself and the shore'.[37]

Maxwell makes the best practical use of this glut, gathering buckets of fry and keeping them as cool as he can 'in the heat of that sunny September'. But he

---

[34] Maxwell, *Ring of Bright Water*, p. 55.
[35] Kathleen Jamie, 'Diary', *London Review of Books*, 33: 14, 14 July 2011, pp. 38–9, https://www.lrb.co.uk/v33/n14/kathleen-jamie/diary (accessed 21 January 2018).
[36] Maxwell, *Ring of Bright Water*, p. 55. [37] Ibid., pp. 55–6.

laments that 'when heaven sends bounty it too often sends monotony'. The 'delight and novelty' of 'the first meal of fried whitebait' rapidly diminish, so that 'the sixth and seventh were cloying'. The arrival of a guest inspires invention, and the windfall is made into 'fish-cakes and fish-pies, into kedgerees and fish-soups, into curries and savouries', until 'one merciful morning' when the buckets of fry 'began to smell' and could be discarded. Travelling to Inverness soon after, he encounters fried whitebait on a hotel menu, and is obliged to leave 'as might one who had perceived a corpse beneath his table'.[38]

A comparison with the similar experience recounted by Walmsley is instructive, chiefly because the wider implications of the glut of fish in Walmsley's autobiography are not considered, other than a parallel with a similarly prodigious catch he witnesses in Senegal, and the general excitement surrounding it, which prompt the reflection that 'fishermen all over the world had something in common'.[39] One has to acknowledge that, in the extracts above, Walmsley's writing is not as well crafted as Maxwell's. But he did write some arresting fiction—and fictionalized 'non-fiction'—in which the topic of fishing is central to his achievements as a regional writer, and also to his moral compass.[40] Walmsley's recollection of the sudden abundance of fish chimes in some ways with his ongoing delight in fishing, the heroism of fisherfolk, and also with his determination to embrace the future with his own brand of internationalism, rooted in primitive kinship. Yet, from a contemporary perspective, he does not seem to make a full or adequate response to the 'snowdrift' of sprats he witnessed in 1914 (and recollected in 1944).

In the Maxwell episode there is a different tenor, and this comparison needs to be approached with a simple historical question in mind: what has happened between 1914/1944 and Maxwell's account of the same freak event occurring in the early 1950s and recorded in 1960? The 'fish-drunk, fish-crazy, fish-happy' actors in the Maxwell scene inhabit a moment of forewarning, as if flouting some interdiction in a folk or fairy tale. The euphoria brings a kind of curse in its wake when Maxwell reflects on the series of predators that have produced this 'silver treacle': the small fry, then the 'flurries of mackerel', then a 'school of porpoises', driven shorewards, in turn, with a single 'bull killer whale' presiding ominously over this catastrophe of predation gone wrong, or, more accurately, predation blindly following its opportunities. The terrible form of the whale, controlling 'the billions of lives between himself and the shore', is an ominous symbol of needless death, and the end of abundance, all figured in Maxwell's account of (enforced) conspicuous consumption, and the disgust it generates, so that it was 'two years

---

[38] Ibid., pp. 56–7.   [39] Walmsley, *So Many Loves*, p. 163.
[40] There is also a powerful celebration of British fishermen in Walmsley's personal account of the role they played in the Second World War, including the rescue from Dunkirk. See Leo Walmsley, *Fishermen at War* (London: Collins, 1941), p. 256.

before [he] could eat whitebait again'.[41] The episode is presented with the economy of a parable, but it is a parable of abundance as a portent of dearth.

Rachel Carson's *Silent Spring* (1962) is usually seen as marking a turning point in international environmental consciousness, its account of the effect of pesticides on bird populations having wider implications for the impact of human action on fragile ecosystems. *Ring of Bright Water* predates *Silent Spring* by a couple of years, and it covertly contributes to the same moment of changing consciousness, its nature writing conventions taking on a new hue, so that—to pursue the current example—the spectacle of abundance is inevitably tinged with the spectre of its opposite: scarcity produced by human need/greed. This is not to say that, in or around 1960, ecological consciousness was instantly born. More generally, the notional date of 1960 as the beginning of our contemporary ecological perspective needs some qualification. The organic movement in Britain certainly predates this—the Soil Association was founded in 1946, but with earlier pre-Second World War roots, so the context for nature prose throughout the twentieth century was imbued with ecological ideas that would provide a legacy for the contemporary view. Notable nature writers such as H. J. Massingham were centrally involved in the organic movement, for example.[42] A contemporary ecological perspective from the 1990s onwards goes beyond roots of this kind, and is informed by the emergence of scientific knowledge that would later instruct our understanding of human impact in the Anthropocene, concerning the long-term effects of pesticides, PCBs, CFCs, radioactive waste, and so on, and (crucially) the relationship between human activity and climate change. But the emergence of the sensibility that informs this contemporary perspective can be discerned in this comparison of Walmsley and Maxwell. It's an imperfect line in the sand; but it seems that, in their respective attitudes to the crucial topic of abundance—in these extraordinary manifestations of it—Maxwell is writing on the cusp of the new, ecological world view, while Walmsley (in the work quoted here) inhabits an earlier moment of innocence.

What I am trying to locate is a shift, a wider understanding—perceived as a generational event—of human culpability. The evolution of Maxwell as a nature writer is an illuminating component of this paradigm shift, as well as an indication of social change. Born into the landed gentry, Maxwell moved away from the culture of hunting—epitomized in his failed 1940s venture in shark fishing, based

---

[41] Maxwell, *Ring of Bright Water*, p. 57. The extravagant estimate is doubtless accurate: shoals of herring 'have been reported in sizes of one cubic mile, containing several billion individual fish'; http://britishseafishing.co.uk/herring/ (accessed 9 February 2018).

[42] Philip Conford, *The Origins of the Organic Movement* (Edinburgh: Floris Books, 2001). This work provoked much debate about the continuity between the early days of the organic movement and its rapid development from the 1970s onwards, a topic that Conford takes up in a later book, *The Development of the Organic Network: Linking People and Themes, 1945-1995* (Edinburgh: Floris Books, 2011).

on the Isle of Soay.[43] As we saw in Chapter 1, Maxwell's change in consciousness began in 1956, according to his biographer Douglas Botting, during a trip with Wilfred Thesiger to the region of the Marsh Arabs in Iraq, an expedition that brought home to Maxwell the misery of human and animal suffering in a harsh environment. Botting suggests that Maxwell extrapolated something emblematic of 'the very system of God's creation itself' from this experience, a bleak vision stemming from the indifference of natural abundance and the contemplation of 'the sheer prodigality of destruction all around him'.[44] It seems to have been a shift centred on the desire to protect individual creatures—or, more in the character of the modern conservationist-naturalist, to champion specific species—in defiance of the indifferent abundant natural order, and the 'prodigality of destruction' at its heart.

Cultural Memory

It is little more than half a century since the emergence in nature prose of an ecological consciousness, as I am defining it here; but even within this short time frame the difficulty of preserving memories that can be mobilized for the purposes of conservation is a pressing topic for nature writers. The configuration of memory in relation to an observer's lifetime can have a devastating impact in nature prose, and especially in understanding the implications of abundance and its loss.

Lloyd and Rapson, in the essay cited above, draw attention to the importance of memory in Kingsolver's *Flight Behaviour*, and especially to the relevance of scholarly attempts 'to raise questions about interconnections between memory and ecology'. In this respect, memory can become a mobilizing force, as in Sebastian Groes's important question about how it can 'be made to be more useful in our conceptualization of climate change, and, perhaps, be used to assuage the impact of climate change, and generate genuine ecocritical mindfulness in our collective consciousness'.[45] But Kingsolver problematizes this resource in the crucial episode of the monarchs' survival when local lore, in the form of Hester's memory of the abundant harbinger flowers, seems to illustrate the human capacity for informed intervention; yet, as we have seen, the knowledge is superfluous because the monarchs find the harbingers, a species-saving food source in this instance, for themselves. Remembered knowledge is thus put in its

---

[43] See Maxwell, *Harpoon at a Venture*.   [44] Botting, *Gavin Maxwell*, p. 183.
[45] Lloyd and Rapson, '"Family Territory" to the "Circumference of the Earth"', p. 924. See Sebastian Groes, 'Introduction to Part III: Ecologies of Memory', in *Memory in the Twenty-First Century: New Critical Perspectives from the Arts, Humanities, and Sciences*, ed. Sebastian Groes (London: Palgrave Macmillan, 2016), pp. 140–6 (p. 140).

place: we sense its importance as a resource, but we also recognize that natural processes are more powerful than human intervention.

In the British context, one of the most powerful mobilizing memories of abundance occurs in Michael McCarthy's *The Moth Snowstorm* (2015), a representative work of new nature writing in the way it interweaves its evocation of nature with autobiography, so that the author's coming-to-terms with his mother's death, but also with the impact of her mental health on his early family life, is achieved by refiguring his lifelong interest in butterflies, which in childhood had been a form of displacement, a means of disengaging from the emotions consequent upon his mother's illness. At the end of the book, the search for butterflies becomes a form of memorial. The book, that is to say, intertwines different scales of memory—personal and public—in a rhetorical effort to stimulate a form of Groes's 'genuine ecological mindfulness'. McCarthy's book is also a fusion of two contrasting moods: the inescapable guilt of a baby boomer who (for all his family difficulties) is privileged to have fallen 'in love with the natural world' in his mid-1950s boyhood, 'right at the end of what one might call the time of natural abundance' in England.[46] The sense of guilt evoked here does not imply direct culpability. The several causes for the demise of wildlife and habitat destruction in England—intensive farming, pesticide use, pollution, climate change—are the consequences of policy, the environmental effects of which are evident only in retrospect. McCarthy's purpose, in the first of the book's governing moods, is to register the severe extent to which fauna has been destroyed, and he does this with especial power through the image in his title:

> There were lots of many things, then. Suburban gardens were thronged with thrushes. Hares galumphed across every pasture. Mayflies hatched on springtime rivers in dazzling swarms. And larks filled the air and poppies filled the fields, and if the butterflies filled the summer days, the moths filled the summer nights, and sometimes the moths were in such numbers that they would pack a car's headlight beams like snowflakes in a blizzard, there would be a veritable snowstorm of moths, and at the end of your journey you would have to wash your windscreen, you would have to sponge away the astounding richness of life.
> (p. 13)

The resonance of this image lies in cultural memory. McCarthy registers surprise 'not just at how many of those over fifty (and especially over sixty) remember it, but at how animated they become once the memory is triggered' (p. 102). It is a powerful, and acutely double-edged, memory: 'it's as if it were locked away in a corner of their minds, and in recalling it and realising it has disappeared, they can

---

[46] Michael McCarthy, *The Moth Snowstorm: Nature and Joy* (London: John Murray, 2015), p. 12. Subsequent references are given in parentheses.

recognise what an exceptional phenomenon it was, whereas at the time, it just seemed part of the way things were' (p. 102). But the animation at the memory of abundance is, surely, almost instantly overwhelmed by the recognition of loss, and then (I am speaking personally) transformed into self-recrimination: *how could I have forgotten something so astounding?* we (or some of us) may ask ourselves. It is a nugget of buried memory that explodes into the indisputable empirical fact of scarcity, registered as a personal failing—of not having borne witness. That is the power of the first mood of *The Moth Snowstorm*, encased in the time-bomb image that must shock out of complacency (probably) the largest demographic component of McCarthy's readership.

The first half of the book ends with a chapter detailing the evidence of how, across Britain, 'abundance, blessed, unregarded abundance, has been destroyed' (p. 88). A key symbol of this destruction is the virtual disappearance of the house sparrow from central London through the twentieth century, a decline presented as a foreshadowing of what may happen to other songbirds (pp. 109–23). The absence is meant to shock, and to seem emblematic of genuine crisis, because the house sparrow, in the popular consciousness, is a fundamental feature of British fauna. In the second half of the book McCarthy seeks to reverse the mood, to cultivate a sense of joy and wonder in the face of environmental dismay, a strategy that includes instances of the 'miraculous survival of abundance' (p. 159), including a bluebell wood encountered in the spring, and the intensity of a blue 'that shocked you' and which 'made you giddy':

> It was a blue that flowed like smoke over the woodland floor, so that the trees appeared to be rising out of it, a blue...constantly morphing in tone with the light and the shade, now lilac, now cobalt, a blue which was gentle but formidably strong, so intense as to be mesmerising...a dozen blue bell-heads nodding on every stem, a hundred thousand stems pressing together in every glade until it ceased to be plants, it was just an overwhelming incredible blueness at the bottom of a wood. (p. 159)

There is a hint of the sublime in the 'smoke'—the suggestion of something unidentified smouldering—as well as the wonder implied in the shifting colour palette. McCarthy reports being so entranced by his bluebell wood that he kept returning to it, but secretively. Hazy about his own motives for the secrecy, he speculates: 'I suppose I felt that declaiming about five successive days of bluebell-peeping would be regarded as eccentric' (p. 169).[47] As the celebration continues, colour is perceived as the 'ultimate abundance' of the natural world (p. 161). But the instances of arresting colour are revered for their rarity. For a comparison to

---

[47] To some commentators, a bluebell wood reveals a lack of ecological diversity. See, for example, George Monbiot, *Feral: Rewilding the Land, Sea and Human Life* (2013; London: Penguin, 2014), p. 95.

the 'brilliant blue' which 'the bluebells contain, in their shade-shifting', when 'the basic colour intensifies itself', McCarthy turns to the Adonis blue butterfly, and to 'the blue of the kingfisher's back', which is 'a blue so bright it appears to be lit from within', and which is distinct from 'the glowing greenish-blue of the folded wings' (pp. 167–8). McCarthy seems deliberately to have built a contradiction into this different abundance, of the colour blue, so that the noteworthy instances are rarities. It seems to underscore the book's central problem, where appreciation is presented as a solitary act (the secretive returns to the bluebell wood), within a dynamic that requires collective action: the power of the moth snowstorm resides in its potential to fuse private and public memory, and so spark a proactive response to ecological catastrophe. Marvelling at the unusual, the exceptional, in nature may reveal contradictory motivation, as the next chapter suggests. Here, it has the effect of reinforcing the pessimism of a book overshadowed by the thinning of species in the Anthropocene, and the gathering evidence for the sixth great extinction event that many biologists believe is underway (pp. 64–5).

Another facet of memory to account for is that of inherited literary tradition. I want to turn to this briefly now, as a prelude to discussion of the main example of nonfictional nature prose in this chapter, Annie Dillard's *Pilgrim at Tinker Creek* (1974), which is located at an important historical juncture, between the emergence of ecological consciousness and the later overwhelming evidence of climate change that informs the composition of later works like Kingsolver's *Flight Behaviour*. This achronological sequence helps to make comparisons as well as to draw distinctions between the different historical moments in play; it also enables me to bring the different texts to bear on each other. For example, there are echoes of *Pilgrim at Tinker Creek* in *Flight Behaviour*, which can be drawn out more clearly in a non-linear argument. But first I need to put Dillard's work in the context of earlier literary antecedents, in the broad field of nature prose. Given that the post-1960 ecological consciousness must reorientate subsequent nature writing on the question of abundance, it is worth briefly tracing the origins of this consciousness through the nineteenth century, in the longer tradition that remains influential in contemporary American writing, the better to account for the 'newness' of more contemporary nature prose. It is surprising how rarely the topic of abundance/scarcity is given extended treatment by literary critics, but one exception is Shawn Loewen, who persuasively shows how American writing about nature—in the work of canonical fiction and nonfiction writers—'registered an apprehension' through the nineteenth century 'that the expansion of the United States was ruining the continent's natural condition'.[48] Loewen traces two contrasting strands in the tradition, as 'some writers continued to invoke a traditional

---

[48] Shawn Loewen, 'The New Canaan: Abundance, Scarcity, and the Changing Climate of Nature Writing in Nineteenth-Century America', *Interdisciplinary Studies in Literature and Environment*, 8 (2001), 1, pp. 97–114 (p. 97).

idea that nature was eternally plentiful', while 'others raised new fears that nature was less bounteous than early settlers had believed'.[49] In this account, 'the discourse of abundance was gradually replaced by the discourse of scarcity as the dominant conception of nature'. Those 'visions of a plentiful land' persisting in the eighteenth century became unsustainable through the nineteenth century, as the growing evidence of ecological damage caused by settlement and industrialism 'could not be easily reconciled with ideas of abundance'. The recognition of scarcity did not necessarily produce an ur-ecological understanding, however, since an alternative discourse 'allowed scarcity to be seen as a normal condition of nature'.[50]

The tension between these two conflicting understandings of scarcity and abundance, as Loewen shows, persisted through the nineteenth century, figuring in the work of the most influential nature writers. Ralph Waldo Emerson, contesting the Malthusian notion that population growth must outstrip any possible rate of increase in food production, saw nature as a self-repairing (and so inexhaustible) machine, while 'a principle of everlasting growth' is evident in Walt Whitman's poetry. A more global perception of abundance eclipsed local instances of depleted resources in Edgar Allan Poe's conviction that 'there will always be natural resources in other parts of the world that may be exploited'. It is tempting to perceive an element of denial in these assertions (as Loewen does), but the impercipience, from the twenty-first-century vantage point, may simply underscore the rapidity with which an ecological consciousness has reversed the complacency of many influential authors.[51] Loewen makes a noteworthy attempt to retrieve the environmental credentials of Herman Melville, arguing that in *Moby-Dick* (1851) he 'draws attention to the contradictions in the discourse of abundance', against his apparent meaning, through the rhetorical device of producing obviously brittle and contradictory arguments in defence of whaling (in the chapter 'Does The Whale's Magnitude Diminish? – Will He Perish?'). For Loewen, this brings Melville tangentially into the company of 'other American writers in the nineteenth century' who 'never doubted that the natural world was finite, even fragile, and that it could be exhausted through human misuse'. The roll call here includes James Fenimore Cooper, George Perkins Marsh (author of the seminal ecological work *Man and Nature*, 1864), and Henry Thoreau, who, in *The Maine Woods* (1864), warned of the dire consequences of excessive logging.[52]

---

[49] Ibid., p. 97.   [50] Ibid., pp. 98–100.   [51] Ibid., pp. 101–4.
[52] Ibid., pp. 104–9. Loewen's essay builds usefully on scattered work on abundance and scarcity in American culture and writing, drawing on: William Cronon, *Changes in the Land: Indians, Colonists, and the Ecology of New England* (New York: Hill & Wang, 1984); Annette Kolodny, *The Lay of the Land: Metaphor as Experience and History in American Life and Letters* (Chapel Hill: University of North Carolina Press, 1975); and David Lowenthal's 'Introduction' to George Perkins Marsh, *Man and Nature* (1864; Cambridge: Belknap Press of Harvard University Press, 1965), pp. ix–xxix.

From this pantheon, Thoreau is certainly the nature writer that readers continue to identify with most strongly; and he is a crucial touchstone for Dillard, as we shall see. But we should not be too quick to make Thoreau seem our contemporary. Indeed, his importance might be better understood in terms of the transitional consciousness he embodies. Lawrence Buell sees Thoreau's whole career as 'a process of self-education in environmental reading, articulation, and bonding', with 'the composition of *Walden*, extending over nearly a decade (1845–1854)', spanning 'the critical stage' of this development. It is this emphasis on *process* that is most significant, because Thoreau's work, understood in these terms, becomes exemplary, 'a record and model of a western sensibility working with and through the constraints of Eurocentric, androcentric, homocentric culture to arrive at an environmentally responsive vision'.[53] This effort of personal re-education resonates powerfully with all of the nature writers examined in this book; and it also implies—to conclude this brief historical excursus in the work of luminaries of American nature writing—that the tradition one writes from must be the focus of critique, to the extent that contemporary knowledge takes us beyond that tradition. The *writing back* of nature writing distinguishes itself from other literary re-evaluations of tradition in its greater emphasis on contemporary scientific understanding—or, in other words, the *current state of nature*. In this section I have conflated different conceptions of cultural memory: individual memories of the nonhuman perceived as a potential resource in the pursuit of conservation; and the literary legacy of nature writing, which contemporary writers retrieve and embellish in the light of fresh ecological knowledge. These two types of cultural memory are frequently brought together in contemporary nature prose, and one of the earliest examples of their thorough integration is Annie Dillard's *Pilgrim at Tinker Creek*, a text that fuses these different forms of memory/knowledge as it fashions exemplary instances of the parable effect.

The Expressive Abundance of *Pilgrim at Tinker Creek*

Thoreau's *Walden* is a dominant influence on, and presence in, Dillard's *Pilgrim at Tinker Creek*, to the point of suggesting an anxiety of influence, which seems to drive her to new forms of verbal dexterity. She announces in chapter 1, 'I propose to keep here what Thoreau called "a meteorological journal of the mind"', and that emphasis on diverse and complex mental states, mutating like weather patterns, is a precise analogy for her writing, rich and elusive of interpretation.[54] Her prose, as Buell so suggestively describes it, 'is a rushy kaleidoscope of perceptual and

---

[53] Buell, *The Environmental Imagination*, p. 23.
[54] Annie Dillard, *Pilgrim at Tinker Creek* (1974; London: Picador, 1976), p. 23. Subsequent references are given in parentheses.

intertextual fragments, precariously contained by a basketry of image motifs'.[55] Some of those 'image motifs' are central to her profoundly ambivalent treatment of abundance in nature.

The significance of abundance to Dillard—and to perceptions of her work—is underscored in the title of a selection of her best-known writings, *The Abundance*.[56] Here, however, 'abundance' does not signal her eye for natural observation only: it identifies, as well, the stylistic exuberance that is characteristic of her work. In his foreword to *The Abundance*, Geoff Dyer accounts for the powerful impression Dillard's work leaves upon her readers by stressing her formal innovation, the uncategorizable nature of her work: 'she alerts us to the possibility of being free of formal conventions that constrain in the guise of enabling'.[57] Partly, this is a way of celebrating her achievement in the annals of nature writing, a genre (Dyer implies) that is prone to self-defeating conventionalism. Finding in her work a vein of comedy—the 'comedy of rapture'—Dyer considers this to be 'a comedy that permits prose and thought to soar while inoculating the rapturous against the three ills of which nature writers should live in permanent dread: preciousness, reverence, and earnestness'.[58] The idiosyncrasy of Dillard's style can be understood as a very early instance of the formal, generic, and stylistic collage that has become commonplace in the twenty-first century—almost de rigueur—especially in nature writing: 'genre-resistant nonfiction may be a recognized genre these days, but Dillard awoke to its possibilities – and attendant difficulties – back in the early 1970s'.[59] In passing, we might observe the literary self-consciousness in Dillard's method, as Dyer indicates, quoting from her journal from the time of composing *Pilgrim at Tinker Creek*: 'we've had the nonfiction novel – it's time for the novelized book of nonfiction'.[60] Dyer's idea of the 'comedy of rapture' in Dillard seems to be another way of explaining the paradoxical effect of conjoining delight and revulsion, awe and wonder, in the modern sublime of nature prose. It is also a way of locating the difficulty of the writing, and the way in which she extends the paradoxical tradition of parable so that the significance of her experience, if we are to see it as in any way exemplary, requires a process of recalibration, an effort of personal re-education.

Before engaging with that bewildering uncertainty, however, I will begin by reflecting on the structural signposts of *Pilgrim at Tinker Creek*, and the guidance they offer to the reader. Buell places stress on Dillard's evocation of the seasonal cycle, equivocal though it is, which serves on balance to 'counter... the vision of a chancy indeterminate universe'.[61] To a degree, 'the seasons supply a macronarrative framework for her pilgrimage, which goes from January to winter solstice, just

---

[55] Buell, *The Environmental Imagination*, p. 237.
[56] Annie Dillard, *The Abundance* (2016; Edinburgh: Canongate, 2017).
[57] Geoff Dyer, 'Foreword' to Dillard, *The Abundance*, pp. xv–xxvi (p. xvii). [58] Ibid., p. xviii.
[59] Ibid., p. xvi   [60] Ibid., p. xvi   [61] Buell, *The Environmental Imagination*, p. 239.

before Christmas'.[62] In Dillard's scheme, it should be noted, this is a very important cultural memory, a specifically Christian calendar, and a Christian pilgrimage, so that the 'second half of the book moves downward into realms of greater and greater emptiness'. The progression to Advent structures Dillard's Christian journey by which 'the soul empties itself of the world in order to prepare for the incursion of God at Christmas'. There is a personal 'emptying' to mirror the emptying of nature: 'the caribou pour out of the hills, the monarch butterflies migrate through the valley, the leaves and birds, like the caribou and butterflies, vamoose'.[63] The bedrock of seasonal certainty allows this superimposition of a Christian calendar over a natural cycle. For Buell, seasonality *transcends* the Christian motifs, and becomes the key to the book's significance: 'her subtle awareness of how seasonality pervades human experience is anything but tribal – a major reinvention of an ancient genre'.[64] But it is a pre-climate-change perspective that supplies Dillard's compositional anchor, a precarious mooring in any twenty-first-century evaluation of the book.

Setting aside the question of seasonality, Dillard's religious credo supplies a different schema that helps explain its dual effects. Buell demonstrates the validity of her assertion that the book 'turns on the Christian distinction between the *via positiva* and *via negativa*', opposing ways of approaching God (or the divine more generally, as this distinction has classical roots), either by loving God's creation (*via positiva*) or by accepting the unknowability of God, as a being beyond human comprehension and morality (*via negativa*).[65] In Dillard's account, this duality supplies a simple structure: 'the first half of the book represents the *via positiva*; the second half, the *via negativa*'. Further, Dillard points out, 'the book has bilateral symmetry', so that 'opposite chapters are paired', with the first and last chapters forming 'a simple frame'. The heart of the dualism comes in the middle of the book, in Dillard's plan:

> The vision culminates in a chapter titled 'Intricacy' – in which the world is seen in all its detail, and loved. This can't last. The center is a little 'Flood' chapter – a narrative break between 'Intricacy' and its twin, 'Fecundity.' In 'Fecundity' the downhill journey begins – the rejection of the world. The soul gags on abundance; the mind quarrels with death.[66]

These two key chapters are analysed more closely below. Here, it is worth observing that the idea of 'emptying' the self is a negation of the world and its ghastly abundance (ghastly for reasons that will become apparent). Yet this

---

[62] Ibid., p. 241.
[63] Karla M. Hammond, 'Drawing the Curtains: An Interview with Annie Dillard', *Bennington Review*, 10 (1981), pp. 30–8 (p. 32).
[64] Buell, *The Environmental Imagination*, p. 242.   [65] Ibid., p. 240.
[66] Hammond, 'Drawing the Curtains', p. 32.

emptying is also a form of 'letting go' (*Pilgrim*, p. 40), an opening of oneself to impressions without preconceptions or analysis.[67]

The irresolvable contradiction here is that one cannot will a visionary state of this kind into being, since to do so involves the very preconception and cognitive process that are absent in the visionary moment. Cardone acknowledges the artifice of Dillard's method: the vision of nature may involve 'a total negation of the self', and yet, because 'it is impossible to continuously hush one's awareness', the visionary perception of nature 'is presented as a glowing instant that vanishes in a second'.[68] The intellect obstructs the visionary embrace of that which 'apparently goes against morality and is characterized as pain, loss, and death', that which 'outlines a Creator who is totally other than human and who does not provide solace but terror'.[69] The idea is that, by stilling the intellect, the fact of fecundity, 'the tangible proof that nature's free creation cannot be stopped' can be embraced so that 'the theme of eating and being eaten acquires a completely different meaning in the *via creativa*; it turns into an act of union with nature'.[70] Yet this 'mystical union' is registered as profoundly ambivalent, not least because of the careful crafting of *Pilgrim at Tinker Creek* which makes the visionary moments seem artfully stage-managed.[71]

I turn now to look in more detail at some of the most resonant passages in *Pilgrim at Tinker Creek* with these problematic aspects in mind: the self-conscious structuring of the book; and the logical contradiction of willing oneself into a receptive visionary state. In the eighth chapter, 'Intricacy', in which Dillard asserts that 'the world is seen in all its detail, and loved', she finds a way of celebrating natural abundance by restricting her vision. This strategy is related to the method articulated in chapter 2, 'Seeing', when Dillard finds she can detect the minnows in the Creek far better by squinting and watching for movement of light: blurring her eyes, she sees 'a new world', including 'the linear flashes' of the minnows, 'gleaming silver, like stars being born at random down a rolling scroll of time'. This produces one of the visionary moments characteristic of the book: 'something broke and immediately opened. I filled up like a new wineskin. I breathed an air like light; I saw a light like water. I was the lip of a fountain the creek filled forever; I was ether, the leaf in the zephyr; I was fleshflake, feather, bone' (pp. 40–1). Emphasizing the visionary and mystical quality of this method of

---

[67] Anastasia Cardone, 'Where the Twin Oceans of Beauty and Horror Meet: An Aesthetic Analysis of Annie Dillard's *Pilgrim at Tinker Creek*', Ecozon@, 7 (2016), 2, pp. 85–97 (p. 90). Cardone cites Arthur Schopenhauer, *The World as Will and Representation*, vol I, ed. and trans. Judith Norman, Alistair Welchman, and Christopher Janaway (Cambridge: Cambridge University Press, 2010), p. 19: Cardone posits some roots of Dillard's idea in 'Arthur Schopenhauer's pure subject of knowledge', where the subject's consciousness is filled with contemplation of the object, until absorption in it is complete. Relinquishing the self, 'the pure subject turns into the perfect mirror of the object and gets a glimpse of the eternal Platonic idea, the objective condition of the aesthetic experience'. This aesthetic effect, which allows 'the subject to merge with the object', is the essence of Dillard's method.

[68] Cardone, 'Where the Twin Oceans of Beauty and Horror Meet', p. 91.   [69] Ibid., p. 93.
[70] Ibid., p. 95.   [71] Ibid., p. 96.

seeing, Dillard writes: 'when I see this way I see truly' (p. 41). The opening of self involves a complex of sensual empathy, and it is this version of 'negative capability', in Keatsian terms, that permits a meaningful approach to the ways in which abundance can overwhelm the intellect. In the 'Intricacy' chapter, the restricted vision becomes a form of self-discipline to manage the potentially overpowering effect of the 'network of detail', the 'extravagance of minutiae': 'if you can't see the forest for the trees, then look at the trees; when you've looked at enough trees, you've seen a forest, you've got it' (p. 119). By donning blinkers, it becomes possible to celebrate a world 'created abundantly, extravagantly', by marvelling at its detailed intricacies.

Dillard considers the idea of intricacy, or 'texture', as the possible signpost for the route of her religious quest, since the 'texture of the world, its filigree and scrollwork' suggest 'a beauty inexhaustible in its complexity'. It is this beauty, she indicates, 'which trains me to the wild and extravagant nature of the spirit I seek' (p. 127). Yet the extravagant texture of the world, imagined through time and evolution, produces a major psychological problem for Dillard, because while, as she puts it, 'beauty itself is the fruit of the creator's exuberance that grew such a tangle', she is mindful that 'grotesques and horrors bloom from that same free growth' (p. 133). In the tenth chapter, 'Fecundity', in which (in Dillard's plan cited above) 'the soul gags on abundance', the revulsion implicit in this trepidation is given full expression. At the beginning of this chapter Dillard recalls watching 'two huge luna moths mate', the male 'hunching repeatedly with a horrible animal vigor'. By watching, Dillard claims responsibility for 'the consequences', which turn out to be a nightmare vision, not initially signalled as a nightmare but, rather, as an event that follows the mating of the moths:

> And then the eggs hatched and the bed was full of fish. I was standing across the room in the doorway, staring at the bed, and a thousand chunky fish swarmed there in a viscid slime. The fish were firm and fat, black and white, with triangular bodies and bulging eyes. I watched in horror as they squirmed three feet deep, swimming and oozing about in the glistening, transparent slime. (pp. 144–5)

Dillard now suggests that 'the landscape of the intricate world that [she has] painted is inaccurate and lopsided', because it is 'too optimistic', and in effect too easily consoling to find 'in complexity... the fringes of beauty, and in variety... generosity and exuberance' (p. 145). For Dillard, fecundity and predation are two sides of the same coin—this is established early in the book when she recounts, from her natural-history reading (Jean-Henri Fabre), the mating ritual of the praying mantis, the female slowly devouring the male during the act of copulation (p. 61). Dillard's most haunting image of predation, which resurfaces in the 'Fecundity' chapter, is the frog sucked dry by the giant water bug. In the first chapter the horror of this encounter is registered, as Dillard discovers a frog that isn't moving: 'as I looked at him, he slowly crumpled and began to sag. The spirit vanished from his eyes as if snuffed' (p. 19). Transfixed by this 'monstrous and terrifying thing', Dillard watches 'the taut, glistening skin on his shoulders ruck, and rumple, and fall'. The most appalling thing is the 'oval shadow...behind the drained frog' which 'glided away' (p. 19). As she concludes her consideration of the 'ugly subject' of fecundity, Dillard reminds us of the episode, telling us that she has been 'sapped by various strong feelings about the incident almost daily for several years': the abundant world of fecundity and predation is morally enervating (p. 159).

In the Introduction to this book, I discussed the furore surrounding the fabrication of the water bug episode, the fact that Dillard presented as a first-hand experience an episode that she had gleaned from her reading; and I implied that the episode is an exemplary instance of cultivated paradox in contemporary nature prose, by virtue of its performance of transformation. We can add to this impression of representativeness by observing that the performance/fabrication produces a prime example of the performative quality identified by Hillis Miller as the distinguishing linguistic feature of secular parable, and which is absent from religious parable: the performative places emphasis on textual construction, not on a constative assertion of abundant religious wisdom. The water bug episode is also an exemplary instance of the parable effect, although it underscores the challenge that can be offered to human morality in such effects. The parable effect offers a distinctive fusion of textuality and mimesis; accordingly, the performative quality of the water bug episode is just one element of the hybrid knowledge it produces. It is an instance of book knowledge posing as experience, and so its textuality is informed by a posited extralinguistic basis. Indeed, the furore about Dillard's duplicity—and the duplicity itself—serve to emphasize the paradoxical combination of textuality and its real-world underpinning. Parable effects, in a particular form of ecomimesis, resist the confines of textuality and encourage us to engage with the experiences of insight and revelation inspired by real-world events (even those 'experienced' at second hand), while they sound an echo of divine authority. The abundance of knowledge in these effects is made manifest by the capacity of abundant/fecund nature—which can inspire horror as well as wonder, as Dillard's revulsion in this episode reveals—to stimulate the metaphorical abundance of new complex understanding. The complexity of such understanding reveals 'true' or 'false' judgements to be facile.

The knowledge revealed by the experiences recounted in *Pilgrim at Tinker Creek* is irreducibly ambivalent. One way of explaining the ambivalence of Dillard's book, and the contradictions exposed by her visionary effort, is—in the broadest terms—to observe the clash between the secular and the religious. The stilling of the intellect, the setting aside of intellectual engagement that is integral to Dillard's attempted visionary state, is difficult to square with the hard-headed ecological consciousness that she is also working towards. In this connection,

James McClintock considers the extent to which Dillard's Christianity distances her from the American nature writing tradition, 'since nature writers and, more broadly, conservationists, environmentalists, and students of American responses to nature have consistently held the Judeo-Christian tradition responsible for land abuse'. Dillard does not seem to share their rejection of the anthropocentricity inherent in this tradition.[72] Yet, for McClintock, the uniqueness of Dillard stems from the idiosyncratic way in which she circumvents this problem. She works 'within meditative traditions' as she 'prepares for mystical reconciliation by mingling Judeo-Christian rituals and traditions with the conventional ways of encountering nature recorded in nature writing'. In short, 'she is an off-beat Christian who walks in nature and reads science as part of her preparation for vision'.[73] As Margaret Loewen Reimer sees it, 'the paradox and incongruity' make *Pilgrim at Tinker Creek* 'a scientific study overlaid with spiritual contemplation, an examination of natural phenomena which leads the author to an encounter with the Divine'.[74] It seems right to situate Dillard within a secular tradition of nature writing, but without losing a sense of the intensity of the visionary impulse: indeed, it is this very impulse that accounts for her enduring influence on contemporary nature prose. The effort in this connection is the difficult task of infusing awe with rationality without losing the intensity of effect that we might associate with scientific or analytical data, on the one hand, or with the mystical sense of engagement with nature on the other. This is to approach the paradox of the parable effect from another direction, pinpointing the biblical tradition as a key cultural memory in its composition. In Dillard's work, it is the religious trope of enlightenment and conversion—which also informs a secular context—that informs her parable effects, and which enables her to gesture towards a resolution of her contradictory response. Such resolution is very much in the spirit of the paradoxes I have been remarking upon throughout this study, moments in which apparently contradictory impulses or ways of comprehending are fused in an irresolvably complex moment of vision, a vision that encapsulates the contemporary predicament.

That claim may be rigorously tested if I try to bring it to bear on Dillard's most challenging example of projecting a form of 'conversion' through an encounter with abundance. This involves an image that forces the religious and the scientific into proximity, in the presentation of the locust in her twelfth chapter, 'Nightwatch'. The discovery in 1921 that locusts are actually grasshoppers—there are several species that become gregarious and mutate in drought conditions—is a detail from natural history that epitomizes Dillard's profound

---

[72] James I. McClintock, *Nature's Kindred Spirits* (Madison: University of Wisconsin Press, 1994), p. 89.
[73] Ibid., p. 90.
[74] Margaret Loewen Reimer, 'The Dialectical Vision of Annie Dillard's *Pilgrim at Tinker Creek*', *Critique*, 24 (1983), 3, pp. 182–91 (p. 182).

ambivalence about natural abundance. She quotes Joel 2:3, the biblical verse that best condenses the devastation of a locust swarm, following drought: 'A fire devoureth before them; and behind them a flame burneth: the land is as the garden of Eden before them, and behind them a desolate wilderness; yea, and nothing shall escape them' (p. 184). Dillard includes an account of a man asleep in a horde (the collective noun she uses here) of locusts, who is woken immediately by friends, but is still 'bleeding from the throat and wrists' when he stands up (p. 185). Although locusts do not attack people, this account of being smothered by the unstoppable progress of, probably, the most feared abundant phenomenon in nature supplies the setting for Dillard's ambitious attempt to think through and beyond her revulsion, at the end of this chapter:

> What if I stood awake in a swarm? I cannot ask for more than to be so wholly acted upon, flown at, and lighted on in throngs, probed, knocked, even bitten. A little blood from the wrists and throat is the price I would willingly pay for that pressure of clacking weights on my shoulders, for the scent of deserts, groundfire in my ears – for being so in the clustering thick of things, rapt and enwrapped in the rising and falling world. (p. 195)

The fusion of the Christian and the scientific appreciation of/revulsion towards natural abundance results in self-negation, through which aversion is overcome in an impersonal acceptance of the temporary composition of the individual, understood as an impermanent configuration of matter in the 'rising and falling world'. Yet there is also something too studied about this imagined event for the moment to qualify as a 'visionary' state attained by the suspension of the intellect. On the contrary, Dillard is self-consciously producing an image that reasserts the intellectual effort of accepting abundance, which must involve accepting all of nature—a swarm of locusts included—and acknowledging one's place in the cycle of death, predation, parasitism. One can extrapolate from this moment because it has the air of a parable—as a problem or riddle to be solved—which again alerts us to its intellectual construction, requiring an interpretive effort to extract the positive significance from an imagined personal dissolution in the 'thick of things', the world of natural abundance. This is a parable effect, in the contemporary sense of an embraced paradox, because the moment of vision, in which integration with nature is glimpsed, also requires the intellectual assertion that signifies the banishment of humanity from the natural cycle.

The influence of Dillard's work on more recent formulations of the ecological paradox—which are usually secular in orientation, while still cultivating the kind of opacity of knowledge implicit in biblical parable—can be illustrated by another consideration of Kingsolver's *Flight Behaviour*, which contains several clear echoes of *Pilgrim at Tinker Creek*. Both texts emphasize the effort of personal growth in response to nature; both explore the competing claims of science and religion; and both contain a flood that reorientates the reader's effort of interpretation. The most arresting point of comparison, however, is the response to the monarch butterflies in their abundance. In *Pilgrim at Tinker Creek* it is the migration of the monarchs, 'in full force for five days', that generates the culminating reflections on the personal journey through the seasonal cycle: 'for those five days I was inundated, drained', writes Dillard:

> Time itself was a scroll unravelled, curved and still quivering on a table or altar stone. The monarchs clattered in the air, burnished like throngs of pennies, here's one, and here's one, and more, and more.... It looked as though the leaves of the autumn forest had taken flight, and were pouring down the valley like a waterfall, like a tidal wave... And when the monarchs had passed and were gone, the skies were vacant, the air poised. The dark night into which the year was plunging was not a sleep but an awakening, a new and necessary austerity, the sparer climate for which I longed. (p. 225)

Once more, in the manner of a parable, there are points of difficulty to decipher and interpret. The altar stone implies the sacrifice denoted by personal relinquishment, perhaps, the finitude of an individual life revealed as 'a scroll unravelled'. The 'tidal wave' simile of the monarchs keeps in view Dillard's ambivalence in the face of abundance (threatening as well as inspiring), while the association between the butterflies and the leaves of the forest conjures an image of autumn process unfolding all at once, another image of time concertinaed, also conjoining awe and wonder. If the 'sparer climate' left after the migration implies a spiritual emptying in Dillard's Christian credo, it also creates a vacancy in which the absence of abundance is felt, and an appetite for the repetition of the cycle is engendered; and in that appetite for repetition the essence of Dillardian paradox resides.

The Opacity of the Parable Effect

I will conclude this chapter by pondering further the significance of the parable dynamic in contemporary nature prose, and the apparent oddity of the suggestion that parables are anything other than transparent in their meaning. Indeed, it has become commonplace to assume that the message of a parable is easily deduced, despite the original opacity of biblical parable. A touchstone here is the widely accepted definition of a parable given in the online Oxford English Dictionary: 'a simple story used to illustrate a moral or spiritual lesson, as told by Jesus in the Gospels'.[75] In the printed full OED definition of parable, however, there is a

---

[75] https://en.oxforddictionaries.com/definition/parable (accessed 7 March 2018).

slightly different implication: 'a fictitious narrative or allegory... by which moral or spiritual relations are typically figured or set forth, as the parables of the New Testament'.[76] The stress on *simplicity* in the illustration of a lesson is notably absent in this definition. The emphasis on a 'lesson'—enlightenment, knowledge, wisdom—is complicated (as in the examples of parable effect I have been concerned with) by the element of *figuration*. What is at stake in modern parable is clearly signalled in this emphasis on the manner of the telling, the foregrounding of performative textuality.

For a further illustration, and to extend the range of examples, I will switch tracks for a moment and consider a different genre—science fiction—in which contemporary dilemmas can be directly, and so transparently, addressed in imaginary settings. A good illustration is Octavia Butler, and her parable novels, *Parable of the Sower* (1993) and *Parable of the Talents* (1998). The main character of these works, Lauren Olamina, invents a utopian religion that addresses the contemporaneous concerns of California in the 1990s, overshadowed by social collapse and ecological disaster, in a futuristic projection. Her religion, Earthseed, works on a utopian principle of 'noneugenic human biological evolution', as David Morris puts it, where biological changes are 'invited, rather than designed'.[77] Most troubling to the ecologist, perhaps, is the colonizing of other planets as a solution to earth's problems as part of 'the Destiny' Earthseed promotes. My aim here, however, is not to engage with the nuanced debates of Butler scholars about the utopian or dystopian implications of Butler's *Parable* novels, but rather to ponder a different paradox that brings me back to the 'Parable of the Talents' in Matthew and the exclusivity of knowledge/enlightenment. Commenting on the parable novels of Butler, Marlene Allen places emphasis on the social utopian foundation of Earthseed as a religion 'that is founded upon the principle of equal access to education in a futuristic society where only the wealthiest Americans are formally educated'.[78] In this sense, Butler is able to yoke together her two key concerns: African American history and impending ecological disaster. On the one hand, Earthseed embodies 'a parable for how we might avoid the "boomeranging" of history' and repeated ethnic oppression; but it also rehearses the 'techniques we might use to survive through the impending environmental, societal, and economic crises that are destined to evolve as a result of our current actions (or inactions)'.[79] Knowledge and education are the resources for this ambitious utopian project. Yet, at the same time, it cannot be realized as a universal project. Morris draws attention to Olamina's

---

[76] I am using a two-volume 'Compact Edition', dated 1971.
[77] David Morris, 'Octavia Butler's (R)evolutionary Movement for the Twenty-First Century', *Utopian Studies*, 26 (2015), 2, pp. 270–88 (p. 271).
[78] Marlene D. Allen, 'Octavia Butler's Parable Novels and the "Boomerang" of African American History', *Callaloo*, 32 (2009), 4, pp. 1353–65 (p. 1354).
[79] Ibid.

belief 'that Earth-bound humanity' will repeat its mistakes, and that 'a small group needs to break away' to colonize other worlds. As a consequence, he argues, for all its suggestiveness for the utopian imagination, 'it would be easy to see Earthseed as a religious movement whose transcendence requires exclusivity... the collectivity Olamina hopes for can never be total'.[80] This is apparently a different paradox to Dillard's, although it is composed of a similar tension between social and ecological frames of need. It also embodies an element of the parable effect that I detect in nature prose, but here at the level of theme: instead of evoking the exclusivity of wisdom in biblical parable, as a secular space to be filled through the performative work of self-development/education, Butler invents a pragmatic religion that requires exclusivity to succeed: the ideational structure serves to compromise the ends that it enunciates.

In the work of Dillard and Kingsolver, the parable effects are *themselves* the focus of interpretation, and this makes the ecological ideas less easily identifiable, in contrast to the thematic emphasis in Butler. There is a paradox at the end of *Flight Behaviour* that illustrates this point, and which also reveals another interesting comparison with the quixotic and irreducibly ambivalent effects of *Pilgrim at Tinker Creek*. The story of Dellarobia Turnbow can be read, as we have seen, as a way of foregrounding the desirability of social mobility through education, specifically as a way of complementing the retrieval of the commons through local knowledge. The ending of the novel, however, may close down that possibility. Yet for many readers Dellarobia's prospects, as the flood waters rise, are unresolved. This seems to be the sense of the comparison of her fate with that of the monarchs: 'they would gather on other fields and risk other odds, probably no better or worse than hers' (p. 433). Because the ending indicates that the monarchs may have survived in sufficient numbers to avoid extinction at this juncture—there are 'maybe' a million of them, the minimum necessary—we might reasonably infer that Dellarobia could endure, and that she could have a different future after a college career. The flood, however, suggests otherwise. It has biblical resonances, in a novel prone to biblical reference, so we must also feel that these rapidly rising waters symbolize the total destruction humanity has brought upon itself. For Linda Wagner-Martin, 'it seems clear that Dellarobia does not survive', even if 'the reader does not know how much of her family dies in the flooding'. She concludes, 'there will be no more Dellarobia'.[81] If the ending is less clear-cut

---

[80] Morris 'Octavia Butler's (R)evolutionary Movement', p. 285.
[81] Linda Wagner-Martin, *Barbara Kingsolver's World: Nature, Art, and the Twenty-First Century* (New York: Bloomsbury, 2014), p. 197. Wagner-Martin seems to base this conviction partly on a response Kingsolver gives in an interview, where she indicates 'there will be no further adventures of Dellarobia'. To my ear—given that this is a discussion about the author's future projects—this sounds more like the denial of a sequel than a comment on *Flight Behaviour*. See 'Barbara Kingsolver's Flight of Fancy for the Real World', *The Herald*, 1 June 2018, http://www.heraldscotland.com/arts_ents/13107339.Barbara_Kingsolver_s_flight_of_fancy_for_the_real_world/ (accessed 7 March 2018). The online article is unsigned; Wagner-Martin attributes it to Jackie McGlone.

than this suggests, Wagner-Martin is surely right about the shift of emphasis—or, perhaps, the way the ongoing logic of the novel surfaces in the ending, with the natural clearly displacing the human, so that 'the most pressing question' on 'the last page' is centred on the plight of the monarchs: 'how many are left?'[82] This is a notable instance of the novel resisting its anthropocentric straitjacket, and adopting the guise of the 'environmentally oriented work' in Lawrence Buell's definition. Indeed, *Flight Behaviour* may display all four of the key elements in Buell's 'checklist', and which he sees as a way of accounting more obviously for the achievements of environmental nonfiction, rather than the novel.[83] For Wagner-Martin, *Flight Behaviour* is punctuated with straightforward parables that relate to Kingsolver's governing theme, about 'the differences' made 'possible as people avail themselves of factual information, even though they still differ radically as they attempt to discern *what* that information means'.[84] Yet, by refocusing attention on the planetary dilemma, and overshadowing the plot of class mobility, Kingsolver loosens the knot by which the novel's parable effects tie personal growth through learning and understanding—the secular equivalent of conversion—to the promotion of ecological consciousness: it is in the complication of the parable effect that nature prose of this kind avoids the 'preciousness, reverence, and earnestness' that Dyer warns nature writers against.

Perhaps the most obvious episode in *Flight Behaviour* that is seemingly transparent in advancing an associated 'lesson' involves the Mexican family, the Delgados, befriended by Dellarobia's son Preston. But this also cultivates elements of the more nuanced parable effect I have been tracing, and the episode is complicated by a difficulty related to the problem of exclusivity that becomes irresolvable in the parable novels of Octavia Butler. On a surface reading, the Delgados seem to perform a straightforward function in Kingsolver's novel. They are keen to see the monarchs, and it transpires that they are refugees, driven from the same site in Mexico that supplied the overwintering site for the butterflies before the flooding and the mudslides that destroyed the butterflies' habitat (pp. 98–103). In this 'key plot device', as Wagner-Martin puts it, the Delgados have been driven to migrancy by the same environmental catastrophe.[85] The association between the butterflies and the Delgados goes further: their livelihood was based on intimate knowledge of the species, working as guides to those who wished to come and view the monarchs in their abundance.

Taken at face value, this mini-parable (perceived as a lesson, in the more straightforward understanding of parable) exhorts us to respect human migrancy, which, like migrancy in nature, may be a consequence of climate change, and a bid

---

[82] Wagner-Martin, *Barbara Kingsolver's World*, p.3.
[83] Buell, *The Environmental Imagination*, pp. 7–8. Buell's account of the key elements of an environmentally orientated work is discussed in the Introduction above.
[84] Wagner-Martin, *Barbara Kingsolver's World*, p. 11.   [85] Ibid., p. 8.

for survival: that simple message is hard to resist, since the Delgados are refugees from the same site and the same natural disaster that has displaced the monarchs. Yet we must also reflect that their livelihood depended on the same opportunistic exploitation of the monarchs that is planned by Dellarobia's townsfolk (p. 255). The Delgados have a respect for, and reverence of, the monarchs, and this distinguishes them from the townsfolk, and sets them on slightly higher moral ground; but we are made aware that their lives in Mexico were also, to a degree, implicated in the same exploitative and parasitic human endeavours—in this case ecotourism—that threaten natural abundance everywhere.[86] The simple parable becomes hazy, and mutates into a more complex parable effect, since the knowledge or enlightenment that can produce purposive, redemptive action—whether it is the knowledge that elicits sympathy for human migrancy or the environmental awareness that promotes conservation—is forestalled by the global constraints that blur the social and moral distinctions we began to glimpse. The status of the Delgados as a 'key plot device', and the embodiment of a simple parable, unravels as the equivocation of the parable effect displaces the easy wisdom needed to make their significance unambiguous. The reader is wrong-footed, left to address the horror of the contemporary moment without having recourse to easily grasped solutions.

In Frank Kermode's account, the inbuilt equivocation of parable is representative of the obscurity of *all* narrative, and this implies some commonality between religious and secular parable, and highlights the key role of interpretation. Kermode argues that 'parable...may proclaim a truth as a herald does, and at the same time conceal truth like an oracle'. This 'double function' or 'simultaneous proclamation and concealment' is a precise way of accounting for the parable effects that have concerned me here.[87] I might have expected this paradoxical double function to be more pronounced in fictional texts, since nonfictional nature prose ostensibly asserts a greater purchase on material ecology. Yet this has not been the case: the nonfiction has also, and in equal measure, conjoined proclamation and concealment in ways that tax exegesis. In the most complex instances, as we have seen, the resulting paradox becomes the kernel of insight itself, the embodiment of a contemporary world view.

Tim Dee's Starlings

It might be felt that my chief example of nonfictional nature writing in this chapter—Dillard's *Pilgrim at Tinker Creek*—is too exceptional, too unusual it its

---

[86] The father had contributed to census work on the butterflies in Mexico (p. 100); but 'thousands of people' had come as tourists to see them (p. 101).
[87] Kermode, *The Genesis of Secrecy*, p. 47.

fluctuating responses to natural abundance to be a representative instance of the parable effect as I am defining it. So, as a final illustration of this formal phenomenon, I will turn to a celebrated contemporary nature writer, Tim Dee, and a very familiar instance of abundance: the murmuration of starlings. This phenomenon is familiar or common in the sense that it is commonly remarked upon;[88] but 'common' must be understood as a relative term for a bird considered to be endangered.[89] Tim Dee's account of the murmuration, my final example of the parable effect, is remarkable is making us see this phenomenon afresh. His account is framed by a seasonal understanding, much as Dillard's appeal to seasonality shapes the idea of rebirth: he visits his chosen starling roost, on the Somerset Levels on the winter solstice, when the starlings 'put away...the year', in anticipation of spring, 'more light; a future; repairs; song, nests and eggs'.[90] This bird's perspective contrasts with Dee's susceptibility to the 'freezing' evening (p. 121), and its effect on his mood, 'cold and alone' (p. 120). But the veteran birder is driven by anticipation of the spectacle, in this celebrated site, hosting perhaps 'the largest ever gathering of birds in Britain', and where 'eight million' starlings 'were counted, somehow, in one roost here' in the previous year (p. 122). As the end-of-day flight before roosting commences, Dee tries to convey the majesty of the phenomenon of thousands of starlings, 'as they wheeled and gyred en masse', beginning with 'the sound of their wings turning', which 'swept like brushes across a snare drum' (p. 124). The spectacle itself is treated with equal invention, as 'great ductile cartwheels of birds were unleashed across the sky' (pp. 124–5). The sudden pulsations of a murmuration are superbly caught here, and in the metaphor of the 'black bloom' that 'burst from the seedbed of birds' (p. 125).

Yet Dee also feels he is not up to the task of conveying, fully, the purport of the happening: 'I could feel my brain slowing as it tried to compute the organising genius of what was in front of me.... I was to sit a maths exam in a room drawn by Escher. I couldn't do it' (p. 125).[91] Dissatisfied with his efforts (although we might demur), Dee turns to a fascinating metaphor in the soundscape of Thomas Tallis's forty-part motet *Spem in alium* (1571). This is an extraordinary piece of music—'there is nothing else in the English repertoire quite like it', as Roger Bray and Philip Cave declare—but it is also an extraordinary choice

---

[88] I counted nine items about starling murmurations on the BBC website since 2016, among other pieces on the bird: the fascination with the murmuration endures, even if it may be seen as a regular filler on a slow news day; https://www.bbc.co.uk/search?q=starlings#page=3 (accessed 15 March 2018).

[89] Starling populations have declined steeply in Northern Europe. In Britain and Ireland, the decline is estimated at 80% since 1969. See Peter Holden and Tim Cleeves, *RSPB Handbook of British Birds*, 4th edn (London: Bloomsbury, 2014), p. 277.

[90] Tim Dee, *The Running Sky: A Birdwatching Life* (London: Jonathan Cape, 2009), p. 121. Subsequent references are given in parentheses.

[91] The Dutch graphic artist M. C. Escher is famous for his representations of impossible objects, the illusion of perspective, and the paradox of infinity. The M. C. Escher Foundation's web address is mcescher.com/foundation/ (accessed 16 March 2018).

for Dee, as the piece embodies Tallis's well-known Catholic purpose, in defiance of religious oppression, the forty parts apparently 'referring to years in the wilderness after which the true faith would be restored'.[92] Its uniqueness, however, has to do with its unconventionality, the separate voices rising and falling, crescendos building and then fading, in an apparently unstructured way. In short, it is carefully planned, with coded intentions, and yet it gives the impression of unpredictability.[93] Dee makes specific reference to the 'recording made in 1962 in King's College Chapel in Cambridge', the tempo of which seems important to his purpose, to see if 'its eleven and a half minutes of singing' could 'light the black midwinter night and the black midwinter starlings' (p. 125).[94] He then makes this piece, and this recording, the purest metaphor for a murmuration, since it 'doesn't describe what the flock does. It is the flock' (p. 125). The lyricism of Dee's writing in this passage needs to be read in context, and in full, but this extract will give an impression of what he achieves:

> The sound catches and swirls towards us, becomes a striving, and floats and opens further... It is huge and everywhere, but tilted and very close.... The voices arrive from all corners, unfolding and bending, in relay and alone. Forty throats open. They sing together and against one another, and then against one another and together again. It is a wind blowing out of paradise. It is a vast river of warm stone and dark skies, of sea silver, of black and sheen and matt and dust and lisping and echoes and news and pain, and it deepens beyond voices until the great stone room is singing its own song, and its sound goes brightly down beneath the building into the earth and then rebounds, coursing up the vaulting into the winter night.   (pp. 125–6)

The analogy within this extended metaphor is based on a poetic but also descriptive account of this unusual music, with its unpredictable script for the individual parts—'the voices arrive from all corners'—in which possible discord may suddenly be resolved into harmony—'they sing together and against one another'—and where the lilting volume vacillates between precision and sudden power—'its sound goes brightly down... and then rebounds'. All of these observations are suggestive analogies for the starlings' flight, where individual virtuosity is absorbed into a collective order that shape-shifts, by turns, slowly, and then suddenly, producing sudden 'bursts' of movement. Yet Dee is also importing into this metaphorical construct an *exchange* between culture and nature, so

---

[92] Roger Bray and Philip Cave, sleeve notes to Thomas Tallis, 'Spem in alium', 'Lamentations', 'Mass and Motets', Magnificat, dir. Philip Cave (Linn Records, 2000) CKO 075, p. 10 .

[93] In addition to the parallel between the number of voices and 'years in the wilderness', the piece may also have been written 'in honour of the Duke of Norfolk (a staunch Catholic, executed in 1572)'. Ibid.

[94] It is just under ten minutes in the recording made by 'Magnificat' directed by Philip Cave.

that Tallis's composition itself can be understood by the comparison, which reveals it as 'a vast river' embracing all of nature—'stone', 'skies', 'sea', 'dust'—as well as the experiences and communications of the birds, their 'lisping', 'echoes', 'news', and 'pain'. Dee's writing here concentrates the essence of the parable, in that the experience suggests overwhelming knowledge that is hard to attain, a feeling we have to embrace when he gives up his effort of straight description and resorts to his musical metaphor. The divinity that Tallis's music aspires to—it is 'a wind blowing out of paradise'—lends the moment the spirituality-in-nature that recurs in such moments.

Yet there is also something very particular about the cultural event that forms the edifice of Dee's extended metaphor: one performance in a specified sacred place. The acoustic capacity of King's College Chapel transcends itself in this recording, Dee suggests, to contribute to the resonance and the union of sight and sound, in a fusion of culture and nature: 'the great stone room is singing its own song'. But we also have a sense of feeling excluded: we can listen to the recording, but we *were not there*, just as we did not witness the particular flight before roosting that Dee recounts for us. The emphasis is strongly on the *mediation* in the echo of a parable here, which gestures towards its referents but cannot deliver them for us, just as the knowledge is felt to be ultimately out of our reach. In this sense, the moment conforms to Hillis Miller's sense that all 'kinds of parable tend to be parables about parable'.[95] Dee makes a bold attempt to break the circularity at the end of the chapter, when he brings together a series of artistic touchstones that he has used to demonstrate the personal enrichment he feels through the cultural mediation of his engagement with birds:

> Keats's sparrow is dead. Yet every time I read his words, as every time I hear Nick Drake and his sparrows, or hear the singing made in King's College Chapel in 1962, I am restored to life, as I was in the dark of midwinter, at the year's midnight, on Westhay Moor amid starlings. (p. 136)

The first reference here is to Keats's letter to Benjamin Bailey (22 November 1817), a key document in the aesthetics of Romanticism, and in the formulation of Keatsian negative capability, in which Keats claims the sight of a sparrow at his window inspires the kind of empathic engagement bordering on personal dissolution that we have seen Annie Dillard striving for: 'I take part in its existence', writes Keats of the sparrow, 'and pick about the gravel'.[96] The second reference is to the sparrows that can be heard singing at the beginning of Nick Drake's song

---

[95] Hillis Miller, *Tropes, Parables, Performatives*, p. 139.
[96] John Keats, *Poetry and Prose*, introduction and notes by Henry Ellershaw (1922; Oxford: Clarendon Press, 1969), p. 166.

'Fly', on the tape recorded at his home.[97] These dead birds (specimens of a now endangered species), dead artists—and another recording—reignite the sense of wonder in the union Dee gives us of the starlings and the Tallis recording. *More mediation* is the route to restoration, because if each of these cultural prompts assists Dee in his quest for greater proximity to nature, then culture can be embraced as a conduit, not a barrier. The writing is exceptional and performative in itself, while also trading on the virtuosic performances it evokes. It is a studiously textual ecomimetic parable effect, forcing a link to knowledge of the referent, in the familiar pattern of secular parable in which the capacity for understanding—spiritual enlightenment in biblical parable—is also an appreciation of the literal natural abundance that provides a metaphorical framework in biblical parable: in the parable effects of contemporary nature prose literal and metaphorical understanding are forced together. Dee leads us by personal example, and this is a feature of much 'voice-driven' nature writing, in which the vicarious aspect, common to all imaginative writing, is transformed into an intensely heightened feature: we feel close to the experience that, as a textual construction, must elude us. This produces an elegiac effect that is often not—or not just—a consequence of our sensibility about environmental degradation but also a sense of being excluded from the fullness of experiences so powerfully evoked by the 'I' that guides us.

---

[97] This version of the song (1969) was released on *Time of No Reply* (Hannibal Records, 1986), HNBL 1318.

4
Rarity

Taken as a pair, this and the preceding chapter are influenced by the scientific understanding that, as Eric Dinerstein puts it, 'the interplay of rarity and abundance is central to understanding patterns of nature'.[1] Much of this chapter uses evidence-based observation about the nonhuman world to contextualize reflections on rarity found in contemporary nature prose. It is this context that produces a distinctively contemporary cultural fascination with the connection between the abundance and rarity of species, characterized by another variety of contained paradox, akin to the parable effects explored in the previous chapter, where we saw how natural and ideational worlds are forced together through a twin understanding of abundance, connoting the plenitude of the natural world (or the capacity for plenitude), as well as a surfeit of knowledge. In the case of rarity, the contained paradox yokes intense appreciation together with the vertiginous fear of total ecological catastrophe. The dread induced by the realization that abundance can easily collapse into rarity, and then extinction, is a startlingly new cultural preoccupation. Nature prose is repeatedly forced to engage with this haunting pattern, producing effects which are partly conditioned by culpability in the facts of ecological collapse, offset by a tortured, but potentially redemptive, cultivation of wonder—redemptive because such wonder is the foundation of the conservationist impulse. It is in the interplay of abundance and rarity that this new aesthetic space emerges, revealing anxieties that have become internalized.

The several implications of rarity that are relevant to the arguments in this chapter are all apparent in Kathleen Jamie's celebrated *Findings* (2005). Describing the appeal of watching peregrines, she ascribes it to 'their rarity', suggesting that 'the peregrine flickers at the edge of one's senses, at the edge of the sky, at the edge of existence itself'.[2] Different kinds of extremity are associated here: the buried instinctive connection with the nonhuman ('the edge of one's sense'); the elusive and compelling behaviour of the animal itself ('at the edge of the sky'); and the vulnerability of this species in the wider context of mass extinction ('the edge of existence itself'). Three kinds of rarity are thus deliberately elided: the neglected impulse to connect; the privilege of seeing remarkable

---

[1] Dinerstein, *The Kingdom of Rarities*, p. 3.
[2] Kathleen Jamie, *Findings*, pp. 46, 47. Jamie is following J. A. Baker's use of the term 'flicker' in relation to this species. See *The Peregrine, The Hill of Summer, and Diaries: The Complete Works*, ed. John Fanshawe (London: HarperCollins, 2015).

Nature Prose: Writing in Ecological Crisis. Dominic Head, Oxford University Press. © Dominic Head 2022.
DOI: 10.1093/oso/9780192870872.003.0005

behaviour when we do; and the reality of species' vulnerability that overshadows our reflection. The elision forces us to see our own responses as inextricably related to the fate of individual species, and the global crisis that the fate of each species illuminates. It is a terse and poetic way of conveying a truism of ecological thought, and also a variation on the kinds of aesthetic form already considered in previous chapters. Jamie here enables us to pause and be impressed with the verbal dexterity and the event it captures, even in the midst of our concern with the purport of what we are reading. This simultaneous appreciation of the human and the nonhuman is related to the paradoxes of the contemporary texts discussed below, where a full response to the nonhuman is shown to depend on the interaction of apparently contradictory forces.

Jamie's subtle emphasis on form hints, then, at the textual principle I am proposing as a specific sign of the contemporary; and the extent of this self-consciousness is thrown into relief by the topic of rarity and extinction. This is one way of addressing the concerns expressed by Amitav Ghosh about the formal incapacity of contemporary writing. Ghosh characterizes the current era as 'the time of the Great Derangement', an exasperated expression of the general cultural failure to register the effects and implications of climate change.[3] The failure of serious literary fiction is his main concern: he argues that major climate change events seem melodramatic in the world of serious literary fiction, because the modern novel is characterized by its probability, its commitment to the surface regularity of bourgeois life, so that its particular form of mimesis is designed to *conceal* the 'scaffolding of exceptional moments', those events that actually create narrative interest.[4] Ghosh's call for a new kind of mimesis, one in which what is happening in the nonhuman realm is revealed rather than concealed, is answered by the instances of extinction narrative discussed here, though perhaps in a more ambivalent form than Ghosh might desire. Whether fictional or nonfictional, these texts *internalize* the cultural denial, or derangement, of which Ghosh writes, so that the claims of the nonhuman are held in tension with the formal anthropocentric emphases that threaten to overwrite such claims. This is a very specific ecological form of self-consciousness, in which the gestures of ecomimesis, towards the construction of an outer world, are always conditioned by the shadow of human limitation, where textual analogues are found for real-world destructiveness.

In this distinctive manner of emphasizing textuality, extinction-related narratives—even in the most popular forms of nonfictional nature writing—reveal a surprising point of contact with the deconstructive end of the ecocritical spectrum. In the texts discussed in this chapter there is an ultimate conviction not

---

[3] Amitav Ghosh, *The Great Derangement: Climate Change and the Unthinkable* (Chicago: University of Chicago Press, 2017), p. 11.
[4] Ibid., pp. 9, 17, 23.

just that a nonhuman world exists but also that writing can encourage us to engage with it;[5] but this 'world' in contemporary nature prose is never fixed—it mutates along with our evolving scientific understanding of the human impact on it—and the forms of ecomimesis through which 'the world' is conjured for us are always conditioned by the building blocks of textual construction and the foregrounding of mediation. In the insistence on the physical nonhuman world there is a different emphasis to that found in deconstructive ecocriticism; but the mutating forms of ecomimesis in nature prose betray a shared conviction about the centrality of textual form to the process of engagement.

Jamie has a simple way of challenging ideas about outer ecomimesis: she also wants us to look *inward* when we think of rarity, and she finds a literal way of signalling the self-conscious inwardness that I have been discussing. This complementary emphasis to her observation of wild nature is apparent in the 'Surgeons' Hall' chapter of *Findings*, where she describes the exhibits in the Playfair Hall at the Royal College of Surgeons of Edinburgh, gruesome relics of medical history presented as marvels and as a challenge to our usual perception that 'the natural world [is] "out there", an "environment"'. Rather, these diseased body parts—gruesome rarities preserved in jars—'show us the forms concealed inside', the nature within (p. 141). Yet Jamie betrays equivocation in this chapter, notably in relation to the eminent men—and they are all men—who had built this collection. She wonders 'if the early anatomists regarded their collections with the same pride as do the collectors of stamps or tin toys' (p. 136); yet, for all her healthy suspicion of patriarchal institutions, the 'Surgeons' Hall' chapter registers the impersonal pursuit of knowledge, and the common goal of understanding nature that stems from individual professional satisfaction. To the central ambivalence in nature prose that appreciates rare things—the delight at rarity in the nonhuman realm which brings with it the shadow of extinction—we can add another from the cultural realm: the ambivalence about the habit of collecting. There is a sorry history of natural history collecting, and not always conducted by amateurs, in which the pursuit of rarities (eggs, feathers, horns, and so on) is a causal factor in extinction.

The Shadow of Extinction

To get a sense of this pattern which connects abundance and rarity, and the implications for contemporary responses to nature in cultural terms, I will begin with an example with well-known ramifications, especially for the American

---

[5] For an account of deconstruction's suspicion about the 'world' and 'worlding', however, see Timothy Morton, 'Deconstruction and/as Ecology', in *The Oxford Handbook of Ecocriticism*, ed. Greg Garrard (Oxford: Oxford University Press, 2014), pp. 291–304 (pp. 296–300).

psyche: the fate of the passenger pigeon. The reason why the passenger pigeon remains a haunting non-presence—it has generated its own shelf of concerned nature writing—is that it condenses the recurring historical pattern of abundance sliding through rarity to extinction in a short space of time, so short that credulity is stretched. The suddenness of this extinction intensifies our sense of the acute vulnerability of species to human interference and predation, because the passenger pigeon was the commonest bird in the world in the nineteenth century—by the measure of population, rather than global range—but was extinct by 1914. The extinction event is also unusual: the last known specimen, named Martha, had been bred in captivity, and died in Cincinnati Zoo on 1 September 1914.[6] To be able to pinpoint the moment of a species' extinction makes the passenger pigeon a particularly poignant instance, because extinction is usually shrouded in uncertainty.[7]

The vastness of passenger pigeon flocks, in eyewitness accounts, is hard to reconstruct in our mind's eye: unlike the examples considered in the previous chapter, the species that is 'synonymous with abundance' can never be seen.[8] We have instead to wrestle with the task of translating statistics into meaningful imaginings. The largest recorded nesting site of these gregarious birds (Wisconsin, 1871) was said to have 'covered 850 square miles (slightly larger than the English county of Herefordshire)', and to have contained 176 million adult birds.[9] The flocks were bigger, producing an abundance that may well exhaust our capacities of visualization. Can we really picture a flock in flight, probably more than a mile wide, 240 miles in length, and possibly containing in excess of 2 billion pigeons? Audubon compared such spectacles to an eclipse of the sun.[10] The sound alone of so many wings overhead was awe-inducing in first-hand accounts, drawing comparison with a tornado.[11] Such abundance meant that the passenger pigeon was a popular food source, hunted on an industrial scale. The most populated nesting sites also gave rise to killing frenzies, in which casual

---

[6] Among other sources, I am drawing on two books that were published to mark the centenary of Martha's death: *A Message from Martha* (London: Bloomsbury, 2014) by Mark Avery, a British ornithological expert; and *A Feathered River Across the Sky: The Passenger Pigeon's Flight to Extinction* (New York: Bloomsbury, 2014) by Joel Greenberg, a more scholarly book by a Chicago-based expert. The passenger pigeon's demise, caused chiefly by deforestation and hunting, is a stark reminder of the ecological consequences of civilization's expansion, and a dramatic depletion of the ecology in the Eastern US in particular.

[7] Accounts of the last passenger pigeon identified *in the wild* are less definitive, but stop in 1902, according to Joel Greenberg, if we restrict the reckoning to specimens 'for which all salient facts are known and the identification is beyond dispute'. See Greenberg, *A Feathered River Across the Sky*, p. 170.

[8] Ibid., p. 166.

[9] Ibid., p. 60.

[10] Ibid., pp. 63, 66. In Michael McCarthy's summary of the relevant literature the extent is slightly different: some migrating flocks were 'estimated to be a mile wide and perhaps 300 miles long', possibly containing a billion birds, taking 'several days to pass a given point'. See Michael McCarthy, *Say Goodbye to the Cuckoo* (London: John Murray, 2009), p. 215. Charlie Elder cites the same example of lost abundance in *While Flocks Last* (London: Bantam Press, 2009), pp. 13–14.

[11] Greenberg, *A Feathered River Across the Sky*, pp. 12, 50.

individuals armed with guns and clubs would join the slaughter alongside the commercial 'harvesting' of pigeons and their squabs. One notorious such event occurred in Petoskey, Michigan, in 1878, where the unfettered killing may have accounted for 5 million birds.[12]

The fate of the passenger pigeon stimulates fear of human-sponsored extinction and dearth: among cautionary environmental tales it is the *ne plus ultra*. Yet in the feelings this historical narrative arouses, in the usual manner of its telling—horror, shame, fear—it is as much concerned with human subjectivity as it is with objective ecological questions. This is an instructive example of how culture mediates perceptions of nature; but where the emphasis should lie is a matter of debate. In her deliberation on extinction Ursula Heise argues that 'biodiversity, endangered species, and extinction are primarily cultural issues, questions of what we value and what stories we tell, and only secondarily issues of science'.[13] Heise places emphasis on 'the imaginative webs that surround endangered species' and asks us to see how animals (especially) become 'cultural tools'.[14] She suggests that 'modern environmentalists' rely on repetitive 'story templates' in which 'modern society has degraded a natural world that used to be beautiful, harmonious, and self-sustaining and that might disappear completely if modern humans do not change their way of life'. In these narratives, 'the awareness of nature's beauty and value is intimately linked to a foreboding sense of its looming destruction', conveying the sense of 'a precious, beautiful, and fragile natural world at risk'.[15] This emphasis on the cultural construction of rarity has purchase in the context of the end-of-nature argument, according to which nature as an entity quite separate from human intervention can no longer be said to exist: what we have instead, in this argument, is a 'pervasively domesticated natural world'.[16] The perception of value and beauty *in* rarity is then bounded by the cultural moment. And such a response points to a paradoxical circularity in the social function of endangerment and extinction narratives, where the conservationist's appreciation of rarity might be said to depend on the human depredation of the environment for creating the conditions of rarity in the first place. Yet the paradox is not so much that we are encouraged to cherish the rarity we have produced, but rather that we are encouraged to cherish *as natural* the rarity that is caused by cultural processes: the paradox resides in the narrative structure rather than in the world—in the *story* of rarity. The challenge, perhaps, is to learn to see the representational paradox of rarity as residing *simultaneously* in narrative form *and* in the world, as another instance of complex ecomimesis.

---

[12] Avery, *A Message from Martha*, pp. 119, 120; In Greenberg's account of the savagery in Petoskey, 'by April and May' in 1878 'pigeon mania had infected everyone', logic no longer applied, and the market was saturated with an oversupply of pigeons, 'forcing dealers and merchants to give them away for free'. See Greenberg, *A Feathered River Across the Sky*, p. 141.
[13] Heise, *Imagining Extinction*, p. 5.   [14] Ibid., p. 6.   [15] Ibid., p. 7.   [16] Ibid., p. 11.

More typically in extinction narratives, culture and nature are seen in opposition, generating a tone of panic and/or self-righteousness that is hard to resist. This can result in polemic, as in Ashley Dawson's short account of the sixth mass extinction. Dawson presents this specifically in relation to the effects of capitalism, although he places that urgent context in the longer history of the demographic expansion and impact of Homo sapiens, from 'the late Pleistocene wave of extinctions' onwards.[17] It is the modern era since 1500 and the consequences of European imperialism leading into the present moment that exercise him chiefly, in common with many commentators on extinction. In Dawson's terms, it was 'the expansion of capitalist social relations through European colonialism and imperialism' that pushed 'regional environmental catastrophes to a planetary scale'.[18] Where some authorities debate how many species the world contains— and what constitutes a species in the first place—Dawson, working with the urgency of polemic, reproduces the headline statistics: 'the Earth is losing about a hundred species a day'; and the World Wildlife Fund estimates that 'the number of wild animals on Earth has halved over the past forty years'.[19] In writing of this urgent kind there is a clear desire to shake up our perceptions. An important issue here is raised by J. B. MacKinnon in his appropriation of the concept of 'change blindness' or shifting baseline syndrome—the effect that prevents us from registering the degradation of the nonhuman environment, because each generation experiences less and has a world view that is impoverished in relation to the previous one, with lower expectations about biodiversity.[20] It is this depletion of human experience that helps facilitate environmental degradation because the bar is constantly being lowered against which expectations can be measured, thus weakening outrage and resistance.

If this is seen as a cultural problem—the failure of memory vis-à-vis the nonhuman—it begs the question of what might constitute a cultural solution, and the means necessary to shore up memory, a problem raised in the previous chapter in connection with cultural memory and books such as Michael McCarthy's *The Moth Snowstorm*. But the emphasis on human culpability in the more urgent writing about extinction can appear to take us beyond cultural solutions. Franz Broswimmer rehearses the argument that Homo sapiens as a species took itself out of the gradual process of biological evolution at the point at which it developed the skill of language, and the ability to act and communicate.

---

[17] Ashley Dawson, *Extinction: A Radical History* (New York: OR Books, 2016), p. 23.
[18] Ibid., p. 41.
[19] Ibid., pp. 9, 64. Dawson is quoting Franz J. Broswimmer's, *Ecocide: A Short History of the Mass Extinction of Species* (New York: Pluto, 2002), p. 1, and the *WWF Living Planet Report 2014*, which states that 'in less than two human generations, population sizes of vertebrate species have dropped by half'; https://wwf.panda.org/discover/knowledge_hub/all_publications/living_planet_report_timeline/lpr_2014/ (accessed 27 March 2018).
[20] J. B. MacKinnon, *The Once and Future World: Nature as it Was, as it Is, as it Could Be* (New York: Houghton Mifflin Harcourt, 2013), pp. 20–1.

At that point in human development, perhaps around 60,000 years ago, human conscious intent began to impose itself on the nonhuman environment, making killing and destruction not only more systematic but essentially a cultural undertaking.[21] Elizabeth Kolbert agrees with this account of the significance of language development, suggesting that the use of 'signs and symbols to represent the natural world' enabled humans to push 'beyond the limits of that world'. She conveys the potency of language, as a sign of humanity's inherent destructiveness, by inviting us to 'picture a poacher in Africa carrying an AK-47 or a logger in the Amazon gripping an ax, or, better still, you can picture yourself, holding a book in your lap'.[22] The book, in this line of thinking, becomes not just the ultimate embodiment of humanity's alienation from the nonhuman but also the final manifestation of the root cause of our catastrophically destructive potential. This is a deliberately challenging rhetorical flourish; but it has the air of a 'final verdict' that could condemn all writing. Contemporary nature prose has to function in the context where such a charge is in the air, and to fashion a complex form of articulation that embraces culpability, ameliorating it in the process.

Extinction, then, casts a long shadow over the attempts by nature prose writers to draw inspiration from the appreciation of rarity: if there is a final analysis in which the inception of culture is perceived as the root cause of the sixth mass extinction, we may as well save our breath. Yet the narrative of rarity reveals important potential as a cultural construction in productive debate with the yearning for an untrammelled natural world: that dynamic is suggestive of intriguing negotiations. A novel written on the cusp of this contemporary dilemma is Julia Leigh's *The Hunter* (1999). This enigmatic novel, about an unnamed man in pursuit of the last Tasmanian tiger, offers a haunting re-evaluation of the problem of extinction.[23] The presentation of Leigh's hunter, known simply as 'M', anticipates the pessimism of Kolbert and Broswimmer: on his first search for the tiger he thinks back to the emergence of the human hunter in this region after the last ice age, on a plateau 'teeming with animals, great fauna now extinct'.[24] His identification with hunting, with 'what his ancestors have always done, and done well', brings him 'the kind of comfort and satisfaction another man might derive from leafing through a set of family photo albums' (p. 31). The association between domestic human organization and the extinctions of other species—that which is explicit in the analyses of Broswimmer and

---

[21] Broswimmer, *Ecocide*, pp. 27-8.

[22] Elizabeth Kolbert, *The Sixth Extinction: An Unnatural History* (2014; London: Bloomsbury, 2015), p. 266.

[23] Until recently it was assumed that the thylacine, or Tasmanian tiger—a species of marsupial predator eventually confined to Tasmania—was hunted to extinction by humans and the human introduction of the dingo to Australia. The last thylacine held in captivity died in 1936, the presumed date of the species' extinction; however, there have been occasional unconfirmed sightings since then.

[24] Julia Leigh, *The Hunter* (1999; London: Faber & Faber, 2000), p. 30. Subsequent references are given in parentheses.

Kolbert—is buried in the psyche of Lee's hunter. And, anticipating Dawson, this hunt is put in the destructive context of capitalism, in the guise of biotechnology: M's mission, on behalf of a shadowy corporation, has sinister implications:

> By studying one hair from a museum's stuffed pup, the developers of biological weapons were able to model a genetic picture of the thylacine, a picture so beautiful, so heavenly, that it was declared capable of winning a thousand wars.
> (p. 40)

Genetic science is here conceived as achieving godlike insights ('so beautiful, so heavenly'), with the inscrutable power to achieve both wonderful and terrible results, as shown in M's uncertainty about what will be done with any sample he may gather: 'whether it will be a virus or antidote, M does not know, cannot know and does not want to know' (p. 40). It is significant that he divests himself of moral responsibility: the identity of the human hunter behoves him to act blindly, helpless to influence the eventual outcome of his actions; but the amorality of the hunter is also marked by cultivated skills, notably M's competence as a shape-changer—he 'swallows the beast', performing 'his favourite trick' of inhabiting its physique (p. 91)—an acquired destructive understanding of the wild. In the scene of the killing, however, M's responses to the tiger also reveal a sense of kinship and a feeling of reverence. When he first has the tiger in his gun sights he knows 'that he is a killer, and that he, too, will be killed' (p. 162), an atavistic thought that puts him momentarily back in the food chain, at the tertiary trophic level.[25] The killing, he feels, is somehow both 'beautiful' and 'terrible' at the same time, echoing the godlike hubris of technoscience, whose agent he is.

Something else is glimpsed, however, in M's response as he recognizes the 'impassable, unimaginable gulf between life and death': having caused an actual extinction, M, looking at the dead tiger, finds that 'her stillness is obscene' (p. 164). This is a moment of great power in the novel, but it is merely a brief philosophical interlude for the hunter: M unpacks his 'surgical kit' and proceeds to harvest the tiger's blood, ovaries, and uterus, storing them in custom-built tubes and vials (pp. 165-6). Leigh presents us with a scene in which an archetypal hunter—an embodiment of both ancient and contemporary destruction—knowingly consigns a species to extinction, recognizing the obscenity of the moment, but then shrugs it off to finish his task.

M is obviously emblematic of humanity; and the indifference of the people he encounters—whether they are aggressive, dysfunctional, or self-absorbed—is also emblematic of larger human disengagement (or derangement). Yet there is also a chilling immediacy about Leigh's precise evocation of a singular moment of

---

[25] Carnivores that eat other carnivores, but which can be preyed upon by 'apex predators', are 'tertiary consumers' in a simple trophic chain.

extinction; and, because M is the main focalizer of this novel, we are made to engage with the suspense of the hunt and the prosecution of the mission. Richard Kerridge suggests that Leigh introduces a 'twist' to the 'traditional format of the Hemingwayesque hunting tale' in that 'the reader is likely to hope desperately that the hunter will fail'.[26] That is partly the case; but this right-minded feeling is also compromised by the lure of the hunting-tale format, spawning a disorientating tension. Where polemical work about extinction has the effect of haranguing the reader, Leigh's fiction puts us through the contradictory responses of man-the— hunter—lethal, calculating, and reverential all at once. To the extent that we are made to identify, in part, with these several reactions and moods, the power of the novel rests on the chill of recognition we may feel, and our sense of culpability in the moment of extinction. In this sense the local is given a global significance. A recurring theme of the reviews of Leigh's novel was its failure to convey a convincing impression of the Tasmanian landscape.[27] But this may be an unreasonable expectation in a short, crystalline novel of this kind; and the crucial point here—and the local anchor for the universalism—is that the Tasmanian tiger remains a significant part of local folklore. Yet the novel poses questions in its oscillation between the particular and the universal, the local and global, thus making extinction a problem of representation.[28] The tendency of fiction towards abstraction and metaphor can dilute real-world political commitment; but these tendencies are brought together, embodied in the different connotations of the folklore of the Tasmanian tiger, now both a regional and 'global icon of extinction', which continues to inspire quests to prove its survival.[29]

A different perspective to that of M emerges (in outline only) from the work of Jarrah Armstrong, the naturalist who precedes M looking for the tiger, on a more sympathetic mission, but who dies in the process. On his hunting trips, M has a base at the Armstrong home, which is in a state of bereaved chaos, with Jarrah's wife, Lucy, sedated and in the throes of a severe breakdown. M develops an

---

[26] Richard Kerridge, 'Narratives of Resignation: Environmentalism in Recent Fiction', in *The Environmental Tradition in English Literature*, ed. John Parham (Aldershot: Ashgate, 2002), pp. 87–99 (pp. 97–8).

[27] For a summary of these objections see Tony Hughes-d'Aeth, 'Australian Writing, Deep Ecology and Julia Leigh's *The Hunter*', *Journal of the Association for the Study of Australian Literature* (2002), 1, pp. 19–31 (p. 19); https://openjournals.library.sydney.edu.au/index.php/JASAL/article/view/9652 (accessed 20 November 2018).

[28] In Scott Brewer's reading, the global thinking about extinction is potentially short-circuited by Leigh's cultivation of metaphor. The problem is resolved through an intensification of 'metaphoric abstraction' that underscores 'the gaps in our representations of place' and 'constructs a peculiar aesthetic of loss'. See Scott Brewer, 'A Peculiar Aesthetic: Julia Leigh's *The Hunter* and Sublime Loss', *Journal of the Association for the Study of Australian Literature* (2009); https://openjournals.library.sydney.edu.au/index.php/JASAL/article/view/10157/10055 (accessed 20 November 2018). Brewer's sophisticated application of the sublime to *The Hunter* is worth reading.

[29] See Brooke Jarvis, 'The Obsessive Search for the Tasmanian Tiger', *The New Yorker*, 2 July 2018; https://www.newyorker.com/magazine/2018/07/02/the-obsessive-search-for-the-tasmanian-tiger (accessed 21 November 2018).

ambivalent relationship with the family, exploiting the daughter's belief that he may find her father (he finds his remains, but does not reveal this), and fantasizing about a role for himself as a surrogate father. Jarrah is the author of a work entitled *Bioethics for Another Millennium* (p. 74), and his work on 'energy and matter', on how 'everything is transformed', is an obvious counterpoint to M's exploitative fieldwork (p. 107).[30] This emphasis on the material world, and the recycling of matter, causes M to reflect that, 'if everything is transformed then what is extinction?' (p. 107); but the reader will not be satisfied by this piece of sophistry, which seems, in context, to justify the hunter's mission. But it also casts doubt upon Jarrah's idealistic materialism—championed by the hippies who descend on the Armstrong home—as a philosophy without purchase on the real.

In several ways *The Hunter* challenges pastoral ideas about sympathetic growth through contact with the nonhuman—an idea the novel asks us to reject. As Tony Hughes-d'Aeth points out, we are given a series of false signals about the possibility of M's redemption in conventional humanist terms—'the promise of redemption remains dangled before the reader throughout the novel', as he puts it—but his apparently 'inhuman' identity is the only fully realized identity.[31] Rather than a '"character", within the humanist precepts of this idea', capable of growth and development, M is an 'agent' more akin to the 'android-hero' of 'the *Terminator* film series' (which is expressly evoked in the novel (p. 126)).[32] M reveals a chink in his mercenary armour when he begins to imagine himself taking the place of Jarrah in the Armstrong family home; but he loses this sentiment after weeks alone in the wilderness, when 'the melancholia deep inside him – the bucolia – works its way to the surface like a bullet or splinter being slowly expelled from a wound'. Now 'he comes to think of his fondness for Lucy and the children as an aberration' (p. 147). The coinage 'bucolia'—as a special form of 'melancholia'—suggests profound sadness for the loss of the bucolic perspective, a lament that a simple appreciation of the countryside is no longer available. When M's 'bucolia' 'surfaces'—and is expelled—he gains clarity of eco-dystopian purpose, no longer hampered by false sentiment. Again, Leigh is eclipsing the humanist tradition of the novel to encapsulate a longer human story, in which sentiment—the love, trauma, death of individual humans—is a distraction from man's consistent role of terminator, unable to desist in the prosecution of extinctions. But there is more to 'bucolia' than this: it is also the

---

[30] Jarrah's work is only briefly mentioned, but it seems to anticipate, or offer an ecological root for, the new materialism, in which matter is conceived as 'possessing its own modes of self-transformation, self-organization, and directedness, and thus no longer as simply passive or inert'. See Diana Coole and Samantha Frost, 'Introducing the New Materialisms', in *New Materialisms: Ontology, Agency, and Politics*, ed. Coole and Frost (Durham, N.C.: Duke University Press, 2010), pp. 1–45 (p. 10). Alternatively, it could be argued that Jarrah's ideas embody a contemporary (and secular) reconfiguration of the transcendentalists' idea of the oversoul, which transcends individual consciousness, and to which one returns on death.

[31] Hughes-d'Aeth, 'Australian Writing', p. 23.   [32] Ibid., p. 25.

emotional and nostalgic connection to the dissolving natural world, Leigh's way of identifying the disorientation of contemporary ecological consciousness. M is able to act as an exterminator because he is able to divest himself of such debilitating sentiment. The power of this novel resides in the effects that implicate us, forcing us into M's shoes as we try to resist him; and in that resistance we see how to distinguish ourselves from him. But the required response is contradictory to some degree, as we are obliged to embrace the confused predicament of our times, our 'bucolia'.

On the face of it, this makes *The Hunter* a distinctively contemporary ecological novel, by virtue of the contained paradox that it adopts to explicate its context. Leigh's emphasis on the atavistic hunting impulse, now felt to be a primary cause of the sixth mass extinction event, is pitted against the hope invested in the intellectual understanding of ecology. Our forced identification with the former, while we incline towards the latter, produces a more complex understanding of the predicament encoded in that term 'bucolia'. But this reading is partly dependent on the scientific moment of its conception. At the time of publication, hunting was presumed to be instrumental in the extinction of the thylacine: Leigh draws on the late twentieth-century status of this species, as iconic victim of human bloodlust, as she finds a contemporaneous equivalent to the ancient hunter in the unethical operations of biotechnology. When the thylacine's gene sequence was eventually captured in 2017, however, the scientific basis of the novel was undermined.[33] Subsequent research uncovered a genetic weakness in the thylacine that may have made it susceptible to climatic changes, so that the reduction of its range, and eventual disappearance, may have had a background contributory cause, downplaying the significance of hunting.[34] This is a rich irony: the intellectual understanding that Leigh holds out as a resource of hope eventually came in the guise of the bioscience that aroused her suspicion. And one eventual aim of the research, far from effecting the extinction of a species, is to clone and reintroduce the thylacine, controversial though that aim may be.[35]

The extent to which we see *The Hunter* as anachronistic, overtaken by science, is a matter for debate: the role of hunting as a major cause of extinction more generally is incontestable; and it may be that Leigh has good reason to question the

---

[33] Andrew J. Pask et.al., 'Genome of the Tasmanian tiger provides insights into the evolution and demography of an extinct marsupial carnivore', *Nature Ecology & Evolution*, 2 (2018), pp. 182–92; https://www.nature.com/articles/s41559-017-0417-y (accessed 27 November 2018).

[34] See Cheryl Jones, 'Climate killed thylacine on mainland Australia', *Cosmos*, 28 September 2017; https://cosmosmagazine.com/palaeontology/climate-not-dingoes-killed-the-thylacine-on-mainland-australia (accessed 21 November 2018).

[35] See Nerissa Hannink, 'Secrets from Beyond Extinction: The Tasmanian Tiger', 12 December 2017; https://pursuit.unimelb.edu.au/articles/secrets-from-beyond-extinction-the-tasmanian-tiger (accessed 21 November 2018). On genome sequencing as the first step towards cloning and reintroduction see John Pickrell, 'Tasmanian Tiger Genome May Be First Step Toward De-Extinction', *National Geographic*, 11 December 2017; https://news.nationalgeographic.com/2017/12/thylacine-genome-extinct-tasmanian-tiger-cloning-science/ (accessed 21 November 2018).

ethical grounding of commercialized biotechnology. Even so, the complication of the causes of the thylacine's extinction weakens the book's mimetic architecture, and this is an indicative example of the ways in which contemporary nature prose stands on the shifting ground of scientific knowledge.

Naming and Collecting

Since its inception in the seventeenth century, modern nature writing has been wrestling with the problem of knowledge, and the shifting basis of its authority. One aspect of this knowledge dilemma is the status of the amateur naturalist: nature writing has always had the capacity to focus attention on the separation between, and sometimes the convergence of, amateur and scientific natural history. But it is in the *union* of the two that some contemporary nature prose achieves its most powerful effects. Avian experts like Mark Avery understand the importance of data to the conservation of species, and the role that amateur birdwatchers—'birders'—play in gathering this data. This is a relatively recent phenomenon: Michael McCarthy records that national bird censuses started operating in the 1960s and were certainly galvanized by the concerns about the poisoning of birds raised by Rachel Carson in *Silent Spring* (1962).[36] This kind of activity points to elements that must be aligned in order to connect the recognition of rarity with the imperative of conservation: the urgency of producing authoritative data; the relationship between amateur and professional naturalism; and the primary role of a scientific approach to nature. But this last issue produces serious difficulties for nature writers who are pursuing an *immersive* approach to wild nature, and for whom scientistic authority can be an obstacle. From the perspective of biology, the classification and naming of species is fundamental, the beginning of the process by which science comes to understand the role of a species, its interaction with other named species, and the ecological function this interplay has. Without the classification and naming of species, ecosystems cannot be scrupulously investigated and understood, and conservation becomes impossible. As Christopher Kemp succinctly puts it, 'how can we protect an animal we haven't named?'[37] In fiction, however, the common-sense vantage point of contemporary ecology becomes less clear-cut. The exemplary instance of this major

---

[36] McCarthy, *Say Goodbye to the Cuckoo*, p. 193. McCarthy shows how forms of bird census and recording have had to improve and evolve. Because these forms of recording are relatively new, the fact of rapid decline in bird species has only been recently proven. See ibid., pp. 193–214. Conor Mark Jameson recalls that the Common Birds Census was 'just being launched' in 1962 (later superseded in Britain by the Breeding Bird Survey), prior to the British publication of *Silent Spring* in 1963, but also how Carson's book brought home 'the full extent of the issues involved'; see *Silent Spring Revisited* (London: Bloomsbury, 2012), pp. 26, 27.

[37] Christopher Kemp, *The Lost Species: Great Expeditions in the Collections of Natural History Museums* (Chicago: University of Chicago Press, 2017), p. xvi.

caveat—and an important precursor of twenty-first-century equivocations—is John Fowles's portrayal of the lepidopterist/abductor Frederick Clegg in his first novel, *The Collector* (1963). Clegg's fascination with 'catching a rarity' and 'setting' it in his collection of pinned dead butterflies is overtly paralleled with his capture of Miranda and her death as his prisoner.[38] Quite bluntly, Fowles suggests that the programmatic disciplines of taxonomic science interfere with the proper engagement with natural beauty, equating science with misogyny in the process.[39]

The Collector is not in the same category as Fowles's more complex novels.[40] Yet it is the urgency with which its thematic content is presented that is of interest here. Miranda expresses hatred for 'people who collect things, and classify things and give them names and then forget all about them', drawing a parallel with art criticism in which categorization is the focus—'they call a painter an impressionist or a cubist or something'—without attending to the artist 'as a living individual painter' (p. 55). Miranda's world view has been fashioned by her artist-mentor and would-be lover, George Paston, for whom art collectors are 'anti-life, anti-art, anti-everything' (p. 123). Paston places emphasis on the 'inmost heart' of an artist, and is dismissive of technical accomplishment (p. 159);[41] and in this he is made to enunciate much of Fowles's own views, including those to be found in the other text I want to consider here, *The Tree* (1979), an essay on nature and the problem of naming that has profound implications for nature prose and how we consider the topic of rarity. Here Fowles makes the same comparison between approaches to art and nature made by the characters in his first novel, complaining that 'our approach to art, as to nature, has become increasingly scientised ... during this last century'.[42] He rails against the process of 'labelling, classifying, analysing' by which artworks are reduced to 'specimens for "setting"' like moths and butterflies, so that—in the analysis of both art and nature—emphasis is wrongly placed 'on the created, not the creation' (pp. 55, 57).[43] He also identifies a kind of fall from the state of immersion in nature, so that persistent 'question-boundaries',

---

[38] John Fowles, *The Collector* (1963; London: Vintage, 1998), pp. 9, 44, 274. Subsequent references are given in parentheses.

[39] A nuanced understanding of Fowles's complaint is needed, if we are to keep in view his own accomplishments as an amateur naturalist. On this topic see Thomas M. Wilson, *The Recurrent Green Universe of John Fowles* (Amsterdam: Rodopi, 2006).

[40] Shyamal Bagchee is surely correct that *The Collector* is 'less distinguished than *The Magus*, *The French Lieutenant's Woman*, and *Daniel Martin*', and that its 'pronounced thematic and moralistic content' is not difficult to identify. See Syhamal Bagchee, 'The Collector: The Paradoxical Imagination of John Fowles', *Journal of Modern Literature*, 8 (1980–1), 2, pp. 219–34 (p. 219). Yet Bagchee still finds in *The Collector* 'a relatively complex philosophy of life' and an 'ironical technique' that is 'quite thorough' (p. 234).

[41] In this way, Fowles emphasizes creative individuality in *The Collector*, an anthropocentric conviction.

[42] John Fowles, *The Tree* (1979; Toller Fratrum: Little Toller Books, 2016), p. 55. Subsequent references are given in parentheses.

[43] Literary critics are included in the ranks of these 'professional explainers' for their propensity to reduce an 'original text to a corpse' by means of the 'long introduction' to set texts—a form of 'anatomy lesson' (p. 56).

consequent upon our habit of naming and classifying, distract us from 'the total experience and the total meaning of nature' (pp. 38, 39). Yet the line of argument in *The Tree* is eventually blurred, so that it becomes less a polemic against the process of naming and more a deliberation on how we are *necessarily* imprisoned by words.[44]

The book concludes with a staged scene in which Fowles withdraws into an isolated copse within Wistman's Wood on Dartmoor, and—as he puts it—'the botanist in me' provokes the habit of classification, so that he labels several species of flora (giving the Latin name for one), before withdrawing into the experience, 'the namelessness, the green phosphorus of the tree'. The experiment confirms his conviction that 'this namelessness is beyond our science and our arts because its secret is being not saying'. *The Tree* ends with this emphasis on the 'inalienable otherness' of nature as ineffable (pp. 98, 100). It contains Fowles's longest published passages of sustained nature prose; but it is presented as a demonstration of the impossibility of nature writing. As Fowles withdraws from Wistman's Wood, the experience of being in the silent copse, within the state of namelessness, recedes, 'already becoming an artefact, a thing to use' (p. 101).

For Fowles, this is related to a wider cultural problem, a form of alienation that can be demonstrated concisely with reference to the genre of the nature film, in which 'natural reality' is presented not just 'through other eyes', since the problem of vicarious experience is compounded by the selectivity, 'in which the novelty or rarity of the subject plays a preponderant part in choice and treatment' (p. 44). Rarity, then, becomes the key aspect of *commodification* in the presentation of the natural, and of the alienation of the viewer from the very thing he or she may seek affinity with.[45] Fowles's trip to Wistman's Wood, as recorded in *The Tree*, demonstrates for him the unsatisfactory and temporary nature of the *willed* immersive state. Pondering this problem, Thomas Wilson turns to David Abram to suggest a solution: Abram also 'sees the written word as creating a distance between humans and the natural world', but seeks to recuperate the 'participatory experience of non-human animals and the earth' found in 'tribal and indigenous societies'. Such experience might be imitated, for example, when

---

[44] The problem of language in its application to the nonhuman is not an unfamiliar perspective in ecocritical literature. Catriona Sandilands, for example, considers the experience of nature to be an 'unrepresentable kernel around which discourse circulates but which language can never fully apprehend'. See *The Good-Natured Feminist: Ecofeminism and the Quest for Democracy* (Minneapolis: University of Minnesota Press, 1999), p. 203.

[45] The impasse of *The Tree* has to do with Fowles's interest in Zen-like modes of experience. On this topic see Thomas Wilson's thoughtful contrast between Fowles's attitude and that of his contemporary, Gary Snyder—'more heavily influenced by Zen Buddhism'—for whom forgetting 'one's self for a moment' allows 'access to a less regressively language-bound way of being in the world' without inhibiting attempts to articulate that experience: Thomas Murray Wilson, 'The Writer Who Gave up on Names: John Fowles's Unwarranted Hostility Toward Nature Writing', *Interdisciplinary Studies in Literature and Environment*, 15 (2008), 1, pp. 135–51 (pp. 139–40).

nature writing 'underscores the soundscapes of particular ecosystems'.[46] For some nature writers, such as Abram, a version of primitivism is needed to facilitate the immersive state of being.

Fowles's complaint does not reckon with this route to solving the problem of distancing, however, because he has a different preoccupation. In the process of naming and categorization he sees a parallel in the alienation of 'most modern societies', in which people are 'brainwashed' to become 'highly acquisitive'; moreover, they are, he feels, trained to enjoy 'the act of acquisition' more than 'the fact of having acquired', since the pursuit is always of the new (p. 39). This sounds like a familiar critique of capitalist societies, and the function of built-in obsolescence in the regulation of consumption; but Fowles then immediately links this pursuit of new objects, when others become stale, to the 'context of nature' and the pursuit of 'new species and experiences' when 'everyday ones grow mute with familiarity'. This, suggests Fowles, is the 'unhappy legacy' of Victorian science, obsessed with 'exact taxonomy' (p. 40). Fowles thus presents us with a psychological prison in the realization that the desire to embrace the exceptional and rare aspects of wild nature may be tainted in advance by the habits of consumerism and the primary emphasis placed on economic growth in modernity. This is an instructive instance of how contemporary nature prose exposes the ways in which its own discourses might be compromised, as it ponders the paradoxes consequent upon cultural influence. The focus for Fowles, within that larger predicament, is the psychological straitjacket built into the work of taxonomy, and which is revealed in the habits of the collector.[47] The challenge, then, is to seek ways that enable us to embrace, rather than deny, our cultural influences and social habits—the things that partly define us—and to reorientate them in an environmentally purposive way.

The evolution of the natural history collection reveals a changing relationship to the quality of rarity, and a certain historical irony. Natural history collectors, as Susan Pearce points out, 'descended directly from the sixteenth-century gatherers of natural curiosities' with a change of direction in 'the last quarter of the seventeenth century, away from the "rarities", now seen as the sports and peculiarities of nature, and towards Nature herself, envisaged as an intricate but sensible pattern of corresponding and differing forms'.[48] Inspired by Carl

---

[46] Ibid., pp. 146, 151.

[47] This concern about naming and taxonomy—a scientific approach perceived as an obstacle to the engagement with nature—is a recurring concern in different modes of nature writing, something that dismays Dana Phillips. Commenting on Richard Nelson's problem with naming birds—specifically his reflection on how the distraction of trying to identify a flock of seabirds prevents him from actually seeing them—Phillips expresses puzzlement about the 'desire for a more perfect union with nature', asking 'why can't we just relax, enjoy the view, and identify the birds, too?' See Phillips, *The Truth of Ecology*, p. 223. Phillips is discussing Richard Nelson's *The Island Within* (San Francisco: North Point Press, 1989).

[48] Susan M. Pearce, *On Collecting: An Investigation into Collecting in the European Tradition* (London: Routledge, 1995), p. 264.

Linnaeus, such collecting focused on the classification and systematic ordering of nature's diversity. The irony of the historical cycle here is that such collections, already within the era of the sixth mass extinction event when they are established, are now storehouses of rare specimens, some of which have (or will) become extinct in the wild before they were (or are) identified. In another paradox, this irony is offset by the utopian ideal of the collection, conceived as a resource or storehouse of increasing ecological significance—an ethical goal which elevates collecting to a position of supreme importance for the conservation of nature.

Natural history, however, inspires contrasting forms of collecting. The roots of this distinction for the contemporary context, as Fowles indicates, lie in the Victorian enthusiasm for natural history, and the rise of the amateur collector. The personal collection of specimens, imperfectly labelled or stored, has little scientific value in comparison to the carefully curated museum collection, ready to make its evidence available to the insights of tomorrow's science. Yet this dichotomy between 'good' and 'bad' collecting is not simply based on historical progress. Kirk Wallace Johnson has identified diametrically opposed *contemporary* attitudes to the same collection—the rare bird specimens housed in the Natural History Museum at Tring—in his investigation of the major theft of rare bird skins carried out by an obsessive salmon fly-tier.[49] To the perpetrator of the act— and to others absorbed with the Victorian art of salmon-fly-tying—the liberation of feathers from rare or extinct birds, feathers needed for the practice of their art in its purest form, outweighs the claims of science. In Johnson's summary, 'some fly-tiers had questioned why, with hundreds of thousands of bird skins, museums needed so many "copies" of the same bird – they'd be better off selling them, wouldn't they?' In the course of his investigation, Johnson comes to understand the scientific basis of collecting, explained to him by the curators at Tring through a series of headline moments: Alfred Russel Wallace and Charles Darwin 'had drawn upon' the birds in the Tring collection 'to formulate their theory of evolution through natural selection'; the gradual thinning through time of shells in the egg collection provided evidence of the damage caused by DDT pesticides; 'feather samples' collected over a 150-year period 'were used to document the rising mercury levels in the oceans'; and now, by examining 'the concentration of carbon and nitrogen isotopes', scientists can 'reconstruct entire food webs throughout history' with important implications for conservation. In short, 'the birds held answers to questions that hadn't even yet been asked', as indicated by the importance of the Tring collection to 'the budding field of de-extinction', which 'relies in part upon extracting DNA from museum specimens in order [such is the hope] to bring lost birds like the Passenger Pigeon back to life'.[50] From

---

[49] Kirk Wallace Johnson, *The Feather Thief: Beauty, Obsession, and the Natural History Heist of the Century* (London: Hutchinson, 2018).
[50] Ibid., pp. 176–7.

this perspective, the theft was 'a natural history disaster of world proportions'.[51] The stubborn refusal of some fly-tiers to acknowledge the scientific importance of the collection reveals how the lure of natural rarity can cloud the intellect and generate an overwhelming desire to render a public collection private. Johnson extrapolates from these contrasting attitudes to identify fundamental human attitudes to nature collecting. On the one hand, there are those for whom 'the march of scientific progress would forever present new ways of looking at the same ancient skins'; and, ranked against these optimists, stand 'the centuries of men and women who looted the skies and forests for wealth and status, driven by greed and the desire to possess what others didn't'. For Johnson, these contrasting attitudes to nature collecting indicate 'a war between knowledge and greed'.[52]

If Johnson pins down the villainy in natural history collecting, Christopher Kemp locates its heroism. He makes us imagine a taxonomist, working in a dusty archive, someone who 'for the past several years...has immersed herself in the almost imperceptible differences that define the species within a particular genus'. It is she who has the eye 'to see patterns emerging', and to 'see something completely new' that is 'half-hidden among the centuries-old specimens'.[53] Such heroism, it should be noted, requires a certain resistance to contemporary methods. Kemp indicates that DNA barcoding will doubtless replace more traditional methods of naming, with regard to species difference, but what the mere process of classification misses is everything: 'by itself a bar code is as meaningless as a single musical note in isolation: nothing can be inferred from it'.[54]

As subsequent sections in this chapter will show, contemporary nature prose brings together elements of these contrasting impulses inherent in the act of collecting. Sometimes the urge to collect is presented as entirely benign. Robert Macfarlane, for example, presents the collection of natural objects while walking—'stones and other talismans'—as a way of consolidating a personal memory map, 'a way both to remember and to join up [his] wild places'.[55] For the professional scientist, collecting is also fundamentally purposive because meaningful work on species depends on the existence of physical specimens in collections, many of which are hidden in museum drawers, collected but waiting to be 'discovered'—to be recognized as new or significant. There remains to be addressed, however, Fowles's suspicion, shared by other commentators, about the motivation of the collector and the consequences of collecting—suspicions that extend beyond the fetishism of groups such as salmon-fly-tiers. Academic accounts of collecting have

---

[51] Ibid., p. 154.   [52] Ibid., p. 254.   [53] Kemp, *The Lost Species*, pp. 221–2.
[54] Ibid., p. 221. In some less sceptical accounts emphasis is placed on DNA sequencing to suggest that nature has an underlying textual structure. See, for example, Morton, 'Deconstruction and/as Ecology', pp. 291–6.
[55] Macfarlane, *The Wild Places*, pp. 87–8. Macfarlane shows that his collecting habit pales in comparison with that of Roger Deakin, 'an inveterate scavenger' of both crafted and natural artefacts (p. 105).

focused on museum studies, where the emphasis has often been on the different motivations of collectors, and the psychological implications of the subject–object relation. Very often the emphasis has been negative, identifying shades of domination or fetishism in the collector's psyche. The larger utopian ambitions of a natural history collection may not be properly registered in these analyses, but it is still worth considering the extent to which the charges laid at the collector's door are germane to that field.

These charges are detailed succinctly in an essay by narratologist Mieke Bal, who evaluates the received wisdom that 'collecting is an essential human feature that originates in the need to tell stories, but for which there are neither words nor other conventional narrative modes'.[56] This sets up an immediate inequality, because if 'collecting is a story, and everyone needs to tell it', it is at the same time 'obvious that not every human being is, or can afford to be, a collector'.[57] This may have some relevance to the fly-tier's theft of feathers, but less to the impersonal objectives of a natural history collection, or, indeed, to the motivations of the amateur in the era of citizen science, whose personal list-making—which requires knowledge and leisure, but not conspicuous wealth—may also contribute to national or international databases and the role they play in conservation. Yet in Bal's account the aesthetic dimension of collecting underscores the problem of privilege, because the cultivation of a collection's aesthetic profile requires an escape from the urgencies of the world. (Contrarily, one might argue that the natural history collection is predicated on an aesthetic that is designed precisely to address urgent global issues, by cultivating an appreciation of the nonhuman.) Bal's account focuses on the role of an individual collector, but she also considers how the collector's dubious motivations might be manifest in the public presentation of a collection:

> Deceptively, collections, especially when publicly accessible, appear to 'reach out', but through this complex and half-hidden aspect they in fact 'reach in', helping the collector – and, to a certain extent, the viewer – to develop their sense of self while providing them with an ethical or educational alibi.[58]

This suggestion that engaging with a collection puts the viewer in a collusive relationship with the collector is intriguing. The pretension of an ethical or educational motive is revealed as a mask, and the development of the self emerges as a kind of crime, requiring an 'alibi'. Given Bal's stress—analogous to Fowles's—on 'the intersection of psychic and capitalist fetishism' in the motivation of the collector, whose appropriation of property is concealed by the 'ameliorations' of

---

[56] Mieke Bal, 'Telling Objects: A Narrative Perspective on Collecting', in *The Cultures of Collecting*, ed. John Elsner and Roger Cardinal (London: Reaktion Books, 1994), pp. 97–115 (p. 103).
[57] Ibid. [58] Ibid., p. 105.

collecting's conventions, it makes some sense to view self-definition as a crime.[59] But this opposition between ethics and the self is troubling. It has some affinity with the anthropocentric/ecocentric opposition at the heart of so many ecocritical debates; and, once again, the challenge is to think beyond the binary, to find a way of bringing ethics and self together, or to descry a more productive dialogic interaction between the two.

In an essay about collecting, which is suggestive for the challenge I have just outlined, Noël Valis finds her memories of the Woolworth's store in Toms River, New Jersey, rekindled by reading Kazuo Ishiguro's *Never Let Me Go*, where Woolworth's is just as appealing to the clone Kathy as it was to Valis as a girl in the 1950s. Her memory of the marbles in their bin, even though she didn't collect them personally, inspires the reflection that 'in the moment that you see, hear, and touch something, the idea of collecting is already there; it preexists the collection itself'.[60] Valis remains mindful of the disturbing connotations of collecting—and of Woolworth's as a human depository—when she reminds us that Clegg in Fowles's *The Collector* 'finds his second specimen, Marian, behind the sweet counter at Woolworth's'. Valis is also conscious of the problematic theories about collecting, views 'that have one thing in common: they see it as a form of inadequacy'.[61] But she is also aware of a compelling counterview on collecting afforded us by Walter Benjamin, whose aphorism about the collector in his essay 'Unpacking My Library' is germane here: 'ownership is the most intimate relationship that one can have to objects. Not that they come alive in him; it is he who lives in them.'[62] It may be that a personal library is a special case, a very obvious source of benign self-realization in the way that, say, a collection of teaspoons may not be;[63] yet this would be to ignore Benjamin's thoughts about the collecting impulse per se: Valis argues that in *The Arcades Project* Benjamin 'thought collecting was at least partly biologically driven, pointing to the nest building of birds'.[64] In this suggestion, collecting reveals the vestige of some ancient genetic memory rather than the sheen of capitalist alienation that Fowles identifies in *The Tree*. But if we accept the suggestion that collecting signals some atavistic impulse, it would, presumably, have to do with a different form of acquisitiveness in the more elemental context of survival.

---

[59] Ibid., p. 115.
[60] Noël Valis, 'Collecting, the Rescue of Things, and the Human', *Yale Review*, 100 (2012), 3, pp. 67–85 (p. 68).
[61] Ibid., p. 71.
[62] Walter Benjamin, *Illuminations*, ed. Hannah Arendt, trans. Harry Zohn (London: Pimlico, 1999), p. 69.
[63] By implication, the instance of the personal library contradicts the arguments cited above, in which the development of language in Homo sapiens leads eventually to planetary destruction. Valis shares the current perspective of much nature prose, in which hope is invested in knowledge.
[64] Valis, 'Collecting, the Rescue of Things, and the Human, p. 79.

This is not, ostensibly, the focus of Valis's essay, which is concerned with the way in which 'memory and collecting go together' in pressing social contexts. It is not just that 'the collecting of things and things themselves play a fundamental role in creating the human'. More particularly, collecting can be seen as part of an impulse that *protects the human from oppression*, because the 'necessary relation between things and people is especially compelling in a time of repression'.[65] The impulse to collect has this embryonic social function, stemming from its role in facilitating self-definition. The human–object relation is not just a form of triangulation, of situating ourselves in space; it is more than this because the objects of our lives are also infused with our memories, and this insight has the power to overwhelm our niggles about the alienating effects of collecting. As Valis puts it, more poetically: 'we gather ourselves up in the same way we gather objects or memory itself'. In other words, 'discovery of the object' is also 'discovery of the self'.[66] But how is this self-realization different from the 'crime' Mieke Bal identifies, at the point where psychic and capitalist forms of fetishism intersect? One answer lies in Valis's illustration of 'the deep attachment characters form to objects and the complicated relation between possessing and being human'; she reminds us of the importance of Kathy's favourite tape cassette in *Never Let Me Go*, containing the song that gives the novel its title, and which is the source of one of that novel's most affecting scenes, as we recognize Ishiguro's purpose to reveal the humanity of Kathy, the clone. With reference to both *Never Let Me Go* and Orwell's *Nineteen Eighty-Four*, Valis deftly shows how the idea of a collection, linked to memory and the self, can be a defence—perhaps the only or last defence—against the dystopian drive to dehumanize: 'the self as a collection of things is continually needing to be rescued'.[67] Valis is not writing about nature prose; but her emphasis on the self as a collection of things has affinity with the eclectic structure of much contemporary nature writing, where objects in the landscape, or in a dwelling place, or in a museum, have a cumulative function in the personal quest to define and nurture an engagement with wild nature.[68] That which is deemed worthy of collection, of course, is often imbued with the qualities of rarity, so—if we accept the logic of Valis's argument about collecting—rarity can then take on a different significance, informing a personal quest that is not necessarily a sign of appropriation, especially if we consider the era of environmental crisis to be a time of oppression, requiring us to muster whatever resistance we can.[69]

---

[65] Ibid., pp. 69, 70.   [66] Ibid., p. 84.   [67] Ibid., pp. 78, 85.
[68] A good example is Adam Thorpe's *On Silbury Hill*, discussed in the Introduction.
[69] Among the sources of that oppression, we must include the political structures that are resistant to Green policies.

Quest Narratives

There is a popular subgenre of contemporary nature writing in which the pursuit of the rare is turned into a personal quest. A close inspection of this trend reveals a series of tensions that further illuminate the apparently opposed features I have been discussing, notably private versus public collecting and the role of the amateur in the face of scientific authority. The impulse to collect may be a necessary trait for those with an interest or knowledge in a specific phylum in nature, or class within a phylum. The larger question I wish to keep in view is the extent to which the naturalist's desire (or need) to collect can be seen as a manifestation of the human resistance proposed by Valis. I will return here to the example of butterflies, in an extension of my reflection on the charge levelled in Fowles's *The Collector*: that the lepidopterist epitomizes the deadening effect of scientific taxonomy.

The popularity of lepidoptery in Britain may be partly due to the distinctly achievable task of collecting the modest number of fifty-eight or fifty-nine species of butterfly resident in Britain.[70] A 'collection' for amateur lepidopterists is now usually a set of digital photographs rather than the series of mounted specimens favoured by Victorian amateur naturalists. In the twenty-first century, the quest to see/collect all of the British butterflies has found a focus in what Michael McCarthy dubbed 'The Great British Butterfly Hunt' when he was Environment Editor of *The Independent*. This was a challenge to readers to spot all of the British species in the summer of 2009.[71] His own attempt at the challenge is punctuated with a personal dedication to his mother each time he spots a different species.[72] It is a moving memorial, and one which intertwines personal and environmental destiny, in (apparently) a rhetorical ploy to resolve the book's central paradox—which, in various guises, is also the central dilemma of contemporary nature prose—the perceived incompatibility of anthropocentric and ecocentric needs.

---

[70] The count is fifty-nine if it includes the Réal's Wood White, found only in Northern Ireland, and which is distinct from the Wood White found in England. It has now been identified as a different species, the Cryptic Wood White. See Patrick Barkham, 'The Butterfly Isles Effect', *Butterfly*, 128 (Summer, 2018), pp. 30–1 (p. 31). The count of fifty-eight or fifty-nine includes two regular migrants, the Painted Lady and the Clouded Yellow. The number of species in Europe is 'approximately 560' according to *The Millennium Atlas of Butterflies in Britain and Ireland*, p. 2. These tallies are always subject to change. Some butterflies are at the northern extent of their range in Britain, which is why the species count is relatively small.

[71] 'The Great British Butterfly Hunt' has since become something of an institution. The idea was not entirely novel, however. Robin Page chronicles his attempt to see all of the British species in a single year in *The Great British Butterfly Safari* (Barton: Bird's Farm Books, 2003), while Phil Hall's five-year quest (2006–10) is recounted in *The Five-Year Butterfly Hunt* (Taunton: Brambleby Books, 2016).

[72] McCarthy, *The Moth Snowstorm*, pp. 232–8. Subsequent references are given in parentheses.

This example of the mode of nature therapy is so structured to suggest that the trauma of his bereavement is simultaneously personal and ecological.[73]

A similar rhetorical manoeuvre is apparent in Patrick Barkham's *The Butterfly Isles* (2010), an account of his own attempt at 'The Great British Butterfly Hunt'.[74] Barkham's book offers the revealing self-analysis of an obsessive aurelian, and an honest evaluation of the appeal of rarity to the collector. Barkham summarizes the appeal of nature observation for a boy in relation to 'scarcity, rarity, unpredictability and the boundless obsessive possibilities in creating lists and ticking things off'. At the same time, Barkham understands, rarity is also a sign of impending ecological collapse. In his lifetime this is marked most obviously by the fate of the species I mentioned in the Preface to this book, the Small Tortoiseshell. It is the first butterfly he sees on his year's quest, and also the most familiar species from his childhood, when Small Tortoiseshells could be seen in their 'dozens' by 'anyone...who had a garden at home', but this butterfly is now becoming a rarity.[75] Barkham's quest narrative is thorough, and presented with skill and enthusiasm, so that each of the species is individuated and intriguing. Of more interest, however, are those moments when the quest narrative breaks down. In one such moment, Barkham encounters an elderly couple on the Isle of Wight, and they observe together his current quarry, the Glanville Fritillary. The husband, who records his butterfly sightings for personal pleasure, exudes delight at meeting 'someone else who loved butterflies and was seeking what he had just found'. His simplicity and modesty, writes Barkham, 'made my mission to find all fifty-nine species during the course of one summer seem both frivolous and greedy'.[76] In such moments, where Barkham allows the mask to slip, he invites us to ponder the extent to which his project—and, in effect, the subgenre to which it belongs—is overshadowed by the simplicity of a different kind of amateur naturalist, prioritizing wonder over the catalogue. Yet the value of his own approach is tacitly reasserted in the book's coda, which records a sighting of the

---

[73] Richard Mabey's *Nature Cure* (2005; London: Vintage, 2015) is an early example of the latest nature therapy trend in Britain.

[74] Barkham undertakes his quest in 2009, but seems to have conceived of his project on his own. For Barkham, the correct tally is fifty-nine species, though he adds a sixtieth in a coda to the book (see below). Patrick Barkham, *The Butterfly Isles: A Summer in Search of our Emperors and Admirals* (London: Granta, 2010), p. 312; 'The Great British Butterfly Hunt' was launched by *The Independent* on 7 April 2009: see Michael McCarthy, 'Join the Great British Butterfly Hunt', https://www.independent.co.uk/environment/nature/uk-butterflies/join-the-great-british-butterfly-hunt-1665114.html (accessed 17 May 2018).

[75] Barkham, *The Butterfly Isles*, pp. 4, 40. Barkham records his first sighting, a Small Tortoiseshell, on 15 March 2009 (p. 339). The Small Tortoiseshell is in rapid decline, especially after the appearance of a parasitic fly since 1998, now finding Britain warm enough as a habitat, but also possibly because of other factors related to global warming, making this butterfly potentially 'one of the first victims of climate change'; ibid., pp. 42–3. The fly in question, the *Sturmia bella*, lays eggs on nettles where the Small Tortoiseshell caterpillars will eat them, the grubs hatching inside them: a fly emerges from the host chrysalis rather than a butterfly (p. 42).

[76] Ibid., p. 123.

rare migrant, the Queen of Spain Fritillary. This rarity gives Barkham cause to speculate, in a crafted and ambiguous ending, that climate change might temporarily allow other species (such as the Queen of Spain) to take up residence in Britain: 'British butterfly history unfolding before our very eyes', as he puts it.[77] It is the thoroughness of his approach, the persistence that leads him to a rarity beyond the anticipated catalogue, that produces his antithetical insight, a marvel that is also a foreboding.

As in McCarthy's book, the personal story intersects with the quest: Barkham breaks up with his girlfriend, possibly because she is concerned about becoming a 'butterfly widow'.[78] He gives a brief indication that they are reunited before the end of the book, but even before their break-up he has had an intimation that his relationship might be threatened by his obsessive lepidoptery.[79] Where McCarthy seeks to interweave the collector's quest with personal healing, Barkham suggests a point of imbalance between collecting and the personal life. Another way of fusing natural history and the personal story is apparent in the memoir of renowned naturalist and lepidopterist Matthew Oates, a specialist in the study of the Purple Emperor. Oates gives us a different insight into the lure of rarity and the nature of the preoccupation that develops through a lifetime partly devoted to an interest in a single species. For most amateur naturalists the Purple Emperor is a very rare butterfly.[80] Indeed, to see one, you need to take a trip to a known woodland habitat and take some foul-smelling lure to entice specimens down from the tree canopy. However—with the confidence of the expert—Oates writes that the Emperor is 'wrongly regarded as a great rarity', presumably because it is not at the point of extinction, which is partly due to the efforts of conservationists.[81] But this is the relative perspective of someone who is constantly seeking a greater rarity, a subspecies of the Emperor, the all-purple aberration *iole* in which the white wing markings are absent: Oates explains his fascination with the *iole* since boyhood,[82] and this is established as his personal quest species, his life quest in essence.[83]

The *iole* aberration remains his goal until he recalls the episode, on a July day in 2009, when he believes he has seen it. He recounts the trance-like state of consciousness this experience produces, a period of '25 minutes, into which was packed all the intensity of fifty years of butterflying'. His diary entry says: '*I've no*

---

[77] Ibid., p. 336. [78] Ibid., pp. 125, 313. [79] Ibid., p. 124.

[80] This butterfly is found in Asia as well as Europe, but in Britain it has declined in population significantly since the Victorian era. In *The Millennium Atlas of Butterflies in Britain and Ireland*, it is listed as a species of conservation concern, with a very sparse distribution map confined to southern England (pp. 188–91).

[81] Matthew Oates, *In Pursuit of Butterflies: A Fifty-Year Affair* (London: Bloomsbury, 2015), p. 400.

[82] Ibid., p. 34.

[83] Oates recalls the day in 1970 from his schooldays when, as he puts it, 'the Monarch of all the butterflies and the Emperor of the Woods finally entered my life'. It is a moment of personal transformation: the specimen, he writes, 'patrolling the high oak edge, flies on within my soul'. Ibid., p. 45.

idea what happened to me for an hour... I was in a waking dream.'[84] It turns out to be a semi-illusion, however, because he has actually seen a different aberration, the *lugenda*, on which some white wing markings remain. At this point in the narrative, the personal species quest is reasserted: 'once I finally encounter this miraculous chimera [the *iole*] I will give up butterflying, for the dream will then have been fulfilled'.[85] It does not happen; and the fulfilment of the dream cannot really be countenanced, within the terms of this narrative, because it would signal the end of butterflying, the end of Oates's focal engagement with nature. The book concludes with a mystical description by Oates of himself in the third person, and the Wordsworthian 'ministry' of his immersion in nature. The taxonomy of lepidoptery, the impulse of the collector, and the format of the quest narrative are all suddenly revealed as the means to this larger end: 'was it an Emperor, or an Admiral perhaps, or more? It mattered little, for the naming of something is only one small part of the experience of it'.[86] Oates intends his example as a naturalist to encourage others to 'seek depth of experience', beyond the cataloguing and the quests, and this is part of Oates's larger ecological imperative to mend 'the relationship between people and Nature'.[87] It is the lure of the quest narrative that structures our reading, however, and—in a relatively simple antithetical effect—we remain attached to the pursuit that Oates exhorts us to relinquish.

This pattern—in which the collector's urge to discover all the rarities and so achieve a complete catalogue is unsettled by a more profound form of encounter—recurs in the quest genre more widely. This contradictory mode comprises a self-conscious exposure of the constraints of the format combined with a quiet, if apologetic, insistence on its usefulness. There is a still more explicit collapse of the quest in Peter Marren's *Chasing the Ghost: My search for all the wild flowers of Britain* (2018). The subtitle outlines the quest, which is, more specifically, to find the fifty species that have eluded renowned naturalist Marren throughout a lifetime of flower finding, within a year. It is planned to end with the search for the most elusive of all—and Marren's personal 'Holy Grail'—the aptly named Ghost Orchid, which may or may not be extinct.[88] The quest fails, with six species remaining elusive.[89] This is partly due to ill health—the illness and death of Marren's mother, and then the collapse of his own health, with symptoms apparently exacerbated by the stress of grief and the pressures of the quest itself, which assumes less importance, especially after his mother's death. She was his 'first wild-flower mentor and companion', and her passing makes the project seem less significant.[90] In the concluding section detailing the search for the Ghost Orchid, which has not been seen in Britain since 2009, Marren reflects on the

---

[84] Ibid., p. 389. [85] Ibid., p. 390. [86] Ibid., pp. 464, 466. [87] Ibid., pp. 452, 462.
[88] Peter Marren, *Chasing the Ghost: My search for all the wild flowers of Britain* (London: Square Peg, 2018), p. 22.
[89] Ibid., pp. 264, 272. [90] Ibid., p. 242.

futility of the project, which 'had been doomed from the start'. On the grounds of ill health, he indicates there will 'probably be no more quests' for him,[91] and this allows a different conception of our engagement with wild nature to take prominence: 'if I do ever see a Ghost, it will be a new experience, not a codicil to a failed quest', he concludes, and ends by encouraging his readers to approach botany in a similar spirit, to 'find your own journey of flowers, perhaps a lifelong one', and thereby 'a new appreciation of life', in stark contrast to the list-ticking habit of his childhood, and the approach taken by the competitive 'pan-listers' in the ranks of contemporary amateur naturalists.[92] *Chasing the Ghost* is the story of a personal revelation, opened up by Marren's intimations of mortality, or personal extinction, which make the nature quest, at best, the means to a more reflective and less egotistical immersion in the nonhuman. Yet Marren's condemnation of the collecting impulse may be more equivocal than it seems for the obvious reason that the quest has facilitated what is felt to be a more responsive approach to wild nature.[93]

It is the aim of each of these quest narratives to stage an exemplary series of encounters with nature that might inspire readers, and in which the idea of the quest is the means to a different end. The real accomplishment for them all, as Barkham puts it, is to have received 'the gift of becoming, for a moment, here and there at least, a small, harmonious part of the natural world'.[94] Yet this process of displacing the quest, and the collecting instinct that gives rise to it, leaves a crucial aspect of these human engagements with wild nature unresolved: the instinct to collect is also an expression of the need to enfold and protect, a means of connecting the human family with the natural 'family' that is the collector's focus. The need of such a bridge can also be understood with reference to Valis's conception of the self as a collection of things. Oates locates his lifelong interest in the Purple Emperor to a day in childhood in 1970; for Barkham, the memory of a Small Tortoiseshell in the family garden is a moment of origin that connects him with contemporary anxieties about climate change; for McCarthy and Marren, their quests are also memorials to their mothers. At the same time, the naming of species, the spark of collecting, is the means by which the naturalist's evolving engagement with the wild is defined: the collecting impulse is the source of self-definition, even as it is recognized as a convenient tool to advance another kind of engagement. Yet this convergence of motivation, suggestive of

---

[91] Ibid., pp. 272, 273.   [92] Ibid., pp. 274, 276, 11, 26–7.

[93] In a less obsessive quest, *Dragonflight: In Search of Britain's Dragonflies and Damselflies* (London: Bloomsbury, 2013), Marianne Taylor focuses on the forty species of regular breeding British odonata (dragonflies and damselflies), with hints of encounters with rarer 'vagrant' species. Personal suffering, again, recalibrates the quest when the end of a relationship interferes with the completion of the project (pp. 171, 180–1); and the chance sighting of a rare bird, a Baillon's crake, when Taylor is unsuccessfully seeking the southern migrant hawker, emphasizes the serendipitous engagement with natural rarity (pp. 207, 218–19).

[94] Barkham, *The Butterfly Isles*, p. 313.

tension and potential contradiction, is not fully developed in the popular quest genre; but it loosely defines the components of another form of paradox in contemporary nature prose. I will conclude this section with a discussion of two texts in which this convergence of motives, and the ambivalence of the quest, yield some powerful formal results—a novel, and then a first-hand account.

A possibly extinct species from the south-east US, the ivory-billed woodpecker, is (in a sense) the main protagonist in Chris White's debut novel, *The Life List of Adrian Mandrick* (2018). The ivory-bill's status on the IUCN Red List has been changed from 'extinct' in the 1990s to 'critically endangered' from 2000 on account of 'strong' but 'controversial' claims for the persistence of the species based on occasional sightings in Arkansas and Florida.[95] White trades on the uncertain status of the ivory-bill, on the cusp of extinction due to habitat depredation, in the portrayal of her main human protagonist, the expert birder Adrian Mandrick, who stands to improve his ranking in 'the North American birding region' from third to first by adding the ivory-bill to his personal 'life list' of catalogued sightings.[96] Ostensibly, nature is used to illuminate the human events; but White finally inverts this conventional pattern of framing nature in fiction. Adrian's obsessive birding is evidently that form of collecting that induces alienation. Appropriately, he works as an anesthesiologist (an anaesthetist in Britain), able to feed his addiction to painkillers with bogus prescriptions, a habit that is linked to his estrangement from his mother who, he believes, had abused him as a child. As he succumbs to his addiction, a progression exacerbated by the death of his mother, so does he alienate himself from his wife and children. The obsession with the 'life list' is another form of anaesthetic (p. 96).

Yet birding is the route to his salvation. This begins when he becomes sympathetic to the posts of a novice birder on the 'Backyard Birder's chat room' whose ineptitude had previously drawn his scorn. This anonymous novice, who is evidently stalking Adrian online, turns out to be his estranged father, luring him to a meeting with the promise of an encounter with the ivory-bill. When Adrian's parents broke up, his father had planted the seed of the thought that Adrian's mother had sexually abused him when he was very small; now the father wishes to make amends for the false accusation, made when he was 'twisted up with what [he] couldn't have' (p. 250). There is no ivory-bill in the location to which Adrian has been lured; but his father, Dean, gives him the gift of the precious species in the form of a photograph from his childhood, taken when Adrian was on a birding expedition with his mother, in which the rare woodpecker can be plainly seen

---

[95] The IUCN is the International Union for Conservation of Nature. For details of the ivory-billed woodpecker, or *Campephilus principalis*, see http://www.iucnredlist.org/details/22681425/0 (accessed 3 February 2022). It was still listed as 'Critically Endangered' in 2022, but with the qualification of being 'possibly extinct' in the US.

[96] Chris White, *The Life List of Adrian Mandrick* (New York: Touchstone, 2018), p. 16. Subsequent references are given in parentheses.

(pp. 259–60). It is the same photograph mentioned at the beginning of the novel, when his mother had tried to show Adrian that the photograph revealed the distinctive marking of the rare bird, and not the 'common Pileated Woodpecker' with its similar marking (pp. 2–3). That childhood memory is retrieved from myth at the novel's end, so that the ivory-bill, which makes this uncertain appearance in the first few paragraphs, and haunts much of the subsequent action, now reappears at the novel's end—if only in the photograph—confirming its materiality in Adrian's experience.

The fact that this confirmed sighting gives Adrian the longest life list amongst the North American birding fraternity, the most complete personal collection, is made insignificant when he hands over his precious book of sightings to his wife, Stella, 'for safekeeping', a first gesture in trying to rebuild their marriage (p. 264). He extracts the photograph of the ivory-bill, however, and Stella suggests that he takes it with him. Gesturing at it, his eyes brimming with tears, Adrian says, 'those birds are all gone...they're so much more fragile than anybody thought' (pp. 264–5). This is the most affecting moment in the book, and it mitigates some of the plot contrivances by displacing the human interest, a recurring feature of fictional nature prose. We remain invested in the possibility of the family being reunited, in the realization of Adrian's desire 'to nurture and protect his own two children', righting the wrong of his own wrecked childhood (p. 265). In this sense, his mother's photograph of the rare ivory-bill becomes a time capsule of care, making the healing a possibility, and to this extent the human and the natural are deftly interwoven. Yet White is also splitting them apart: the bird was extant in Adrian's childhood, but is now extinct, he has realized. Its presence as the book's main preoccupation, a shadowy protagonist that drives Adrian's ambition and then, unexpectedly, redeems his childhood, dissolves in Adrian's acceptance of the brute fact of its absence. The utility of the ivory-billed woodpecker for White, structuring the human drama, also dissolves, a gesture that unsettles the novel's modus operandi and refocuses our attention on the fact of extinction, a mood anticipated at the beginning of the seventeenth chapter, when White (or her authorial narrator) breaks the frame and presents us with 'the cold, hard facts' of extinction as 'a black-and-white equation': 'no amount of financial wizardry, artistic genius, media glitz, religious feeling, or political heft can influence it once it's reached critical mass' (p. 262). This is the intellectual setting of Adrian's tears of remorse, remorse for the loss of a species that has defined his life in conflicting ways—the falsity of the life list set against the healing balm of the photograph, which provides evidence simultaneously of the bird's earlier existence and his mother's care. But the species is now understood to have been experiencing its own demise through his lifetime. The remorse can then be seen as an apology for the culpable anthropocentrism of his story—and the novel's design—but also as a way of laying claim to that narrative through the other experience that remorse prepares for: redemption. It is a definitively indissoluble contemporary paradox.

The South African conservationist Vernon Head offers an equally thoughtful and nuanced account of rarity's lure in his quest adventure to find what he calls 'the rarest bird in the world', the Nechisar nightjar.[97] The justification for giving the Nechisar nightjar this status of unmatched rarity is that it is a species known to exist, but which had never been seen, because the only collected specimen is a single detached wing held in the museum at Tring. For Head, the single wing is the ultimate enticement, 'spark[ing] imagination and dreams': 'this small wing', he writes, 'was to become my own personal story of birdwatching' (p. 22). The Tring collection inspires him to a lyrical celebration of the natural history museum per se, and of the discipline it enshrines. It is, he writes, 'a powerful cultural cathedral of logic', and 'a beautiful educational view of the wilderness, talking of wild mystery, telling of a way of seeing nature by naming things' (p. 26). As the source of scientific enquiry, museums 'are home to the pioneers who search the wilderness for our lost past and our lost future, reminding us of the importance of the pristine' (p. 27). That word 'pristine' epitomizes Head's infectious lyricism: he means something more than 'unspoilt wilderness' by it, a complex quality that combines the purity of the wild with an admonishment aimed at the perpetrators of habitat depredation. Purity, in this conception, is another irreducibly antithetical term.

Head thoroughly inhabits the Adrian Mandrick world view fictionalized by Chris White; indeed, he exceeds it in his reflection on the 'lifer' (that is, another specimen added to the birdwatcher's life list):

> Lifer is a big word for us. It sits alongside words like rarity, extinction, even love. Seeing a lifer is a special moment, an accomplishment, the end of a particular journey and the beginning of the next, a pause in time to wonder and celebrate the diversity and fecundity of life. It is a profound moment, but fleeting. (p. 37)

Head's unequivocal celebration of the intellectual disciplines—and obsessions—of both birdwatchers and natural historians distinguishes his book from the other quest narratives considered here. He is aware of the 'numbers game' played by some birdwatchers; but he emphasizes the sublimation of this process, and the significance 'of what it means to truly watch enquiringly', so that the list becomes a kind of portal to the thorough immersion in the nonhuman that all questers are seeking. For Head, 'each name is a story of an interaction, a time of connection with the pristine' (that loaded, ambivalent term), but also the route to 'an understanding of our place in the system of natural things' (pp. 121–2). He is afforded an example of what this might mean when he encounters cows being

---

[97] Vernon R. L. Head, *The Search for the Rarest Bird in The World* (Oxford: Signal Books, 2015). Subsequent references (in parentheses) are to this edition. As 'Head' is a relatively uncommon surname, I should point out that there is no relation (as far as I know).

herded 'on the plain at Nechisar' (p. 141), with birds feeding on the parasitic insects on the cows' bodies. More precisely, 'men herded cattle and cattle herded men': it is a 'herd of cattle and men and birds' (p. 146). This simple and pre-modern scene of cooperation, apposite for this place on the 'very edge of the cultivated and farmed, on the edge of our human world, the furthest places humans occupy', affords him an intimation that 'people are a part of the pristine' (p. 146). There is a sense in which the perception of this idealized human state—combining the twin perspectives of pre-modern integration and contemporary ecological critique—is the true heart of the quest; it is certainly preparatory to the brief encounter with 'the rarest bird in the world' that Head and his colleagues on the expedition are finally granted, and which inspires in him an extraordinary epiphany:

> I flew up to be with the bird, possessing it in an air of partnership, talking to it like a friend. I climbed with the bird into the higher air, private air. We glanced below at the car like a little ship, squatting solidly, grey and foreign, bursting with torch-light flickers: little twitching candle flames. And I watched myself down there with my fellow birdwatchers, all looking up into the stars. I could see myself smile, and feel the glow. I became different. The buoyancy of wings was everywhere, padding my mind as the bird and I floated together, bobbing about.
>
> (p. 154)

The delight, and the *construction* of the delight, are simultaneously palpable; and so the epiphany is also a non-epiphany, the notional sudden insight compromised by its careful preparation and precise recapitulation. Head draws on the out-of-body sensations reported by those who have had a near-death experience, as well as on the long-standing literature in which bird flight is imagined and infused with human reflection.[98] It is, however, the assertion of the union with the bird—the 'partnership', friendship, togetherness—that makes this moment seem wilful, producing a resistant reader. Head, however, insists on the importance of this extremely rare and fleeting moment of just 'six seconds', but 'the most exciting six seconds of a lifetime' (p. 155). What he is doing is celebrating the constructions to which we must have recourse, as the only means of worthwhile connection: 'naming is how we find our way through the physical landscape and the landscape of the mind...we are enriched in the act of naming' (p. 162). The source of such enrichment is concentrated in the rarity:

> The rarity embodies all that is threatened, and reminds us of a shrinking world. The rarity speaks of evolution and of the fleeting existence of species. The rarity

---

[98] Richard Bach's fable *Jonathan Livingston Seagull* (New York: Macmillan, 1970) is perhaps the most famous example of the attempt to infuse bird flight with profound human meaning.

has become a treasured living symbol of the precious, of change. It reminds us of the temporariness of life and of life's different forms. Sprinkled in the wilderness around us, these rarities lie hidden – the special ones, the keepers of the untamed, the last gatekeepers of the pristine. (pp 181–2)

This is a remarkable attempt to reclaim rarity as a quality to celebrate and to dignify the quest narrative. Rarity is a stark reminder of extinction, but also a sign of evolution. If we cherish the rare, it also reminds us of the processes of wild nature, and our modest place (as individuals) within it. And, if approached with proper scientific understanding, rarity educates us about the integrative essence of ecosystems: 'when we look upon the rare, diversity is confirmed; and we value the common more' (p. 183).

The effect of Head's book is to produce a rather different kind of ambivalence to that generated in the texts considered earlier. There is the dialectical impulse that Richard Shelton detects, which resides in Head's ability to transcend the 'austere requirement[s]' of 'academic ornithology' on the one hand, and 'the twitchers' soulless obsession with ticking off lists of rarities' on the other. Head shows us, says Shelton, 'how both approaches may be combined and enhanced in a way which recaptures the spirituality of a Gilbert White or a Thomas Bewick'.[99] But there is also something richer that goes beyond the reclamation of a style through this synthesis of modes. Head's lyricism seeks to afford us a glimpse of the 'pristine', a response that is partly dependent on the temporary or partial suspension of our intellectual faculties, as we allow the rhetorical flow to carry us; at the same time, retrieving the associations of the pristine depends on the reassertion of the intellect. Head has fashioned a form, in other words, that embraces the *feeling* of our predicament in the world of ever increasing scientific sophistication in the comprehension of ecology (one element of the pristine), but which also reveals the faint possibility of sharing, self-consciously, the state enjoyed by the herders on the plain.

Rethinking Rarity

In the examples I have discussed, rarity can connote several slightly different, but interrelated, things: an extinct or threatened species; a personal quest to find a species, and to extend a collection of sightings (the 'life list'); an immersive experience in the nonhuman, where the rarity could reside in the perception rather than the phenomenon observed; and a personal revelation, which may lead the observer to an enriched (if self-conscious) state of communion with the

---

[99] Richard Shelton, 'On the Wing', *Times Literary Supplement*, 5898, 15 April 2016, p. 28.

wild. In the remainder of this chapter I will look more closely at the implications of these forms of cultural appropriation; but first it may be prudent to reconsider the definition of rarity in biological science, which conditions the understanding of each of these appropriations.

A short definition of rarity seems simple enough: a species that is deemed to be rare 'occupies a narrow geographic range, has a low abundance, or exhibits both traits', as Dinerstein explains.[100] It is not always recognized, however, that 'many, many species on Earth are rare'—possibly 'as much as 75 percent of all species'— so that the problem facing conservationists is to distinguish between rarity caused by human interference and effects that might be reversed or addressed, on the one hand, and rarity that is simply an inevitable state of affairs, a consequence of blind ecological process, on the other.[101] The picture is complicated by the Homogenocene, the term that describes the new ecological state partly defined as the Anthropocene. The latter refers to the current period in which the human impact on nature is deemed to be so pervasive that it will characterize a new geological era. The Homogenocene, more narrowly, identifies the consequences of human interference in the range and habitat of species. Human action facilitates the spread of species beyond their original range, so that 'natural habitats around the world, full of invasive species, begin to resemble one another'. The condition of rarity in this homogenized world 'could mean something much different from when these same species first appeared in relative isolation'.[102] Rarity can also be caused by geology, as when (for example) rugged, isolated terrain causes a species to divide, and mutate and adapt to very specific habitats. Such divergence can lead to the birth of a new species in a process known as 'speciation'.[103] In the tropics, Dinerstein observes, 'many species...naturally occur at low population densities and hence are rare'. This can be due to 'the sheer number of species' in an ecosystem which results in 'a kind of diffuse competition in which the interactions of many species keep others in a limited range or at a low density'. Geography, geology, 'isolation and speciation' are all 'engines of rarity'.[104] The different conditions of rarity—and the fact that it is not always a consequence of human interference—gives an additional reason for viewing the collecting impulse indulgently: the desire for the rare species is not always linked to human depredation, in that ironic vicious circle. Even so, Dinerstein alerts us to 'the allure of the rare', our propensity to be 'seduced by rarity and novelty', which for naturalists— professional and amateur—can lead to the construction of 'quest species', and the 'single-minded pursuit' of the kinds considered in the previous section.[105] In my consideration of *how* nature prose makes us rethink the relationship between

---

[100] Dinerstein, *The Kingdom of Rarities*, p. 4. A third condition of rarity is the loyalty of a species to a particular habitat (p. 86).
[101] Ibid., p. 4.   [102] Ibid., p. 6.   [103] Ibid., pp. 18–19.   [104] Ibid., pp. 44, 46.
[105] Ibid., pp. 11–12.

rarity and extinction, by attending to those textual effects that might produce new knowledge in readers, I am questioning the dominance of the *what*, the environmental agenda, in isolation.

There is a difference, however, between the attempt to identify some of the formal characteristics of this emergent genre and a more insistent culturalism, such as Heise's provocative emphasis on biodiversity and extinction as *cultural constructions*, embedded within 'endangerment narratives' that, for Heise, promote an interest in species that have broad appeal, the 'charismatic megafauna' or 'flagship species' that are 'good tools in campaigns to raise public awareness', but which, when singled out, can serve to obscure the plight of other species without the same appeal, species which may be 'more endangered or more crucial for ecosystemic functioning'.[106] Such narratives, in this argument, become detached from the task of promoting ecological understanding. Heise identifies a reliance on the conventions of elegy and tragedy so that 'the endangerment of a particular species comes to function as a synecdoche for the broader environmentalist idea of nature's decline as well as for the stories that communities and societies tell about their own modernization'. Viewed as 'part of the cultural history of modernity', these narratives, argues Heise, reveal a different kind of crisis.[107] The generic conventions take these narratives beyond their referents, so that 'what is lost... is not just particular ties to nature but also particular stories about these ties, so that thinking about extinction becomes a story about the loss of stories'.[108] One could argue that the texts examined above, such as Julia Leigh's *The Hunter*, illustrate Heise's point about the selective single-species account: the charismatic Tasmanian tiger, or thylacine, with its popular and iconic appeal, is a choice selection, and the novel might be said to falsify the fact of extinction—manufacturing a narrative of loss—especially after the subsequent DNA sequencing led to speculation that qualified the role of hunting in the thylacine's demise. I suggested above that the shifting knowledge base weakened *The Hunter*'s purchase on biological reality; yet Leigh's powerful study of the hunter's psyche retains its force by implicating the reader in the history of extinctions, with the thylacine standing merely as one example. And the 'bucolia' Leigh implies we must embrace points to more than cultural loss. Bucolia *does* embrace an emotional and nostalgic response to the endangered world, it is true; but it also requires of us a self-conscious and informed understanding of the current disorientating times. In such antithetical effects—Vernon Head's idea of the 'pristine' is another example—we find a fusion between cultural and scientific responses, rather than a false prioritization. The endangerment narratives considered here do not eclipse the fact of extinction. They sometimes *do* lament the demise of their

---

[106] Heise, *Imagining Extinction*, p. 24.   [107] Ibid., p. 32.   [108] Ibid., p. 45.

own conditions of possibility, but they remain focused on the facts of endangerment, even while they make rarity a focus of self-conscious reflection.

The emphasis in the readings in this chapter has been on a mode of expression in which apparently opposed tendencies—self- and collective interest, anthropocentric and ecocentric views—are embraced to convey a full account of the human response to natural rarity. This aesthetic, in which the dubious is absorbed rather than denied, serves to highlight and redeem human foibles instead of seeking to expunge them. As a final example, I end this chapter with a reading of a novel by Barbara Kingsolver, *Prodigal Summer*, which seeks a comparable route to the resolution of competing perspectives on rarity. Indeed, rarity is the organizing principle in Kingsolver's novel, and this has different facets. The most obvious elements are those that broach environmental and political agendas, and this can make the novel seem didactic, as is often the case with Kingsolver; but these strands are ultimately resolved in unpredictable ways, as she complicates her message. That message can seem obvious, at a macro political level, with an easily detectable commentary on the problem of farming, and the threat of 'extinction' confronting this occupation in the region that Kingsolver knows best. Her method, underpinned by her 'academic training in evolutionary biology and ecology', results in a novel with seemingly clear political ambitions, 'a blueprint for saving the small family farm and for restoring ecological balance in a southern Appalachian bioregion that is struggling to survive', as Suzanne Jones puts it.[109] This apparently straightforward mimetic mood, in which Kingsolver the scientist recuperates rural skills, in fact belies the guile of Kingsolver's craft, which hinges on the way its apparent didacticism fades, leading the reader into a less certain response.[110]

The surface didacticism consolidates around Kingsolver's attempt to encourage us to 'reform the way we live and the way we think about home', in Kristin Van Tassel's words. The focus on the female farmer is central to this ideological promotion of a 'new pastoral' which celebrates, against the odds, 'the possibility of returning to an agrarian life, one that is ecologically healthy and socially equitable'.[111] At this level of ideas, the novel appears to debate alternative conceptions of farming, as well as engaging with the US tradition of nature writing, notably by rearticulating Aldo Leopold's 'land ethic'.[112] These organizing ideas

---

[109] Suzanne W. Jones, 'The Southern Family Farm as Endangered Species: Possibilities for Survival in Barbara Kingsolver's *Prodigal Summer*', *Southern Literary Journal*, 39, (Fall, 2006), 1, pp. 83–97 (p. 84). Jones puts Kingsolver in the ranks of 'southern environmentalist writers' including Wendell Berry and Janisse Ray (p. 83).

[110] This formal operation is comparable to, but more extensive than, the displacement of anthropocentrism detected in *Flight Behaviour* in the previous chapter.

[111] Kristin Van Tassel, 'Ecofeminism and a New Agrarianism: The Female Farmer in Barbara Kingsolver's *Prodigal Summer* and Charles Frazier's *Cold Mountain*', *Interdisciplinary Studies in Literature and Environment*, 15 (2008), 2, pp. 83–102 (p. 91).

[112] As we have seen in previous chapters, Leopold's land ethic 'changes the role of *Homo sapiens* from conqueror of the land-community to plain member and citizen of it'. See Leopold, *A Sand County*

seem unequivocal, anthropocentric, and without much purchase on the topic of rarity. Yet Kingsolver gradually complicates her themes through a series of richer individual plot lines. These narrative strands are conditioned by facets of rarity, and the ways in which encounters and engagements with rarity have a causal effect in changing the consciousness of Kingsolver's characters. Priscilla Leder shows how each of the novel's three interwoven stories contains 'a kind of parallel ecosystem', and that in each case the central protagonist 'emerges from solitude' as their place in their own ecology is defined.[113] This is well said; but what needs to be stressed is that, in each case, it is *rarity* that supplies the route to enhanced ecological functionality, whether this is perceived in managed nature or in the cultural systems that are invested in it.

One of the commanding features in Kingsolver's landscape is a giant hollow chestnut log, felled by the grandfather of Garnett Walker.[114] As a retirement project, Walker—widowed and increasingly senile—sets himself the task of reintroducing the American chestnut, presumed to have been made extinct by 1950, having succumbed to Asian fungal disease (p. 129). By 'crossing and backcrossing' American chestnuts (preserved in seed stock) with the disease-resistant Chinese variety, Garnett hopes to restore 'the landscape of his father's manhood' (p. 130). Garnett's confusion is partly signalled by this patriarchal thought, but chiefly by his creationist views (p. 186), at odds with his horticultural practice, which involves imitating evolutionary processes of selection, as his neighbour Nannie Rawley points out (p. 280). His own quest for a rare specimen is realized when Nannie tells him there are two surviving American chestnuts in her wood-lot, and a potential source of an 'infusion of fresh genetic material ... for his program' (p. 343). The ideological conflict between pesticide enthusiast Garnett and Nannie, a certified organic producer, is effectively nullified by Garnett's drive to reintroduce and improve an extinct species. He grapples with a realization about natural balance when he reflects on the proximity of these surviving American chestnuts: 'now that he thought about it, if those trees had been shedding pollen all along they might already have helped him out, infusing his fields with a little bit of extra diversity' (p. 343). In a quid pro quo, the rarity that Garnett already possesses is a stack of obsolete hand-cut roof shingles, which

---

Almanac, p. 204. On this aspect of Kingsolver's novel see Peter S. Wenz, 'Leopold's Novel: The Land Ethic in Barbara Kingsolver's *Prodigal Summer*', *Ethics and the Environment*, 8 (2003), 2, pp. 106–25. Priscilla Leder (following Michael Pollan) suggests that Kingsolver extends the Leopold tradition by privileging a 'garden ethic' over a 'wilderness ethic', thereby promoting a conscious adaptation to different circumstances, and a principle of management, or responsible husbandry, in which the human actor must be conscious of his or her separation from nature. See Priscilla Leder, 'Contingency, Cultivation, and Choice: The Garden Ethic in Barbara Kingsolver's *Prodigal Summer*', *Interdisciplinary Studies in Literature and Environment*, 16 (2009), 2, pp. 227–43 (pp. 231–2). Leder is drawing on Michael Pollan's *Second Nature: A Gardener's Education* (New York: Dell, 1991).

[113] Leder, 'Contingency, Cultivation, and Choice', p. 227.
[114] Barbara Kingsolver, *Prodigal Summer* (New York: HarperCollins, 2000), p. 82. Subsequent references are given in parentheses.

are eventually used to repair Nannie's roof (pp. 135, 373). These shingles, originally shared by Garnett's and Nannie's fathers, contribute to the rapprochement, and the historical restoration of cooperation between the two families.

The novel's lesson in rewilding is conveyed by the coyotes, whose appearances punctuate the narrative; but Kingsolver transcends her discursive theme by virtue of the bond with the coyotes felt by the wildlife biologist Deanna Wolfe. In this way, Kingsolver moves her readers from the simple message that rare predators must be preserved/reintroduced in the interests of ecological balance to a perspective of affinity: with Deanna as our surrogate, we progress from the intellectual grasp of humanity's pragmatic dependence on wildlife, intensified by our comprehension of its rarity, to a sense of identification with this instance of rarity, so that rarity becomes the route to an energizing—and integrative—mode of perception. Deanna feels the need to articulate her bond with the coyotes precisely in terms of this progression, and closing of distance, so that her aim is 'not to dissect their history and nature' because 'she had done that already', but, rather, 'what she craved to explain was how much they felt like family' (p. 203). In a dramatic final withdrawal from the mode of didactic realism, Kingsolver narrates the last chapter from a coyote's point of view, displacing the human perspective with a different form of ecomimesis, but also forcing the reader to identify with a coyote's priorities, through anthropomorphic projection: 'she loved the air after a hard rain, and a solo expedition on which her body was free to run in a gait too fast for companionship' (p. 441). Here we are asked to embrace the vitality of wild being, but also to sense its tensions, where a pack animal can also thrive on solo freedom.[115]

Kingsolver's emphasis on the importance of diversity in ecosystems is the underlying principle that knits together individual instances of rarity, in a cumulative pattern of meaning. This pattern also allows her to develop the contemporary trope in which human migrancy finds parallels in the nonhuman realm: again, that parallel is drawn through the figure of rarity. Despite the damage done by the introduction of some non-native species and organisms (notably the Asian fungus that killed off the American chestnut), knowledge-based ecological improvements reveal hope, as in the migration of the coyote to southern Appalachia, a new larger predator that might restore balance to the food chain. In this way, Jones suggests, Kingsolver 'breaks down simplistic oppositions between natives and non-natives, preparing readers to see the beneficial nature of the human exotic that she introduces in the character of Lusa Maluf Landowski', who is a rich ethnic hybrid, of Arabic and Jewish descent: her mother's parents 'were Palestinian', and her

---

[115] Dilia Narduzzi has demonstrated an extended parallel between Deanna and the female coyote, which is especially evident in the repeated descriptions in the first and last chapters. See Dilia Narduzzi, 'Living With Ghosts, Loving the Land: Barbara Kingsolver's *Prodigal Summer*', *Interdisciplinary Studies in Literature and Environment*, 15 (2008), 2, pp. 59–81 (pp. 75–6).

father's were 'Jews from Poland' (p. 151).[116] An 'exotic' human thus becomes the valuable rare specimen in the transposition of an ecological principle to the consideration of human continuity, since it is Lusa who has the capacity to save the Widener family farm, restoring balance through her own 'widening' faculties: enlarging the variety of farming activities; embracing ecologically sound methods; and extending the conception of 'family'.

There is, of course, something schematic about this biological hybridity; but this gives Kingsolver another opportunity to complicate her pattern. The abiding and most resonant impression of Lusa takes us beyond the neat ecosystem analogy, through a more unsettling analogy that emerges from her sexuality. This is also a resolution of Kingsolver's dialogue with Annie Dillard's *Pilgrim at Tinker Creek*. In *Prodigal Summer* there is an extended riposte to Dillard's seminal chapter 10, 'Fecundity', and the revulsion (discussed in Chapter 3 above) that flows from Dillard's dream about the Luna moths mating 'with a horrid animal vigor', and which mutates into a vision of 'a thousand chunky fish' hatching from eggs into 'a viscid slime' (*Pilgrim*, p. 144). In *Prodigal Summer*, a series of dreams about the Luna moth and fecundity chart the integration of Lusa into the southern Appalachian environment, as a social and natural being, through her sexuality.

The significance of the Luna moth in Lusa's mental development is explained by one of her last memories of her husband, Cole. After one of their regular rows, a few days before his fatal accident, she senses him across the fields picking flowers for her. She is sitting by her bedroom window, so it is easy to read this passage and assume it is something she has seen. But that is not how it is described: she detects 'a potent rise of scent as her young husband reached out his muscled arm for a branch of flowers' (p. 46). Lusa marvels at this, deciding 'this is how moths speak to each other', telling 'their love across the field by scent' (p. 47). Unable to sleep in the days after Cole's funeral, Lusa accepts a sleeping pill from her sister-in-law, Jewel, which produces an erotic dream in which a Luna moth-man makes love to her in a field, and again she emphasizes the non-verbal communication that was the essence of her bond with Cole: 'his scent burst onto her brain like a rain of lights, causing her to know him perfectly. *This is how moths speak to each other. The wrong words are impossible when there are no words*' (p. 79). The dream is a recurring one, and it involves Lusa's willed memories of Cole morphing into the 'comforting presence' with 'the silky, pale-green wings of the stranger who had first come to her after the funeral' (p. 345). Like the American chestnut and the coyote, the Luna moth is a motif that links the separate narrative threads while also expounding the novel's ecological argument, although it is more a motif that

---

[116] Jones, 'The Southern Family Farm as Endangered Species', p. 85.

is increasingly *felt* rather than intellectualized:[117] the rarity of the moth resides in the perception of it. Deanna Wolfe is also transfixed by the Luna moth in an episode when she catches 'the unusual sight of a Luna moth flying in the daytime'. Its arresting wings, 'like a pair of pale hickory leaves caught in an updraft', cause her to hold her breath (p. 65). She is moved by these moths, even though they are 'common enough up here', 'because of their size and those pale-green, ethereal wings tipped with long, graceful tails. As if they were already ghosts, mourning their future extinction' (p. 66). Deanna's response is a blend of intellectual effort and immediate response: the sight of this moth prompts a childhood memory of a wounded Luna, with a 'ferocious face' that horrified her, making her reflect on 'how a mystery caught in the hand could lose its grace'; but her 'preconceived affection for the Luna' enables her to 'hold on' (p. 66). Here Deanna is made to flirt with the kind of horror that disables Annie Dillard in her extreme sensitivity to the Luna's animal vigour; but Deanna defeats the thought, retaining the appreciation embodied in the construction of the rare experience.

In this chapter I have been concerned with identifying effects that encapsulate the dilemma of contemporary consciousness, but which suggest a degree of sanguinity in their ability to balance contending impulses, rather than an escape from eco-catastrophe through sanitized aesthetic order. Such narrative balance is a specific form of self-assertion—of the collector, the quester, the observer—in which the discovery of order, pattern, or the grain of the collection is simultaneously the key to self-definition, *and* a challenge to the repressive disorder of extinction: such a defiant challenge, that is to say, is internalized through gathering and understanding. This is also to acknowledge that the human fascination with rarity in nature may have to do with our constant desire for diversion, novelty. Adam Thorpe catches this trait succinctly in his poem 'Sighting', when the delight in observing a sea otter cannot be sustained when it is spotted repeatedly: Thorpe concludes the poem with regret at his failure to share in the continuous amazement he perceives in the otter.[118] The poem's narrator, imprisoned by the propensity to be bored by the familiar, is banished from the elusive immersive state of consciousness, or wonder, which—as the texts considered in this chapter have shown, with a more redemptive mindset—may well depend upon the continual pursuit of the rare, the unusual. At the same time, the lure of the rare tangentially evokes the pragmatic need for biodiversity as the driver of conservation, revealing another crucial aspect of contemporary ecological consciousness that has its roots in the appreciation of rarity. This redemptive view of rarity stands in stark contrast with John Fowles's characterization of

---

[117] Paul Mirocha's beautiful artwork for the first edition gives the Luna moth pride of place on the inside cover in a montage of moths and beetles. In this way, the novel includes its own field guide to this species, archly building a bridge between real and imagined perceptions of it.

[118] Adam Thorpe, 'Sighting', in *Voluntary* (London: Jonathan Cape, 2012), p. 5.

the pursuit of the rare, as a sign of the colonization of thought by commodity fetishism. But such 'redemption' is only one possible implication of an inconclusive and ambivalent world view, formally encoded, in which the appreciation of mutating nature is inseparable from a consciousness of the history of human depredation. This realization—an internalization and acceptance of our paradoxical times—is a cultural gesture of defiance against the looming oppression broadcast by the era of extinctions. Because human culpability is a necessary component of these paradoxical and contradictory effects, the instances of nature prose discussed in this chapter may seem to fall some way short of the utopian hopes of the emerging extinction studies, epitomized in the 'multispecies community' that Thom van Dooren identifies.[119] But in failing to achieve that ideal, they accurately register the ambivalence of their cultural moment.

---

[119] Thom van Dooren, *Flight Ways: Life and Loss at the Edge of Extinction* (New York: Columbia University Press), p. 41.

Conclusion
Transformations

The central feature of contemporary nature prose, as each chapter in this survey shows, is that it seeks to inspire new perceptions of, or greater engagements with, the nonhuman world through complex and paradoxical moments of realization. In Chapter 1, for example, we saw how Dan Boothby, one of Gavin Maxwell's followers, concludes *Islands of Dreams* with complex nostalgia for the moment when starting up a programme of conservation—of participating in the vitality of that movement—was a source of hope rather than a rearguard action: the site of that earlier moment in Scotland, and the literary tradition associated with it, is shown to be inspiring even while it is dismantled. The writers considered in Chapter 2 wrestle with ambivalent feelings towards the exclusive tradition of nature writing, and find ways of reclaiming and reinvigorating literary modes that have been racially exclusive. In one notable dynamic, illustrated well in Lauret Savoy's *Trace*, mourning practices (or their absence) are simultaneously a sign of racist oppression and the route to ecological inclusiveness. The reflections on abundance considered in Chapter 3 were accounted for by the concept of 'parable effects', moments of complex 'enlightenment' in which literal and metaphorical understanding are forced together, so that our feeling for the natural world is intensified *because* of the thoroughness with which cultural mediation is evoked, as in Tim Dee's comparison of a murmuration of starlings with *Spem in alium* by Thomas Tallis. In Chapter 4, the interplay of rarity and abundance in nature was shown to have parallels in cultural habits related to natural history and to human self-definition, such as taxonomy and collecting. Vernon Head's *The Search for the Rarest Bird in the World* epitomizes how writers of nature prose redeem ostensibly blameworthy habits (such as the 'collecting' impulse of the birder), so that problematic concepts, such as the idea of the 'pristine' in nature, can be made to speak in vital ways to our feeling of uncertainty in a world haunted by extinction. What these readings have in common is the attempt to identify moments of paradoxical insight in which *transformations in thinking* are encouraged, but by a circuitous intellectual route whereby sometimes antithetical perceptions are recognized as being contained in a holistic form. While such effects have always been a staple component of literary expression, they have a special resonance as a way of both embracing our ecological predicament and stimulating reflection upon it. The emphasis on textual paradox requires interpretive effort in a mediated route to interaction with nature, a brand of ecomimesis that makes textual difficulty both the catalyst of transformation and a source of hope, as evidenced in the work of the writers considered throughout this book.

The precise *vehicle* of transformation is often that familiar literary trope, the moment of revelation or epiphany. Taken at face value, such moments constitute a strategy aimed at the perceived alienation of modern citizens from nature, in which the marvellous otherness of the nonhuman is laid bare. We can recapture something elemental in our dealings with nature, such moments may seem to imply, by sloughing off our garb of intellectual preconception. While such moments have figured throughout this book, they have also been revealed as the locus of contradiction in nature prose, and this contradiction receives more extended treatment in this concluding chapter. We might ask, simply: how can carefully crafted writing—or writing that cannot help but carry the intellectual burden of its time—replicate and inspire spontaneous transformative encounters? And, in light of the self-evident contradiction between that which is crafted and that which is spontaneous, we might feel some sympathy with the views of Dana Phillips, who judges (apropos of Annie Dillard) that nature writers present the nonhuman 'all aglow and awash in mystery' in these supposedly revelatory moments, a tendency that results, Phillips argues, in 'bad faith' in nature writing, where 'the natural world' is represented 'as alien, and therefore as something impossible to address, much less capture, in words – even when the words it uses to describe the natural world are in fact wonderfully eloquent and evocative'.[1] In this view, the most problematic aspect is that the contradiction structurally built in to the nature epiphany—the contradiction of writing the inexpressible—induces numinous wonderment and leads us away from useful scientific knowledge about the nonhuman.

The nature epiphany appears very different, however, if it is *not* taken at face value, as this survey has shown. What if nature writers are trading on ambiguity in such moments? What if they are, consciously or subconsciously, writing from the imperative of our paradoxical ecological predicament? How do we view the revelatory moment in contemporary nature prose if we put it in the context of the long literary tradition of such moments, especially the complex or ambiguous 'non-epiphanies' beloved of modernist writers, in which the contradictory or competing issues at stake are put into arresting configurations? This complicates the common perception that nature writers are apt to lead their reader towards an epiphanic experience of wonder. It also raises the possibility that the contemporary nature epiphany emphasizes the *difficulty* of the transformative experience and serves to heighten awareness of the complexity in the human relationship with the nonhuman. To illustrate these effects, *Nature Prose* concludes with a

---

[1] Phillips, *The Truth of Ecology*, pp. 190, 218–19.

discussion of apparently transformative moments in the growing literature about the wild and 'rewilding', a mode which often posits a radical transformation of both environment and consciousness: some of these texts represent perhaps the most significant test of the claim that culture can be embraced as a conduit, not a barrier to productive understanding of nonhuman nature. As in other chapters, I range beyond this nonfictional subgenre, and embrace other forms of writing in the developing discussion, including fiction and divers cultural commentaries on the contemporary understanding of nature.

Self-conscious Rewilding

In *Feral* (2013) George Monbiot makes the persuasive case for the concept of environmental rewilding by amassing and synthesizing examples from the available evidence in the field. By contrast, *personal* rewilding is shown by Monbiot to depend on a willed state, where the visionary potential is hamstrung by consciousness. This is a familiar impasse in nature writing, as we have seen throughout this book—most notably, perhaps, in the paradox presented by Annie Dillard in *Pilgrim at Tinker Creek*. Monbiot makes use of personal revelation in a very specific way, however, in a form of constructed 'insight'. His book makes a strong case for the reintroduction of large predators and other 'missing' species, and especially for restoring trophic chains in Britain by restoring predators and large herbivores;[2] and the key element of personal transformation is Monbiot's way of overcoming public hesitancy. Ostensibly, he remains mindful of the moral 'constraints' within which we operate; and when he presents his table of the species that might be reintroduced in Britain, he emphasizes the need for 'widespread public consent', 'wide-ranging consultation', 'public safety issues', 'political difficulties', and so on. Yet, deliberately pulling against this mood of liberal restraint, there is an emphasis on reclaiming the feral as a state of mind, as in the episode when he is stalking flounder with a spear and finds himself 'transported by the thought – the knowledge – that I had done this before'. The sudden moment of insight is rooted in this 'genetic memory', asserted as an 'irreducible component of our identity', however much such impulses are (often necessarily) 'suppressed by thought'.[3] We are asked to embrace the paradox of self-conscious rewilding, the reclamation of instinct as a mental effort; but we may also recognize this as a campaigning conservationist's strategy, a rhetorical device designed to eclipse the public safety issues.

Early in his book Monbiot gives an account of a solo fishing expedition, paddling a kayak downriver and into the open sea.[4] An essential feature of an

---

[2] Monbiot, *Feral*, p. 9.   [3] Ibid., pp. 9, 81, 48, 126–7, 33–4.   [4] Ibid., pp. 14–22.

adventure in personal rewilding such as this is to encounter—and embrace—the threat of danger posed by exposure to the elements. He paddles for three hours 'straight out to sea' and is evidently dangerously tired by the time he heads back to land. He recalls his first similar journey into Cardigan Bay when he landed a greater weever onto his boat, the poison from which causes extreme pain and immobility—enough to prevent a single fisherman from paddling back to shore. And when he tries to negotiate his way back upriver, he is nearly drowned when his kayak is caught between rocks. The episode ends with an emphasis on Monbiot the hunter, returning to his car with his catch of mackerel, filleting and consuming three fish raw, with some left over, so that 'for the first time on the boat that summer I had caught more energy than I had used'. Monbiot has not exactly returned himself to the food chain; but he has exposed himself to mortal danger from the elements, and from sea creatures, so that this experience of hunting emulates a wild existence. But it is a self-conscious and willed reinsertion of the self into a wild state, an emphasis on his *frame of mind* that is caught in the most remarkable passage in these pages, when, after paddling out to sea for 6 or 7 miles, Monbiot has to go a little further to find 'the peace' he seeks. When he paddles a course to insert himself amidst a flock of fifty shearwaters on the sea's surface, 'not feeding – just looking', 'the faint sense of loneliness that had crept up on me as I headed away from land dispersed'. He continues, 'every time I go to sea I seek this place, a place in which I feel a kind of peace I have never found on land'. It is not a specific place—it's 'a here that was always different but always felt the same'—so what he is seeking is a state of mind produced by moving through and beyond isolation from human company to the point of communion with the animal world.[5] It is when Monbiot is in the company of the shearwaters, feeling the affinity of hunting through need, that he makes the transition to the wild or feral state he wishes to promote. This is a quintessential non-epiphany, in which the revelation is a studied part of Monbiot's promotion of psychological rewilding, something we can grasp only by seeing its functionality, and the predetermined interpretation of the moment's significance. This is also part of Monbiot's political strategy, to entice the reader to wish for the same 'revelation' by vicarious inducement.

A related treatment of the nature epiphany is found in Jay Griffiths' *Wild* (2006), her account of personal rewilding involving journeys into extreme landscapes, following what she calls 'the first command', which is 'to live in fealty to the feral angel'.[6] At the outset she addresses the paradox that bedevils all attempts to reintegrate with wild nature: 'we are – every one of us – a force of nature, though sometimes it is necessary to relearn consciously what we have never forgotten'.[7] In this conception, the paradox disappears from view: the conscious

---

[5] Ibid., pp. 16–17, 19–20, 21, 22, 16.
[6] Jay Griffiths, *Wild: An Elemental Journey* (2006; London: Penguin, 2008), p. 2.   [7] Ibid., p. 5.

effort is *necessary* to achieving the desired state, rather than an interference that makes it unattainable, although this may be to smooth over the difficulty too easily, as we shall see. The centrality of human consciousness—or, rather, an *expanded* state of consciousness—to Griffiths' conception of the wild state is made very clear: 'to me all these suggest wildness; the wild-mindedness of hallucinogens, the wildness of sex, the unboundedness necessary to creativity, and the essentialness of them all'.[8] It is a highly self-conscious project: the state of wildness is implicitly linked to the creative articulation of it, so that *Wild*, the book, becomes the single best expression of the state it envisages, a state that will have less direct relevance to the more mundane lives of most of its readers. As with Monbiot, the rhetorical strategy is one of enticement. It is also worth noting that Griffiths deploys a conventional set of associations for the writer's creative inspiration: artificially induced states of heightened consciousness; the imperative to transgress or innovate (in the pursuit of 'unboundedness'); and the association between creativity and sexuality.

The episode in which Griffiths might be said to transcend this literary self-consciousness—and supplant it with a more visceral demonstration of her conviction about wild insight produced through a heightened state of awareness—is the one in which she takes ayahuasca ('pronounced "eye-er-*wass*-ka"', she helpfully clarifies), 'a powerful hallucinogenic drug widely used by shamans throughout South America', and which is believed to show the user his or her personal 'path', or 'a map of your life'.[9] This appears to happen for Griffiths—not on her first use of ayahuasca, but on a subsequent 'trip'—when she has the vision of a jaguar on the High Street in Oxford, and feels herself 'shape-shifting' to become the jaguar, 'aware it was a hallucination', but grasping it as 'a slanted, metaphoric truth'. The Bodleian Library becomes the focus of the vision, inspiring 'untetherable rage' at the careful storage of 'the dry knowledge of years, *while the Amazon burns*'. As a jaguar, she 'stalk[s] in' to the Radcliffe Camera, 'the centre of a centre of Western learning', and roars 'in anger and disgust at how my culture can know so little for knowing so much'.[10] The symbolic rejection by an Oxford graduate of the seat of her learning while hallucinating in the Amazon has a pithy force; at the same time, the epiphany implied in this experience seems 'ready-made', less a revelation induced by hallucination, more a *conscious retrieval* of the 'wild' or instinctive state, its significance clearly signposted. We might glimpse an enactment of David Abram's celebration of the 'shaman's ecological function, his or her role as intermediary between human society and the land', a role 'not always evident to Western researchers';[11] but the structured performance, and the

---

[8] Ibid., p. 27.
[9] Ibid., p. 11. Peter Matthiessen calls ayahuasca 'a hallucinogen of morbid effect'. See *The Snow Leopard*, p. 49.
[10] Griffiths, *Wild*, pp. 97–8.   [11] Abram, *The Spell of the Sensuous*, pp. 10, 8.

interpretive sheen, bind the role to the written tradition it purports (in a sense) to position itself against.

Griffiths' adventures reflect revealingly on Western habits; but they are not elusive of interpretation. Rather, they are presented as easy to grasp, in the manner of a self-help book, so that personal rewilding becomes a conscious personal choice, based on rational critique, rather than a sudden *change* of consciousness. The experience of reading *Wild*, for most of us, will be a *vicarious* engagement with her 'elemental journey'; and this intellectualization is an inevitable corollary of the book's construction: revelation necessarily loses its radical potency, but reveals its meaning through the performance of (and commentary on) personal change. The point here is not the obvious and indisputable fact that writing is mediation; rather, it is that these non-epiphanies, in the manner of fictional engagement, entice us to enter a scenario of imagined intensity, while also alerting us to the literary embedding that puts the desired engagement out of our reach, a reading experience that requires us to go on and evaluate the significance of our desire. We might think of this cultivated form of non-epiphany as a mode of managed paradox. The frame paradox is the persisting but unattainable desire for non-verbal, unselfconscious immersion in nature; the corresponding literary paradox is the *re-presentation* of immersive revelatory moments, a mode in which the spontaneity of the revelation is short-circuited. These corresponding elements of paradox—situational and literary—combine to create a managed paradox in the sense that they invite interpretation of the impasse they register, and so are oriented towards some form of intellectual resolution in which the impossible desire for immersion is sidestepped, even while it is stimulated.

The intellectualization of the immersive experience is especially clear in Charles Foster's *Being a Beast* (2016), a fascinating attempt to experience the world from the perspective of animals. It is also a representative work of hybridized and self-conscious new nature writing by virtue of its reliance on a variety of sources. In Foster's summary of this literary collage, his efforts draw on a combination of 'neuroscience', 'a bit of philosophy', as well as 'a lot of the poetry of John Clare'.[12] The emphasis is very much on trying to understand the physiology of a series of animals—badger, otter, fox, red deer, swift—and to imitate their experience of landscape on the basis of his informed theories and assumptions about the animals' behaviour. Foster is well aware that actual integration with the animal world is not possible: as he says, 'shamanic transformation possibly aside, there will always be a boundary between me and my animals' (p. 6). His method is 'simply to go as close to the frontier as possible and peer over it with whatever instruments are available' (p. 7). The book is noteworthy because of its application of physiology, which allows Foster to claim 'close evolutionary cousinhood' with

---

[12] Charles Foster, *Being a Beast* (London: Profile Books, 2016), p. xi. Subsequent references are given in parentheses.

'most of the animals in this book', on the basis of 'the battery of sense receptors we all bear' (p. 7). In this way, for example, Foster can assert that he would have the same experience as a fox, if they were both to step on a piece of barbed wire, because of their similar 'pain receptors', 'electronic impulses', and 'more or less identical tracts in the peripheral and central nervous systems' for mental processing (p. 9). The science sponsors Foster's experiments in the limits of empathy with the nonhuman.

Foster's stated mantra is that humanity is an integral part of nature, although this is really a hypothesis that his book significantly qualifies. When he is imagining himself into the life of a swift, he can proceed (he asserts) because 'no qualification other than occupancy of a shared world is necessary for me to write about swifts'. He finds this 'a great relief, because swifts are the ultimate other [living, as they do, for extended periods solely in the air]. I can write about them only because I am other too or (depending on my mood) because nothing is other' (p. 182). That *nothing is other* would be a genuine revelation—not to mention a profound challenge to a nigh sacred shibboleth of literary theory—a revelation that would unleash 'our capacity for vicariousness', which Foster sees as 'infinite': 'empathise enough with a swift and you'll either become one or (which may be the same thing) you'll be able to rejoice so much with the screeching race round the church tower that you'll not mind not being one yourself' (p. 209). Of course, as Foster knows, this is not the same thing: the rejoicing spectator is pointedly excluded from the action. The book is structured around qualified, overthought, or failed epiphanic connections, and a less joyous mood emerges from Foster's failures. This is most pronounced in his final remarks about red deer, which, he concludes, are 'victims'. Consequently, 'their landscape is the landscape of victims, and invisible except through victims' eyes'. Foster's failure to be a victim 'vitiate[s] the enquiry' (p. 178). His attempts to 'become' a red deer are compelling partly because of his shame at having participated in stag hunts in his past. This enables him to pronounce, with authority, on the assumption 'that being an effective predator helped me to know something about my prey species'. Foster has learned to see this idea as 'very wrong' (p. 156); and this moment of clarity is also a form of atonement, which is related to his failure to inhabit the animal as victim: it retains its otherness, and Foster withdraws to the level of social critique.

There is an overtly literary context to Foster's revelations and attempts at integration with other animals. He distinguishes himself from Henry Williamson and Gavin Maxwell, 'those true masters of otter writing', as he calls them, but claims as an advantage over them that 'I don't like otters very much'. This enables him to avoid the combination of anthropocentrism and egocentrism he clearly detects in Maxwell's depiction of 'rollicking, boisterous otter friends who wouldn't ask him too much about himself and could be cuddled on lonely Hebridean nights' (p. 71). Foster is entirely unsentimental about otters, seeing them as merely 'circuit boards'

(p. 78), expressing the 'intuition' that they 'suffer less than badgers, foxes or dogs'. This 'deeply unscientific' (p. 79) distinction seems a calculated manoeuvre, one designed to establish a cordon sanitaire around his work, protecting it from the taint of anthropomorphism associated with the venerable English tradition of writing about otters. Yet in that gesture, that self-conscious marking of literary territory, Foster reveals the limits of empathy and integration. The other remains other; and this suggests another way of accounting for the managed paradox I described above. Foster's book presents a series of such moments, which are controlled engagements with otherness. Irresolution has to be the governing mood: a fully immersive epiphanic encounter, were such a thing possible, would be undesirable, since complete affinity—and ultimate integration—would dissolve otherness. In an alienated state, by contrast, the respect of otherness is retained, and the realm of environmental ethics, instigated in Leopold's 'land ethic', remains viable.

Foster's failure to connect with the deer, and the rejection of hunting-as-empathy, are rebuttals of the conventional wisdom found in 'most poaching books', in which, as Nick Richardson points out, the poacher 'must be sensitive to the smallest details in his environment'.[13] David Abram develops this idea in his celebration of primitivism, in which the potential of language is also retrieved in the service of rewilding. Abram shows that hunting 'for an indigenous, oral community' requires harmony with an environment, a habit of immersion that is mirrored in oral culture, where the spoken language, in its 'rhythms, tones and inflections', is itself attuned 'to the contour and scale of the local landscape'.[14] There is something appealing in Abram's project of '*taking up* the written word, with all of its potency, and patiently, carefully, writing language back into the land'.[15] Yet we may wonder if this is an exemplary instance of our contemporary predicament, the desire, which appeals even while we know it to be impossible, to retrieve the primitivist potential in written language. Abram ends his book with the metaphor of the task ahead—'planting words, like seeds'—but then gives us a brief paragraph, a prose poem, as an illustration of such 'planting'. It is a modest paragraph, comprising a description of a floating alder leaf bumping into the leg of a wading blue heron. It does not seem revelatory—indeed, it is disappointing in its understatement. Yet that is also the intent: this illustration, in its simplicity, exemplifies a kind of non-intrusive immersive experience—Abram is 'drawn into the spread of silence'—in which the human observer is enfolded 'within a common flesh, a common story'.[16] This is a beautifully poised moment, and one that illustrates perfectly the paradox of the nature non-epiphany, haunted by the desire for oneness that words can convey only sketchily, as Abram implicitly concedes here.

---

[13] Nick Richardson, 'Eels in Their Pockets', *London Review of Books*, 37: 24, 17 December 2015, pp. 33–4 (p. 33).
[14] Abram, *The Spell of the Sensuous* (1996; New York: Vintage, 1997), p. 140.   [15] Ibid., p. 273.
[16] Ibid., p. 274.

Wolves and People

Rewilding requires us to reconceptualize wilderness, once eloquently described by Gary Snyder as 'a *place* where the wild potential is fully expressed, a diversity of living and nonliving beings flourishing according to their own sorts of order'.[17] The human interference in 'wilderness', and the subsequent desire to find a place within it, require us to modify this definition, and arrive at a different understanding of jeopardy: the peril of being exposed to the trophic chain once more, in which risk is (or would be) produced partly by human experimentation. The psychological power and resonance of rewilding thus stems from a significant recalibration of a centuries-old human perception, so that 'keystone species, once viewed by human beings as a direct threat', and which have been 'displaced or driven to the edge of extinction', are reintroduced into new 'wilderness' areas.[18] Personal transformation then becomes a testing of limits, of how far one can progress towards an integration with the nonhuman by accepting the concomitant danger. Over the centuries, in both European and North American culture, the wolf has been the animal used most consistently to appraise human interaction with the wild, and so this section examines two texts concerning wolves, one fictional and one nonfictional: Sarah Hall's novel *The Wolf Border* (2015), and the nature-writing classic *Of Wolves and Men* (1978) by Barry Lopez.

Hall's *The Wolf Border* is an important exploration of the parameters within which personal rewilding might be experienced. The return of Rachel Caine from the US to her native Cumbria, to oversee the introduction of grey wolves on the estate of a wealthy English landowner, Thomas Pennington (the Earl of Annerdale)—she has been working on a similar project in Idaho—neatly introduces a parallel between human 'reintroduction' and the re-establishment of a once-native species. A puzzle for any reader of *The Wolf Border*, however, is why this and other related parallels between the wolves and the human drama are not sustained; but first it might be helpful to consider the achievement of the book as a form of commentary on its context. Lord Pennington is modelled on real-world rewilders, such as Paul Lister, the English multimillionaire who would like to reintroduce large predators, including wolves, at his Alladale Wilderness Reserve in Scotland.[19] Thomas Pennington is in a similar position—having the wealth and the land to facilitate an enclosed exercise in rewilding—yet he is also a skilful Tory politician who can make things happen, and this political dimension of the novel

---

[17] Gary Snyder, *The Practice of the Wild* (San Francisco: North Point Press, 1990), p. 12.

[18] Dawson, *Extinction*, p. 65. Dawson has significant reservations about rewilding because it 'relies on the thoroughgoing manipulation and commodification of nature, and as such dovetails perfectly with *biocapitalism*' (p. 77).

[19] See https://alladale.com/conservation/vision_mission/ (accessed 18 April 2018). For a longer account of imaginative treatments of Scotland's future that includes discussion of Hall's novel, see Timothy C. Baker, 'Writing Scotland's Future: Narratives of Possibility', *Studies in Scottish Literature*, 42 (2016), 2, pp. 248–66.

overlays the rewilding theme.[20] The implications of independence become a primary focus, and the practical means for Pennington to realize his ambition of letting wolves loose, rather than into a managed estate: he contrives to set them free from their enclosure, knowing they will migrate north, and that their likely route will take them in to Scotland, where the moment in which new legislation is being devised makes it possible for him, with Rachel's expert intervention, to secure safe passage for the wolves to a site 'north of Loch Lomond, west of Ben Nevis, to the sea', where they will serve to control the deer population.[21] Improbable though this is, Hall clearly sees an opportunity for rewilding in an emerging nation, a sense that 'Scotland's independence gives it the opportunity to revert to something more primal, more authentically unmanaged', as Alex Clark puts it.[22] Yet she also projects a situation in which politics subsumes the gesture. Indeed, this is part of Pennington's calculations, assuming the wolf will become 'a new icon for a new nation' (p. 423).[23]

The political strand is relatively straightforward. The novel becomes richer through the analogies between the wolves and the human protagonists, a relative emphasis that parallels the treatment of environmental and human rewilding in Monbiot's *Feral*. Readers will be looking for such analogies, especially in the portrayal of Rachel and her parallel reintroduction into England. She also returns as an expectant mother—pregnant after a one-night stand with a friend and colleague in Idaho—and this gives scope for Hall to present the 'discovery' of Rachel's maternal self as she is overseeing the breeding of the grey wolves at Annerdale, and the development of their first litter. (It is these wolves and their cubs that will form the first wild pack in the new independent Scotland.) These obvious analogies lead to greater complexity when they begin to break down. If there is something free and 'wild' in Rachel's initial independence from her family, and in her uncomplicated sexuality—her inclination for sex without commitment makes her seem to be both predator and prey simultaneously (pp. 38–41)—the novel sees her become increasingly domesticated: in her relationship with Alexander, her vet boyfriend and his daughter; in her decision finally to let the father of her baby know of the child's existence; and, especially, in her efforts to rekindle a relationship with her brother and then to save him from his drug addiction. We might wonder if these are 'pack' instincts, a productive analogy

---

[20] The Scottish independence referendum takes place during the novel's action, and it is possible that the novel went to press before the vote (although it was published afterwards, in March 2015, while the referendum for Scottish independence took place on 18 September 2014), so the 'yes' vote in the world of Hall's novel might be predictive, rather than part of a parallel reality.

[21] Sarah Hall, *The Wolf Border* (London: Faber & Faber, 2015), p. 420. Subsequent references are given in parentheses.

[22] Alex Clark, 'In Search of Wilderness', *The Guardian*, 1 April 2015, https://www.theguardian.com/books/2015/apr/01/the-wolf-border-by-sarah-hall-review (accessed 11 April 2018).

[23] Monbiot makes the case for the reintroduction of wolves in the Scottish Highlands, an environment 'which has all the characteristics required': the desirable levels of deer population; low density of human population; and relatively few roads. See *Feral*, p. 116.

with the wolves; but we might equally interpret the new domestication of Rachel as the means by which the analogy is dismantled, a process that comments on the rewilding scheme itself, which is not truly wild but managed within defined human parameters. Professionally, Rachel wants the wolves to be unleashed, of course: she is desirous of that new edge to consciousness that rewilding posits, a point 'where the streetlights end and wilderness begins'. This is, in one meaning, 'the wolf border' (p. 234). But the wolf border, at this level of traceable literary theme or motif, is also internal, and equally compromised.

Rachel sees the temptation to perceive analogies between human and wolf behaviour, especially in connection with sexual rivalry and breeding, but considers them 'not helpful', and this is a clue for the reader (p. 221). If Hall seems to brandish overt analogies between the wolves and her human characters, only to relinquish them, she also leaves something unresolved by virtue of that process, and this is where the richness of the novel emerges; because in that space of irresolution, Hall does something unnerving by drawing on—or at least relying on—the mythology of wolves. In this respect James Kidd is right to suggest that, in Hall's hands, the wolves 'inhabit liminal spaces' between 'wilderness and civilisation'; their liminality chimes with unresolved aspects of the plot, and this enables Hall to use the idea of wolves to 'transgress the boundary between reality and the imagination'.[24] Early in the novel Rachel dreams of wolves in a wildlife park to which her mother took her when she was a child. A wolf, in its enclosure, elicits from her what seems to be a primal fear:

> The god of all dogs. It is a creature so fine, she can hardly comprehend it. But it recognises her. It has seen and smelled animals like her for two million years. It stands looking. Yellow eyes, black-ringed. Its thoughts nameless. She holds the fence but the fence has almost disappeared; she is hanging in the air, suspended like a soft offering. Any minute it will be upon her. (p. 6)

As she runs, in the dream, back and forth in front of the enclosure, the wolf becomes 'an echo, a mirror', tracking her movements: 'it turns as she turns, runs as she runs', until she demands to know, in dream logic, '*What are you doing?*' Waking from the dream, rational thought intervenes, so that 'already she knows' the answer to her question: 'her brain is restarting. That creature of the outer darkness—of geographic success, myth and horror, hunted with every age's weapon, stone axe, spear, sprung-steel trap, and semi-automatic—was playing' (p. 7). The ecologist's admiration intervenes and stifles the elemental response: the wolf maintains the genetic impulse to play in the hunt, even when faced with its

---

[24] James Kidd, 'A mysterious, gripping dance with wolves', *The Independent*, 26 March 2018, https://www.independent.co.uk/arts-entertainment/books/reviews/the-wolf-border-by-sarah-hall-book-review-a-mysterious-gripping-dance-with-wolves-10135394.html (accessed 11 April 2018).

worst adversary, her reasoning suggests; and this is also an artificial situation—the enclosure forcing the proximity that a wolf in the wild, fearful of man, would avoid. But before the sheen of reasoned admiration intervenes, Rachel's more visceral response conjoins fear and vitality, making them interdependent, and in a way that anticipates the vitality of her adult life: 'pre-erotic fear. The heart beneath her chest jumps, smells bloody' (pp. 6–7).

The dream epiphany intertwines Rachel's adult work with wolves and a childhood memory, as her mother confirms: *'There were wolves in the park for a while. Don't you remember? You kids used to torment them. One of them got out, created havoc'* (p. 8). This bridge between the dream and the world of the novel suggests a formative moment that has informed Rachel's career choice. It also contributes to the motif of escape, and the dissolution of borders; but the more significant consequence of linking the dream with Rachel's reality is to further the exploration of internal rewilding. Yet the visceral and spontaneous character of the dream epiphany is already compromised. Rachel's dream describes an adult perception of the tormenting of an animal; yet to the child the engagement with the wolf—as its mirror, its echo—is much more serious, the experience of an animal encounter, provoking an atavistic response. As one of its strands, the novel continues to cultivate an atavistic fear of wolves; but this is also conditioned by the sheen of cultural preconception, an element that is given emphatic expression in a later dream when Rachel envisions 'an impossible number' of wolves forming 'a super-pack, like a modern fable'. She pictures them in fields, appearing to be like 'black water', in which 'the body of a cow floats, its ribs lathed raw, like the beams of a boat', and then running through an urban scene, in 'tortured' action, with 'snarling fights' and 'terrible injuries' (p. 364). The epiphanic force of this dream is coloured by environmental concerns. It revisits the vitality of internal rewilding, and rapprochement with the animal, which here tips over into the old mythology of the wolf as an unstoppable predator and a threat to human civilization, devouring livestock and invading settlements. It is a bleak moment in which the inherited tradition of folklore informs a new modern fable, a cultural layer which distances this dream from the earlier one when the resurfacing of childhood fear allows a direct engagement with the wild to be briefly glimpsed. The progression of the novel, in keeping with Rachel's own thought that human–wolf analogies are 'not helpful', works to dilute the revelatory force of personal rewilding suggested by that earlier dream, as Rachel is made to confront the human alienation from nature.

One objective of Barry Lopez's *Of Wolves and Men* (1978) is to discredit the kind of mythology and folklore about wolves that informs Rachel's later dream fable; but it is also a complex, resonant, and contradictory book that puts a fresh complexion on our predicament of paradox. The demystifying of wolf mythology is the most straightforward element. Lopez argues, for example, that the common belief that wolves are 'bloodthirsty' and sometimes kill more than they need is part of a broader false analysis in which 'their hunting behavior' is seen 'in human terms'.[25] The insistence that 'wolves are wolves, not men' colours much of Lopez's analysis; but it pinpoints a European misperception, not a native one, and this is where the contemporary resonance of the book lies, in its comparative analysis of European and indigenous cultures. In contrast to the critique of European attitudes, a different way of seeing is discerned in primitivist practices—a reversal in which humans are seen in wolf terms. Lopez traces close correspondences between wolves and Native American and Inuit peoples, revealing an affinity that 'aligns wolf and primitive hunter'.[26] For example, the semi-nomadic Nunamiut people of northern Alaska are said to have an equivalent knowledge of the territory they share with wolves.[27]

Lopez's interest in primitivism leads him to the theme that interests me most, here: a perception of mortality that is quite alien to the European perspective, and which resolves the question of danger/jeopardy that rewilding narratives inevitably move towards. Indeed, the boldest human–wolf parallel Lopez draws concerns the notion of 'appropriate death' in the primitive hunter's world view, and the relationship this has to the 'conversation of death' Lopez perceives in the looks exchanged between a wolf and its 'major prey species'. He considers this 'a ceremonial exchange' in which both animals 'choose for the encounter to end in death', and which signals 'a sacred order'. On this topic, we approach something closer to a genuine revelation (for the Western mind) about the human relationship to nature; but it brings with it its own obvious paradox: life is enriched by the embrace of death.

Lopez draws a parallel with 'Native American cultures' which 'in general stressed that there is nothing wrong with dying, one should only strive to die well'. Such an attitude 'was rooted in a different perception of ego' [than that of Europeans/colonizers].[28] There is an obvious slippage here: the parallel between hunter and wolf is displaced by a parallel between hunter and prey, in the situation (say) where a native warrior must confront death in battle with another tribe. Yet Lopez is also trading on the inconsistency of the reasoning. He proceeds to identify the importance of primitivist belief in a collectivist principle that has a parallel in the social organization of wolves: the realization that 'as the individual grows stronger, the tribe grows stronger, and vice versa' is precisely that which 'made the wolf such a significant animal in the eyes of hunting peoples'.[29] Although Lopez doesn't labour this point, it follows that the individual acceptance of 'appropriate death' by a native hunter, for the good of the tribe, is a necessary

---

[25] Barry Lopez, *Of Wolves and Men* (London: J. M. Dent, 1978), p. 63. One reason Lopez cites for the apparently irrational 'surplus killing' undertaken by wolves is that put forward by Hans Kruuk: if the hunting impulse doesn't follow its normal course, 'the sequence jams'. For example, if 'unseasonably deep snow or an excessively dark night interferes, if game animals can't, or won't, flee – the predator just keeps killing' (pp. 56–7).
[26] Ibid., pp. 63, 88.   [27] Ibid., p. 86.   [28] Ibid., pp. 94, 95.   [29] Ibid., p. 105.

component of the collectivist principle. Such acceptance, moreover, implies an affinity between primitivist philosophy and the natural cycle, even if the 'predator', for an indigenous hunter/warrior, is likely to be a human from another tribe. We might demur, and reflect that tribalism is an impediment to human collectivism. But I am not concerned too much here with the blind spot other commentators have detected in Lopez's treatment of indigenous and primitivist cultures.[30] It is not so much that we find in Lopez a problematic instance of self-division, a writer wholly distrustful of the Western cultural influences he cannot escape. Rather, he wants to implicate us in that self-division, and make us feel the worth of the synthesis of cultures that he calls for at the end of the book.

To move us through these contradictory perceptions, Lopez gives an account of how Euro-Americans have presided over a very different presentation of death in the extermination of wolves and other animals in eighteenth- and nineteenth-century America; and he wants to implicate us in the killing impulse because 'we forget how little, really, separates us from the times and circumstances in which we, too, would have killed wolves'. The recurring idea of contemporary nature prose, the problem of disconnection, is here configured as a failure to understand the place of death:

> In the nineteenth century when the Indians on the plains were telling us that the wolf was a brother, we were preaching another gospel. Manifest Destiny. What rankles us now, I think, is that an alternative gospel still remains largely unarticulated. You want to say there never should have been a killing, but you don't know what to put in its place.[31]

This implies that we cannot easily divest ourselves of the garb that still reflects the colonizer's 'destiny' to tame wilderness, and to impose the order of civilization upon it. In this sense, the misperception of death is a root cause of the disconnection of European thought from the nonhuman. Lopez wants to foster in us 'a view of the human world in which the natural world' is 'deeply reflected', an 'integrated' view that can produce 'an utter calm, a sense of belonging'.[32] Integration of this kind cannot countenance principles of control or extermination, which embody the opposite of the non-egotistical acceptance of mortality, the quality that emerges as a primary source of ecological wisdom in *Of Wolves*

---

[30] Dana Phillips, for example, finds in the work of Barry Lopez a key example of retrograde primitivism, 'which turns a blind eye on the barbarism that inevitably infects all cultures to some degree, whether they actually are so-called primitive cultures or not'. See Phillips, *The Truth of Ecology*, p. 225.

[31] Lopez, *Of Wolves and Men*, p. 138. 'Manifest Destiny' was the nineteenth-century conviction that the expansion of the United States' dominion was destined by God, an ideology that 'justified' the displacement of indigenous Americans as well as the exploitation of nature. See https://www.britannica.com/event/Manifest-Destiny (accessed 5 July 2021).

[32] Lopez, *Of Wolves and Men*, p. 113.

and Men. Extermination, by contrast, is a manifestation of insecurity. This recuperation of indigenous ecological wisdom is worth revisiting because it offers a corrective or supplementary view to the more recent discussions of death explored in the next section. For Lopez, the mistreatment of wolves, and the insecurity it has revealed, pinpoints the human failure to interact sympathetically with the nonhuman:

> The motive for wiping out wolves (as opposed to controlling them) proceeded from misunderstanding, from illusions of what constituted sport, from strident attachment to private property, from ignorance and irrational hatred. But the scope, the casual irresponsibility, and the cruelty of wolf killing is something else. I do not think it comes from some base, atavistic urge, though that may be a part of it. I think it is that we simply do not understand our place in the universe and have not the courage to admit it.[33]

In addressing the need to 'understand our place in the universe' Lopez strives for a profundity that is nebulous; but he tries to outline a form of resolution by calling for a fusion of ideas that is contradictory. As we have seen, the impetus of much of the book is to privilege indigenous over European understanding, and especially to show how European projections of the wolf reveal a form of self-hatred and a profound disconnection from the nonhuman. In the final segment of his account, however, he envisions an amalgamation of 'the benevolent wolf' of the Native American tradition, and the 'malcontented wolf of most European fairy tales'. Such a 'synthesis', Lopez suggests, might prompt a change of great enormity in man, indicating 'he had finally quit his preoccupation with himself and begun to contemplate a universe in which he was not central'.[34] The components of this proposed synthesis become clearer in the book's 'epilogue', where Lopez wants us 'to allow mystery' within the realm of the Western biological sciences, and thereby stimulate them to produce 'real knowledge, not more facts'.[35] Intuition and mystery stimulate the imagination, for Lopez. But the key to this wisdom is the way in which death informs our world view.

Intimations of (Im)mortality

My heading for this section is intended to refocus this book, in its concluding pages, on the literary construction of ideas about human engagement with the nonhuman, and the desire for a transformative experience in which a reconceptualization of mortality might suggest a kind of 'immortality': Lopez's formula for

---

[33] Ibid., p. 196.   [34] Ibid., p. 270.   [35] Ibid., pp. 284.

wisdom implies a Whitmanesque celebration of the natural cycle.[36] I am alluding here, however, to Wordsworth's ode 'Intimations of Immortality', in which a rather different sense of immortality emerges, less clear-cut that the impersonal planetary reinterpretation of 'death' in Whitman. Wordsworth registers how age distances us from an elemental or instinctual feeling of oneness still remembered in childhood: the adult mind, encumbered especially by encroaching death, cannot regain the sense of childhood immortality. Yet the poem's final revelation is that the appreciation of natural beauty is felt all the more keenly by the adult burdened by an awareness of mortality, a paradox centred on the conflict between nostalgic remembrance, on the one hand, and the desire to live in the moment again, on the other: we regain an intimation of the feeling of immortality we once had, which has more meaning in our self-conscious adulthood, but which is also more fleeting as a consequence.

Wordsworth's paradox is resolved in some measure by the presumed permanence of art, but the contemporary paradox of nature prose cannot be resolved in like fashion, in an era dominated by thoughts of impermanence. Instead, we have effects that amount to an intensification of Wordsworth's revelation (itself a kind of non-epiphany). Reflections on nature now seem to press for a revelatory encounter still more urgently, driven by a broader sense of looming mortality in the era of extinctions, while raising the bar of self-consciousness. In *Being a Beast*, Foster's chapter on the badger seeks to bring together ideas of mortality, appropriate inhabitation, and ecological wisdom. He emphasizes the badger's '*intense localness*', partly bestowed by its 'exact relationship' to its native wood 'in both space and time', but also by the longevity of badgers' 'hillside dynasties', a nativeness that means 'their bodies are built from the recycled earth of a few acres'. Badgers are thus 'the embodiment of the genius loci' for Foster (pp. 62–3). Emulating a badger, living in a specially constructed 'sett', Foster achieves a key moment of revelation in his project, acclimatizing himself to lying 'in the dark, surrounded by the scratching and humming and thrashing of animals that would one day eat me', a state of mind from which 'it was a small enough step not to mind being eaten, and not to mind being in, or getting towards, the state in which one is eaten'. Such a state would be truly revelatory, because 'once you're there, you're at last a proper ecologist, knowing your place, all eco-colonialism gone' (pp. 40–1).

This sanguine approach to mortality draws inspiration from the badger's life cycle, the recycling of matter, and a life lived in proximity to other decaying badgers, who are apt to die inside their setts. Foster translates that moment of egotistical relinquishment while 'being a badger' into a more conventional notion

---

[36] *Leaves of Grass* exists in different versions and many editions. See Ed Folsom, 'Whitman Making Books/ Books Making Whitman: A Catalog and Commentary', https://whitmanarchive.org/criticism/current/anc.00150.html (accessed 5 July 2021).

of generational life-and-death in human communities, where 'localness means that you weave round your mouldering ancestors'. The proposition is that we can continue to 'settle in a place and by living sufficiently completely to each moment, die completely to each moment too, so that the place becomes littered with our own corpses, and we can fix our landscapes by reference to their graves' (p. 64). Yet we are also aware of how this benign notion of being (and dying) in place is at odds with the nature of contemporary human existence, where persecution, climate change, economic insecurity, and globalization conspire to make indigeneity an increasingly quaint concept. Foster's celebration of the inevitability of death embellishes an intuition from his boyhood, when the discovery of a dead fox produces his first horrified intimation of mortality, followed by an inchoate grasp of animal splendour preserved in death: 'this very, very dead fox is more alive than a correspondingly dead dog', he claims to have reflected, leading to the realization that 'if I wanted to be like a fox I could do it by, first of all, being very alive (which was a comfort), or by being splendidly dead (which is a rather stranger comfort)' (p. 113). But this is also the intuition of the taxidermy collector, a correspondence that reminds us of Foster's hunting days. His childhood memory cannot reproduce Wordsworth's intimation of immortality because it seems to chime with his earlier adult self; but this is another important moment of non-revelation, yoking together a posited ideal state with an implied consciousness of the human flaws that must always distance us from it.

Such paradoxes, in various guises, have been shown to encapsulate the contemporary predicament throughout this book. My emphasis here is on how the treatment of mortality, in relation to the amorphous concept of ecological wisdom, makes such paradoxes both necessary and productive. They emphasize a complex transitional state, the sense of being human as a work in progress, thrown into relief by the desire for transformation. The need for transition, however, does not lose its urgency: the very piquancy of the literary effects that have concerned me, these intensely felt, non-epiphanic approximations of unrealized transformation, are ways of encapsulating the difference between reality and utopia. In Chapter 2 we saw how the predicament of ethnic exclusion, concentrated so deftly in Lauret Savoy's *Trace*, reorientates the ethical grounding of environmental thought, especially through a consideration of ancestry and mourning. Here I want to consider what this project contributes to the trend in contemporary writing, in which death, mourning, and consolation are revisited. In *Trace* there is a contradictory assemblage of ideas—acknowledged as such—in which (for example) wildly divergent timescales, human and geological, are brought together in such a way as to suggest parallels between different forms of oppression, caused by racism and by environmental degradation. How far such a rhetorical construction can hold together is unclear; or, rather, the threat that it might dissolve is central to the challenge it poses, its ethical grounding perceived as important yet evanescent, simultaneously.

CONCLUSION 197

If the victims of racism articulate grief in parallel forms—that is, the grief for the end of nature, a grief hard-won, and claimed despite the fact of dispossession, and filtered through the pain of familial injustice—then there is a tacit assertion of different levels of grief. And this obliges us to look again at the literary tropes of mourning, grieving, and consolation. David James gives us a poignant example of how grief changes our perspective, in a quotation from Julian Barnes's *Levels of Life* (2013), when Barnes is reflecting on his wife's terminal illness: the threat of ecological catastrophe offers no alternative framework of understanding, and no immediate consolation: 'what did I care about saving the world if the world couldn't, wouldn't, save her?'[37] Implicitly, the presentation of this understandable petulance demonstrates how grief is a leveller (quite against the idea of different levels). Without discrimination, the rawness of grief destroys order, ethical frameworks of meaning, and sources of consolation. In the writing of the memoir, however, an alternative aesthetic framework of meaning emerges, as James explains: 'Barnes's scepticism about the consolations of restorative patterns doesn't altogether neutralize' his hope, or his 'artistic investment' in the patterns words can make. A dialogic space is thus created in which the text can work against itself, to create an alternative form of solace, which might admit concern for the context of ecological catastrophe. As James has it, 'this is memoir at its most discursively self-conscious: simultaneously aware of its own salvage work and of the propensity for symbolic patterning to offer the solace of sense-making'.[38]

Barnes's exploratory juxtaposition of mourning on different scales—personal and planetary—opens up a more nuanced attempt to grapple with mourning than is found in some of the climate-crisis and end-of-civilization writing (such as Robert Bringhurst's) quoted earlier in this book. In another example of this more direct mode of expression, Roy Scranton suggests that 'the only way to keep alive our long tradition of humanistic enquiry is to learn to die'.[39] This involves extrapolating from the ancient focus on the problem of one's individual death in Western philosophy so that 'the question of individual mortality...is universalised and framed in scales that boggle the imagination'. The acceptance of one's own death, for Scranton, involves the 'letting go of our predispositions and fear'. This is an extension—or contemporary resiting—of the stance advocated by Lopez in *Of Wolves and Men*: 'learning to die as a civilisation', writes Scranton, 'means letting go of this particular way of life and its ideas of identity, freedom, success, and progress'. In this sense, learning to die is a way of revealing that global capitalism, and the civilization it has built, is in its death throes. And this

---

[37] Julian Barnes, *Levels of Life* (London: Jonathan Cape, 2013), p. 74.
[38] David James, *Discrepant Solace: Contemporary Literature and the Work of Consolation* (Oxford: Oxford University Press, 2019), p. 93.
[39] Roy Scranton, *Learning to Die in the Anthropocene: Reflections on the End of a Civilisation* (San Francisco: City Lights Books: 2015), p. 108.

relinquishment also has a larger, communal goal: letting go of the self is 'the first step' towards 'participation in a larger collective self' which Scranton traces back 'to our first moments in Africa 200,000 years ago'. Articulated in this way, the acceptance of death that allows us to recognize our place in an ongoing human story may have universal sources and potential: 'We are humanity. We are the dead. They have become us, as we will become the dead of future generations.'[40]

I have shown how indigenous wisdom reveals an approach to death and mourning that anticipates Scranton's critique of the focus on individual death in Western philosophy. This is related to Robert Pogue Harrison's demonstration, discussed in Chapter 2, that a less egocentric understanding of death may already be inscribed in Western mourning practices, a parallel view that is also implicit in the work of Louis Owens and Lauret Savoy, and their exploration of cultural rapprochement in an ecologically sound reckoning with death. Scranton's objective in promoting a longer view of historical kinship is to put the brief period of industrialization in perspective, so that our recent switch to 'a carbon-based energy economy' may be seen as an aberration, an interruption to our established 'photosynthetic-based energy economy' to which we will have to return if we survive as a species.[41] This hope for human life, a recalibration of the Western humanist tradition, also hinges on our 'keeping communion with the dead', in a way that may be common to both Western mourning practices and traditional indigenous wisdom.[42] And yet the felt need to 'universalize' individual mortality in this argument has a chillingly clinical air, an aestheticization of death in which an intellectual form of impersonal mourning *supplants* the visceral nature of actual grief. In this sense, such arguments seem to have some affinity with the death drive that Louis Owens sees as a determining feature of Euro-American literature in general, and more specifically as an attribute of writing about Native American culture, willing cultural death and suppressing culpability, in a kind of self-fulfilling prophecy. In contrast to Barnes, the paradox of conflicting levels of grief/mourning is set aside.

A progression beyond Barnes's paradox, by way of an ambivalent repurposing of elegiac forms, is at work in Helen Macdonald's *H is for Hawk* (2014), as David James shows. At the surface level, *H is for Hawk* is about Macdonald's process of grieving for her father, while learning to train a goshawk; but it simultaneously underscores a series of impersonal themes, not least of which are embodied 'in her frank warnings about romanticizing the countryside', and the eventual ambivalent summation of this theme in her investigation of 'how one might love the countryside without being implicated' in that romanticization. This gives a distinctively ecological hue to the tensions that James sees as explaining 'what elegy in our contemporary moment does', tensions 'between rescinding affective repair and

---

[40] Ibid., pp. 20, 24, 93, 94.   [41] Ibid., p. 34.   [42] Ibid., p. 108.

cautiously entertaining solace'.[43] One dimension of these tensions is to complicate the same apparent dichotomy between personal grief and planetary catastrophe contested by Julian Barnes. For Macdonald, the difficulty in this connection lies in our limited human purview:

> We are very bad at scale. The things that live in the soil are too small to care about; climate change too large to imagine. We are bad at time, too. We cannot remember what lived here before we did... Nor can we imagine what will be different when we are dead. We live out our three score and ten, and tie our knots and lines only to ourselves.[44]

Set against our tendency to lead narrow lives, an important strand of Macdonald's book bridges the gap between personal grief and mourning for nature, an idea embodied in her reflection on hunting with hawks, when she perceives that 'the puzzle that was death was caught up in the hawk, and I was caught up in it too' (p. 160). In such moments, the writer is drawn into the circle of mortality, in which human and animal destinies are intertwined. A process of empathic engagement enables Macdonald to resolve personal grief by letting it inform her evolving reflections on nature. Recalling her reactions at an art exhibition, she describes the exhibit of a stuffed Spix's macaw, an extinct species, 'lying on its back in a glass box in an empty room'; but this sight—'the loneliest thing [she has] ever seen'—leads her away from thoughts about extinction and to the traumatic memory of her father's corpse (pp. 181–2). Yet animal extinction and human mortality are bound together in the episode, a connection predicated upon Macdonald's progression from a pragmatic view of hunting to a position of taking responsibility for her hawk's killings, to a realization that, as she puts it, she is 'accountable to myself, to the world and all the things in it' (p. 197). Reflections on grieving, death, killing, and extinction orientate the writer towards a more holistic understanding of her ecological position.

This is not a seamless or fully resolved stance but, rather, an exploration of the tensions and ambivalences of the literature of mourning, attuned to the contemporary context of environmental responsibility. The first point of affinity with the texts written from a position of ethnic exclusion (the mode I wish to resonate at the end of *Nature Prose*) is the working through of impossibly divergent timescales, so that (in Barnes's case) personal grief no longer jars with climate catastrophe, and that (in Macdonald's case) the exposure of the ecological carelessness of our 'three score [years] and ten' can provoke a more philosophical reflection on the era of mass extinctions, explicitly connected to familial

---

[43] James, *Discrepant Solace*, pp. 95, 99, 100.
[44] Helen Macdonald, *H is for Hawk* (London: Jonathan Cape, 2014), p. 265. Subsequent references are given in parentheses.

mourning. In this way, *H is for Hawk* (especially) illustrates a recurring feature of contemporary nature writing: the repurposing of the forms of consolation that appear as a form of temporary relief or respite, where the unimaginable timescales of evolution, or cosmic cataclysm, put our era of climate crisis and mass extinctions into a perspective that enables us to evaluate and accept them more dispassionately. Here personal grief remains firmly in the frame, jarring with impersonal philosophical reflection in a thoughtful paradox.

In Savoy's *Trace* there is a comparable deployment of disparate frameworks of meaning, notably in the epilogue when Savoy compares her own alienation with that of the fossil of an unclassified species, as we saw in Chapter 2. By comparison with *H is for Hawk*, *Trace* registers a more sudden and dramatic refusal of (in this case) divergent timescales: in an arresting rhetorical gesture in Savoy's epilogue, woman and fossil are presented *as kin* in a moment on earth, aliens together. This is an impossible moment of willed, fantastic rapport, which may help us to understand the intensity of aesthetic feeling—on the question of belonging in place—that distinguishes Savoy's work from Macdonald's: where challenging different perspectives are worked through in Macdonald's book, in an incomplete process, they are presented as simultaneously necessary and impossible by Savoy, in an intensification of the same paradoxical relationship. In this way, *Trace* condenses a contradictory dilemma familiar in contemporary nature prose into a new form of aesthetic concentration.

Such a recalibration hinges partly on how racism keeps unlimited (geological, cosmic) temporal reflections in check. Pertinent here is an essay on film and affect by Allyse Knox-Russell, which opens up the question of how grieving for nature might be calibrated with respect to ethnicity and wealth. In this line of thinking, the first obstacle is the very different kind of grief required of us in facing up to environmental crisis. In this overwhelming 'time of climate change and species extinction' we have to confront 'unique temporal obstacles for grief work as it is usually practiced'. We have to work with a mental construction which is 'something like a permanent condition of the past, present, and future', learning to 'grieve that which hasn't yet been lost' while grappling to understand 'a complex set of interactions between human behavior and the earth's atmosphere that cannot be easily clarified or explained'.[45] The reconceptualization of grief has immediate benefits, over and above the obvious relinquishment (to the extent that we may still cling to this) of optimism based on better futures promised by current models of oil-based capitalism. Allyse Knox-Russell's conception of 'futurity without optimism' obliges us to suppress egocentric as well as anthropocentric

---

[45] Allyse Knox-Russell, 'Futurity Without Optimism: Detaching from Anthropocentrism and Grieving Our Fathers in *Beasts of the Southern Wild*', in *Affective Ecocriticism: Emotion, Embodiment, Environment*, ed. Kyle Bladow and Jennifer Ladino (Lincoln: University of Nebraska Press, 2018), pp. 213–32 (pp. 213, 214).

perceptions of grief. And yet, in a parallel and contrary dynamic, it also brings environmental justice into focus because the environmental crisis has disproportionately affected devalued lives: we must also grieve, in less philosophical terms, for 'racialized human lives', conscious as we must be that climate crisis is being 'borne overwhelmingly by the poor and nonhuman, while the privileged – those considered most fully "human" – protect themselves at the expense of abandoning the rest'.[46] Once death is accepted in non-egocentric terms, as an aspect of holistic environmental thinking, we open the door to equality in grief, and a clearer understanding of the ways that 'racialized human lives' obstruct ecological wisdom.

The attempt to link an appropriate perception of death with an end to racism, and also with ecological wisdom, is also found in Barry Lopez's *Horizon* (2019), a culmination of a lifetime of thinking about human interaction with the nonhuman. He argues that to realize the ultimate goal for humanity, to find 'a fitting, not a dominating, place' in 'the natural world', requires receptiveness to other human cultures, as well as an 'acute awareness of human foibles' that have fashioned the 'world view' and 'wisdoms' of those cultures 'not associated with modern technologies'.[47] Our collective goal will be advanced, he suggests, by privileging the wisdom of those closest to death—elders—who share features across different cultures. Elders, he suggests, are empathic; accessible; good listeners; and humble. This is a difficult case to make in a world where youthful environmentalism sometimes seems to embody the best way forward, in contradistinction to the perceived failure of 'elders' in the developed world. Of course, this is a way of forgetting the many hard campaigns environmentalists have been mounting for generations, a form of amnesia that is related to the impression Lopez has, that revered elders have disappeared in 'modern cultures', perhaps because humility is no longer sufficiently valued, but especially because they might 'tell us a story we [don't] want to hear'.[48] Obliquely, this points to the true knub of paradox in contemporary nature prose: again and again such moments invite us to confront and recast (but not relinquish) our most cherished material desires: for the genius loci; to belong; for an immersive experience; and, finally, to live.

Coda

My examples in this concluding chapter have been leading towards a demonstration of the *function* of paradox in nature prose. I do not want to overemphasize this capacity, however: the tenor of this book has been on how complex crystallizations of contradictory pulls, conflicting emotions, and divers kinds of resolve

---

[46] Knox-Russell, 'Futurity Without Optimism', p. 214.
[47] Barry Lopez, *Horizon* (London: Bodley Head, 2019), p. 45.   [48] Ibid., p. 312.

are framed in nature prose, not as blueprints for action but, rather, as a demonstration of how paradoxical literary effects find a new kind of configuration in nature prose to articulate and debate our contemporary dilemma. In a way, these effects are related to the contemporary movement that Barry Lopez has defined through a comparison with taphonomic research, the study of burials or biological remains. In the field, an example of such research might involve the reconstruction of the circumstances surrounding an animal's death, in an effort 'to put back together what nature or man has taken apart, to make something whole and integrated again out of its remnant parts'. By analogy, Lopez argues, 'such a formal inquiry into disintegration and the attempt to achieve reintegration is an emerging force in the arts today, just as it is in archaeology and field biology'.[49] In some respects, contemporary nature prose has a place in this new emerging cultural force; but the implied utility doesn't quite do justice to the radical uncertainty of the contemporary that I detect in nature prose, and the way in which that uncertainty is embraced as a sign of the contemporary moment.

For a final example of the origins of contemporary nature prose, and to pinpoint its place in literary history, I turn to Vladimir Nabokov. Brian Boyd makes an important distinction between Nabokov and Samuel Beckett that helps this attempt at periodization. The terrain they share is considerable, as Boyd suggests, as 'the foremost writers of the mid-twentieth century'. Both began writing 'just after the heyday of the great modernists, Joyce, Proust, and Kafka'—male modernists, that is, with which they have most in common—and continued publishing 'to the emergence of postmodernism as a fashion and a formula'. They also point towards the 'transnational' moment, we might also note, from another similarity Boyd observes: 'both wrote major works in two languages (Russian and English, English and French) and translated them from one language into the other'. And yet, Boyd concludes, 'their visions were polar opposites': where Beckett 'saw life as a terminal illness and human thought, speech, and action as a babble amid meaninglessness', Nabokov 'saw life as a "great surprise" amid possibly greater surprises'.[50] The peculiar infusion of lepidoptera within literature is one way of accounting for Nabokov's distinctive aesthetic, and this may reveal something very significant about the engagement of nature prose—its literary effects—more generally. For Boyd, it is the vision of the naturalist that supplies the positivity of Nabokov's world view, reflected in the arrangement of his art, pulling him in the opposite direction to the existential crisis of the Beckettian vision, so that, for Nabokov, 'only the ridiculously unobservant could

---

[49] Ibid, p. 453.

[50] Brian Boyd, 'Nabokov, Literature, Lepidoptera', in *Vladimir Nabokov, Nabokov's Butterflies: Unpublished and Uncollected Writings*, ed. Brian Boyd and Robert Michael Pyle, new trans. by Dmitri Nabokov (London: Allen Lane, 2000), pp. 1–31 (p. 1). 'Great surprise' is a quotation from *Pale Fire*.

be pessimists in a world as full of surprising specificity as ours'.[51] To illustrate this I will consider a profound moment in Nabokov's simply titled essay 'Butterflies', in which he describes the experience of appreciating nature as a form of timelessness, as (in a sense) I did in the Preface to this book:

> The highest enjoyment of timelessness – in a landscape selected at random – is when I stand among rare butterflies and their food plants. This is ecstasy, and behind the ecstasy is something else, which is hard to explain. It is like a momentary vacuum into which rushes all that I love. A sense of oneness with sun and stone. A thrill of gratitude to whom it may concern – to the contrapuntal genius of human fate or to tender ghosts humouring a lucky mortal.[52]

Feeling oneself to be outside of time allows the familiar desires of nature prose to be momentarily realized: integration with place, immersion in the nonhuman, a sense of immortality. Inevitably, the epiphany is compromised, the luck is fleeting; yet the realization of these desires is intensified by the encroaching consciousness of their ephemerality. And when the world of time and intellect reimposes itself, in such moments, we are still left with a sense of wonder about being among rare butterflies and plants, but with the admixture of a resolve: to protect them.

---

[51] Boyd, 'Nabokov, Literature, Lepidoptera', p. 19.
[52] Vladimir Nabokov, 'Butterflies', in *Nabokov's Butterflies: Unpublished and Uncollected Writings*, pp. 81–97 (p. 97).

Bibliography

Abram, David, *The Spell of the Sensuous* (1996; New York: Vintage, 1997).
Alarcón, Francisco X., 'Reclaiming Ourselves, Reclaiming America', in *The Colors of Nature: Culture, Identity, And The Natural World*, ed. Alison H. Deming and Lauret E. Savoy (Minneapolis: Milkweed Editions, 2002), pp. 28–48.
Allen, Marlene D., 'Octavia Butler's Parable Novels and the "Boomerang" of African American History', *Callaloo*, 32 (2009), 4, pp. 1353–65.
Ansell, Neil, *Deep Country: Five Years in the Welsh Hills* (London: Penguin, 2011).
Ansell, Neil, *Deer Island* (Toller Fratrum: Little Toller Books, 2013).
Ansell, Neil, *The Last Wilderness: A Journey Into Silence* (London: Tinder Press, 2018).
Ansell, Neil, *The Circling Sky: On Nature and Belonging in an Ancient Forest* (London: Tinder Press, 2021).
Anzaldúa, Gloria, *Borderlands/La Frontera: The New Mestiza*, 2nd edn (1987; San Francisco: Aunt Lute Books, 1999).
Asher, Jim, Martin Warren, Richard Fox, Paul Harding, Gail Jeffcoate, and Stephen Jeffcoate, eds., *The Millennium Atlas of Butterflies in Britain and Ireland* (Oxford: Oxford University Press, 2001).
Avery, Mark, *A Message from Martha* (London: Bloomsbury, 2014).
Bach, Richard, *Jonathan Livingston Seagull* (New York: Macmillan, 1970).
Bagchee, Shyamal, '*The Collector*: The Paradoxical Imagination of John Fowles', *Journal of Modern Literature*, 8 (1980–1), 2, pp. 219–34.
Baker, J. A., *The Peregrine, The Hill of Summer, and Diaries: The Complete Works*, ed. John Fanshawe (London: HarperCollins, 2015).
Baker, Timothy C., 'Writing Scotland's Future: Narratives of Possibility', *Studies in Scottish Literature*, 42 (2016), 2, pp. 248–66.
Bakhtin, M. M., *The Dialogic Imagination*, trans. Caryl Emerson and Michael Holquist (Austin: University of Texas Press, 1981).
Bal, Mieke, 'Telling Objects: A Narrative Perspective on Collecting', in *The Cultures of Collecting*, ed. John Elsner and Roger Cardinal (London: Reaktion Books, 1994), pp. 97–115.
Barkham, Patrick, *The Butterfly Isles: A Summer in Search of our Emperors and Admirals* (London: Granta, 2010).
Barkham, Patrick, 'The Butterfly Isles Effect', *Butterfly*, 128 (Summer, 2018), pp. 30–1.
Barnes, Julian, *Levels of Life* (London: Jonathan Cape, 2013).
Benjamin, Walter, *Illuminations*, ed. Hannah Arendt, trans. Harry Zohn (London: Pimlico, 1999).
Bennett, Jane, *Thoreau's Nature: Ethics, Politics, and the Wild* (London: Sage, 1994).
Bennett, Jane, *The Enchantment of Modern Life: Attachments, Crossings, and Ethics* (Princeton: Princeton University Press, 2001).
Berman, Marshall, *All That is Solid Melts into Air: The Experience of Modernity* (London: Verso, 1983).
Bernardin, Susan, 'Wilderness Conditions: Ranging for Place and Identity in Louis Owens' *Wolfsong*', *Studies in American Indian Literatures*, 10 (1998), 2, pp. 79–93.

Beston, Henry, *The Outermost House: A Year of Life on the Great Beach of Cape Cod* (1928; London: Pushkin Press, 2019).
Bladow, Kyle, and Jennifer Ladino, eds., *Affective Ecocriticism: Emotion, Embodiment, Environment*, (Lincoln: University of Nebraska Press, 2018).
Blythe, Ronald, 'Introduction' to Adrian Bell, *Silver Ley*, 'Twentieth Century Classics' edn (Oxford: Oxford University Press, 1983), pp. vii–xx.
Böhme, Gernot, *Für eine ökologische Naturästhetik* (Frankfurt am Main: Suhrkamp, 1989).
Böhme, Gernot, *Atmosphäre* (Frankfurt am Main: Suhrkamp, 1995).
Boothby, Dan, *Island of Dreams: A Personal History of a Remarkable Place* (London: Picador, 2015).
Botting, Douglas, *Gavin Maxwell: A Life* (1993: London: HarperCollins, 1994).
Bourne, Joel K., *The End of Plenty: The Race to Feed a Crowded World* (New York: W. W. Norton, 2015).
Bowen-Mercer, Carrie, 'Dancing the Chronotopes of Power: The Road to Survival in Linda Hogan's *Power*', in *From the Center of Tradition: Critical Perspectives on Linda Hogan*, ed. Barbara J. Cook (Boulder: University Press of Colorado, 2003), pp. 157–77.
Bowes, John P., *The Choctaw* (New York: Chelsea House, 2010).
Boyd, Brian, 'Nabokov, Literature, Lepidoptera', in Vladimir Nabokov, *Nabokov's Butterflies: Unpublished and Uncollected Writings*, ed. Brian Boyd and Robert Michael Pyle, new trans. by Dmitri Nabokov (London: Allen Lane, 2000), pp. 1–31.
Brande, David, 'Not the Call of the Wild: The Idea of Wilderness in Louis Owens's *Wolfsong* and *Mixedblood Messages*', *American Indian Quarterly*, 24 (2000), 2, pp. 247–63.
Bray, Roger, and Philip Cave, sleeve notes to Thomas Tallis, '*Spem in alium*', '*Lamentations*', '*Mass and Motets*', Magnificat, dir. Philip Cave (Linn Records, 2000), CKO 075.
Brewer, Scott, 'A Peculiar Aesthetic: Julia Leigh's *The Hunter* and Sublime Loss', *Journal of the Association for the Study of Australian literature* (2009), Special Issue: Australian Literature in a Global World, https://openjournals.library.sydney.edu.au/index.php/JASAL/article/view/10157/0 (accessed 20 November 2018).
Bringhurst, Robert, and Jan Zwicky, *Learning to Die: Wisdom in the Age of Climate Crisis* (Saskatchewan: University of Regina Press, 2018).
Broswimmer, Franz J., *Ecocide: A Short History of the Mass Extinction of Species* (New York: Pluto, 2002).
Buell, Lawrence, *The Environmental Imagination: Thoreau, Nature Writing, and the Formation of American Culture* (Cambridge, Mass.: Belknap Press, 1995).
Bunting, Madeleine, *Love of Country: A Hebridean Journey* (London: Granta, 2016).
Butler, Octavia, *Parable of the Talents* (1998; London: Women's Press, 2000).
Butler, Octavia, *Parable of the Sower* (1993; New York: Grand Central, 2007).
Byrd, Richard E., *Alone* (New York: G. P. Putnam's Sons, 1938).
Callaway, Henry, *The Religious System of the Amazulu* (1870 facsimile repr., Cape Town: Struik, 1970).
Campbell, Gordon, *The Hermit in The Garden: from Imperial Rome to Ornamental Gnome* (Oxford: Oxford University Press 2013).
Cardone, Anastasia, 'Where the Twin Oceans of Beauty and Horror Meet: An Aesthetic Analysis of Annie Dillard's *Pilgrim at Tinker Creek*', *Ecozon@*, 7 (2016), 2, pp. 85–97.
Carson, Rachel, *Silent Spring* (1962; London: Hamish Hamilton, 1963).
Carson, Rachel, *The Sense of Wonder* (1965; New York: HarperCollins, 1998).

Chakrabarty, Dipesh, *The Climate of History in a Planetary Age* (Chicago: University of Chicago Press, 2021).
Cheney, Jim, 'Truth, Knowledge and the Wild World', *Environmental Ethics*, 10 (2005), 2, pp. 101–35.
Clark, Alex 'In Search of Wilderness', *The Guardian*, 1 April 2015, https://www.theguardian.com/books/2015/apr/01/the-wolf-border-by-sarah-hall-review (accessed 11 April 2018).
Clark, Timothy, *The Cambridge Introduction to Literature and the Environment* (Cambridge: Cambridge University Press, 2011).
Conford, Philip, *The Origins of the Organic Movement* (Edinburgh: Floris Books, 2001).
Conford, Philip, *The Development of the Organic Network: Linking People and Themes, 1945–1995* (Edinburgh: Floris Books, 2011).
Coole, Diana, and Samantha Frost, 'Introducing the New Materialisms', in *New Materialisms: Ontology, Agency, and Politics*, ed. Coole and Frost (Durham, N.C.: Duke University Press, 2010), pp. 1–45.
Cowley, Jason, 'Editor's letter: the new nature writing', *Granta*, 102, Summer 2008, pp. 7–12.
Cronon, William, *Changes in the Land: Indians, Colonists, and the Ecology of New England* (New York: Hill & Wang, 1984).
Crumley, Jim, 'Mike Tomkies, Nature Writer Who Immersed Himself in the Wildest of Terrain', *The Scotsman*, 21 October 2016, https://www.scotsman.com/news/obituary-mike-tomkies-nature-writer-who-immersed-himself-wildest-terrain-647953 (accessed 30 June 2021).
Crutzen, Paul J., and Eugene F. Stoermer, 'The Anthropocene', *IGBP Newsletter*, 41(2000), pp. 17–18.
Cushman, H. B., *History of the Choctaw, Chickasaw and Natchez Indians*, ed. Angie Debo (1899; Stillwater: Redlands Press, 1962).
Davies, Catrina, *Homesick: Why I Live in a Shed* (London: riverrun, 2019).
Dawson, Ashley, *Extinction: A Radical History* (New York: OR Books, 2016).
Dee, Tim, *The Running Sky: A Birdwatching Life* (London: Jonathan Cape, 2009).
Dee, Tim, ed., *Ground Work: Writings on Places and People* (London: Jonathan Cape, 2018).
Deming, Alison H., and Lauret E. Savoy, eds., *The Colors of Nature: Culture, Identity, And The Natural World* (Minneapolis: Milkweed Editions, 2002).
Dillard, Annie, *Pilgrim at Tinker Creek* (1974; London: Picador, 1976).
Dillard, Annie, *The Abundance* (2016; Edinburgh: Canongate, 2017).
Dinerstein, Eric, *The Kingdom of Rarities* (Washington DC: Island Press, 2013).
Dixon, Melvin, *Ride Out the Wilderness: Geography and Identity in Afro-American Literature* (Urbana: University of Illinois Press, 1987).
Dooren, Thom van, *Flight Ways: Life and Loss at the Edge of Extinction* (New York: Columbia University Press, 2014).
Drake, Nick, *Time of No Reply* (Hannibal Records, 1986), HNBL 1318.
Dwyer, Margaret, 'The Syncretic Impulse: Louis Owens' Use of Autobiography, Ethnology, and Blended Mythologies in *The Sharpest Sight*', *Studies in American Indian Literatures*, 10 (1998), 2, pp. 43–60.
Dyer, Geoff, 'Foreword' to Annie Dillard, *The Abundance* (2016; Edinburgh: Canongate, 2017), pp. xv–xxvi.
Elder, Charlie, *While Flocks Last* (London: Bantam Press, 2009).

Elsner, John, and Roger Cardinal, eds., *The Cultures of Collecting* (London: Reaktion Books, 1994).
Fleckinger, Angelika, *Ötzi, the Iceman* (Vienna and Bolzano: Folio, 2014).
Folsom, Ed, 'Whitman Making Books/ Books Making Whitman: A Catalog and Commentary', https://whitmanarchive.org/criticism/current/anc.00150.html (accessed 5 July 2021).
Foster, Charles, *Being a Beast* (London: Profile Books, 2016).
Fowles, John, *The Collector* (1963; London: Vintage, 1998).
Fowles, John, *The Tree* (1979; Toller Fratrum: Little Toller Books, 2016).
Frere, Richard, *Maxwell's Ghost: An Epilogue to Gavin Maxwell's Camusfeàrna* (1976; Edinburgh: Birlinn, 2011).
Garrard, Greg, ed., *The Oxford Handbook of Ecocriticism* (Oxford: Oxford University Press, 2014).
Garrard, Greg, 'Conciliation and Consilience: Climate Change in Barbara Kingsolver's *Flight Behaviour*', in *Handbook of Ecocriticism and Cultural Ecology*, ed. Hubert Zapf (Berlin: de Gruyter, 2016), pp. 295–312, https://www.academia.edu/39752480/Conciliation_and_Consilience_Climate_Change_in_Barbara_Kingsolvers_Flight_Behaviour (accessed 2 December 2018).
Ghosh, Amitav, *The Great Derangement: Climate Change and the Unthinkable* (Chicago: University of Chicago press, 2017).
Goodbody, Axel, 'Risk, Denial and Narrative Form in Climate Change Fiction: Barbara Kingsolver's *Flight Behaviour* and Ilija Trojanow's *Melting Ice*', in *The Anticipation of Catastrophe: Environmental Risk in North American Literature and Culture*, ed. S. Mayer and A. Weik von Mossner (Heidelberg: Universitätsverlag Winter, 2014), pp. 39–58, https://purehost.bath.ac.uk/ws/portalfiles/portal/123429557 (accessed 12 February 2018).
Gordimer, Nadine, *The Conservationist* (London: Jonathan Cape,1974).
Greenberg, Joel, *A Feathered River Across the Sky: The Passenger Pigeon's Flight to Extinction* (New York: Bloomsbury, 2014).
Greenblatt, Stephen, *Marvelous Possessions: The Wonder of the New World* (Oxford: Clarendon Press, 1991).
Griffiths, Jay, *Wild: An Elemental Journey* (2006; London: Penguin, 2008).
Groes, Sebastian, 'Introduction to Part III: Ecologies of Memory', in *Memory in the Twenty-First Century: New Critical Perspectives from the Arts, Humanities, and Sciences*, ed. Groes (London: Palgrave Macmillan, 2016), pp. 140–6.
Guattari, Félix, *The Three Ecologies* (1989; London: Bloomsbury, 2018).
Hall, Phil, *The Five-Year Butterfly Hunt* (Taunton: Brambleby Books, 2016).
Hall, Sarah, *The Wolf Border* (London: Faber & Faber, 2015).
Hammond, Karla M., 'Drawing the Curtains: An Interview with Annie Dillard', *Bennington Review*, 10 (1981), pp. 30–8.
Hannink, Nerissa, 'Secrets from Beyond Extinction: The Tasmanian Tiger', University of Melbourne website, 12 December 2017, https://pursuit.unimelb.edu.au/articles/secrets-from-beyond-extinction-the-tasmanian-tiger (accessed 21 November 2018).
Harris, Michael, *Solitude: In Pursuit of a Singular Life in a Crowded World* (London: Random House, 2017).
Harrison, Robert Pogue, *The Dominion of the Dead* (Chicago: University of Chicago Press, 2003).
Head, Dominic, 'Ecocriticism and the Novel', in *The Green Studies Reader: From Romanticism to Ecocriticism*, ed. Laurence Coupe (London: Routledge, 2000), pp. 235–41.

Head, Dominic, *The Cambridge Introduction to Modern British Fiction, 1950-2000* (Cambridge: Cambridge University Press, 2002).
Head, Vernon R. L., *The Search for the Rarest Bird in The World* (Oxford: Signal Books, 2015).
Heise, Ursula K., *Sense of Place and Sense of Planet* (Oxford: Oxford University Press, 2008).
Heise, Ursula K,. *Imagining Extinction: The Cultural Meanings of Endangered Species* (Chicago: University of Chicago Press, 2016).
Herman, Judith Lewis, *Trauma And Recovery: The Aftermath of Violence—From Domestic Abuse to Political Terror* (New York: Basic Books, 1992).
Hoare, Philip, 'Introduction' to Henry Beston, *The Outermost House: A Year of Life on the Great Beach of Cape Cod* (1928; London: Pushkin Press, 2019), pp. ix–xxiii.
Hogan, Linda, *Power* (New York: Norton, 1998).
Holden, Peter, and Tim Cleeves, *RSPB Handbook of British Birds*, 4th edn (London: Bloomsbury, 2014).
Houser, Heather, 'Knowledge Work and the Commons in Barbara Kingsolver's and Ann Pancake's Appalachia', *Modern Fiction Studies*, 63 (2017), 1, pp. 95–115.
Hughes-d'Aeth, Tony, 'Australian Writing, Deep Ecology and Julia Leigh's *The Hunter*', *Journal of the Association for the Study of Australian Literature* (2002), 1, pp. 19–31 (p. 19), https://openjournals.library.sydney.edu.au/index.php/JASAL/article/view/9652 (accessed 20 November 2018).
Ireland, Julia A. 'Annie Dillard's Ecstatic Phenomenology', *Interdisciplinary Studies in Literature and Environment*, 17 (2010), 1, pp. 23–34.
James, David, *Discrepant Solace: Contemporary Literature and the Work of Consolation* (Oxford: Oxford University Press, 2019).
Jameson, Conor Mark, *Silent Spring Revisited* (London: Bloomsbury, 2012).
Jamie, Kathleen, *Findings* (London: Sort Of Books, 2005).
Jamie, Kathleen, 'A Lone Enraptured Male', *London Review of Books*, 30:5, 6 March 2008, pp. 25–7.
Jamie, Kathleen, 'Diary', *London Review of Books*, 33:14, 14 July 2011, pp. 38–9, https://www.lrb.co.uk/v33/n14/kathleen-jamie/diary (accessed 21 January 2018).
Jarvis, Brooke, 'The Obsessive Search for the Tasmanian Tiger', *The New Yorker*, 2 July 2018, https://www.newyorker.com/magazine/2018/07/02/the-obsessive-search-for-the-tasmanian-tiger (accessed 21 November 2018).
Johnson, Kirk Wallace, *The Feather Thief: Beauty, Obsession, and the Natural History Heist of the Century* (London: Hutchinson, 2018).
Johnson, Kurt, and Steve Coates, *Nabokov's Blues: The Scientific Odyssey of a Literary Genius* (Cambridge, Mass.: Zoland Books, 1999).
Jones, Cheryl, 'Climate killed thylacine on mainland Australia', *Cosmos*, 27 September 2017, https://cosmosmagazine.com/palaeontology/climate-not-dingoes-killed-the-thylacine-on-mainland-australia (accessed 21 November 2018).
Jones, E. A., ed., *Hermits and Anchorites in England, 1200-1500* (Manchester: Manchester University Press, 2019).
Jones, Suzanne W., 'The Southern Family Farm as Endangered Species: Possibilities for Survival in Barbara Kingsolver's *Prodigal Summer*', *Southern Literary Journal*, 39, (Fall, 2006), 1, pp. 83–97.
Keats, John, *Poetry and Prose*, introd. and notes by Henry Ellershaw (1922; Oxford: Clarendon Press, 1969).
Kemp, Christopher, *The Lost Species: Great Expeditions in the Collections of Natural History Museums* (Chicago: University of Chicago Press, 2017).

Kermode, Frank, *The Genesis of Secrecy: On the Interpretation of Narrative* (Cambridge, Mass.: Harvard University Press, 1979).

Kerridge, Richard, 'Narratives of Resignation: Environmentalism in Recent Fiction', in *The Environmental Tradition in English Literature*, ed. John Parham (Aldershot: Ashgate, 2002), pp. 87–99.

Kerridge, Richard, 'Nature Writing', in *The Cambridge Companion to Prose*, ed. Daniel Tyler (Cambridge: Cambridge University Press, 2021), pp. 214–32.

Kidd, James, 'A mysterious, gripping dance with wolves', *The Independent*, 26 March 2018, https://www.independent.co.uk/arts-entertainment/books/reviews/the-wolf-border-by-sarah-hall-book-review-a-mysterious-gripping-dance-with-wolves-10135394.html (accessed 11 April 2018).

Kilpatrick, Jacquelyn, ed., *Louis Owens: Literary Reflections on His Life and Work* (Norman: University of Oklahoma Press, 2004).

Kincaid, Jamaica, *My Garden (Book)* (New York: Farrar, Straus & Giroux, 1999).

Kingsolver, Barbara, *Animal Dreams* (1990; London: Abacus, 1992).

Kingsolver, Barbara, *Prodigal Summer* (New York: HarperCollins, 2000).

Kingsolver, Barbara, *Flight Behaviour* (London: Faber & Faber, 2012).

Knight, Richard L., and Suzanne Riedel, eds., *Aldo Leopold and the Ecological Conscience*, (Oxford: Oxford University Press, 2002).

Knox-Russell, Allyse, 'Futurity Without Optimism: Detaching from Anthropocentrism and Grieving Our Fathers in *Beasts of the Southern Wild*', in *Affective Ecocriticism: Emotion, Embodiment, Environment*, ed. Kyle Bladow and Jennifer Ladino (Lincoln: University of Nebraska Press, 2018), pp. 213–32.

Kolbert, Elizabeth, *The Sixth Extinction: An Unnatural History* (2014; London: Bloomsbury, 2015).

Kolodny, Annette, *The Lay of the Land: Metaphor as Experience and History in American Life and Letters* (Chapel Hill: University of North Carolina Press, 1975).

Krupat, Arnold, *Ethnocriticism: Ethnography, History, Literature* (Berkeley: University of California Press, 1992).

LaLonde, Chris, *Grave Concerns, Trickster Turns: The Novels of Louis Owens* (Norman: University of Oklahoma Press, 2002).

Leder, Priscilla, 'Contingency, Cultivation, and Choice: The Garden Ethic in Barbara Kingsolver's *Prodigal Summer*', *Interdisciplinary Studies in Literature and Environment*, 16 (2009), 2, pp. 227–43.

Leder, Priscilla, ed., *Seeds Of Change: Critical Essays on Barbara Kingsolver* (Knoxville: University of Tennessee Press, 2013).

Leigh, Julia, *The Hunter* (1999; London: Faber & Faber, 2000).

Leopold, Aldo, *A Sand County Almanac and Sketches Here and There* (1949; Oxford: Oxford University Press, 1987).

Licence, Tom, *Hermits and Recluses in English Society, 950–1200* (Oxford: Oxford University Press, 2011).

Lindo, David, *Tales From Concrete Jungles: Urban Birding Around the World* (London: Bloomsbury, 2015).

Lindo, David, *The Urban Birder* (2011; London: Bloomsbury, 2018).

Lister-Kaye, John *The White Island* (London: Longman, 1972).

Lloyd, Christopher, and Jessica Rapson, '"Family Territory" to the "Circumference of the Earth": Local and Planetary Memories of Climate Change in Barbara Kingsolver's *Flight Behaviour*', *Textual Practice*, 31 (2017), 5, pp. 911–31.

Loewen, Shawn, 'The New Canaan: Abundance, Scarcity, and the Changing Climate of Nature Writing in Nineteenth-Century America', *Interdisciplinary Studies in Literature and Environment*, 8 (2001), 1, pp. 97–114.
Lopez, Barry, *Of Wolves and Men* (London: J. M. Dent, 1978).
Lopez, Barry, *Horizon* (London: Bodley Head, 2019).
Lowenthal, David, 'Introduction' to George Perkins Marsh, *Man and Nature* (1864; Cambridge: Belknap Press of Harvard University Press, 1965), pp. ix–xxix.
Lyotard, Jean-François, *The Postmodern Condition: A Report on Knowledge*, trans. Geoff Bennington and Brian Massumi (1979; Manchester: Manchester University Press, 1984).
Mabey, Richard, in *The Unofficial Countryside* (1973; repr. Wimborne Minster: Little Toller Books, 2010).
Mabey, Richard, *Nature Cure* (2005; London: Vintage, 2015).
Mabey, Richard, *Turning the Boat for Home: A Life Writing About Nature* (London: Chatto & Windus, 2019).
McCarthy, Michael, *Say Goodbye to the Cuckoo* (London: John Murray, 2009).
McCarthy, Michael, 'Join the Great British Butterfly Hunt', *The Independent* 7 April 2009, https://www.independent.co.uk/environment/nature/uk-butterflies/join-the-great-british-butterfly-hunt-1665114.html (accessed 17 May 2018).
McCarthy, Michael, *The Moth Snowstorm: Nature and Joy* (London: John Murray, 2015)
McClintock, James I., *Nature's Kindred Spirits* (Madison: University of Wisconsin Press, 1994).
Macdonald, Helen *H is for Hawk* (London: Jonathan Cape, 2014).
Macfarlane, Robert, *The Wild Places* (London: Granta Books, 2007).
McGlone, Jackie [unsigned],'Barbara Kingsolver's Flight of Fancy for the Real World', *The Herald*, 1 June 2018, http://www.heraldscotland.com/arts_ents/13107339.Barbara_Kingsolver_s_flight_of_fancy_for_the_real_world/ (accessed 7 March 2018).
McKenna, Virginia, 'Afterword' to Gavin Maxwell, *The Ring of Bright Water Trilogy*, ed. Austin Chinn (London: Puffin Books, 2001), pp. 405–8.
MacKinnon, J. B., *The Once and Future World: Nature as it Was, as it Is, as it Could Be* (New York: Houghton Mifflin Harcourt, 2013).
Maehr, David *The Florida Panther: Life and Death of a Vanishing Carnivore* (Washington DC: Island Press, 1997).
Magherini, Graziella, *La Sindrome di Stendhal* (Milan: Feltrinelli, 1992).
Marren, Peter, *Chasing the Ghost: My search for all the wild flowers of Britain* (London: Square Peg, 2018).
Marsh, George Perkins, *Man and Nature* (1864; Cambridge: Belknap Press of Harvard University Press, 1965).
Matthiessen, Peter, *The Snow Leopard* (1978; London: Vintage, 1998).
Maxwell, Gavin, *A Reed Shaken by The Wind* (London: Longmans, Green & Co., 1957).
Maxwell, Gavin, *Ring of Bright Water* (London: Longmans, 1960).
Maxwell, Gavin, *The Rocks Remain* (London: Longmans, 1963).
Maxwell, Gavin, *Raven Seek Thy Brother* (London: Longmans, 1968).
Maxwell, Gavin, *Harpoon at a Venture* (1952; Harmondsworth: Penguin, 1984).
Maxwell, Gavin, *The Ring of Bright Water Trilogy*, ed. Austin Chinn (London: Puffin Books, 2001).
Menzies, Charles R., ed., *Traditional Ecological Knowledge and Natural Resource Management* (Lincoln: University of Nebraska Press, 2006).
Miller, J. Hillis, *Tropes, Parables, Performatives: Essays on Twentieth-Century Literature* (Hemel Hempstead: Harvester, 1990).

Monbiot, George, *Feral: Rewilding the Land, Sea and Human Life* (2013; London: Penguin, 2014).

Morris, David, 'Octavia Butler's (R)evolutionary Movement for the Twenty-First Century', *Utopian Studies*, 26 (2015), 2, pp. 270–88.

Morton, Timothy, *Ecology without Nature: Rethinking Environmental Aesthetics* (Cambridge, Mass.: Harvard University Press, 2007).

Morton, Timothy, *Hyperobjects: Philosophy and Ecology after the End of the World* (Minneapolis: University of Minnesota Press, 2013).

Morton, Timothy. 'Deconstruction and/as Ecology', in *The Oxford Handbook of Ecocriticism*, ed. Greg Garrard (Oxford: Oxford University Press, 2014), pp. 291–304.

Murphy, Patrick D, *Farther Afield in the Study of Nature-Oriented Literature* (Charlottesville: University Press of Virginia, 2000).

Murray, Walter J. C., *Copsford*, introd. Raynor Winn (1948; Toller Fratrum: Little Toller Books, 2019).

Nabokov, Vladimir, *Nabokov's Butterflies: Unpublished and Uncollected Writings*, ed. Brian Boyd and Robert Michael Pyle, new trans. by Dmitri Nabokov (London: Allen Lane, 2000).

Narduzzi, Dilia, 'Living With Ghosts, Loving the Land: Barbara Kingsolver's *Prodigal Summer*', *Interdisciplinary Studies in Literature and Environment*, 15 (2008), 2, pp. 59–81.

Nelson, Melissa, 'Becoming Métis', in Alison H. Deming and Lauret E. Savoy, eds., *The Colors of Nature: Culture, Identity, and the Natural World* (Minneapolis: Milkweed Editions, 2002), pp. 146–52.

Nelson, Richard, *The Island Within* (San Francisco: North Point Press, 1989).

Norton, David, ed., *The New Cambridge Paragraph Bible* (Cambridge: Cambridge University Press, 2005).

Oates, Matthew, *In Pursuit of Butterflies: A Fifty-Year Affair* (London: Bloomsbury, 2015).

Outka, Paul, *Race and Nature from Transcendentalism to the Harlem Renaissance* (New York: Palgrave Macmillan, 2008).

Owens, Louis, *Other Destinies: Understanding the American Indian Novel* (Norman: University of Oklahoma Press, 1992).

Owens, Louis, *The Sharpest Sight* (Norman: University of Oklahoma Press, 1992).

Owens, Louis, *Wolfsong* (1991; Norman: University of Oklahoma Press, 1995).

Owens, Louis, *Mixedblood Messages: Literature, Film, Family, Place* (Norman: University of Oklahoma Press, 1998).

Owens, Louis, *I Hear the Train: Reflections, Inventions, Refractions* (Norman: University of Oklahoma Press, 2001).

Owens, Louis, 'Burning the Shelter', in Alison H. Deming and Lauret E. Savoy, eds., *The Colors of Nature: Culture, Identity, and The Natural World* (Minneapolis: Milkweed Editions, 2002), pp. 142–5.

Page, Robin, *The Great British Butterfly Safari* (Barton: Bird's Farm Books, 2003).

Parham, John, ed., *The Environmental Tradition in English Literature* (Aldershot: Ashgate, 2002).

Pask, Andrew J., et al., 'Genome of the Tasmanian tiger provides insights into the evolution and demography of an extinct marsupial carnivore', *Nature Ecology & Evolution*, 2 (2018), pp. 182–92, https://www.nature.com/articles/s41559-017-0417-y (accessed 27 November 2018).

Pearce, Susan M., *On Collecting: An Investigation into Collecting in the European Tradition* (London: Routledge, 1995).

Pearse, Andrew, *Seeds of Plenty, Seeds of Want: Social and Economic Implications of the Green Revolution* (Oxford: Oxford University Press, 1980).
Phillips, Dana, *The Truth of Ecology: Nature, Culture, and Literature in America* (New York: Oxford University Press, 2003).
Pickrell, John, 'Tasmanian Tiger Genome May Be First Step Toward De-Extinction', *National Geographic*, 11 December 2017, https://news.nationalgeographic.com/2017/12/thylacine-genome-extinct-tasmanian-tiger-cloning-science/ (accessed 21 November 2018).
Pollan, Michael, *Second Nature: A Gardener's Education* (New York: Dell, 1991).
Purdy, John, '*Wolfsong* and Pacific Refrains', in Jacquelyn Kilpatrick, ed., *Louis Owens: Literary Reflections on His Life and Work* (Norman: University of Oklahoma Press, 2004), pp. 175–94.
Raine, Anne, 'Du Bois's Ambient Poetics: Rethinking Environmental Imagination in *The Souls of Black Folk*', *Callaloo*, 36 (2013), 2, pp. 322–41.
Raine, Kathleen *The Lion's Mouth: Concluding Chapters of Autobiography* (London: Hamish Hamilton, 1977).
Reddy, Jini, *Wanderland: A Search for Magic in the Landscape* (London: Bloomsbury, 2020).
Reed, T. V., 'Toward an Environmental Justice Ecocriticism', in the *Environmental Justice Reader: Politics Poetics and Pedagogy*, ed. Joni Adamson, Mei Mei Evans, and Rachel Stein (Tucson: University of Arizona Press, 2002), pp. 145–62.
Reimer, Margaret Loewen, 'The Dialectical Vision of Annie Dillard's *Pilgrim at Tinker Creek*', *Critique*, 24 (1983), 3, pp. 182–91.
Richardson, Nick, 'Eels in Their Pockets', *London Review of Books*, 37: 24, 17 December 2015, pp. 33–4.
Roorda, Randall, *Dramas of Solitude: Narratives of Retreat in American Nature Writing* (Albany: SUNY Press, 1998).
Ruffin, Kimberley N., *Black on Earth: African American Ecoliterary Traditions* (Athens: University of Georgia Press, 2010).
Sandilands, Catriona, *The Good-Natured Feminist: Ecofeminism and the Quest for Democracy* (Minneapolis: University of Minnesota Press, 1999).
Savoy, Lauret, *Trace: Memory, History, Race, and the American Landscape* (Berkeley: Counterpoint, 2015).
Savoy, Willard, *Alien Land* (1949; Boston: Northeastern University Press, 2006).
Scheese, Don, *Nature Writing: The Pastoral Impulse In America* (New York: Twayne Publishers, 1996).
Schopenhauer, Arthur, *The World as Will and Representation*, vol I, ed. and trans. Judith Norman, Alistair Welchman, and Christopher Janaway (Cambridge: Cambridge University Press, 2010).
Schwartzstein, Peter, 'Iraq's Marsh Arabs Test the Waters as Wetlands Ruined by Saddam are Reborn', *The Guardian*, 18 January 2017, https://www.theguardian.com/global-development/2017/jan/18/iraq-marsh-arabs-test-the-waters-wetlands-ruined-by-saddam-reborn-southern-marshes.
Schweizer, Harold, *Rarity and the Poetic: The Gesture of Small Flowers* (London: Palgrave Macmillan, 1915).
Schweninger, Lee, 'Landscape and Cultural Identity in Louis Owens' *Wolfsong*', *Studies in American Indian Literatures*, 10 (1998), 2, pp. 94–110.
Schweninger, Lee, *Listening to the Land: Native American Literary Responses to the Landscape* (Athens: University of Georgia Press, 2008).

Scranton, Roy, *Learning to Die in the Anthropocene: Reflections on the End of a Civilisation* (San Francisco: City Lights Books, 2015).

Sethi, Anita, *I Belong Here: A Journey Along the Backbone of England* (London: Bloomsbury, 2021).

Shelton, Richard, 'On the Wing', *Times Literary Supplement*, 5898, 15 April 2016, p. 28.

Smith, Jos, *The New Nature Writing: Rethinking the Literature of Place* (London: Bloomsbury, 2017).

Snyder, Gary, *The Practice of the Wild* (San Francisco: North Point Press, 1990).

Soper, Kate, *What is Nature? Culture, Politics and the Non-human* (Oxford: Blackwell, 1995).

Stepto, Robert B., 'Foreword' to Willard Savoy, *Alien Land* (1949; Boston: Northeastern University Press, 2006), pp. vii–xix.

Stevenson, Sheryl, 'Trauma And Memory In *Animal Dreams*', in *Seeds Of Change: Critical Essays On Barbara Kingsolver*, ed. Priscilla Leder (Knoxville: University of Tennessee Press, 2013), pp. 87–108.

Stewart, Iain, 'Introduction' to Frank Fraser Darling, *Island Years, Island Farm* (1940, 1943; Toller Fratrum: Little Toller Books, 2011), pp. 13–17.

Storr, Anthony, *Solitude* (1988; London: HarperCollins, 1997).

Tassel, Kristin Van, 'Ecofeminism and a New Agrarianism: The Female Farmer in Barbara Kingsolver's *Prodigal Summer* and Charles Frazier's *Cold Mountain*', *Interdisciplinary Studies in Literature and Environment*, 15 (2008), 2, pp. 83–102.

Taylor, Marianne, *Dragonflight: In Search of Britain's Dragonflies and Damselflies* (London: Bloomsbury, 2013).

Tesson, Sylvain, *Consolations of the Forest: Alone in a Cabin in the Middle Taiga*, trans. Linda Coverdale (2011; London: Penguin, 2014).

Thorpe, Adam, *Ulverton* (London: Secker & Warburg, 1992).

Thorpe, Adam, *Voluntary* (London: Jonathan Cape, 2012).

Thorpe, Adam, *On Silbury Hill* (Toller Fratrum: Little Toller Books, 2014).

Thoreau, Henry David, *The Portable Thoreau*, ed. Carl Bode (London: Penguin, 1982).

Tomkies, Mike, *Look Stranger*, dir. Colin Morris, BBC 1975, https://www.youtube.com/watch?v=zDRW8HOygD0.

Tomkies, Mike, *Last Wild Place* (London: Jonathan Cape, 1984).

Tomkies, Mike, *Between Earth and Paradise* (1981; London: Jonathan Cape, 1991).

Tomkies, Mike, *Last Wild Years* (London: Jonathan Cape, 1992).

Valis, Noël, 'Collecting, the Rescue of Things, and the Human', *Yale Review*, 100 (2012), 3, pp. 67–85.

Vizenor, Gerald, ed., *Narrative Chance: Postmodern Discourse on Native American Indian Literatures* (Albuquerque: University of New Mexico Press, 1989).

Wagner-Martin, Linda, *Barbara Kingsolver's World: Nature, Art, and the Twenty-First Century* (New York: Bloomsbury, 2014).

Walmsley, Leo, *Fishermen at War* (London: Collins, 1941).

Walmsley, Leo, *So Many Loves: An Autobiography* (London: Collins, 1944).

Watt, Ian, *The Rise of the Novel: Studies in Defoe, Richardson and Fielding* (London: Chatto & Windus, 1957).

Wenz, Peter S., 'Leopold's Novel: The Land Ethic in Barbara Kingsolver's *Prodigal Summer*', *Ethics and the Environment*, 8 (2003), 2, pp. 106–25.

Weschler, Lawrence, *Mr Wilson's Cabinet of Wonder* (1995; Vintage: New York, 1996).

White, Chris, *The Life List of Adrian Mandrick* (New York: Touchstone, 2018).

Williams, Raymond, *People of the Black Mountains*, 2 vols (London: Chatto & Windus, 1989–90).
Williamson, Henry, *The Flax of Dream* (London: Faber & Faber, 1936).
Williamson, Henry, *Goodbye West Country* (Boston, MA: Little, Brown & Co., 1938).
Wilson, Thomas Murray, *The Recurrent Green Universe of John Fowles* (Amsterdam: Rodopi, 2006).
Wilson, Thomas Murray, 'The Writer Who Gave up on Names: John Fowles's Unwarranted Hostility Toward Nature Writing', *Interdisciplinary Studies in Literature and Environment*, 15 (2008), 1, pp. 135–51.
Wood, Michael, 'Saddam Drains the Life of the Marsh Arabs', *The Independent*, 27 August 1993.
Youngs, Tim, *The Cambridge Introduction to Travel Writing* (Cambridge: Cambridge University Press, 2013).

Index

Table entries that span two pages (e.g., 52–53) may, on occasion, appear on only one of those pages.

Abram, David 155–6, 187
abundance 25–6, 105–42, 144–6, 172–3, 180–1
Alarcón, Francisco X. 81
Alladale Wilderness Reserve 188–9
Allen, Marlene 134–5
ambiguity 2–3, 43, 60, 65–6, 80, 90–1, 93–4, 109, 181–2
American Indian 13–17, 82–98, 191–4
Ansell, Neil 28–9, 39–42, 60–8
 Deep Country 39–42, 60
 Deer Island 29, 60–2
 Last Wilderness, The 28–9, 62–6
Anthropocene 1–2, 5, 21–2, 104, 109, 119, 122–3, 172–3, 197n.39
anthropocentrism 7, 17–18, 135–6, 143, 159–60, 162–3, 168, 174–5, 186–7, 200–1
anthropomorphism 17–18, 40–1, 176
Anzaldúa, Gloria 81
Avery, Mark 145n.6, 153–4

Bach, Richard 170n.98
Bailey, Benjamin 140–1
Bakhtin, Mikhail 91
Bal, Mieke 159–61
Barkham, Patrick 162n.70, 163–4, 166–7
 Butterfly Isles, The 163–4
Barnes, Julian 197–200
 Levels of Life 197–8
Barrie, J. M. 51–2
 Peter Pan 51–2
Beckett, Samuel 202–3
Benjamin, Walter 160
 Arcades Project, The 160
 'Unpacking My Library' 160
Bennett, Jane 37–8, 52
Berman, Marshall 1–2
Bernardin, Susan 88–9
Beston, Henry 38–9
 Outermost House, The 38–9
binary oppositions 8, 11–16, 30–1, 42, 60, 63–4, 86n.47, 93–4, 159–60
black writing/identity 69–81, 101–2

Blythe, Ronald 27
Bodleian Library 184–5
Böhme, Gernot 11n.24
Boothby, Dan 56, 180–1
 Island of Dreams 56–9, 180–1
Botting, Douglas 43–4, 54, 119–20
Bourne, Joel 112
Bowen-Mercer, Carrie 17
Boyd, Brian 202–3
Brande, David 89
Bray, Roger 138–9
Bringhurst, Robert 97–8, 102–3, 197–8
Broswimmer, Franz 147–9
Buell, Lawrence 8, 21, 72, 126–7, 135–6
Burke, Gillian 69n.6
Butler, Octavia 134–6
 Parable of the Sower 134–5
 Parable of the Talents 134–5
Byrd, Richard E. 32–3

Cardone, Anastasia 127–8
Carson, Rachel 63, 119, 153–4
 Silent Spring 119, 153–4
Cave, Philip 138–9
Chakrabarty, Dipesh 1–2, 21–2, 104
Cheney, Jim 18n.43
Clark, Alex 188–9
Clark, Timothy 11–12
collecting 144, 156–62, 180–1
contradiction 3–6, 10–11, 30–1, 65–6, 85–6, 91, 122–4, 128–31, 166–7, 181, 194, 196, 200–2
Cooper, James Fenimore 124
Cowley, Jason 21–2
Cushman, H. B. 95–7

Dakobed/Glacier Peak 86, 88–94, 103–4
Darwin, Charles 157–8
Davies, Catrina 28n.4
Dawson, Ashley 147
Dee, Tim 69–70, 137–41, 180–1
Deming, Alison 70

218 INDEX

Dillard, Annie 9–10, 12, 17, 24–5, 113, 123–33, 135–8, 177–8, 181–2
   Abundance, The 126
   Pilgrim at Tinker Creek 9–10, 12, 17, 24–5, 123–33, 135–8, 177, 182
Dinerstein, Eric 142, 172–3
Dixon, Melvin 72
Dooren, Thom van 178–9
doubleness 1–2, 38–9, 42–3, 59, 76
Drake, Nick 140–1
Du Bois, W. E. B. 101–2
   Souls of Black Folk, The 101–2
Dwyer, Margaret 95–6
Dyer, Geoff 126, 135–6

ecocentrism 7, 159–60, 162–3, 174
ecological crisis 1–2, 5–6, 21–2, 25–6, 30–1, 36–9, 43, 60, 63–4, 83, 97–8, 102–3, 109, 115n.28, 122–3, 142–3, 161, 197–201
ecomimesis 3–4, 12–13, 21–6, 76, 105, 130, 140–1, 143–4, 146, 176, 180–1
Emerson, Ralph Waldo 124
Environmental Justice 72
epiphany and non-epiphany 12, 27–8, 38–9, 59, 87–8, 169–70, 181–5, 187, 191, 195, 203
exclusivity 4, 25–6, 67–104
extinction 48–9, 63, 83–4, 97–8, 102–4, 106, 108, 110, 122–3, 135–6, 142–53, 164, 167–8, 174, 178–81, 188, 195, 199–201

Fabre, Jean-Henri 129–30
fiction and nonfiction 5, 7–10, 21–6, 30–1, 33–4, 72, 126, 143, 181–2, 188
Foster, Charles 185–7, 195–6
   Being a Beast 185–7, 195–6
Fowles, John 153–61, 178–9
   Collector, The 153–5, 160
   Tree, The 154–6, 161
Frere, Richard 54–5

Garrard, Greg 105–6
genius loci 29–30, 36, 38–9, 41–2, 61–2, 195, 201
geology 1–2, 76, 99–100, 102–4, 172–3, 200–1
Ghosh, Amitav 143
Gordimer, Nadine 96n.88
Gramsci, Antonio 109–10
Grand Canyon 74–5, 77, 84–6, 101–2
'Green Revolution' 111–12
Griffiths, Jay 183–5
   Wild 183–5
Groes, Sebastian 120–1

Hall, Sarah 188–91
   Wolf Border, The 188–91

Harris, Michael 32–3
Harrison, Robert Pogue 98–101, 198
Head, Vernon 169–71, 173–4, 180–1
   Search for the Rarest Bird in the World, The 169–71, 173–4, 180–1
Heise, Ursula 13–14, 29–31, 146, 173–4
Herman, Judith Lewis 82
Highland Clearances 44–5, 53–4, 64
Hogan, Linda 13–17, 24–5, 68–9
   Dwellings 16–17
   Power 13–17, 24–5, 68–9
homelessness 52–3, 60–2, 64–8, 103–4
Homogenocene 172–3
Houser, Heather 109–10
Hughes-d'Aeth, Tony 151–2
humanism 3–4
hyperobjects 115

Independent, The 162–3
indigenous knowledge 13–17, 83–95, 191–4
Industrial Revolution 21–2
International Union for Conservation of Nature (IUCN) 167
Inuit people 191–2
Ishiguro, Kazuo 160–1
   Never Let Me Go 160–1
ivory-billed woodpecker 167–8

James, David 197–9
Jamie, Kathleen 35–6, 117, 142–4
   Findings 36, 142–4
Jefferies, Richard 54–5
Johnson, Kirk Wallace 157–8
Jones, Suzanne 174, 176–7
Joyce, James 12, 202–3
   Dubliners 12
Jura, Isle of 29

Kafka, Franz 202–3
Kant, Immanuel 74–6, 101–2
   Observations on the Feeling of the Beautiful and Sublime 75
Keats, John 128–9, 140–1
   negative capability 128–9, 140–1
Kemp, Christopher 153–4, 158
Kermode, Frank 113n.23, 137
Kerridge, Richard 10, 149–50
Kincaid, Jamaica 71–3
   My Garden (Book) 71–2
Kingsolver, Barbara 82–4, 95–6, 98–9, 105–10, 123–4, 132–3, 135–7, 174–9
   Animal Dreams 82–4, 98–9
   Flight Behaviour 105–10, 123–4, 132–3, 135–7
   Prodigal Summer 174–9

Knox-Russell, Allyse 200–1
Kolbert, Elizabeth 147–9
Krupat, Arnold 93–4

LaLonde, Chris 94–5, 97
Leder, Priscilla 174–5
Leigh, Julia 148–53, 173–4
   Hunter, The 148–53, 173–4
Leopold, Aldo 17–18, 77–80, 90, 101–2, 174–5, 186–7
   land ethic 17–18, 79, 90, 101–2, 174–5, 186–7
   Sand County Almanac, A 77–8
lepidoptery 121–3, 153–5, 162–5, 202–3
Lindo, David 69n.6
Linnaeus, Carl 71–3, 156–7
Lister, Paul 188–9
Lister-Kaye, John 55–6
   White Island, The 55–6
literary criticism 2–3, 11–13
Lloyd, Christopher 109, 120–1
Loewen, Shawn 123–4
Lopez, Barry 188, 191–4, 197–8, 201–2
   Horizon 201–2
   Of Wolves and Men 188, 191–4, 197–8
Luna moth 177–8

Mabey, Richard 20–1, 63
   Nature Cure 63
McCarthy, Michael 121–3, 147–8, 153–4, 162–3, 166–7
   Moth Snowstorm, The 121–3, 147–8
McClintock, James 130–1
Macdonald, Helen 198–200
   H is for Hawk 198–200
Macfarlane, Robert 34–6, 73–4, 158–9
   Wild Places, The 34–6
MacKinnon, J. B. 147
Manifest Destiny 193
Marren, Peter 165–7
   Chasing the Ghost 165–6
Marsh, George Perkins 124
Marx, Karl 1
Massingham, H. J. 119
Matthiessen, Peter 18–21, 24–5
   Snow Leopard, The 18–21, 24–5
Maxwell, Gavin 43–50, 54–5, 64, 116–20, 180–1, 186–7
   Raven Seek Thy Brother 48–50
   Ring of Bright Water 45–8, 50–1, 54–6, 116–19
   Rocks Remain, The 47–9
Melville, Herman 124
mestizo/mestiza 81
Miller, J. Hillis 113–15, 130, 140

modernism 181–2, 202–3
modernity 1–2, 27, 45–6, 51–2, 156, 173–4
Momaday, N. Scott 90, 100–1
   'American Land Ethic, An' 90
Monarch butterfly 105–10, 120–1, 126–7, 132–3, 135–7
Monbiot, George 122n.47, 182–3, 189–90
   Feral 122n.47, 182–3, 189–90
Morris, David 134–5
mortality, *see* mourning
Morton, Timothy 12–13, 97–8, 115
   Ecology without Nature 97–8
mourning 95–104, 180–1, 194–201
murmuration of starlings 137–40, 180–1
Murphy, Patrick D. 6n.7, 9–10
Murray, Walter J. C. 27–8, 59
   Copsford 27–8

Nabokov, Vladimir 202–3
natural history 5, 22, 71–3, 83–5, 103–4, 144, 156–60
Natural History Museum at Tring 157–8, 169
nature 3–8, 186
nature writing 5–6, 8–13, 30–7, 41–2, 45–6, 48–9, 53–5, 59–61, 63–5, 68–80, 101–2, 104, 123–6, 130–1, 137–8, 140–1, 143–5, 153–6, 174–5, 182, 188
Nechisar nightjar 169–71
new nature writing 1, 21–2, 34–5, 39–42, 44–5, 87, 104, 121, 161–2, 185–6, 199–200
Nutkins, Terry 47

Oates, Matthew 164–7
odonata 166n.93
Ornsay, Isle 54–5
Orwell, George 29, 161
   Down and Out in Paris and London 29
   Nineteen Eighty-Four 29, 161
otter 43–4, 46–9, 56–8, 60–3, 178–9, 185–7
'Ötzi the Iceman' 22–5
Outka, Paul 72, 80
Owens, Louis 68–9, 84–98, 198
   I Hear the Train 84–6
   Mixedblood Messages 86, 91
   Sharpest Sight, The 68–9, 95–8
   Wolfsong 88–95

parable and parable effects 26, 111–15, 130–42, 180–1
paradox 2–6, 28–31, 33, 38–9, 42–3, 48–9, 56–7, 59–60, 69, 71–2, 76–7, 80–3, 93–6, 101–5, 107–8, 110, 114–15, 126, 130–7, 142–3, 146, 152, 156–7, 162–3, 166–8, 178–87, 191–2, 194–6, 198–202

passenger pigeon 144–6, 157–8
Pearce, Susan 156–7
Pearse, Andrew 111–12
performative 10–11, 33–5, 114–15, 130, 133–5, 140–1
Phillips, Dana 8–12, 18, 30–1, 41, 156n.47, 181
Poe, Edgar Allan 124
post-humanism 3–4
postmodernism 202–3
primitivism 118, 155–6, 187, 191–3
Proust, Marcel 202–3
Purple Emperor butterfly 164–7

quest narratives 162–71

racism 4, 69, 73–83, 101–2, 104, 107, 180–1, 196–7, 200–1
Raine, Anne 101–2
Raine, Kathleen 49–50
Rapson, Jessica 109, 120–1
rarity 25–6, 142–81
Reddy, Jini 73–4
    Wanderland 73–4
Reimer, Margaret Loewen 130–1
remoteness 25–66
rewilding 26, 44–5, 65–6, 176, 181–92
Richardson, Nick 187
Robin Hood's Bay 115–16
Romanticism 67–8, 75, 107, 140–1
Roorda, Randall 33–4, 36–7
Ruffin, Kimberley 69

Savoy, Lauret 70, 74–80, 83, 95–6, 99–104, 107, 180–1, 196, 198, 200
    Trace: Memory, History, Race, and the American Landscape 74–80, 99–104, 180–1, 196, 200
Savoy, Willard 78–80
    Alien Land 78–80
Schaller, George 18–20
Scheese, Don 5–6
Schweninger, Lee 13–15, 90
science fiction 134–5
Scottish independence referendum 189n.20
Scranton, Roy 197–8
Sethi, Anita 73–4
    I Belong Here 73–4
Shelton, Richard 171
shifting baseline syndrome 147
Skye Bridge 54–6
Small Tortoiseshell butterfly vii, 163–4, 166–7
Smith, Jos 36

Snyder, Gary 155n.45, 188
Soay, Isle of 43–4, 119–20
sojourner 37–42, 52
solitude 31–42
Soper, Kate 3–4
speciation 172–3
Stepto, Robert 78–9
Stevenson, Sheryl 82
Stewart, Iain 44–5
Storr, Anthony 31–3
sublime, the 44–5, 74–6, 80, 84–6, 101–2, 107–9, 122–3, 126, 150n.28

Tallis, Thomas 138–41, 180–1
    Spem in alium 138–41, 180–1
taphonomy 201–2
Tasmanian tiger, *see* thylacine
Tassel, Kristin Van 174–5
Taylor, Marianne 166n.93
Tesson, Sylvain 38–9
    Consolations of the Forest 38–9
Thesiger, Wilfred 43–4, 119–20
Thoreau, David Henry 32, 36–9, 51–2, 124–6
    Walden 36–9, 51–2, 125–6
Thorpe, Adam 22–5, 178–9
    On Silbury Hill 22–5
    'Sighting' 178–9
    Ulverton 22–4
thylacine 148–53, 173–4
Tomkies, Mike 50–4, 64
    Between Earth and Paradise 51–3
    Last Wild Place, A 51–4
    Last Wild Years 53–4
traditional ecological knowledge, *see* indigenous knowledge
transcendentalism 67–8, 75
transformations 25–6, 88–9, 180–203
trauma 71–2, 75–6, 78, 80–5, 98–9, 151–2, 162–3, 199
trickster 91, 93–5

Valis, Noël 160–2, 166–7
Vizenor, Gerald 91, 93–4

Wagner-Martin, Linda 135–6
Wallace, Alfred Russel 157–8
Walmsley, Leo 115–16, 118–19
    So Many Loves 115–16, 118–19
White, Chris 167–9
    Life List of Adrian Mandrick, The 167–8
Whitman, Walt 124, 194–5
Williamson, Henry 51–2, 186–7
    fascism 51–2

Flax of Dream 51–2
  Dream of Fair Women, The 51–2
  Pathway, The 51–2
Wilson, Thomas 155–6
Winn, Raynor 27–8
wolves 188–94
Woolworth's 160

Wordsworth, William 164–5, 194–6
World Wildlife Fund 147

Youngs, Tim 18–19

Zen Buddhism 18–21, 40, 155n.45
Zwicky, Jan 103